Multilevel Citizenship

The Right to Consular Protection of EU Citizens Abroad

P.I.E. Peter Lang

Bruxelles · Bern · Berlin · Frankfurt am Main · New York · Oxford · Wien

Eva-Maria Poptcheva

Multilevel Citizenship

The Right to Consular Protection of EU Citizens Abroad

This publication has been peer-reviewed.

1 avenue Maurice, B-1050 Brussels, Belgium
info@peterlang.com; www.peterlang.com

ISBN 978-2-87574-168-4
D/2014/5678/45

Printed in Germany

Library of Congress Cataloging-in-Publication Data. Poptcheva, Eva-Maria, author. Multilevel citizenship : the right to consular protection of union citizens abroad / Eva-Maria Poptcheva. p. cm. Includes bibliographical references and index. ISBN 978-2-87574-168-4 (alk. paper) 1. Citizenship--European Union countries. 2. Civil rights--European Union countries. 3. Diplomatic and consular service, European. I. Title. KJE5124.P67 2014 323.6094--dc23 2014013871.

Bibliographic information published by "Die Deutsche Nationalbibliothek".

"Die Deutsche Nationalbibliothek" lists this publication in the "Deutsche National-bibliografie"; detailed bibliographic data is available on the Internet at <http://dnb.de>.

Table of Contents

Preface

The book of Eva-Maria Poptcheva addresses questions of utter importance for the way forward of European integration. The conviction that the future of the European Union towards a real federation passes inevitably through a positively construed 'Union of Rights', making citizens believing again in the European project, is in the centre of this book. The book acknowledges rightfully the stage in which European integration is at this moment by not trying to impose a rather idealistic concept of a federal Union citizenship, conceived of by the hierarchical relationship between national, supranational and international norms, but understands to combine both citizens' aspiration to be part of a community entitling to certain rights, as well as Member States' legitimate interest to remain Masters of core state competences inherent to their state sovereignty, and the strive of the international community to see observed the rules of the game between international law subjects. This is the great achievement of the paradigm of 'multilevel constitutionalism' – it allows us to overcome the shortcomings of the current stage of the European Union architecture, somewhere on the way to a federal union.

The multilevel-constitutionalism approach has turned into a quasi-philosophical paradigm, into a being and time, to put it with Heidegger's words, seeking to explain in an abstract-juridical way the interplay of legal orders within one and the same subject. Nowadays, it is no longer possible to employ a legal approach to the analysis of a right without taking into account that the applicable normative framework features diverse levels of legal production, and, as shown by the European constitutional doctrine, needs to deploy its paramount efficacy ensuring to its right-holders the best possible protection. And there lies the greatest achievement of this book: it breaths new live into the legal-philosophical concept in applying the multilevel-constitutionalism approach to a concrete institution of law – the right to consular protection of Union citizens abroad.

Mrs Poptcheva's book embarks on a challenging journey of meticulously identifying the relationships between legal norms deriving from national, European Union and international law and practices, which only in their multilevel interplay construe the right to consular protection of Union citizens as an EU fundamental right. A great challenge and at the same time an achievement of the book is the lack of other constitutionalist analysis of the right to consular protection, having the constitutionalist relinquished the examination of consular protection under the law of the European Union to the foreign affairs science, depriving it in this way of a dogmatic analysis that does justice to its constitutional character as a right deriving from the Union citizenship status. The analysis of the elements construing consular protection as a right, turning it into an identifiable institution of law that cannot be desnaturalised, shows the potential that this right offers in times of globalisation to the protection of persons in distress, which was left in the past to the mercy of the political discretion. This book is therefore the first monograph offering a dogmatically founded analysis of the configuration elements of the right to consular protection (right holders, exercise, guarantees, etc.) providing scientific evidence for its character as a fundamental right, against the attempts of both some Member States and parts of the scientific community to write it off as a mere State discretion and denying it the advantages implied by the rights deriving from Union citizenship.

But the book goes beyond the mere appraisal of a fundamental right and frames the analysis of all Union citizenship rights under consideration of the symbiotic relation between the Union citizenship status as a constitutional paradigm and the rights flowing from that status. The book is visionary in the way it extrapolates the findings surrounding the dogmatic framework of the right to consular protection as a fundamental right, conceived of through the interplay of legal norms belonging to diverse legal orders, to the analysis of Union citizenship as 'multilevel citizenship'. The book converts in this way the analysis of the right to consular protection into a case in point for the construction of multilevel citizenship as a constitutional paradigm best suited to explain the quasi-federal setting of Union citizenship in a triangle of legal relationships between Union citizens, Member States and the European Union.

The book's innovative spirit is owed not only to the constitutionalist approach to the right to consular protection embedded in the dogmatic environment of Union citizenship as a constitutional status, but also in the coherent analysis of all legal norms operating within the provision of consular protection, including the 28 Member States' legal norms and practices. Inspired by a study on the national rules governing consular protection in the EU Member States conducted by the Instituto Europeo de Derecho for the former Directorate General Justice, Freedom and Security of the European Commission, Mrs. Poptcheva undertook a major challenge in seeking to identify the dogmatic consequences of the divergent level of juridification of the right to consular protection in the Member States for the legal design of consular protection under the law of the European Union. There are not many scholars living up to the challenges posed by comparative analysis in the way done in this book by Mrs Poptcheva, not least owing to her background as a real European lawyer, being a Bulgarian national with a German law degree from the Albert-Ludwigs-University in Freiburg i.Br., and holding a European PhD in Law from the Autonomous University of Barcelona.

The comparative analysis requires indeed not only an understanding of the differences between the Member States' legal cultures but also a mastery of a methodology enabling us to establish existing differences but also to positively construe a common European model. The book thus successfully strikes a balance between Union citizens' strive for protection not only from their own country but also from other Member States on the one side, and the practicability of such aspirations under due account of the general interest to be observed by the EU Member States on the other side, making of this book, despite its coherent dogmatic approach, an indispensable guide for all actors operating in the field of consular protection.

As the supervisor of Mrs Poptcheva doctoral thesis, I am very glad about the publication of this book, as a culmination of a research initiated in a European project, followed by a doctoral thesis defended at the Universidad Autónoma de Barcelona with the highest distinction. It is a rigorous work and at the same time forward-looking to a future in which we, the Union citizens, wish to relate ourselves as such not only when we move across the Member States but also beyond EU territory, since consular protection, as a citizenship right, identifies us as such and makes us holders of a common legal baggage vis-à-vis the whole international community.

The focus of the present book on Union citizenship and the rights flowing from the "fundamental status of Union citizens" is more than adequate in the current crisis bedeviling the European project. Today, the easy recourse to the moral and economic crisis is a demagogic charge against institutions, against the application of the law, against European integration. If we would listen to the many messages that overflood the media, we would see that, in many cases, all evil comes from Europe. And the alarm calls are made to discredit the democratic systems that we have implemented in Europe in recent decades. While acknowledging the difficulties and the mistakes done, that are present in our integration process, it is necessary to send a message of warning against populism, nationalism and other 'isms' that inundate us, just now, when we have to renew the legitimate representation of European citizens in the shape of the European Parliament. As recognized amongst those who want Europe to remain a bastion of defense of the values included in the Lisbon Treaty, we are also facing the challenge of reinventing the EU's institutional architecture and our legal system and to bring all this nearer to the citizens.

Prof. Dr. Teresa Freixes

Professor of Constitutional Law at the Autonomous University of Barcelona

Jean Monnet Chair *ad personam*

Abbreviations

ECHR	European Court of Human Rights
ECR	European Court Reports
EDT	Emergency Travel Document
EEAS	European External Action Service
EEC	European Economic Communities
EU	European Union
ICJ	International Court of Justice
TEC	Treaty on European Communities
TEU	Treaty on European Union
TFEU	Treaty on Functioning of the European Union
VCDR	Vienna Convention on Diplomatic Relations

Acknowledgements

I would like to thank Prof. Dr. Teresa Freixes for her personal and professional guidance and commitment to my research work. My deepest gratitude also to Prof. Dr. Yolanda Gómez for her advice and support. My thanks go also to Prof. Dr. Francesc de Carreras, Prof. Dr. José Carlos Remotti and Prof. Dr. Juan Carlos Gavara from the Autonomous University of Barcelona, as well as to Prof. Dr. Matt Henn and Prof. Dr. Elspeth Berry from the Nottingham Trent University. I would also like to express my gratitude to Prof. Dr. Alessandra Silveira, Prof. Dr. Pascuale Policastro, Prof. Dr. Markus Helfrich and Dr. Matthias Hartwig for the review of the previous drafts of this monograph.

Finally, special thanks to my parents, Svetla and Alexandar, as well as to my husband, Pablo, for their unconditional support and love.

Chapter I

Complexity vs. Relevance of Consular Protection

Union citizenship has evolved – since its entrenchment first in the Treaty establishing the European Community by the 1992 Treaty of Maastricht, and, with the entry into force of the Treaty of Lisbon on 1 December 2009, also in the Treaty on European Union (TEU)[1] – into the motor for a new stage and a new type of European integration creating an "ever closer union among the peoples of Europe".[2] European integration ushered in this new age by creating a direct link between the citizens of the Member States and the European Union, with the aim of fostering a sense of identity with the Union by strengthening the protection of the rights and interests of the nationals of its Member States.[3] This direct political link between Union and Member States' nationals was established through the introduction of a citizenship of the Union.[4] The rights deriving from Union citizenship are in effect granted constitutional status by being enshrined in the Treaties themselves and became together with the central political status of the citizens the source of democratic legitimacy of the Union.[5] This new approach in

1 Article 9 of the Treaty on European Union (modified by the Treaty of Lisbon): "In all its activities, the Union shall observe the principle of the equality of its citizens, who shall receive equal attention from its institutions, bodies, offices and agencies. Every national of a Member State shall be a citizen of the Union. Citizenship of the Union shall be additional to national citizenship and shall not replace it."

2 Article A section 2 of the Treaty of Maastricht (Article 1 para. 2 of the consolidated version of the Treaty on European Union): "This Treaty marks a new stage in the process of creating an ever closer union among the peoples of Europe, in which decisions are taken as openly as possible and as closely as possible to the citizen."

3 As testimony to their importance, the provisions on citizenship were placed immediately after the introductory provisions of the Treaty of Rome, even before the four freedoms making up the internal market, such as Article 6 EC-Maastricht which prohibits discrimination on the grounds of nationality, and Article 7A EC (formerly 8 A EEC), which provides for the establishment of the internal market *inter alia* for persons.

4 Article B of the Treaty of Maastricht (Article 2 of the consolidated version of the Treaty on European Union: "The Union shall set itself the following objectives:

[...]

– to strengthen the protection of the rights and interests of the nationals of its Member States through the introduction of a citizenship of the Union;"

5 PERNICE, I., "The Treaty of Lisbon: Multilevel Constitutionalism in Action", in *The Columbia Journal of European Law*, Vol. 15, No. 3 (2009), pp. 385 et seq.

the European integration process prompted many scholars to proclaim the rise of a new "Union of Rights" replacing the former Union based mainly on the Common Market rules.[6]

Union citizenship describes the relationship between the nationals of the EU Member States and the European Union, which, like national citizenship, is characterised by competences for action of the EU institutions towards Union citizens on the one side, and citizens' rights, duties and political participation on the other side. By this means the gap between the increasing impact on Union citizens caused by EU action as well as by measures adopted under the former second (Common Foreign and Security Policy)[7] and third pillars of the European Union (Police and Judicial Cooperation in Criminal Matters), and the protection of rights and participation in democratic processes, as traditionally and almost exclusively national matters, shall be bridged.

Union citizenship is aimed to increase people's sense of identification with the Union by fostering a sense of European identity.[8] This European identity is based on a community of interests, improving substantially the legal position of the citizens vis-à-vis the European Union and the Member States through citizenship rights, and by drawing increasingly on these same European citizens to strengthen the democratic legitimacy of the EU decision-making. For the latter, the necessary European political consciousness is again narrowly linked to the impact of EU citizens' rights on their lives.

According to Article 20 of the Treaty on the Functioning of the European Union (TFEU),[9] as well as Article 9 TEU (as modified by the

6 WOLLENSCHLÄGER, F., *Grundfreiheit ohne Markt*, Tübingen 2007; SCHÖNBERGER, C., *Unionsbürger. Europas Föderales Bürgerrecht in vergleichender Sicht*, Tübingen 2005; DÖRR, D./ DREHER, M., *Europa als Rechtsgemeinschaft*, Baden-Baden 1997; MAGNETTE, P., *La Citoyenneté européenne: Droits, politiques, institutions*, Bruxelles, 1999.

7 See for instance the Judgment of the Court of Justice of the European Communities in the case *Kadi* on so called targeted sanctions, such as freezing of funds, adopted by the Council of the European Union in connection, for example, with combating terrorism, where the Court held that the appellant was directly and individually concerned by the measures adopted within the framework of the Common Foreign and Security Policy, Judgment of the Court of Justice of 03.09.2008 in joined cases C-402/05 P and C-415/05 PC, *Yassin Abdullah Kadi and Al Barakaat International Foundation v. Council of the European Union*, ECR 2008, p. I-06351, para. 241.

8 Ad hoc Committee on "A People's Europe", "Adonnino Report "A People's Europe", Luxembourg 1985, prepared according to the mandate issued by the Fontainebleau European Council of 25 and 26 June 1984, in *Bulletin of the European Communities Supplement*, 7/85, p. 7. Available at: <http://www.ombudsman.europa.eu/en/resources/historicaldocument.faces;jsessionid=2FAF476D7F307335E43A6D9ED8D8862D> (23.07.2013).

9 Ex-Article 17 of the Treaty establishing the European Community. The Treaty establishing the European Community has been renamed in Treaty on the Functioning of the

Treaty of Lisbon), every person holding the nationality of a Member State is a citizen of the Union.[10] Nationality is defined according to the national laws of the Member States.[11] Citizenship of the Union is additional[12] to national citizenship but does not replace it, and it gives rise for a number of rights in addition to those stemming from citizenship of a Member State.[13]

European citizenship confers on every European citizen an individual right to move and reside freely without reference to an economic activity. With the Treaty of Maastricht also came additional electoral active and passive rights in European and local elections as well as the right to petition the European Parliament and to complaint before the European Ombudsman. Besides, recently the Treaty of Lisbon introduced a new citizens' right into the TEU: the citizens' initiative giving Union citizens the right to take the initiative of inviting the European Commission, within the framework of its powers, to submit any appropriate proposal on matters where citizens consider that a legal act of the Union is required for the purpose of implementing the Treaties.[14]

But the Treaty of Maastricht went to introduce provisions applicable even beyond the borders of the then European Community and established

---

European Union by the Treaty of Lisbon. For more details please see below.

10 Article 20 of the Treaty on the Functioning of the European Union:

"Citizenship of the Union is hereby established. Every person holding the nationality of a Member State shall be a citizen of the Union. Citizenship of the Union shall be additional to and not replace national citizenship."

11 This is in keeping with the Judgment of the Court of Justice in the case *Micheletti v. Delegación de Gobierno en Cantabria* (case C-369/90, ECR 1990, p. 4239) where it held that Spain could not prevent the plaintiff establishing himself in its territory by refusing to recognise his Italian nationality, on the grounds that his primary nationality was his Argentinean nationality.

12 The Treaty of Lisbon amended the wording of ex-Article 17 TEC stipulating that "Citizenship of the Union shall complement" national citizenship. The notion "complementary" was replaced by the notion "additional".

13 It should be noted that although Article 20 para. 2 TFEU (ex-Article 17 TEC) stipulates that "Citizens of the Union shall enjoy the rights and be subject to the duties provided for in the Treaties", no duties for the EU citizens have been established so far by the Treaties.

14 Article 11 para. 4 of the Treaty on European Union (modified by the Treaty of Lisbon):

"Not less than one million citizens who are nationals of a significant number of Member States may take the initiative of inviting the European Commission, within the framework of its powers, to submit any appropriate proposal on matters where citizens consider that a legal act of the Union is required for the purpose of implementing the Treaties.

The procedures and conditions required for such a citizens' initiative shall be determined in accordance with the first paragraph of Article 24 of the Treaty on the Functioning of the European Union."

a citizens' right with an extraterritorial character by conferring upon Union citizens the right to ask for the help of any Member State represented in a third country if their own Member State is not represented there.

Globalisation, entailing a steadily growing number of EU citizens travelling to third countries (which are not members of the EU), as well as recent humanitarian crises caused by natural disasters, armed conflicts or terrorist attacks such as those in Thailand as consequence of the Indian Ocean tsunami on 26 December 2004, the Bali bombings on 23 July 2005, the 2006 Lebanon conflict, the 2008 Georgia conflict, the Haiti earthquake in January 2010 and the earthquake in Japan in March 2011, as well as the uprisings in Tunisia, Egypt and Libya in spring 2011 and recently the Syrian conflict demanded the attention of the EU institutions to this fourth block of EU citizens' rights, those on protection by diplomatic and consular representations abroad. In particular the tsunami and the Lebanese crisis impressively demonstrated that even the most traditional, widest and best organised national consular services could not cope with these situations on their own.[15]

As a result, the right to consular protection became a focal point of European policy, being a possible remedy to the challenges of globalisation and of its accompanying phenomena. The growing number of Union citizens living in and travelling to third countries outside the EU and the grave crisis situations involving a large number of EU citizens from different EU Member States on the one side face on the other side the fact that not every Member State is represented by a diplomatic and/or consular mission in every third country. There are currently only three countries in which all 28 Member States are represented (China, Russia and the United States of America). Member States' diplomatic and consular representations are especially limited in Central America and the Caribbean, Central Asia and Central and West Africa. A maximum of ten Member States are represented in 107 of the 166 third countries in the world.[16] Some Member States have more than 100 representations (France, Germany and the United Kingdom) in third countries while others have less than ten (Estonia, Latvia, Malta and Luxembourg).[17]

15 PORZIO, G., "Consular Assistance and Protection: An EU Perspective", in *The Hague Journal of Diplomacy*, 3 (2008), pp. 93, 94.

16 EUROPEAN COMMISSION, Action Plan 2007-2009 "Effective consular protection in third countries: the contribution of the European Union", Communication from the Commission to the European Parliament, the Council, the European Economic and Social Committee and the Committee of the Regions of 05 December 2007, COM(2007)767 final, p. 2, 3. Available at: <http://eur-lex.europa.eu/LexUriServ/LexUriServ.do?uri=COM:2007:0767:FIN:EN:HTML> (15.08.2010).

17 EUROPEAN COMMISSION, "EU initiative to strengthen consular protection for citizens outside the European Union", MEMO/07/551 of 05 December 2007, p. 3. Available at: <http://europa.eu/rapid/pressReleasesAction.do?reference=MEMO/07/551> (10.03.2010).

There are eighteen countries in which no Member State is represented at all,[18] seventeen countries in which only one Member State is represented[19] and eleven countries[20] in which only two Member States are represented.[21]

Accordingly, the need for consular protection concerns potentially thousands of EU citizens each year since Union citizens are increasingly travelling and living in third countries as tourists, workers, students, etc. The Austrian Presidency of the Council estimated in 2006 that Union citizens make some 180 million trips every year to destinations outside the European Union.[22] Furthermore, between 30 and 50 million citizens reside permanently outside Europe. It is estimated that 8.7% of the EU citizens travelling outside the EU go to third countries where their Member State has no consular or diplomatic representation. Based on the number of trips made annually by EU citizens to third countries, the estimated number of 'unrepresented' Union citizens travelling abroad annually is at least 7 million. In addition, around 2 million EU expatriates live in a third country where their Member State is not represented.[23]

Most Member States do not keep records of the number of requests for consular assistance in third countries. However, on the basis of available data it is estimated that around 0.53% of EU citizens need consular assistance when travelling outside the EU, which would amount to at least 425,000 cases per year.[24] In addition, it is estimated that at least 37,000 of these cases concern Union citizens whose Member States are not represented in the third country.[25] The number of the cases of Union citizens looking for assistance by the embassy or consulate of another EU Member State in a third country is expected to increase during the

---

18 The Bahamas, Bhutan, Dominica, Kiribati, Lichtenstein, Micronesia, Nauru, Republic of Palau, San Marino, St Christopher and Nevis, Tuvalu, The Maldives, The Marshall Islands, Saint Vincent and the Grenadines, Somalia, Swaziland, Tonga, Western Samoa.

19 Antigua and Barbuda, Barbados, Belize, Central African Republic, The Comoros, Djibouti, Gambia, Grenada, Guyana, Kirghizstan, Lesotho, Liberia, Monaco, Sao Tomé and Principe, Solomon Islands, East Timor, Vanuatu.

20 Chad, Equatorial Guinea, Madagascar, Malawi, Mauritius, Santa Lucia, The Seyshelles, Sierra Leone, Surinam, Papua-New Guinea, Niger.

21 EUROPEAN COMMISSION, "EU initiative to strengthen consular protection for citizens outside the European Union", *op. cit.*, footnote 17.

22 Report of the Presidency of the Council of European Union to the European Council "Reinforcing the European Union's emergency and crisis response capacities", 15 June 2006, Document 10551/06, p. 6. Available at: <http://www.consilium.europa.eu/uedocs/cmsUpload/st10551en06.pdf> (03.05.2009).

23 EUROPEAN COMMISSION, Action Plan 2007-2009, *op. cit.*, footnote 16.

24 *Ibidem.*

25 *Ibidem.*

next years due to growing popularity of the EU provisions on consular protection among the citizens of the EU. It should be highlighted in this regard that while a Eurobarometer survey published in 2006 showed that only 23% of those interviewed were aware of the possibilities offered by ex-Article 20 TEC,[26] a Eurobarometer Flash Report of October 2010[27] indicates that an average of 79% of the citizens of the twenty-seven EU Member States are aware of their "right to ask for help at embassies of other EU Member States, if his/her country does not have an embassy there".[28]

In these circumstances, aggravated by globalisation reflected in different patterns such as placement of Union citizens working for multinational companies in third countries, permanent residence of Union citizens in third countries as a consequence of their family links with third-country nationals as well as low-cost travel possibilities leading to an increasing number of Union citizens travelling outside the EU, to places that have not been tourism hotspots during the last decades, the right to consular protection under Union law has steadily gained in relevance while its legal design is continuing being afflicted with legal uncertainty.

The above-mentioned situation attracted the attention of the Austrian Presidency of the Council and originated its report on "Reinforcing the European Union's emergency and crisis response capacities" to the European Council in 2006. Shortly after, in November 2006, the Commission adopted a Green Paper on diplomatic and consular protection of Union citizens in third countries,[29] which sets out ideas to be considered for strengthening the right to consular protection for Union citizens. Furthermore, the right to consular protection and the need "to

---

26 EUROPEAN COMMISSION, Flash Eurobarometer No. 188 on "Consular Protection" of July 2006, p. 9. This survey was requested by Directorate-General for Justice, Freedom and Security and coordinated by Directorate-General Communication. Available at: <http://ec.europa.eu/public_opinion/flash/fl188b_en.pdf> (30.11.2010).

27 EUROPEAN COMMISSION, Flash Eurobarometer No. 294 on "*European Citizenship*" of October 2010, requested by the former Directorate-General for Justice, Freedom and Security (after an administrative reorganisation now DG Justice) and coordinated by the Directorate-General for Communication (DG COMM "Research and Speechwriting" Unit). Available at: <http://ec.europa.eu/public_opinion/flash/fl_294_en.pdf> (30.11.2010).

28 This is the wording chosen by the organisator of the survey. The Member State with the greatest number of citizens aware of the Treaty provisions on consular protection was Finland (92%), followed by Estonia (87%), Italy (87%) and Spain (86%). Respondents from Sweden (66%), France (70%) and the United Kingdom (71%) were the least aware of those provisions. See *Ibidem*, p. 26.

29 EUROPEAN COMMISSION, Green Paper "Diplomatic and consular protection of Union citizens in third countries", COM(2006)712 of 28 November 2006. Official Journal C 30 of 10.02.2007.

ensure its full application" has been evoked in the Stockholm Programme of the Council of the European Union.[30]

Following a public consultation, the Commission presented an Action Plan in December 2007[31] outlining a working programme for the period 2007-2009. The plan focused on enhancing consular protection measures and improving the communication of this right to citizens. To this end, and as a response to the limited knowledge of Union citizens of the possibilities offered by ex-Article 20 TEC, as shown by the above-mentioned Eurobarometer survey in 2006,[32] the European Commission issued a Recommendation to the Member States in December 2007[33] to reproduce the wording of the first sentence of Article 20 TEC in national passports issued after 1 July 2009. The great majority of the Member States followed the Recommendation of the European Commission and included the wording in question into the newly issued passports[34] whereas seven Member States rejected the initiative or have not yet decided how to proceed.[35]

Also in order to raise the awareness of EU citizens about consular protection in third countries, the European Commission launched in November 2010 a web site informing citizens on the protection that could be offered under the law of the European Union.[36] The web site contains a very useful tool for citizens, which allows verifying whether the Member State of nationality is represented by an embassy or a consulate in any country of the world, and provides a list of those Member States with a representation in the third country in question.[37]

---

30 PRESIDENCY OF THE COUNCIL OF THE EUROPEAN UNION, General Affairs Council/European Council, The Stockholm Programme – An open and secure Europe serving and protecting the citizens, Document 17024/09 of 02 December 2009, p. 20. Available at: <http://register.consilium.europa.eu/pdf/en/09/oist17/st17024.en09.pdf> (08.09.2009).

31 EUROPEAN COMMISSION, Action Plan 2007-2009 "Effective consular protection...", *op. cit.*, footnote 16.

32 EUROPEAN COMMISSION, Flash Eurobarometer No. 188 on "Consular Protection" of July 2006, p. 9, *op. cit.*, footnote 26.

33 EUROPEAN COMMISSION, "EU initiative to strengthen consular protection for citizens outside the European Union", *op. cit.*, footnote 17.

34 Austria, Belgium, Bulgaria, Cyprus, France, Germany, Greece, Hungary, Italy, Latvia, Lithuania, Luxembourg, Malta, Netherlands, Poland, Romania, Slovenia, Spain, Sweden, United Kingdom. See Communication from the Commission to the European Parliament and the Council "Consular protection for EU citizens in third countries: State of play and way forward", COM(2011) 149/2, of 23.03.2011, p. 6.

35 Czech Republic, Denmark, Estonia, Finland, Ireland, Portugal, Slovakia. *Ibidem*.

36 See <http://ec.europa.eu/consularprotection/index.action> (06.10.2011).

37 *Ibidem*.

The Action Plan 2007-2009 "Effective consular protection in third countries: the contribution of the European Union" was evaluated in 2010 in the context of the 6th EU Citizenship Report "Dismantling the obstacles to EU citizens' rights".[38] The EU Citizenship Report 2010 highlights that the citizenship' rights have at their disposal a broad and comprehensive legal framework endorsed by the EU's and Member States' political commitment but that the future challenge would be to deal with the practical reality confronting citizens.[39] Much as this statement is true as regarding the right to freely move and reside, the electoral rights, the right to petition and even the recently established right to submit a European Citizens' Initiative,[40] it seems that the right to consular protection is being treated as a 'second-quality right' both in terms of legal rules and of practical effectiveness. Despite the 'hot-button' nature of consular protection in third countries, its provision under Union law is afflicted with a wide range of uncertainty. This has been partly acknowledged in the Action Plan 2007-2009 pointing to several shortcomings both regarding the legal embodiment of the provision of consular protection and its practical implementation leading to an uncertainty regarding the scope of protection to be offered to unrepresented EU citizens due to, *inter alia*, different interpretations of ex-Article 20 TEC (Article 23 TFEU). Taking into account the objective of consular protection to produce relief in a situation of distress, the certainty of Union citizen, whose Member State of origin is not represented in a third country, as regards entitlement and conditions in order to ask the diplomatic or consular mission of another EU Member State for consular protection, is of particular importance. This kind of uncertainty could even lead to the factual impossibility for unrepresented Union citizens to exercise their right to consular protection.

The lack of legal certainty, but also the challenges before the exercise of the right to consular protection in practice, stem on the one side from the complexity of its legal framework involving rules of international law as well as EU law provisions and national rules and practices. But the complexity of the right to consular protection rests not only upon the interaction among all these legal orders involved but also upon the lack of comprehensive legal regulation at EU level and the different degree

---

38 EUROPEAN COMMISSION, EU Citizenship Report "Dismantling the obstacles to EU citizens' rights", COM(2010)603 final of 27.10.2010. Available at: <http://ec.europa.eu/justice/citizen/files/com_2010_603_en.pdf> (13.01.2011).

39 *Ibidem*, pp. 2, 3.

40 See Regulation (EU) No. 211/2011 of the European Parliament and of the Council of 16 February 2011 on the citizens' initiative, published in the Official Journal of the European Union L 65/1 of 11.03.2011.

of juridification of the concept of consular protection in the Member States, being the consular protection domain traditionally governed rather by practices and non-binding internal rules, conferring a wide range of discretion to the officials and other stakeholders, than by comprehensive legal norms with binding character.

On the other side, the pitfalls before the right to consular protection are based on its character as an equal-treatment right raising the question of whether the Treaties have established a subjective right to consular protection regardless of the relevant national rules of the Member States or whether merely a right to equal treatment as compared to nationals is provided, whereby the existence and configuration of the provision of consular protection is governed by the legal rules and practices of each Member State. In this regard, the legal uncertainty concerning consular protection ranges also over the question of who is entitled to be provided with consular protection and what is the beneficiary entitled to.

In the meanwhile the provision of consular protection has been put on a new legal platform with the entry into force of the Treaty of Lisbon on 1 December 2009 amending the Treaty on European Union and the Treaty establishing the European Community.[41] The Treaty of Lisbon involved no change in substance as regards the right to consular protection. Art. 23 TFEU (ex-Article 20 TEC) establishes that:

> Every citizen of the Union shall, in the territory of a third country in which the Member State of which he is a national is not represented, be entitled to protection by the diplomatic or consular authorities of any Member State, on the same conditions as the nationals of that State. Member States shall adopt the necessary provisions and start the international negotiations required to secure this protection.

However, a new second paragraph was included allowing the enactment of directives by the Council in order to facilitate such protection.[42]

Furthermore, for the determination of the legal character and scope of consular protection under EU law, the entry into force of the Charter of Fundamental Rights of the European Union[43] according to Article 6 para.

---

41 The Treaty of Lisbon was signed on 13 December 2007 by the heads of State or Government of the EU Member States. Published in the Official Journal of the European Communities C 306 of 17.12.2007.

42 Article 23 para. 2 TFEU:

"The Council, acting in accordance with a special legislative procedure and after consulting the European Parliament, may adopt directives establishing the coordination and cooperation measures necessary to facilitate such protection."

43 Hereinafter: the Charter. Published in Official Journal of the European Union C 83 of 30.3.2010.

1 of the Treaty on European Union (as amended by the Treaty of Lisbon) should be taken into due account.[44] The inclusion of the citizens' rights, and amongst them also the right to consular protection, into the rights' catalogue of the Charter underpins the constitutional dimension of the rights deriving from Union citizenship and as a result their character as fundamental rights.

This book seeks to offer an analysis of the legal character and configuration of the provision of consular protection abroad taking into account the structural traits of the right to consular protection as a fundamental citizens' right as well as its function as substantive content of Union citizenship and thus as an instrument of creation of an European identity. The justifiable claim of the right to consular protection to qualify as a subjective right equipped with guarantees will be established by employing a coherent dogmatic approach identifying its direct effect, right-holders, substantive scope, guarantees and passive subjects. Moreover, the corner stones of a further legislative development will be outlined offering a future prospective regarding the areas of action of the EU and the Member States in the field of consular protection abroad.

In this sense, the methodology employed in this book seeks to meet the challenges posed by the complex legal structure of consular protection under Union law setting the right to consular protection in the constitutional context of Union citizenship and is aimed at offering a comprehensive analysis of a fundamental right involving in its legal framework multiple legal orders.

Therefore, the next chapter defines the concept of consular protection under Union law accounting for the multilevel context of the right to consular protection stemming from its extraterritorial character on the one side and from the existing international law rules in this field on the other side. To this end, a distinction has been drawn between diplomatic protection under international law and consular protection under Union law establishing the rules of game as to the interaction between Union law and international law provisions. The book then sets the dogmatic framework of the right to consular protection as a subjective right combining a structural and a functional analysis placing the right to consular protection in the context of Union citizenship. Moreover, a dogmatic approach to subjective rights in Union law has been established taking into account the constitutional traditions of the Member States as

[44] Article 6 para. 1 of the Treaty on European Union reads:
"The Union recognises the rights, freedoms and principles set out in the Charter of Fundamental Rights of the European Union of 7 December 2000, as adopted at Strasbourg, on 12 December 2007, which shall have the same legal value as the Treaties."

well as the approach applied by the Court of Justice. In the following, the question of the exercise of the right to consular protection in terms of its direct effect on the relationships between Member States and Union citizens has been examined. Detailed analysis is also offered of the right-holders of the right to consular protection, focusing not only on the conditions to be fulfilled by Union citizens in a third country in order to be entitled to approach the representation of another Member State, but also on the extension of the circle of right-holders to persons who are non-Union citizens with view to the practical effectiveness of the provision of consular protection to Union citizens as well as to other obligations of the Member States towards non-nationals. The substantive scope of the right to consular protection has been established by identifying the powers conferred upon an individual under the right to consular protection in correlation with the obligations imposed upon the Member States. To this end, the national rules on consular protection have been analysed in order to establish the consequences of conceiving of the right to consular protection as a mere equal-treatment right referring in all aspects to national rules and practices on consular protection. The book then addresses the judicial and non-judicial guarantees ensuring the practical effectiveness of the right to consular protection analysing the judicial remedies available in case of an alleged violation of the right to consular protection both before the Court of Justice and in the Member States as well as the instruments of collaboration and cooperation aimed at guaranteeing the bridging of any gaps in the protection of Union citizens abroad. Moreover, the possibilities for the Union to provide consular protection to unrepresented Union citizens by means of the European External Action Service have been critically examined. Finally, the new possibility introduced by the Lisbon Treaty to adopt a Council directive on consular protection has been analysed, offering a proposal for a directive drawing on the shortcomings identified in the previous chapters as well as a critical analysis of the proposal for a directive on consular protection presented by the European Commission.

Chapter II

Conceptualising 'Consular Protection'

1. Framing the Issue

In order to define the legal scope of the provision of consular protection within the framework of the European Union and to examine its consequences for any further legislative action of the European Union and of the EU Member States, the conceptual differences in the field of consular protection need to be identified and analysed. The historical link between diplomatic and consular protection, the concurrence or partial overlapping of legal provisions belonging to different legal orders as well as the different types of protection provided to citizens abroad reflecting the wide range of consular functions, contribute to the complexity of the normative and practical context, in which the EU provisions on consular protection are embedded. This legal and factual complexity makes it necessary to frame the provision of consular protection to unrepresented Union citizens in third countries, taking into account the historical and social context of the legal provisions at their respective level of application (international, European Union and national), the addressees of the measures operating under the different concepts in the field concerned as well as the underlying values and objectives pursued by each of the concepts in question. In this way, consular protection will be conceptualised observing the international obligations of the Member States, the autonomy of the EU legal order as well as the citizens' legitimate interest to be able to effectively enjoy their rights.

2. Multilevel Context of Consular Protection

It is no longer possible to conduct legal analysis without taking into consideration the different legal systems operating at various levels that interact with each other within the subject matter under examination.[1] *A fortiori* it is not possible to study paradigms like consular protection for

---

[1] FREIXES SANJUÁN, T., "Multilevel constitutionalism as general framework for the ascertainment of the legal regulations in the European Union", in *Libertad, seguridad y transformaciones del estado*, Joan Lluís Pérez Francesc (coord.), Barcelona 2009, p. 71.

EU citizens without having regard to the existence of international law rules that might touch upon its legal regulation.

Consular and diplomatic protection, as institutions of law, are on the one side regulated to an important extent by international law rules such as the Vienna Convention on Diplomatic Relations of 1961[2] and the Vienna Convention on Consular Relations of 1963.[3] On the other side, Article 23 TFEU stipulates the right of 'unrepresented' EU citizens to protection by the diplomatic or consular authorities of an EU Member State in a third country. Furthermore, the Member States provide consular and diplomatic protection under law or as a matter of policy within the framework of their internal legal orders so that besides international law and EU law provisions, there are also national provisions on consular and diplomatic protection of different legal rank (constitutional provisions, statutory laws, government regulations, circulars etc.). In this sense, it is safe to say that globalisation has clearly extended its impact to the legal field[4] and that consular protection can be regarded as a case in point of a multilevel legal framework.

The coexistence of these various regulatory levels necessarily implies that their analysis can no longer be carried out separately, but must be done jointly and coherently. Otherwise, any conclusion would be partial or flawed as the analysis failed to take into account the existing interaction between the different legal levels regulating the same subject matter. When it is obvious that States can no longer act alone on the international stage and that the legal relations between the international, European and national levels coincide and interweave, legal science must respond by using interpretative concepts and methods which allow us to provide analytical solutions to legal voids and antinomies, in other words, which help us understanding the legal framework within which both, public authorities and citizens, act in today's complex societies.[5]

---

2 Done at Vienna on 18 April 1961. Entered into force on 24 April 1964. United Nations, Treaty Series, Vol. 500, p. 95.

3 Done at Vienna on 24 April 1963. Entered into force on 19 March 1967. United Nations, Treaty Series, Vol. 596, p. 261.

4 FREIXES SANJUÁN, T., "Multilevel constitutionalism as general framework for the ascertainment of the legal regulations in the European Union", *op. cit.*, footnote 1.

5 FREIXES SANJUÁN, T., "La europeización de los derechos fundamentales", in *La tutela miltilivello dei diritti. Punti di crisi, problemi aperti, momenti di stabilizzazione*, Paola Bilancia/Eugenio De Marco (a cura di), Milano, 2004, p. 21; See also FREIXES SANJUÁN, T., "Multilevel constitucionalism y principios fundacionales de los ordenamientos constitucionales: el caso de España", in *Federalismi e integrazioni sopranazionali nell'arena della globalizzazione; Unione Europea e Mercosur*, Paola Bilancia (a cura di), Milano, 2006, p. 43.

Providing an adequate response to this regulatory confluence from a multilevel perspective entails examining and establishing relationships between regulations regarding a specific subject matter – in this case consular protection – which originate from different legal levels and which should be interpreted and applied coherently and systematically.[6] In order to apply a correct dogmatic approach to the subject matter concerned, the different terminologies and concepts as regards consular and diplomatic protection used at each of the interacting legal levels – international, EU and national – shall be presented and distinguished. This is even more necessary taking into account that the provision of consular protection to Union citizens in third countries has an international legal relevance, *ad extra* the European Union.[7]

2.1. Diplomatic vs. Consular Protection

The history of the consular function is largely associated with that of diplomacy, although consular offices were established well before diplomatic services. According to LEIRA and NEUMANN:[8]

> The consular institution has the particular character of being domestic and international at the same time, but unlike diplomacy it does not form a separate 'third culture'.

Whereas diplomacy has been traditionally seen as an instrument to mediate in cases of estrangement between different cultures stemming from the systemic alienation inherent in international society,[9] the emergence of consular offices was originated by the development of international trade and the economic interest of states, however, not depending on the existence of sovereign states but simply on the existence of certain economic activities, particularly in the shape of long distance trade. This goal-setting of the consular function explains also the fact that consular services precede chronologically considerably the appearance and consolidation of diplomatic services. In this context it is worth mentioning that although first diplomatic relations could be observed already in ancient Greek cities in the shape of certain personal inviolability awarded to envoys

6 See in this sense also POLICASTRO, P., "Constitutionalism, Multi-Level Democracy and Fundamental Values", preface to J. Nergelius, P. Policastro and K. Urata (eds.), *Challenges of Multi-Level Constitutionalims, Proceedings of IVR 21st World Congress, Lund 2003*, Kraków, 2004.

7 JIMÉNEZ PIERNAS, C., "La Asistencia consular al ciudadano de la Unión: de Maastricht a Amsterdam" in *Acción exterior de la Unión Europea y Comunidad Internacional*, Fernando M. Mariño Menéndez (ed.), Madrid, 1998, p. 220.

8 LEIRA, H. / NEUMANN, I.B., "The many past lives of the Consul", in *Consular Affairs and Diplomacy*, J. Melissen and A.M. Fernández (ed.), Leiden/Boston, 2011, pp. 225.

9 DER DERIAN, J., *On Diplomacy: A Genealogy of Western Estrangement*, Oxford 1997, p. 43.

and intermediaries, diplomacy in the modern sense of this notion was not institutionalised until the sixteenth century. The posterior progressive development of the codification of the rules of international law governing diplomatic relations culminated in 1961 in the adoption of the Vienna Convention on Diplomatic Relations signed on 18 April 1961 at the Vienna Conference held in March/April 1961.

The Vienna Convention of 1961 provides a legal framework for the establishment, functioning and termination of diplomatic relations between sovereign states, specifying *inter alia* the functions of the diplomatic missions which shall consist of representing the sending state in the receiving state; protecting in the receiving state the interests of the sending state and of its nationals, within the limits permitted by international law; negotiating with the Government of the receiving state; ascertaining conditions and developments in the receiving state, and reporting thereon to the Government of the sending State; promoting friendly relations between the sending state and the receiving state, and developing their economic, cultural and scientific relations.[10]

The origins of the consular institution can be traced back to ancient Greece, where foreigners living there were choosing *prostates* who acted as their intermediaries in legal and political relations, whereas the need of the Greek city states to protect their trade and their citizens in other cities gave rise to *proxeny*, who was a citizen of the host polity chosen by the citizens of the city whose protection was sought.[11] Both ancient institutions were aimed at the administration of justice to foreign merchants according to the principle of personality of law, i.e. the law applied to a dispute was determined by the status of the subjects involved and not the territory where they pursued their trade.[12]

---

10 Article 13 of the Vienna Convention on Diplomatic Relations:
"1. The functions of a diplomatic mission consist, inter alia, in:
(a) Representing the sending State in the receiving State;
(b) Protecting in the receiving State the interests of the sending State and of its nationals, within the limits permitted by international law;
(c) Negotiating with the Government of the receiving State;
(d) Ascertaining by all lawful means conditions and developments in the receiving State, and reporting thereon to the Government of the sending State;
(e) Promoting friendly relations between the sending State and the receiving State, and developing their economic, cultural and scientific relations.
2. Nothing in the present Convention shall be construed as preventing the performance of consular functions by a diplomatic mission."

11 ZOUREK, J., "Report on Consular Intercourse and Immunities", in *Yearbook of International Law Commission* 1957, Vol. II, Document A/CN.4/108, pp. 71, 73.

12 LEIRA, H. / NEUMANN, I.B., "The many past lives of the Consul", p. 232, *op. cit.*, footnote 8.

Nevertheless, it was not until the eleventh century that the first figure of the consul emerged and developed to its present and more complex structure with the rise of the trade between the Byzantine Empire and several Italian towns (Venice, Amalfi, Genoa and Pisa) as well as with Bulgarian and Russian merchants residing in Constantinople.[13] Special magistrates sent to the Byzantine Empire in charge of settling disputes between their compatriots began to be called "consuls" in the twelfth century.[14]

In the sixteenth century, the centralization of power in the hands of the monarchs and the rise of sovereign fiscal-military states as well as the need to meet the challenges of the international trade led to the transformation of the consuls from representatives of the merchants into state representatives.[15]

In the sixteenth and seventeenth centuries, with the foundation of the diplomatic missions in Europe and its subsequent proliferation, a significant shift in consular powers could be observed, culminating with the publication of the first collection of consular rules,[16] *Ordonnance de la Marine*, by COLBERT in France in 1681, which served as a model in organizing the consular services of many other states. Nonetheless, it was not until 1792 when the United States adopted their first consular laws, Prussia in 1796, Russia in 1820, Great Britain in 1825 and the Netherlands in 1838.[17]

The extraordinary increase of consulates during the nineteenth and twentieth centuries revealed the need for a more precise legal framework, particularly concerning the consular service and the legal status of consuls. It took, however, yet more time until social changes and globalisation spotlighted the need to set up rules for the protection of citizens abroad. After the failure of the first attempts to codify consular law by the

---

[13] ZOUREK, J., "Report on Consular Intercourse and Immunities", p. 73, *op. cit.*, footnote 11.

[14] According to ZOUREK, this kind of special magistrates existed also in China, India and the Arab countries during the VIIIth and IXth century, consulates appeared, however, first in Europe to deal with relations between the Byzantine Empire and the rest of Europe. See ZOUREK, J., "Report on Consular Intercourse and Immunities", *op. cit.*, footnote 11.

[15] LEIRA, H. / NEUMANN, I.B, "The many past lives of the Consul", pp. 237, 238, *op. cit.*, footnote 8.

[16] The earliest codes on consular duties were developed throughout the XI-XIIst centuries, mostly in the form of maritime law compilations, e.g. the Amalfi Tables (*Tabula Amalfitana*), Consulate of the Sea (*Consolato del Mare*), Codes of Lübeck, etc. See ZOUREK, J., "Report on Consular Intercourse and Immunities", *op. cit.*, footnote 11, p. 74.

[17] ZOUREK, J., "Report on Consular Intercourse and Immunities", p. 76, *op. cit.*, footnote 11.

League of Nations in 1928,[18] in 1949, the United Nations International Law Commission considered the inclusion of consular intercourse and immunities as part of its future codification work.[19]

At its seventh session, held at Geneva in 1955, the Commission appointed Mr Jaroslav ZOUREK as Special Rapporteur to commence the review of the matter and draft a set of provisional rules, based on *jus cogens*, national and international law.[20] The draft was divided into four chapters (consular intercourse and immunities; consular privileges and immunities; legal status of honorary consuls and their privileges and immunities; and general provisions), and accompanied by commentaries submitted by member states.[21] Worth mentioning is that during the negotiations, the close relationships with the Vienna Convention on Diplomatic Relations, signed in 1961, were frequently highlighted.

The United Nations Conference on Consular Relations was held in Vienna from 4 March to 22 April 1963 and was attended by delegates of ninety-five States. The Final Act of the Conference was signed on 24 April 1963. The Convention and Optional Protocols remained open for signature until 31 October 1963 at the Federal Ministry for Foreign Affairs of Austria and subsequently, until 31 March 1964, at United Nations Headquarters. The Convention and both Optional Protocols came into force on 19 March 1967.

The Vienna Convention on Consular Relations contains *inter alia* a detailed catalogue of functions of the consular offices which are for instance protecting in the receiving State the interests of the sending State and of its nationals, both individuals and bodies corporate; furthering the development of commercial, economic, cultural and scientific relations between the sending State and the receiving State; issuing passports and travel documents to nationals of the sending State,

18 See League of Nations publication, V. Legal, 04.05.1928, Document A.15.1928.V, p. 43.

19 Report of the International Law Commission on the work of its first Session, 12 April 1949, Official Records of the General Assembly, Fourth Session, Supplement No. 10, Document A/CN.4/13 and Corr. 1-3, in *Yearbook of the International Law Commission* 1949, Vol. I, pp. 278 et seq. Available at: <http://www.un.org/law/ilc/> (02.02.2012).

20 Report of the International Law Commission Covering the Work of its Seventh Session 2 May-8 July 1955, Official Records of the General Assembly, Tenth Session, Supplement No. 9 (A/2934), Document A/CN.4/94, in *Yearbook of the International Law Commission* 1955, Vol. II, p. 19, 42. Available at: <http://untreaty.un.org/ilc/sessions/7/7docs.htm> (02.02.2012).

21 Draft Articles on Consular Relations, with commentaries, in *Yearbook of the International Law Commission*, 1961, Vol. II, pp. 92 et seq. Available at: <http://untreaty.un.org/ilc/texts/instruments/english/commentaries/9_2_1961.pdf> (12.03.2012).

and visas to persons wishing to travel to the sending State; helping and assisting nationals, both individuals and bodies corporate, of the sending State; acting as notary and civil registrar and in capacities of a similar kind, and performing certain functions of administrative nature.[22]

---

[22] Article 5 of Vienna Convention on Consular Relations: "Consular functions consist in:

(a) protecting in the receiving State the interests of the sending State and of its nationals, both individuals and bodies corporate, within the limits permitted by international law;

(b) furthering the development of commercial, economic, cultural and scientific relations between the sending State and the receiving State and otherwise promoting friendly relations between them in accordance with the provisions of the present Convention;

(c) ascertaining by all lawful means conditions and developments in the commercial, economic, cultural and scientific life of the receiving State, reporting thereon to the Government of the sending State and giving information to persons interested;

(d) issuing passports and travel documents to nationals of the sending State, and visas or appropriate documents to persons wishing to travel to the sending State;

(e) helping and assisting nationals, both individuals and bodies corporate, of the sending State;

(f) acting as notary and civil registrar and in capacities of a similar kind, and performing certain functions of an administrative nature, provided that there is nothing contrary thereto in the laws and regulations of the receiving State;

(g) safeguarding the interests of nationals, both individuals and bodies corporate, of the sending States in cases of succession *mortis causa* in the territory of the receiving State, in accordance with the laws and regulations of the receiving State;

(h) safeguarding, within the limits imposed by the laws and regulations of the receiving State, the interests of minors and other persons lacking full capacity who are nationals of the sending State, particularly where any guardianship or trusteeship is required with respect to such persons;

(i) subject to the practices and procedures obtaining in the receiving State, representing or arranging appropriate representation for nationals of the sending State before the tribunals and other authorities of the receiving State, for the purpose of obtaining, in accordance with the laws and regulations of the receiving State, provisional measures for the preservation of the rights and interests of these nationals, where, because of absence or any other reason, such nationals are unable at the proper time to assume the defence of their rights and interests;

(j) transmitting judicial and extrajudicial documents or executing letters rogatory or commissions to take evidence for the courts of the sending State in accordance with international agreements in force or, in the absence of such international agreements, in any other manner compatible with the laws and regulations of the receiving State;

(k) exercising rights of supervision and inspection provided for in the laws and regulations of the sending State in respect of vessels having the nationality of the sending State, and of aircraft registered in that State, and in respect of their crews;

(l) extending assistance to vessels and aircraft mentioned in subparagraph (k) of this article, and to their crews, taking statements regarding the voyage of a vessel, examining and stamping the ship's papers, and, without prejudice to the powers of the authorities of the receiving State, conducting investigations into any incidents which occurred during the voyage, and settling disputes of any kind between the master, the officers and the seamen insofar as this may be authorized by the laws and regulations of the sending State;

Taking on the statement of LEIRA and NEUMANN that the consular institution is domestic and international at the same time,[23] it should be added that it also became a topic covered by European Union law and practice, contributing by this means to its complexity.

The inclusion of the provisions on consular protection of unrepresented Union citizens abroad into the Treaties can be traced back to the proposals of the Adonnino Committee contained in its report on Peoples' Europe[24] in 1985.[25] The committee, chaired by Pietro ADONNINO, an Italian Member of the European Parliament, and launched by the 1984 June European Council summit in Fontainebleau, stated in its final report submitted to the European Council of Milan on 28/29 June 1985 that a Community citizen in need of assistance during a temporary stay in a third country, where his own country is not represented by an embassy or a consulate, should be able to obtain assistance from the local consular representation of another Member State. The Committee recommended that the European Council invite Member States to intensify work for such consular cooperation in third countries and to formulate more precise guidelines.[26] Thereupon, the European Council of Rome of 14 and 15 December 1990 asked in its conclusions the Intergovernmental Conference on Political Union[27] to consider the extent to which, *inter alia*, the right to joint protection of Community citizens outside the Community's borders could

---

(m) performing any other functions entrusted to a consular post by the sending State which are not prohibited by the laws and regulations of the receiving State or to which no objection is taken by the receiving State or which are referred to in the international agreements in force between the sending State and the receiving State."

23 LEIRA, H. / NEUMANN, I.B, "The many past lives of the Consul", p. 225, *op. cit.*, footnote 8.

24 The notion "People's Europe" was adopted from Tindemans' report of 1975 (Section IV: *L'Europe des citoyens*). In his report on the European Union of 29 December 1975, Leo Tindemans, the Belgian Prime Minister, made a plea for greater protection of the rights of Europeans alleging that in order to construct the European Union, in a democratic society not only the political will of the governments of the Member States is necessary, but also the will of the citizens to form a society build on common values and traditions (See Rapport de Leo. M. Tindemans au Conseil européen sur l'Union européenne of 29 December 1975, in *Bulletin of the European Communities 1986*, Supplement 1/76, p. 27.

25 However, the seed of these new provisions was sown at the summit meeting held at Paris in 1974, which first considered the special rights of citizens of Member States.

26 Report submitted to the Milan European Council (Milan, 28-29 June 1985), in *Bulletin of the European Communities 1985*, Supplement 7/85, pp. 18-30.

27 In 1990 two Intergovernmental Conferences were convened to reform the Treaties. One of them focused on the Economic and Monetary Union, the other one, solely on the political Union.

be enshrined in the Treaty so as to give substance to the concept of European citizenship.[28]

It was the Spanish delegation that first presented to the Intergovernmental Conferences, in October 1990, a text on the European citizenship. According to Article 8 of the Spanish proposal of 20 February 1991, every citizen of the Union enjoys, on the territory of third countries, the protection of the Union as well as of every Member State under the same conditions as the nationals of that Member State.[29] Later within the deliberations on the Treaty on European Union (Maastricht) this very progressive proposal of the Spanish delegation, including besides the protection by the Member States also protection provided by the Union itself, was abandoned. Instead, with the Treaty of Maastricht Article 20 (ex-Article 8c TEC)[30] was included into the Treaty establishing the European Community[31] reading:

---

28 Conclusions of the Rome European Council (14 and 15 December 1990), Doc/90/6, p. 7, available at: <http://europa.eu/rapid/pressReleasesAction.do?reference=DOC/90/6&format=HTML&aged=1&language=EN&guiLanguage=en> (05.10.2011).

29 Spanish Delegation, "Proposal of text with articles on European citizenship presented by the Spanish delegation to the Intergovernmental Conference on Political Union (20 February 1991)", in *Revista de Instituciones Europeas (RIE)*, Vol. 18 (1991), p. 405, 408.
Article 8 of the Proposal:
"Every citizen of the Union enjoys, on the territory of third countries, the protection of the Union as well as of every Member State under the same conditions as the nationals of that Member State."

30 Ex-Article 8c of the Treaty establishing the European Community according to the Treaty of Maastricht established: "Every citizen of the Union shall, in the territory of a third country in which the Member State of which he is a national is not represented, be entitled to protection by the diplomatic or consular authorities of any Member State, on the same conditions as the nationals of that State. Before 31 December 1993, Member States shall establish the necessary rules among themselves and start the international negotiations required to secure this protection."

31 The inclusion of the provisions on EU citizenship into the Treaty establishing the European Community seems to be unsystematic taking into consideration that the notion "citizenship of the Union" shall describe (and establish) the relationship between the EU citizens and the European Union and not the European Community. Accordingly, the rules of a proper legislative technique would require the inclusion of those provisions into the Treaty on European Union instead of the Treaty establishing the European Community. However, the view of VILARIÑO PINTOS, whereupon the location of Article 20 TEC is inadequate, cannot be agreed with (VILARIÑO PINTOS, E., "Representación exterior y cooperación diplomática y consular en el Tratado de la Unión Europea", in *Revista de Instituciones Europeas*, No. 2 (1995), Vol. 22, p. 418). The reason for the inclusion of the provisions on citizenship of the Union into the TEC was the attempt to achieve a better level of protection of those rights taking into account that the principles of direct effect (ECJ, case 26/62, *Van Gend & Loos*, Judgment of 5 February 1963, European Court reports (ECR), p. 00001; Case 57/65, *Lütticke*, Judgment of 16 June 1966, ECR 1966, p. 205) and priority of community law over national law (ECJ, Case 6/64, *Costa/ENEL*, Judgment of 15 July 1964, ECR 1964, p. 00585; Case 11/70, *Internationale Handelsgesellschaft*, Judgment of 17 December

> Every citizen of the Union shall, in the territory of a third country in which the Member State of which he is a national is not represented, be entitled to protection by the diplomatic or consular authorities of any Member State, on the same conditions as the nationals of that State. Member States shall establish the necessary rules among themselves and start the international negotiations required to secure this protection.

The Treaty of Lisbon signed on 13 December 2007 and in force since 1 December 2009 introduced no changes into the first sentence of Article 23 TFEU but only into its second sentence, adding a second paragraph.[32] However, the Reform Treaty has brought no clarity to the scope of application of Article 23 TFEU. The question whether Article 23 TFEU refers to consular protection only or also to diplomatic protection is highly controversial in the legal doctrine. Starting point of this discussion is the different wording of Article 23 in the different linguistic versions in the 23 EU official languages of the Treaties. While the majority of the Treaty versions refer to the authorities in charge with the provision of protection to unrepresented EU citizens in third countries ("protection by the diplomatic and consular authorities"),[33] only the German, Polish and Czech versions use the notion "diplomatic and consular protection".[34]

1970, ECR 1970, p. 1125; Case 106/77, *Simmenthal II*, Judgment of 9 March 1978, ECR 1978, p. 629) have been developed by the European Court of Justice only with regard to community law (provisions of the former first pillar). In this way the individuals may invoke these provisions in procedures before the national courts and administrative authorities. Furthermore, the breach of community law by a Member State may give rise for a claim for damages (see for breaches of primary community law ECJ, Joined Cases C-46/93 and C-48/93, *Brasserie du Pêcheur/Factortame*, Judgment of 5 March 1996, ECR 1996, p. 1029). In this context it should be pointed out that the European Court of Justice had under the Treaty establishing the European Community no (general) jurisdiction over the intergovernmental elements of the EU Law (former second and third pillar) so that were the citizens' rights included into the Treaty on European Union, they would have remained outside the scope of jurisdiction of the ECJ. This would have led to a shortening of the protection of those rights (See also OBWEXER, Walter, "Das Recht der Unionsbürger auf diplomatischen und konsularischen Schutz", in *ECOLEX* 1996, pp. 323, 324).

The inclusion of the European citizenship also into the Treaty on European Union by the Treaty of Lisbon (Article 9 of the Treaty on European Union) is due to the abolition of the pillar structure entailing the extension of the jurisdiction of the Court of Justice to the law of the European Union unless the Treaties provide otherwise (Article 19 Treaty on European Union).

32 Please see to the implications of those modifications Chapter IX below.

33 French version of Article 23, para. 1 TFEU: "protection de la part des autorités diplomatiques et consulaires"; Spanish version: "la protección de las autoridades diplomáticas y consulares".

34 German version of Article 23: "genießt ... den diplomatischen und konsularischen Schutz"; Chech version: "právo na diplomatickou nebo konzulární ochranu"; Polish version: "z ochrony dyplomatycznej i konsularnej każdego".

Thus, many authors argue for an "institutional understanding" of Article 23 para. 1 TFEU excluding from its scope of application diplomatic protection.[35] The fact that Article 23 para. 1 TFEU refers not only to consular but also to diplomatic authorities does not dismiss this approach since according to Article 3 para. 2 of the Vienna Convention on Diplomatic Relations, diplomatic missions may also perform consular functions.[36]

In addition, Article 46 of the Charter of Fundamental Rights of the EU adopted for instance in its German version the so called "institutional understanding",[37] leaning towards the majority of linguistic versions of Article 23 TFEU, and reads "*den Schutz durch die diplomatischen und konsularischen Behörden*" (protection by the diplomatic and consular authorities).

Besides, it is worth mentioning that the European Commission argued in its Action Plan 2007-2009 "Effective consular protection in third countries: the contribution of the European Union" rather for a restrictive interpretation of Article 23 TFEU, taking account of the fact that "It appears that the majority of cases in which EU citizens need help in third countries concern consular protection" so that "the Commission will therefore concentrate on improving consular protection of Union citizens in third countries".[38] Notwithstanding, the Commission insured itself against possible future legal developments and thus did not completely exclude diplomatic protection from the scope of protection offered by Article 23 TFEU stating that "This is without prejudice to possible future action in the area of diplomatic protection."

Furthermore, it should be highlighted that Decision 95/553/EC regarding protection for citizens of the European Union by diplomatic

---

35 See e.g. RUFFERT, M., "Diplomatischer und konsularischer Schutz zwischen Völker- und Europarecht", in *Archiv des Völkerrechts*, 35 (1997), p. 472.

36 Article 3 para. 2 of the Vienna Convention on Diplomatic Relations of 1961: "Nothing in the present Convention shall be construed as preventing the performance of consular functions by a diplomatic mission."

37 See RENGELING, H. W. /SZCZEKALLA, P., *Grundrechte in der Europäischen Union. Charta der Grundrechte und Allgemeine Rechtsgrundsätze*, Köln-Berlin-München 2004, p. 940, para. 1147.

38 EUROPEAN COMMISSION, Action Plan 2007-2009 "Effective consular protection in third countries: the contribution of the European Union", Communication from the Commission to the European Parliament, the Council, the European Economic and Social Committee and the Committee of the Regions of 05 December 2007, COM(2007)767 final, p. 7. Available at: <http://eur-lex.europa.eu/LexUriServ/LexUriServ.do?uri=COM:2007:0767:FIN:EN:HTML> (15.08.2012).

and consular representations[39] refers to consular protection only. Article 1 of the Decision establishes that:

> Every citizen of the European Union is entitled to the **consular protection** of any Member State's diplomatic or consular representation if, in the place in which he is located, his own Member State or another State representing it on a permanent basis has no accessible permanent representation, or – accessible Honorary Consul competent for such matters.[40]

Many authors have argued that although Decision 95/553/EC is no secondary Community act but rather an intergovernmental act *sui generis*,[41] it must not contradict the primary EU law provision of Article 23 TFEU since the Decision itself is rooted in the Treaty.[42] This is evidenced by the Preamble of Decision 95/553/EC declaring that it was adopted by the Member States in order to perform the obligation under Article 23 TFEU (Article 8 c TEDC according to the Treaty of Maastricht) to establish the necessary rules among themselves.[43] Accordingly, these authors argue that the limitation on consular protection brought by Decision 95/553/EC would be invalid if the primary EU law provision of Article 23 TFEU embraced both consular and diplomatic protection.

Against the institutional approach to Article 23 TFEU can be argued that even disregarding that all 23 linguistic versions of the Treaties are equally binding,[44] those linguistic versions referring to "protection by the diplomatic and consular authorities" do not lead mandatorily to a limitation of the scope of protection on consular protection only. Rather, the notion "protection" does not imply any restriction in this sense[45] and the terms used in the different language versions of Article 23 allow

---

39 Decision 95/553/EC of the Representatives of the Governments of the Member States meeting within the Council of 19 December 1995 regarding protection for citizens of the European Union by diplomatic and consular representations, published in the Official Journal of the European Communities L 314 of 28.12.1995, pp. 0073-0076.

40 Emphasis added by author.

41 Please see to this dispute Chapter VII below.

42 RUFFERT, M., "Diplomatischer und konsularischer Schutz zwischen Völker- und Europarecht", p. 467, *op. cit.*, footnote 35.

43 Preamble of Decision 95/553/EC: "Desirous of performing the obligation laid down in Article 8c of the Treaty establishing the European Community…".

44 See Article 358 TFEU in conjunction with Article 55 para. 1 TEU: "This Treaty, drawn up in a single original in the Bulgarian, Czech, Danish, Dutch, English, Estonian, Finnish, French, German, Greek, Hungarian, Irish, Italian, Latvian, Lithuanian, Maltese, Polish, Portuguese, Romanian, Slovak, Slovenian, Spanish and Swedish languages, the texts in each of these languages being equally authentic […]".

45 GEYER, F., "The External Dimension of EU Citizenship, Arguing for Effective Protection of Citizens Abroad" in *Centre for European Policy Studies* (CEPS) No. 136, July 2007, p. 5.

both interpretations (diplomatic and consular protection versus consular protection only).[46] If so, the limitation on consular protection provided by Decision 95/553/EC would not contradict to Article 23 TFEU but rather would present an indication of the intention of the Member States as regards the scope of protection under Article 23 TFEU.

However, the limitation on consular protection of the scope of the protection provided under Article 23 TFEU in conjunction with Article 46 of the EU Charter of Fundamental Rights could be indicated by the need to achieve a better coexistence with the relevant international law rules as well as in order to guarantee the widest possible effect of EU provisions.

To this end it is necessary to distinguish between the concepts of diplomatic and consular protection taking into consideration the definitions and interpretations established in this regard by international law rules and the spirit and purpose of the relevant Union provisions.

2.1.1. Triggering Event

According to draft Article 1 of the UN Report of the International Law Commission 2006,[47]

> For the purposes of the present draft articles, diplomatic protection consists of the invocation by a State, through diplomatic action or other means of peaceful settlement, of the responsibility of another State for an injury caused by an internationally wrongful act of that State to a natural or legal person that is a national of the former State with a view to the implementation of such responsibility.

But even already in 1924 the Permanent Court of International Justice, the predecessor of the International Court of Justice from 1922 to 1946, held in its leading case on the jurisdiction of the Court "Mavrommatis Palestine Concessions"[48] that:

> It is an elementary principle of international law that a State is entitled to protect its subjects, when injured by acts contrary to international law committed by another State [...].

---

46 STEIN, T., "Die Regelung des diplomatischen Schutzes im Vertrag über die Europäische Union", in *Der diplomatische Schutz im Völker- und Europarecht. Aktuelle Probleme und Entwicklungstendenzen*, Georg Ress/Thorsten Stein (ed.), Baden-Baden 1996, pp. 97, 98.

47 Report on the work of the International Law Commission's fifty-eighth session (1 May to 9 June and 3 July to 11 August 2006), UN General Assembly, Official Records, Sixty-first Session, Supplement No. 10 (A/61/10). The International Law Commission recommended to the UN General Assembly the adoption of a convention on the basis of the draft articles on Diplomatic Protection. Available at: <http://untreaty.un.org/ilc/reports/2006/2006report.htm>.

48 Judgment of the Permanent Court of International Justice of 30.08.1924, Publications of the Permanent Court of International Justice, Series A, A02, p. 12.

Accordingly, diplomatic protection requires as a precondition an internationally wrongful action of another State. This action does not need to be directed against the State undertaking a diplomatic action but rather the injury of a private interest is capable of serving as an action that is wrongful according to international law. This was confirmed by the judgment of the Permanent Court of International Justice mentioned above stating that the dispute between an individual and a State is sufficient to establish a dispute between that State and the home State of the individual concerned.

In contrast, consular protection in terms of Union law does not require an internationally wrongful action of another State but shall be provided to citizens in distress caused not necessarily by human acts.[49] According to Article 5 para. 1 of Decision 95/553/EC, consular protection shall comprise *inter alia* assistance in case of death, serious accident or illness, arrest or detention and violent crime as well as relief and repatriation in situation of distress. Thus, among the circumstances, that may trigger the provision of consular protection, only the detention and arrest presuppose an action of the host State, while the majority of situations provoking the need of consular protection under Union law refer rather to situations not involving a state action (death, accident, illness, violent crime, etc.).

Accordingly, while the triggering event in case of diplomatic protection is an internationally wrongful act committed by a State, the distress situation requiring consular protection under EU law does not need necessarily to have been caused by an action of the host State but can rather arise without any human influence (e.g. natural disasters).

2.1.2. Nationality Rule and Third States' Consent

Another point of difference between diplomatic and consular protection is the "nationality rule" which means the requirement that claims may be brought by a State on condition that the affected person possesses its nationality.[50] As held by the International Court of Justice in the *Nottebohm* case,[51] this link has to be both genuine and effective. In this

---

49 See to this question the extraordinary analysis of VERMEER-KÜNZLI, A., "Exercising Diplomatic Protection, the Fine Line between Litigation, Demarches and Consular Assistance", in *ZaöRV* 66 (2006), pp. 321, 337.

50 See draft Article 3 para. 1 of the UN Report of the International Law Commission 2006 (A/61/10): "The State entitled to exercise diplomatic protection is the State of nationality." According to Article 4: "For the purposes of the diplomatic protection of a natural person, a State of nationality means a State whose nationality that person has acquired, in accordance with the law of that State, by birth, descent, naturalization, succession of States or in any other manner, not inconsistent with international law."

51 International Court of Justice, case *Lichtenstein v. Guatemala* (*Nottebohm* case), ICJ Reports 1955, p. 23.

regard, it should be pointed out that the "citizenship of the Union" is not a nationality, it is additional to and does not replace national citizenship,[52] and cannot be attributed to a State. Therefore, according to the nationality rule, the EU Member States would not be able to provide diplomatic protection on behalf of non-nationals, even if they were Union citizens.

Consular assistance provided under the Vienna Convention on Consular Relations refers to the nationality of the distressed citizens as well,[53] so that the nationality rule is applicable to both diplomatic and consular protection. The difference is most notably in the possibility to overcome the hurdles involved by it in practice. Under the strict application of the nationality rule, there seem to be no possibility for a Member State to provide diplomatic protection to non-national citizens on behalf of their State of origin. Article 46 of the Vienna Convention on Diplomatic Relations stipulates that:

> A sending State may with the prior consent of a receiving State, and at the request of a third State not represented in the receiving State, undertake the temporary protection of the interests of the third State and of its nationals.

In this case, the provision of diplomatic protection to non-national EU citizens would be conditional upon the previous consent of the third

---

52 Article 20 para. 1 TFEU: "Every person holding the nationality of a Member State shall be a citizen of the Union. Citizenship of the Union shall be additional to and not replace national citizenship."

53 Article 5 Vienna Convention on Consular Relations: Consular functions consist in:

"(a) protecting in the receiving State the interests of the sending State and of its nationals, both individuals and bodies corporate, within the limits permitted by international law;

...

(e) helping and assisting nationals, both individuals and bodies corporate, of the sending State;

...

(g) safeguarding the interests of nationals, both individuals and bodies corporate, of the sending States in cases of succession *mortis causa* in the territory of the receiving State, in accordance with the laws and regulations of the receiving State;

(h) safeguarding, within the limits imposed by the laws and regulations of the receiving State, the interests of minors and other persons lacking full capacity who are nationals of the sending State, particularly where any guardianship or trusteeship is required with respect to such persons;

(i) subject to the practices and procedures obtaining in the receiving State, representing or arranging appropriate representation for nationals of the sending State before the tribunals and other authorities of the receiving State, for the purpose of obtaining, in accordance with the laws and regulations of the receiving State, provisional measures for the preservation of the rights and interests of these nationals, where, because of absence or any other reason, such nationals are unable at the proper time to assume the defence of their rights and interests."

State obtained in the course of international negotiations. However, even after obtaining the consent of the third State, Article 46 of the Vienna Convention on Diplomatic Relations allows for only a temporary protection. The provision of protection on a temporary basis is not what is intended by Article 23 TFEU. Rather, the EU provision pretends to offer protection on a permanent basis to unrepresented EU citizens without the obligation for the Member States to establish own representations in each third country in order to prevent the extension of the temporary protection provided for by Article 46 VCDR to a permanent protection of their nationals in those third States where the Member States concerned are not represented.

Moreover, even if diplomatic protection could be provided in exceptional circumstances, in a concrete case and with the consent of the host State, given the importance of the relationship between States for the resolution of conflicts, it is hardly imaginable that an Union citizen could be provided with the right to ask any of the Member States represented in a third country for diplomatic protection, regardless the tradition of relationships between the Member State concerned and the host State. It is unlikely that any other government than the French one would have been able to launch a diplomatic offensive for the liberation of five Bulgarian nurses and a Palestinian doctor sentenced to death penalty in Libya in 2007.[54] Yet, although Bulgaria has a representation in Tripoli and long-standing relationships with the Libyan government, the personal implication of the then French President, Mr SARKOZY and his then wife, was – together with the support by the former Commissioner for External Affairs, FERRERO-WALDNER, – crucial for the resolution of the conflict.

Conversely, in the case of consular protection, according to Article 8 of the Vienna Convention on Consular Relations only a notification is necessary in order to provide consular protection to non-national citizens on behalf of their State of origin in third States:

> Upon appropriate notification to the receiving State, a consular post of the sending State may, unless the receiving State objects, exercise consular functions in the receiving State on behalf of a third State.

Accordingly, the link between consular protection and nationality is less strong that the one between diplomatic protection and nationality.[55] Therefore only consular protection can be easily rendered to nationals of another EU

---

[54] See also OKANO-HEIJMANS, M., "Changes in Consular Assistance and the Emergence of Consular Diplomacy", in *Consular Affairs and Diplomacy*, Leiden/ Boston 2011, p. 25.

[55] KLEINLEIN, T./ RABENSCHLAG, D., Auslandsschutz und Staatsangehörigkeit, in *Zeitschrift für ausländisches öffentliches Recht und Völkerrecht* (67) 2007, pp. 1227, 1297.

Member State by simply notifying the provision of consular protection to unrepresented non-national EU citizens to the third country concerned.

2.1.3. A Right to Diplomatic Protection under EU Law?

Another difference between diplomatic and consular protection is their legal character. Diplomatic protection has traditionally been considered as an exclusive State right[56] in the sense that a State exercises diplomatic protection in its own right because an injury to a national is deemed to be an injury to the State itself. This approach has its roots first in a statement by the Swiss jurist Emmerich de VATTEL in 1758 that "whoever ill-treats a citizen indirectly injures the State, which must protect that citizen". It was then taken up in a dictum of the Permanent Court of International Justice in 1924 in the *Mavrommatis Palestine Concessions* case:

> By taking up the case of one of its subjects and by resorting to diplomatic action or international judicial proceedings on his behalf, a State is in reality asserting *its own right*, the right to ensure, in the person of its subjects, respect for the rules of international law.[57]

This "fiction"[58] regarding the subjects of the dispute (act affecting an individual causing a dispute between two States) relies on the assumption that not an individual but only the State whose national he/she is, as subject of international law, is entitled to seek redress for an action violating international law. However, while in the early years of international law the individual had no place, no rights in the international legal order, in the meanwhile the individual has become the subject of many primary rules of international law, both under custom and treaty, which protect him at home, against his own Government, and abroad, against foreign Governments.[59]

This has been recognized by the International Court of Justice in the *LaGrand*[60] and *Avena*[61] cases. Although the individual has rights

---

56 It should be noted that in International Law the notion "right" is used also as regards public authorities, unlike Constitutional law where public authorities cannot be holders of rights but rather have powers and competences.

57 Emphasis added by author.

58 VERMEER-KÜNZLI, A., "As If: The Legal Fiction in Diplomatic Protection", in *EJIL* 2008, Vol. 18, No. 1, p. 37.

59 See commentary to draft Article 1 of the UN Report of the International Law Commission 2006 (A/61/10), *op. cit.*, footnote 21.

60 Judgment of the International Court of Justice in the *LaGrand* case (*Germany v. United States of America*), I.C.J. Reports 2001, p. 466, paras. 76-77.

61 Judgment of the International Court of Justice in the case concerning Avena and Other Mexican Nationals (*Mexico v. United States of America*), I.C.J. Reports, 2004, p. 12, para. 40.

under international law, the remedies are few. Diplomatic protection conducted by a State at inter-State level remains an important remedy for the protection of persons whose human rights have been violated abroad. Thus, according to the International Law Commission,[62] this fiction is still necessary since it should be distinguished between primary and secondary rules of international law. The individual has a right not to be tortured or not to be deprived of his or her property without compensation. These rights clearly are not the rights of a State. These rights of the individual, the violation of which may give rise to the exercise of diplomatic protection by his/her national State, belong to the field of primary rules of international law. However, the right of the State to exercise diplomatic protection in response to the violation of such a primary rule of international law by espousing the claim is a secondary rule of international law. As the international legal personality of the individual is incomplete, owing to the limited capacity of the individual to assert his or her rights, the fiction inherent in the *Mavrommatis Palestine Concessions* case is the means employed by international law – a secondary rule – to enforce the primary rule, which protects the undoubted right of the individual. In this sense, diplomatic protection and human rights law complement each other.

In 2005 and 2006, in a series of rulings, the Court of First Instance of the European Communities seemed to defy the reluctance of the international law rules to conceptualise diplomatic protection as an individual right that can be claimed vis-à-vis a State and to establish a new concept of an individual right to diplomatic protection in conjunction with the fundamental rights founded in the law of the European Union. The applicants in the cases *Yusuf*,[63] *Kadi*,[64] *Hassan*[65] and *Ayadi*[66] sought the same legal remedy against Community measures implementing resolutions of the UN Security Council regarding so called "targeted sanctions" against persons and entities allegedly associated with terrorist groups. In all four cases the applicants challenged

62 See Seventh Report on Diplomatic Protection by John Dugard, Special Rapporteur of the ILC of 07.03.2004, A/CN.4/567, p. 4. Available also at: <http://untreaty.un.org/ilc/documentation/english/a_cn4_567.pdf> (03.05.2009).

63 Judgment of the Court of First Instance of 21.09.2005 in the case T-306/01, Ahmed Ali Yusuf and Al Barakaat International Foundation v. Council of the European Union and Commission of the European Communities, ECR 2005, p. II-03533.

64 Judgment of the Court of First Instance of 21.09.2005 in the case T-315/01, *Yassin Abdullah Kadi v. Commission of the European Communities*, ECR 2005, p. II-03649.

65 Judgment of the Court of First Instance of 12.06.2006 in the case T-49/04, *Faraj Hassan v Council of the European Union and Commission of the European Communities*, ECR 2006, p. II-00052.

66 Judgment of the Court of First Instance of 12.06.2006 in the case T-253/02, *Chefiq Ayadi v. Council of the European Union*, ECR 2006, p. II-02139.

Council Regulation (EC) No. 881/2002 of 27 May 2002 imposing certain specific restrictive measures directed against certain persons and entities associated with Usama bin Laden, the Al-Qaeda network and the Taliban,[67] in implementation of Resolution 1267 (1999)[68] and Resolution 1333 (2000)[69] adopted by the Security Council of the United Nations. Paragraph 4(b) of Resolution 1267 (1999) provides that all States shall freeze funds and other financial resources owned or controlled by the Taliban and ensure that neither they nor any other funds or financial resources are made available, by their nationals or by any persons within their territory, to or for the benefit of the Taliban.[70]

All applicants in the cases in question were designated by the Sanctions Committee established by Security Council Resolution 1267 (1999), as the body responsible in particular for ensuring that the States implement the measures imposed by the Committee and for considering requests for exemptions from those measures,[71] as persons whose funds shall be frozen and their names were included into the list in Annex I to Council Regulation (EC) No. 881/2002. The Resolutions of the Security Council in question provided no possibility for an individual included in the list of persons whose funds shall be frozen to challenge that measure

---

67 Council Regulation (EC) No. 881/2002 of 27 May 2002 imposing certain specific restrictive measures directed against certain persons and entities associated with Usama bin Laden, the Al-Qaida network and the Taliban, and repealing Council Regulation (EC) No. 467/2001 prohibiting the export of certain goods and services to Afghanistan, strengthening the flight ban and extending the freeze of funds and other financial resources in respect of the Taliban of Afghanistan, OJ of 29.5.2002, L 139/9.

68 Resolution 1267 (1999) adopted by the Security Council at its 4051st meeting on 15 October 1999, S/RES/1267 (1999), establishing Security Council Committee and imposing limited air embargo and funds and financial assets embargo on the Taliban.

69 Resolution 1333 (2000) adopted by the Security Council at its 4251st meeting, on 19 December 2000, S/RES/1333 (2000) on air and arms embargo, restricted travel sanctions, freezing of funds of Usama Bin Laden and associates.

70 Paragraph 4 (b) of Resolution 1267 (1999) provides that: "All states shall freeze funds and other financial resources, including funds derived or generated from property owned or controlled directly or indirectly by the Taliban, or by any undertaking owned or controlled by the Taliban, as designated by the Committee established by paragraph 6 below, and ensure that neither they nor any other funds or financial resources so designated are made available, by their nationals or by any persons within their territory, to or for the benefit of the Taliban or any undertaking owned or controlled, directly or indirectly, by the Taliban, except as may be authorised by the Committee on a case-by-case basis on the grounds of humanitarian need."

71 Paragraph 6 of Resolution 1267 (1999) the Security Council decided to establish, in accordance with rule 28 of its provisional rules of procedure, a committee of the Security Council composed of all its members ('the Sanctions Committee'), responsible in particular for ensuring that the States implement the measures imposed by paragraph 4, designating the funds or other financial resources referred to in paragraph 4 and considering requests for exemptions from the measures imposed by paragraph 4."

before the Sanctions Committee in charge of the update of the lists. In contrast, the "Guidelines of the [Sanctions] Committee for the conduct of its work" foresees that the petitioners shall approach the government of their country of residence and request the government to forward their request for de-listing to the Sanctions Committee.[72] Accordingly, the petitioners rely on the support by the government concerned in order to file a complaint against their inclusion in the list with targeted sanctions and cannot approach directly the Sanctions Committee.

The Court of First Instance sought to close this gap in the possibilities of direct complaint with the Sanctions Committee by stating in the *obiter dictums* of the rulings in the cases *Yusuf* and *Kadi* that individuals concerned are "dependent, essentially, on the diplomatic protection afforded by States to their nationals".[73] But whereas in the ruling in *Kadi* and *Yusuf* the Court still referred to the discretion of the competent national authorities relating to the right of the person concerned to make his point of view known,[74] in the cases *Ayadi* and *Hassan* one year later the Court held that the Member States, that have been approached with a de-listing request, "are required to act promptly to ensure that such persons' cases are presented without delay and fairly and impartially to the Committee, with a view to their examination…".[75]

The Court of First Instance seemed to derive a Union-tailored 'right to diplomatic protection' from the Member States' obligation pursuant to Article 6 para. 2 TEU[76] to respect the fundamental rights of the

---

72 Security Council Committee Established pursuant to Resolution 1267 (1999) concerning Al-Qaida and the Taliban and Associated Individuals and Entities, Guidelines of the Committee for the conduct of its work of 7.11.2002 with further amendments. Available at: <http://www.un.org/Docs/sc/committees/1267/1267_guidelines.pdf>. Section 8 stipulates:

"(a) Without prejudice to available procedures, a petitioner (individual(s), groups, undertakings, and/or entities on the Committee's consolidated list) may petition the government of residence and/or citizenship to request review of the case. In this regard, the petitioner should provide justification for the de-listing request, offer relevant information and request support for de-listing;"

73 Judgment of the Court of First Instance in the case *Yusuf*, para. 314, *op. cit.*, footnote 63; Judgment of the Court of First Instance in the case Kadi, para. 267, *op. cit.*, footnote 64.

74 *Ibidem*. Judgment *Yusuf*, para. 327.

75 Judgment of the Court of First Instance in case *Ayadi*, para. 149, *op. cit.*, footnote 66; Judgment of the Court of First Instance in case Hassan, para. 119, *op. cit.*, footnote 65.

76 After the entry into force of the Treaty of Lisbon, Article 6 para. 3 Treaty on European Union: "Fundamental rights, as guaranteed by the European Convention for the Protection of Human Rights and Fundamental Freedoms and as they result from the constitutional traditions common to the Member States, shall constitute general principles of the Union's law."

persons, as guaranteed by the European Convention on Human Rights and Fundamental Freedoms and as they result from the constitutional traditions common to the Member States.[77]

However, it is worth noting that the Court of First Instance did not confirm in the present cases a claim founded on a 'right to diplomatic protection' *per se*, at least since the applicants in the cases *Ayadi, Hassan and Kadi* were no nationals of the Member States concerned[78] and the Court referred expressly to diplomatic protection afforded by States "to their nationals".

Moreover, diplomatic protection in terms of international law rules would be applicable vis-à-vis another State but not vis-à-vis an international body, in the present case the Sanctions Committee established by the UN Security Council.[79]

Admittedly, the Court underlined that since the exercise of the fundamental rights of the applicants to be heard by the competent authorities and to effective judicial protection is impossible without the collaboration of the government of their country of residence, the Member States in question shall guarantee the efficiency of the de-listing procedure. However, the effective functioning of any internal procedures in order to guarantee the fundamental rights of the persons affected by targeted sanctions as well as the forwarding of the request of a non-national person by the government of his/her country of residence cannot be regarded as provision of diplomatic protection in terms of international law. The Court rather limited the so called "diplomatic protection" to the obligation of the Member States to pay due attention to the possible violation of fundamental rights and procedural rights of the persons concerned in examining their request for de-listing.

It is therefore rather a question of guaranteeing effectively the exercise of fundamental rights and procedural rights stemming from the rule of law. However, not every act of a State seeking to guarantee the fundamental rights of citizens residing on its territory can be

---

77 See Judgment of the Court of First Instance in case *Ayadi*, para. 146, *op. cit.*, footnote 66.

78 Mr Ayadi is a Tunisian national residing in Ireland, Mr Hassan is a Libyan national residing (detained) in the United Kingdom and Mr Kadi is national of Saudi Arabia who resided temporally in the United Kingdom.

79 Please see Article 1 of the draft articles on diplomatic protection adopted by the International Law Commission, *op. cit.*, footnote 21.

Article 1 Definition and Scope: "For the purposes of the present draft articles, diplomatic protection consists of the invocation by a State, through diplomatic action or other means of peaceful settlement, of the responsibility of another State for an injury caused by an internationally wrongful act of that State to a natural or legal person that is a national of the former State with a view to the implementation of such responsibility."

regarded as diplomatic protection and it cannot be assumed that the intention of the Court of First Instance was to establish such a Union-law-tailored diplomatic protection.[80] The simply forwarding of a petition for de-listing to an international institution, submitted even more by a non-national citizen, does not suppose any further implication of the State concerned in the procedure before the Sanctions Committee[81] and does not represent an act of reparation of a harm caused to the State as a consequence of the harm caused to the petitioner. Rather, as the Court pointed out, the Member State concerned acts in those cases within the framework of an "administrative procedure on several levels, in which the national authorities ... play an indispensable part".[82] Accordingly, the Court did not seek to establish a right to diplomatic protection founded in European Union law[83] but rather affirmed that the discretion of the national authorities in examining the request of the petitioner is not guided by the procedural rules, and therefore without any specifications, established by international law only (Guidelines of the Sanctions Committee) but is delimited by the fundamental rights of the person concerned as guaranteed under Union law.[84] The "diplomatic protection" referred to by the Court of First Instance is therefore not a legal institute appropriate to describe the obligation incumbent upon the Member States to observe the fundamental rights of the citizens when implementing Union law.

---

80 It should be noted in this context that the Court of Justice did not mention diplomatic protection in its ruling on appeal in the cases *Hassan* and *Ayadi*. See Judgment of the Court of Justice of 03.12.2009 in the cases C-399/06 P and C-403/06 P, *Faraj Hassan v. Council of the European Union and European Commission, and Chafiq Ayadi v. Council of the European Union*, ECR 2009, p. I-11393.

81 "Guidelines of the Committee for the conduct of its work", *op. cit.*, footnote 72:
Section 8 d): "The petitioned government may, [...], submit a request for de-listing to the Committee, pursuant to the no-objection procedure;"
Section 8 e): "The Committee will reach decisions by consensus of its members."

82 Judgment of the Court of First Instance in the case *Yusuf*, para. 315, *op. cit.*, footnote 63; Judgment of the Court of First Instance in the case *Kadi*, para. 268, *op. cit.*, footnote 64.

83 Different opinion SIMON, D./ MARIATTE, F., "Le 'droit' à la protection diplomatique: droit fondamental en droit communautaire?", in *Europe*, 2006, Etude 11, pp. 4, 6.

84 See Judgment of the Court of Justice in the case Hassan, where the Court held that: "The Member States must thus ensure, so far as is possible, that interested persons are put in a position to assert their point of view before the competent national authorities when they present a request to be removed from the list. Furthermore, the discretion that it is to be recognised that those authorities enjoy in this respect must be exercised in such a way as to take due account of the difficulties that the persons concerned may encounter in arranging for the effective protection of their rights, having regard to the specific context and nature of the measures affecting them." Judgment of the Court of First Instance in the case *Hassan*, para. 117, *op. cit.*, footnote 65.

In contrast, there are no objections on the part of international law to conceive consular protection under EU law as a right of the individuals and not as a State' power. Quite the contrary, the individual character of consular protection has been explicitly affirmed by the International Court of Justice in the *LaGrand* and *Avena* cases, where the ICJ went to conclude that rights related to consular assistance are not merely rights of states in interstate relations but are also individual rights.[85]

2.1.4. Discretionary Character of Diplomatic Protection

As a consequence of diplomatic protection being a right of the State, it is characterized by the wide scope of discretion of which the State concerned disposes. A State is under international law not obliged to exercise diplomatic protection on behalf of a national who has suffered harm as a result of an internationally wrongful act attributable to another State. The discretionary nature of the State's right to exercise diplomatic protection is affirmed by draft Article 2 of the UN Report of the International Law Commission and has been asserted by the International Court of Justice in the *Barcelona Traction* case:[86]

> The State must be viewed as the sole judge to decide whether its protection will be granted, to what extent it is granted, and when it will cease. It retains in this respect a discretionary power the exercise of which may be determined by considerations of a political or other nature, unrelated to the particular case.

However, due to tendencies within the national legislations (and practices) of the UN members, the ILC draft Article 19 establishes a "Recommended practice" declaring that a State entitled to exercise diplomatic protection "should [...] give due consideration to the possibility of exercising diplomatic protection, especially when a significant injury has occurred". However, this provision is of mere recommendatory and not of prescriptive nature not able to cause any legal consequence to a State not observing this recommendation.[87]

---

85 In the *LaGrand* case the International Court of Justice held that article 36 of the Vienna Convention on Consular Relations "creates individual rights, which by virtue of Article 1 of the Optional Protocol, may be invoked in this Court by the national State of the detained person" (LaGrand (*Germany v. United States of America*), p. 494, para. 77) and in the *Avena* case the Court further observed "that violations of the rights of the individual under article 36 may entail a violation of the rights of the sending State, and that violations of the rights of the latter may entail a violation of the rights of the individual" (Case concerning Avena and Other Mexican Nationals (*Mexico v. United States of America*), p. 26, para. 40).

86 Case concerning the Barcelona Traction Light and Power Company Limited (Belgium v. Spain), Second Phase, Judgment, I.C.J. Reports 1970, p. 4, p. 44.

87 Different opinion VERMEER-KÜNZLI, A., "Restricting Discretion: Judicial Review of Diplomatic Protection" in *Nordic Journal of International Law*, Vol. 75 (2006), p. 93.

Accordingly, being diplomatic protection a power of the State, the decision on whether to take or not an action in defence of the legitimate interests of the individual concerned is at the State's discretion. In this regard, it should be pointed out that the State has a wide scope of discretion, being the overriding consideration of general State's interests over those of an individual a legitimate use of that discretion.

Again, there is no international law rule reserving consular protection to the full State' discretion. Rather, since, as stated above, consular protection may be conceived as an individual right, there is no need to obscure consular protection provided under EU law with unlimited State' discretion.

2.1.5. Interim Findings

The findings in the previous sections show that diplomatic and consular protection feature different embodiments due to their multilevel context, containing legal rules at national, but in particular at international and European Union level. While consular protection shall by provided by diplomatic and consular missions to unrepresented Union citizens abroad in situations of distress that can be caused by human actions, natural disasters or an action of the host State, diplomatic protection in terms of international law requires the existence of an internationally wrongful act of the host State. Moreover, whereas diplomatic protection is provided on a permanent basis only to nationals of the State concerned, the international-law rules on consular protection do not object per se the provision of consular protection to non-national citizens. Another characteristic differentiating consular and diplomatic protection at Union and international level is the discretionary character of diplomatic protection as well as its legal concept as a "State right" that could lead to discrepancies with the provision of protection to unrepresented Union citizens in third countries as a legal position stemming from Union citizenship.

Therefore, it is necessary to determine the relationship between the different possible concepts at Union and international level, establishing any hierarchical relationship between diplomatic protection under international law and consular protection under EU and national law or, otherwise, any rules of coexistence of the different concepts of protection of Union citizens abroad.

2.2. Relationship between International and EU Law Rules

The provision of consular protection to unrepresented Union citizens links together obligations under EU law on the one side and on the other side, due to its extraterritorial character, rules of general and specific public international law. The potential consequence of this concurrence is that the implementation of the obligation under European Union law comes up against the limits drawn by public international law, so that it is necessary to establish first the relationship between those two legal systems in order to establish the conceptual limits of consular protection under European Union law.

The traditional dichotomy between monism and dualism seeking to explain the relationship between international and national law seems not to be able to approach the interaction among international, European Union and national law. While, according to the monism doctrine, international law and national law are part of a single legal order governed by hierarchical rules replacing the need of 'translating' international law into national law,[88] the "dualists" postulate the superiority of the international and national legal systems in their respective sphere of application with the consequence that international law is not automatically incorporated into national law, its application being rather dependent on some form of adopting national act.[89]

KELSEN, as one of the most outstanding representatives of the monist epistemological school, argues that the fact that international law obligates the state to perform certain acts or to adopt certain legal norms, means merely that a contrary act is sanctioned by the international law rules as an unlawful act.[90] However, according to KELSEN national norms violating international law remain valid as even international law provided for no invalidation of norms contrary to international law.[91]

The representatives of the dualist theory draw also on the conflict between obligations emanating from international and national law, which should not be resolved via subordination of one of the legal systems to the other, but rather by co-ordinating the different obligations imposed by two different legal orders.[92]

Yet, both dogmatic approaches offer no rules of game as for the triangular relationship including the interlacement between European Union law and national law, taking into account the supremacy of EU law over national law, as well as the "intersections" between EU law and international law. The supremacy of EU law over national

---

88 KELSEN, H., *Reine Rechtslehre: Einleitung in die rechtswissenschaftliche Problematik*, Aalen 1985, pp. 105-120.

89 FITZMAURICE, G., *Recueil des Cours*, Collected Courses, Volume 92 (1957-II), The Hague 1992, pp. 68 et seq.

90 KELSEN, H., *Reine Rechtslehre…*, p. 114, *op. cit.*, footnote 88.

91 *Ibidem*.

92 FITZMAURICE, G., *Recueil des Cours*, pp. 69 et seq., *op. cit.*, footnote 89.

law, including the national constitutions,[93] created a new paradigm of relationships between legal orders and modified the previous hierarchical or coordination mechanisms between international and national law, interposing itself often between international and national law[94] as a new form of legal order created among sovereign States.

In this context, it should be noted that the European Union is itself a product of international law since, in its origins, it is a product of the relationship between sovereign states with the purpose of creating reciprocal rights and obligations.[95] Nevertheless, it is obvious that the Union has a character different from other traditional arrangements of international law.

Thus, the Court of Justice went to conclude in its leading case *van Gend & Loos*[96] that the EEC Treaty went over and beyond the traditional agreements between International Law actors implying merely obligations between the contracting states. Rather the Community legal order involved new actors with a growingly active rather than a passive roll – the citizens of the Member States of the European Communities. In that connection, the Court stated that this active roll of the people as addresses of the Community provisions, besides the Member States, has been reflected by the establishment of institutions endowed with sovereign rights whose exercise affects not only Member States but also their citizens.[97] Therefore, the Court held that:

> [...] the community constitutes a new legal order of international law for the benefit of which the states have limited their sovereign rights, albeit within

---

93 See Judgment of the Court of Justice of 17.12.1970 in the case 11/70, Internationale Handelsgesellschaft mbH v. Einfuhr- und Vorratsstelle für Getreide und Futtermittel, ECR 1970, p. 1125.

94 See BETHLEHEM, D., "International Law, European Community Law, National Law: Three Systems in Search of a Framework, Systematic Relativity in the Interaction of Law in the European Union", in *International Law Aspects of the European Union*, Martti Koskenniemi (ed.), The Hague/London/Boston, 1998, p. 172.

95 *Ibidem*, p. 178.

96 Judgment of the Court of Justice of 05.02.1963 in the case 26/62, *NV Algemene Transport en Expeditie Onderneming van Gend & Loos v. Netherlands Inland Revenue Administration* (van Gend & Loos), ECR 1963, p. 00001.

97 *Ibidem*. The Court held that: "The objective of the EEC treaty, which is to establish a common market, the functioning of which is of direct concern to interested parties in the community, implies that this treaty is more than an agreement which merely creates mutual obligations between the contracting states. This view is confirmed by the preamble to the treaty which refers not only to governments but to people. It is also confirmed more specifically by the establishment of institutions endowed with sovereign rights, the exercise of which affects Member States and also their citizens. Furthermore, it must be noted that the nationals of the states brought together in the Community are called upon to cooperate in the functioning of this community through the intermediary of the European Parliament and the Economic and Social committee."

limited fields, and the subjects of which comprise not only Member States but also their nationals.[98]

Furthermore, the citizens of the Member States – as citizens of the Union – directly elect Members of the European Parliament, which controls the European Commission and co-decides together with the Council of the European Union upon legislative acts. As highlighted by PERNICE, this kind of provisions for democratic legitimacy as well as the protection of fundamental rights are specific for constitutional public authority rather than for acts of an international organization and hence more state-like features.[99]

Thus, by creating a new legal order, that involves actors different from those inherent to the traditional International Law treaties, and by establishing mechanisms and institutions guaranteeing the rights and interests of those new actors – the nationals of the Member States –, the Community legal order[100] seems not to be "absorbed" into the international-law framework, but is rather governed by own, autonomous, rules that need to be accommodated to the practical and legal realities and demands established by international law rules governing the relationship of the Member States with third countries and other actors of international law.

The Treaties provide for only partially a coordination model between rights and obligations stemming from EU law and international law rules. Tracing back to the *pacta sunt servanda* principle, established *inter alia* by Article 26 of the Vienna Convention on the Law of Treaties of 1969,[101] Article 351 para. 1 TFEU (ex-Article 307 TEC) stipulates a chronological hierarchy between the Constitutive Treaties of the European Communities and other International Law treaties establishing the intangibility of those international treaties concluded by the Member States (or some of them) before the entry into force of the Rome Treaties:

> The rights and obligations arising from agreements concluded before 1 January 1958 or, for acceding States, before the date of their accession, between one or more Member States on the one hand, and one or more third countries on the other, shall not be affected by the provisions of the Treaties.

98 *Ibidem*.

99 PERNICE, I. E. A., "The Treaty of Lisbon: Multilevel Constitutionalism in Action", in *Columbia Journal of European Law*, Vol. 15, No. 3/2009, p. 367.

100 Since the Treaty of Lisbon, the legal order of the European Union.

101 Vienna Convention on the Law of Treaties, done at Vienna on 23 May 1969, entered into force on 27 January 1980. United Nations, Treaty Series, Vol. 1155, p. 331. Article 26 of the Vienna Convention on the Law of Treaties reads: "Every treaty in force is binding upon the parties to it and must be performed by them in good faith."

The provision of Article 351 para. 1 TFEU establishes the principle of international-law loyalty of the European Union on the basis of integration consistent with the rules of international law.[102]

As for the international agreements on consular protection, attention is invited to the fact that the Vienna Convention on Diplomatic Relations and the Vienna Convention on Consular Relations were signed in 1961 and 1963 respectively so that the international agreements concerned do not precede the Rome Treaties of 1958. However, Article 351 para. 1 needs to be teleologically interpreted according to its spirit and purpose so that account being had of the progressive Community integration and thus the gradual development of the Community competences, the provision should be analogically applied to international agreements concluded before the inclusion of a certain subject matter into the Treaties.[103]

Since the provisions on consular protection were included into the Treaty on the European Community by the Treaty of Maastricht in 1993 and the international rules in this regard had already entered into force at that moment, the keynote of Article 351 TFEU applies analogically also to the provision of consular protection under European Union law.

As for the consequences of the 'untouchability' clause it should be pointed out that Article 351 TFEU demands rather the practical concordance between earlier international agreements and the Treaty provisions than the primacy of those agreements over Treaty provisions relating to the same subject matter, which is evidenced by the second paragraph of Article 351 TFEU that establishes merely an obligation of the Member States to eliminate the incompatibilities in question.[104]

Article 351 para. 2 TFEU stipulates an obligation on the part of the Member States and not on the European Union itself. In this context it could be argued that the obligation upon the Member States should refer to the roll of the Member States as contracting parties to the Treaties so that an incompatibility with an older international agreement should be removed by amending the relevant Treaty provisions. However, according to Article 48 EUV not only the Member States but also the European Parliament or the Commission can submit proposals for the amendment of the Treaties to the Council that forward such proposal to

[102] TERHECHTE, J.P., "Kommentar zum Artikel 351 AEUV", in *EU Kommentar*, Jürgen Schwarze (ed.), Baden-Baden 2012, para. 2.

[103] *Ibidem*, para. 16.

[104] Article 351 para. 2, first clause: "To the extent that such agreements are not compatible with the Treaties, the Member State or States concerned shall take all appropriate steps to eliminate the incompatibilities established."

the European Council.[105] Thus, not only the Member States, that need to ratify the amendments to the Treaties, but also several Union institutions are involved in the revision procedure.[106]

Moreover, it should be highlighted that the Treaty of Lisbon introduced a new form of a simplified revision procedure according to which the European Council upon proposal submitted by the Government of any Member State, the European Parliament or the Commission, may adopt a decision amending all or part of the provisions of Part Three of the Treaty on the Functioning of the European Union on internal policies and action of the Union, e.g. on the provisions relating to internal market.[107]

---

105 Article 48 para. 1 and 2 TEU: "The Treaties may be amended in accordance with an ordinary revision procedure. They may also be amended in accordance with simplified revision procedures.

Ordinary revision procedure

2. The Government of any Member State, the European Parliament or the Commission may submit to the Council proposals for the amendment of the Treaties. These proposals may, inter alia, serve either to increase or to reduce the competences conferred on the Union in the Treaties. These proposals shall be submitted to the European Council by the Council and the national Parliaments shall be notified."

106 Please note that the Treaty of Lisbon included for the first time also the European Council as a Union institution. Article 13 para. 1 TEU: The Union shall have an institutional framework which shall aim to promote its values, advance its objectives, serve its interests, those of its citizens and those of the Member States, and ensure the consistency, effectiveness and continuity of its policies and actions.

The Union's institutions shall be:

the European Parliament,

the European Council,

the Council,

the European Commission (hereinafter referred to as 'the Commission'),

the Court of Justice of the European Union,

the European Central Bank,

the Court of Auditors.

107 Article 48 para. 6 TEU: "The Government of any Member State, the European Parliament or the Commission may submit to the European Council proposals for revising all or part of the provisions of Part Three of the Treaty on the Functioning of the European Union relating to the internal policies and action of the Union.

The European Council may adopt a decision amending all or part of the provisions of Part Three of the Treaty on the Functioning of the European Union. The European Council shall act by unanimity after consulting the European Parliament and the Commission, and the European Central Bank in the case of institutional changes in the monetary area. That decision shall not enter into force until it is approved by the Member States in accordance with their respective constitutional requirements.

The decision referred to in the second subparagraph shall not increase the competences conferred on the Union in the Treaties."

Therefore, it can be assumed that by establishing an obligation to eliminate the incompatibilities between international agreements and Treaty provisions upon the Member States and not upon the Union itself, the Treaty stipulates an obligation to resolve any conflicts in favour of European Union law, i.e. not by adapting of the EU law rules but rather by adapting or cancelling of the older international agreements.[108]

The Court of Justice seems to consider the adaptation of the Community provisions as an exceptional option that takes place only under very restrictive conditions. In its judgement in the case *T. Port* the Court held that for a community provision to be deprived of effect as a result of an international agreement, the rights of a third country must have been affected so that the third country concerned must derive from it rights which it can require the Member State concerned to respect.[109] In a more recent case the Court relativised yet the importance of the rights of third countries affected by the Community provisions, stating that the fact that a Member State encounters difficulties in bringing its obligations to a third state in line with its obligations under Community law does not release that Member State from its obligation to adjust, and when necessary to denounce the conflicting agreement.[110] Notwithstanding, it cannot be assumed that the Treaties require the Member States to commit an internationally wrongful action in order to release themselves from an international agreement.[111] In fact, this kind of far-reaching obligation under Article 351 para. 2 TFEU would contradict the principle of international-law-loyalty established by Article 351 para. 1 TFEU.

This approach could be observed also in the case-law of the Court of Justice that has continuously drawn on international law rules as basis for interpretation of Community provisions in order to achieve their peaceful coexistence and to guarantee that Community rules do not hinder Member States to fulfil their obligations under international law. Already in 1972 the Court of Justice held in the judgment in the case *Interfood* that international agreements concluded by the European Community "may be of assistance in interpreting"

[108] KRÜCK, H., "Kommentar zum Artikel 307 EGV", *op. cit.*, footnote 102, para. 10.

[109] Judgment of the Court of Justice of 10.03.1998 in joined cases C-364/95 and C-365/95, *T. Port GmbH & Co. v. Hauptzollamt Hamburg-Jonas*, ECR 1998, p. I-1035.

[110] Judgment of the Court of Justice of 04.07.2000 in the case *European Commission v. Portugal*, ECR 2000, I-5215, paras. 58, 59.

[111] See in this sense also KRÜCK, H., "Kommentar zum Artikel 307 EGV", para. 10, *op. cit.*, footnote 102.

Community rules[112] and went further in its judgment in the case *International Dairy Arrangement* in 1996 establishing the primacy of international agreements concluded by the Community over provisions of secondary Community legislation so that "such provisions must, so far as is possible, be interpreted in a manner that is consistent with those agreements".[113]

Worth mentioning is here the analogy drawn by the Court of Justice between the conform interpretation of Community provisions and international agreements concluded by the Community on the one side and secondary and primary Community law on the other side.[114]

However, consular protection of unrepresented Union citizens in third countries is regulated at international law level by the Vienna Convention on Consular Relations and thus not by an international agreement concluded by the Community/Union itself but by the Member States.[115] Therefore the question arises whether the principles established by the Court of Justice as regarding the interpretation of Community legislation in accordance with agreements to which the Community is a party, are applicable also to other rules of general or specific international law.

The Court upheld this principle of co-operation between Community and international law provisions in the case *Bosphorus* in 1996 where the Court interpreted Regulation No. 990/93 of the Council[116] in line with the

---

[112] Judgment of the Court of Justice of the European Communities of 24.04.1973 in the case 92/71, *Interfood GmbH v. Hauptzollamt Hamburg-Ericus*, ECR 1973, p. 231, 242 (6th ground of the Judgment).

[113] Judgment of the Court of Justice of the European Communities of 10.09.1996 in the case C-61/94, *Commission of the European Communities, v. Federal Republic of Germany*, ECR 1996, p. I-4006, para. 52.

[114] *Ibidem*: "When the wording of secondary Community legislation is open to more than one interpretation, preference should be given as far as possible to the interpretation which renders the provision consistent with the Treaty. Likewise, an implementing regulation must, if possible, be given an interpretation consistent with the basic regulation [...]. Similarly, the primacy of international agreements concluded by the Community over provisions of secondary Community legislation means that such provisions must, so far as is possible, be interpreted in a manner that is consistent with those agreements."

[115] All 28 EU Member States have ratified the Vienna Convention on Consular Relations, see the Status of Signatories and Parties to the Vienna Convention on Consular Relations as at 01.11.2013, available at: <http://treaties.un.org/Pages/ViewDetails.aspx?src=UNTSONLINE&tabid=2&mtdsg_no=III-6&chapter=3&lang=en#Participants>.

[116] Council Regulation (EEC) No. 990/93 of 26 April 1993 concerning trade between the European Economic Community and the Federal Republic of Yugoslavia (Serbia and Montenegro) (OJ 1993 L 102, p. 14. Council regulation (EEC) No. 3300/91 of 11 November 1991 suspending the trade concessions provided for by the Cooperation Agreement between the European Economic Community and the Socialist Federal

resolutions of the Security Council of the United Nations regarding the embargo against the Federal Republic of Yugoslavia.[117] This approach was reiterated also in the judgment in the case *Ebony* relating to the same Regulation.[118]

Nonetheless, both judgements deal with Community legislation implementing, at least partially, resolutions of the Security Council of the United Nations, and thus international law, so that by interpreting Community legislation in accordance with the international rules that originated the implementing Community legislation in question, the Court of Justice merely applied the logic of relationships between basic and implementing rules as stipulated in the judgment in the case *International Dairy Arrangement*[119] mentioned above.

Conversely, the EU provisions on protection of unrepresented Union citizens in third countries have not been included into the Treaties in order to give effect to an international agreement but constitute original Union law. Thus, the question should be posed of whether EU legal rules should be interpreted in a manner consistent with any rules of international law, even when the EU legal rules concerned have not been adopted in implementation of or, in general terms, in order to give effect to an international agreement or customary international law.

The Court of Justice had for the first time to decide on the relationship between Community and international-law rules, without any implementation link between them, in a Law of the Sea case in 1992. In the case *Poulsen and Diva Navigation* the Court of Justice had to deal with a preliminary question on the interpretation of Council Regulation 3094/86/EEC laying down certain technical measures for the conservation of fishery resources.[120] The Court of Justice pointed out that in order to interpret the Regulation in question, account must be taken of all relevant conventional international law as well as of customary international

---

Republic of Yugoslavia, *Official Journal of the European Communities* 1991 L 315, p. 1.

117 Judgment of the Court of Justice of 30.07.1996 in the case C-84/95, *Bosphorus Hava Yollari Turizm v. Ticaret AS v. Minister for Transport, Energy and Communications and others*, European Court Reports ECR 1996, p. 03953, paras. 14, 15.

118 Judgment of the Court of Justice of 27.02.1997 in the case C-177/95, *Ebony Maritime SA, Loten Navigation Co. Ltd v. Prefetto della Provincia di Brindisi and others*, European Court Reports 1997, p. I-1131, paras. 20, 24.

119 Judgment of the Court of Justice of the European Communities of 10.09.1996 in the case C-61/94, *Commission of the European Communities, v. Federal Republic of Germany*, ECR 1996, p. I-4006, para. 52.

120 Council Regulation (EEC) No. 3094/86 of 7.10.1986, laying down certain technical measures for the conservation of fishery resources, published in the Official Journal of the European Communities 1986 L 288, p. 1.

maritime law. The Court argued that the European Community must respect international law in the exercise of its powers and that Community provisions "must be interpreted, and its scope limited, in the light of the relevant rules of international law".[121]

The Court noted that within the interpretation of the provisions of the Regulation in question, great importance should be placed on its objective, stating that "the provision must be interpreted so as to give it [the objective pursued] the greatest practical effect, within the limits of international law".[122]

By emphasizing the importance of the objective of the Union law provision to be interpreted in accordance with international law, the Court has rejected – though not expressly – an interpretation *contra legem*,[123] preventing itself of assuming the role of the Community legislator.

This case-law was upheld in the case *Racke*[124] where the Court held that the rules of customary international law concerning the termination and the suspension of treaty relations by reason of fundamental change of circumstances (*rebus sic stantibus*) are binding upon the Community institutions. The Court of Justice reiterated that the European Community must respect international law in the exercise of its powers[125] and held that although conventional international law is not *per se* integrated into the Community legal order when neither the Community nor all Member States are contracting parties to an international convention, as for instance the Vienna Convention on the Law of Treaties of 1969, the rules of customary international law, codified by that Convention, do form part of the Community legal order.[126]

The case-law of the Court of Justice shows the intention of the Court to seek reconciliation between both legal orders rather than a hierarchical controversy. Nevertheless, the case-law mentioned relates to secondary Union law, i.e. legal provisions adopted by the institutions of the European Union,[127] establishing the obligation of the European Community to observe

---

121 Judgment of the Court of Justice of the European Communities of 24.11.1992 in the case C-286/90, *Poulsen and Diva Navigation*, ECR 1992, I-6048, para. 9.

122 *Ibidem*, para. 11.

123 See in this sense also DÍEZ-HOCHLEITNER, J., *La posición del Derecho Internacional en el Ordenamiento comunitario*, Madrid 1998, p. 87.

124 Judgment of the Court of Justice of 16.06.1998 in the case C-162/96, *A. Racke GmbH v. Hauptzollamt Mainz*, ECR 1998, p. I-03655.

125 *Ibidem*, para. 45.

126 *Ibidem*, para. 24 and 46.

127 While primary Union law consists of those provisions adopted directly by the Member States in their capacity as "constituent authority", meaning the constituent Treaties and the Treaties amending and supplementing them, as well as general principles of law,

the relevant international-law rules when adopting legislation or other measures in exercise of its competences conferred by the Member States.

However, the provisions on consular protection under European Union law are governed by the Treaties themselves, i.e. primary Union law, and not by secondary Union law, so that the principles established by the Court of Justices in the cases *Poulsen and Diva Navigation*, *Bosphorus* and *Racke* cannot be directly applied to the relationship between Treaty provisions and international-law rules on the subject matter concerned.

The primacy of international law rules over Union secondary legislation has been confirmed by the Court of Justice also in the recent judgment on the appeal against the judgment of the Court of First Instance in the cases *Kadi* and *Yusuf* where the Court had to rule on the validity of a targeted sanction in the form of freezing of assets (restrictive measure against natural or legal persons) imposed by a Community Regulation implementing an UN Resolution relating to the combat of terrorism.[128] In both cases the applicants challenged Council Regulation (EC) No. 881/2002 of 27 May 2002 imposing certain specific restrictive measures directed against certain persons and entities associated with Usama bin Laden, the Al-Qaeda network and the Taliban, in implementation of Resolution 1267 (1999)[129] and Resolution 1333 (2000)[130] adopted by the Security Council of the United Nations Resolutions under Chapter VII of the Charter of the United Nations.[131]

Examining the relationship between the international legal order and the domestic legal orders or the Community legal order, the Court

to which also the fundamental rights count, secondary/derived Union law is adopted on the legal basis provided by primary Union law by the institutions of the European Union and must be consistent with the rules of primary Union law (See an overview of the hierarchical structure of the sources of Union law LENAERTS, K./ VAN NUFFEL, P., *Constitutional Law of the European Union*, Robert BRAY (ed.), 2. edition, London 2005, pp. 703 et seq.).

128 Judgment of the Court of Justice (Grand Chamber) of 03.09.2008 in joined cases C-402/05 P and C-415/05 P, *Yassin Abdullah Kadi and Al Barakaat International Foundation v. Council of the European Union*, ECR 2008, p. I-06351.

129 Resolution 1267 (1999) adopted by the Security Council at its 4051st meeting on 15 October 1999, S/RES/1267 (1999), establishing Security Council Committee and imposing limited air embargo and funds and financial assets embargo on the Taliban.

130 Resolution 1333 (2000) adopted by the Security Council at its 4251st meeting, on 19 December 2000, S/RES/1333 (2000) on air and arms embargo, restricted travel sanctions, freezing of funds of Usama Bin Laden and associates.

131 Article 41 of the Charter of the United Nations is worded as follows:

"The Security Council may decide what measures not involving the use of armed force are to be employed to give effect to its decisions, and it may call upon the Members of the United Nations to apply such measures. These may include complete or partial interruption of economic relations and of rail, sea, air, postal, telegraphic, radio, and other means of communication, and the severance of diplomatic relations."

of First Instance ruled that, from the standpoint of international law, the Member States, as members of the United Nations, are bound to respect the principle of the primacy of their obligations under the Charter of the United Nations, enshrined in Article 103 thereof, which means, *inter alia*, that the obligation, laid down in Article 25 of the Charter, to carry out the decisions of the Security Council prevails over any other obligation they may have entered into under an international agreement.[132]

According to the Court of First Instance, that obligation of the Member States to respect the principle of the primacy of obligations undertaken by virtue of the Charter of the United Nations is not affected by the Treaty on the European Community, for it is an obligation arising from an agreement concluded before the Treaty, and so falling within the scope of the untouchability clause of ex-Article 307 TEC (Article 351 TFEU).[133] The Court of First Instance went to conclude that resolutions adopted by the Security Council under Chapter VII of the Charter of the United Nations are binding on the EU Member States which must therefore, in that capacity, take all measures necessary to ensure that those resolutions are put into effect and may, and indeed must, leave unapplied any provision of Community law, whether a provision of primary law or a general principle of Community law, that raises any impediment to the proper performance of their obligations under that Charter.[134]

In the Judgment on appeal the Court of Justice set aside the judgments of the Court of First Instance in the cases *Kadi* and *Yusuf*.[135] The Court reiterated the principles established in the judgements in the cases *Poulsen and Diva Navigation* and *Racke* establishing that the European Community must respect international law in the exercise of its powers and that a measure adopted by virtue of those powers must be interpreted, and its scope limited, in the light of the relevant rules of international law.[136] The Court has confirmed in this way the binding force of international agreements stemming from the principle of

---

[132] Judgment of the Court of First Instance in the case *Kadi*, *op. cit.*, footnote 108, paras. 181-184; Judgment of the Court of First Instance in the case *Yusuf*, *op. cit.*, footnote 107, paras. 231-234.

[133] *Ibidem*. Judgment in case *Kadi*, paras. 185-188, *op. cit.*, footnote 64; Judgment in case *Yusuf*, paras. 235-238, *op. cit.*, footnote 63.

[134] *Ibidem*. Judgment in case *Kadi*, paras. 189, 190; Judgment in case *Yusuf*, paras. 239, 240.

[135] Judgment of the Court (Grand Chamber) of 3.09.2008 in joined cases C-402/05 P and C-415/05 P, *Yassin Abdullah Kadi and Al Barakaat International Foundation v. Council of the European Union*, ECR 2008, p. I-06351, *op. cit.*, footnote 128.

[136] *Ibidem*, para. 291.

interpretation of the Community/Union rules in a manner consistent with the rules established by international law and leading to the primacy of concurrent international rules over acts of secondary Community law.[137]

Nevertheless, the Court held that that primacy at the level of Community law would not extend to primary law, in particular to the general principles of which fundamental rights form part.[138] The Court argued that an international agreement cannot affect the autonomy of the Community legal order, observance of which is ensured by the Court, jurisdiction that the Court has, moreover, already held to form part of the very foundations of the Community.[139]

Although the Court refrained from recalling the landmark ruling in the case *Van Gend & Loos*, in which the Court affirmed for the first time the autonomy of the Community legal order,[140] the Court refused in the judgment on appeal in the case *Kady and Yusuf* the primacy of international agreements over primary Union law and deduced from this basic principle of multilevel interaction among legal norms established already in 1963 a principle of collaboration and complementarity.[141]

By stating that the Treaty is not merely an agreement between States, but an agreement between the peoples of Europe, the Court considered in its ruling in the *Van Gend & Loos* case that the Treaty had established a "new legal order", beholden to, but distinct from the existing legal order of public

---

137 *Ibidem*, para. 307. The Court put forward that ex-Article 300 para. 7 TEC (Article 216, 218 TFEU) provides that agreements concluded under the conditions set out in that article are to be binding on the institutions of the Community and on Member States and thus, by virtue of that provision, supposing it to be applicable to the Charter of the United Nations, the latter would have primacy over acts of secondary Community law (*Ibidem*, para. 306). However, it is to be noted that ex-Article 300 TEC relates to international agreement concluded by the European Community according to a special procedure. Ex-Article 300 TEC (Articles 215, 218 TFEU) is thus not applicable to the United Nations Charter signed in 1945 since the European Communities are not a member of the United Nations but have since 1974 an observer status within the UN. On 3 May 2011, the UN General Assembly adopted Resolution A/65/276 upgrading the status of the European Union's participation in the United Nations allowing EU representatives to present common positions of the Union to the Assembly. Moreover, EU representatives have the right to make interventions during sessions and to be invited to participate in the general debate of the General Assembly. It also permits EU communications relating to the sessions and work of the Assembly to be circulated directly as documents of the Assembly. EU representatives also have the right to present proposals and amendments agreed by EU Member States and to exercise the right of reply.

138 *Ibidem*, para. 308.

139 *Ibidem*, para. 282.

140 Judgment of the Court of Justice in the case *Van Gend & Loos*, *op. cit.*, footnote 96.

141 See HÄBERLE, P., *Pluralismo y Constitución. Estudios de teoría constitucional en la sociedad abierta*, Madrid 2002, p. 263.

international law. In other words, the Treaty has created a municipal legal order of trans-national dimensions, of which it forms the "basic constitutional charter".[142] This does not mean, however, that the Community's municipal legal order and the international legal order "pass by each other like ships in the night".[143] Rather, the Court argued for a loyal cooperation between the obligations deriving from each of both legal orders.

Likewise, the Court did not argue for a hierarchical relationship between the obligations incumbent under international law rules and those under primary Union law in favour of the latter by examining the effects of international agreements within the Community as to whether they are in compliance with the constitutional principles of the Union. Rather, the Court underlined the inviolability of "the principles of liberty, democracy and respect for human rights and fundamental freedoms enshrined in Article 6 para. 1 TEU as a foundation of the Union",[144] being these principles "part of the very foundations of the Community legal order, one of which is the protection of fundamental rights".[145] The Court went to conclude that ex-Article 307 (Article 351 TFEU) cannot justify any challenge to those principles forming part of the very foundations of the Community legal order.[146]

It can be concluded that, although the Court takes great care to respect the obligations that are incumbent on the Community and the Member States by virtue of international law, it seeks to preserve the constitutional framework created by the Treaties.[147] Thus, it would be wrong to conclude that when the Member States are bound by a rule of international law, it must be applied unconditionally in the Union legal order regardless of its autonomy. In the words of Advocate General POIARES MADURO:

> [...] the relationship between international law and the Community legal order is governed by the Community legal order itself, and international law can

142 See also Judgment of the Court of Justice of the European Communities of 23.04.1986 in the case 294/83, *Parti écologiste 'Les Verts' v. European Parliament*, ECR 1986, p. 1353, para. 23.

143 See Opinion of Advocate General POIARES MADURO delivered on 16.01.2008 in the case C-402/05 P, *Yassin Abdullah Kadi v. Council of the European Union and Commission of the European Communities*, ECR 2008, p. I-06351, para. 22.

144 Judgment of the Court of Justice in the case *Kady*, para. 303, *op. cit.*, footnote 128.

145 *Ibidem*, para. 304.

146 The General Court criticised this approach of the Court of Justice in the judgement in the case Kadi II, Judgment of the General Court (Seventh Chamber) of 30.09.2010 in the Case T-85/09, Yassin Abdullah Kadi v. European Commission, ECR 2010, p. 00000, para. 119: "So far as those principles are concerned, the Court of Justice thus seems to have regarded the constitutional framework created by the EC Treaty as a wholly autonomous legal order, not subject to the higher rules of international law – in this case the law deriving from the Charter of the United Nations."

147 Opinion delivered by Advocate General POIARES MADURO in the case *Kady and Yusuf* at appeal, para. 24. See also Opinion of the Court of Justice 2/94, 1996, paras. 30, 34, 35.

permeate that legal order only under the conditions set by the constitutional principles of the Community.[148]

Thus, for the case of consular protection provided to unrepresented Union citizens in third countries, the relevant international agreements, and above all the Vienna Convention on Consular Relations, have no primacy over the correspondent primary Union law in the shape of Article 20, 23 TFEU and Article 35 TEU but rather reconciliation needs to be sought between the international obligations of the Member States on the one side and the autonomy of the EU legal order under particular consideration of its constitutional principles on the other side. In doing so, the reconciliation between the institutes of diplomatic and consular protection in their configuration established by Union and by international law should lead to their best possible unfolding and promote their coexistence as well as cooperation rather than the subordination of one concept to the other,[149] paying particular attention to the thrust of the provisions under Union law and their relevance for the general constitutional principles on which the Union is founded.

2.3. *Best Possible Effectiveness of EU Law in Light of International Law*

Since consular and diplomatic protection are regulated both at international law and EU level, the practical concordance between the legal rules concerned allowing their coexistence shall be aimed at. To this end it should be ascertained whether the EU provisions would unfold more effectiveness if they would cover consular protection only.

The aforementioned differences between diplomatic and consular protection show that while the triggering event in case of diplomatic protection is an internationally wrongful act committed by a State, the distress situation requiring consular protection under EU Law does not need necessarily to have been caused by an action of the host State but can rather arise without human influence.

In addition, under the strict application of the nationality rule, Member States would be able to provide diplomatic protection to unrepresented non-national EU citizens on behalf of their State of origin only after having obtained the consent thereto of the third country concerned. To this end international negotiations would be necessary which would hinder the effectiveness of

---

148 *Ibidem.*

149 This "peaceful coexistence" of legal rules deriving respectively from International or EU Law could be leant towards Konrad HESSE's doctrine on the "practical concordance" seeking to optimize the effect of the colliding legal norms by balancing (weighting) the opposing provisions (See HESSE, K., *Grundzüge des Verfassungsrechts der Bundesrepublik Deutschland*, 20. edition, Heidelberg 1999, para. 72).

the protection of unrepresented EU citizens in third countries.[150] But even if such consent has been obtained, the provision of diplomatic protection on behalf of other States is possible according to International Law only on a temporary basis, which is not what is intended by Article 23 TFEU though. Rather, the EU provision pretends to offer protection on a permanent basis to unrepresented EU citizens without the obligation for the Member States to establish own representation in each third country. On the contrary, in the case of consular protection, only a notification to the host State is necessary in order to provide consular protection to non-national citizens on behalf of their State of origin in third States. Accordingly, only consular protection can be easily rendered to nationals of another EU Member States by simply notifying the provision of consular protection to unrepresented non-national EU citizens to the third countries concerned.

Furthermore, as stated above, diplomatic protection is a State' right based on the "fiction" that the harm caused to its individuals is automatically a harm caused to the State itself, with the consequence that the individual may request the State to provide diplomatic protection but possesses no individual subjective legal position allowing him/her for the enforcement of his/her legitimate interests. In contrast, there are no objections on the part of international law to the conception of consular protection under EU Law as a right of the individuals and not as a State' power. The conception of consular protection as an individual right, whose holders are the EU citizens by themselves, means a stronger legal position. This approach does in turn more justice to the citizens' right character of Article 23 TFEU since all rights deriving from the EU citizenship status are conceived as citizens' rights and not as State powers.

In addition, whilst diplomatic protection has a discretionary nature leaving to the State a wide range of considerations and general interest as reasons suitable to justify the denegation of diplomatic protection, there is no international law rule preserving consular protection from being, at least, not at the full State' discretion.

In this regard, it should be stressed that this absolute discretion, even arbitrariness, characterizing diplomatic protection, is not compatible with the nature of a legal position deriving from Union citizenship[151] whose holders are the EU citizens and not the Member States.

In summary, the protection intended by Article 23 TFEU could be rendered more effectively and would have a more positive bearing on the legal position of EU citizens if the EU Law provisions concerned covered consular protection and not also diplomatic protection. Thus, the limitation

---

150 Please see regarding the direct effect of Article 23 TFEU Chapter IV below.

151 BLÁZQUEZ PEINADO, M. D., *La ciudadanía de la Unión (Los derechos reconocidos en los artículos 8.A a 8.D del T.C.E.)*, Valencia 1998, p. 271.

of the material scope of Article 23 TFEU on consular protection would lead to a reinforcement of the regulatory depth of this legal provision by its personification and subjectivisation. This interpretation of Article 23 TFEU would bring the most practical effectiveness to European Union Law.

Nevertheless, this shall not mean that Member States cannot rely on Article 23 TFEU in order to provide diplomatic protection on behalf of another Member State. However, as evidenced by the previous findings, in this case other standards must apply and further concretisation by the Member States would be needed.

3. Consular Assistance vs. Consular Protection

At the latest with the report "For a European Civil Protection Force: Europe Aid" issued by the former French Minister for Foreign Affairs and Member of the European Commission, Michel BARNIER in 2006,[152] the wide range of legal, political and technical concepts of protection of Union citizens abroad has been evidenced. The BARNIER' Report addresses different types of actions in emergency situations not only in third countries but also within the European Union and delivers proposals reaching from the establishment of an European civil protection force as a response to major risks (e.g. earthquakes, nuclear accidents, pandemics)[153] to the creation of "consular flying guards",[154] placing emphasis rather on the role that the European Union could undertake as well as on the cooperation among the Member States[155] than on the possibilities offered by the EU provisions on consular protection.

Although Article 20[156] and 23[157] TFEU refer to 'protection' by diplomatic and consular missions of unrepresented Union citizens abroad, the notion 'consular assistance' seems to be politically more

152 Mr BARNIER was entrusted with the writing of the Report by the then President of the European Council, Mr Wolfgang SCHÜSSEL and the President of the European Commission, Mr José Manuel BARROSO. See Annex 1 – Mission statement to the Report available at: <http://ec.europa.eu/archives/commission_2004-2009/president/pdf/rapport_barnier_en.pdf>.

153 *Ibidem*, p. 12.

154 *Ibidem*, p. 23.

155 *Ibidem*, p. 22.

156 Article 20 para. 2 (c) TFEU: "(c) the right to enjoy, in the territory of a third country in which the Member State of which they are nationals is not represented, the protection of the diplomatic and consular authorities of any Member State on the same conditions as the nationals of that State".

157 Article 23 para. 1 TFEU: "Every citizen of the Union shall, in the territory of a third country in which the Member State of which he is a national is not represented, be entitled to protection by the diplomatic or consular authorities of any Member State, on the same conditions as the nationals of that State."

welcomed than the one of 'consular protection' when the protection of Union citizens abroad is concerned, mainly by the authorities of some Member States as an attempt to constrict the expectations of the citizens that could be raised by the notion 'protection'. Therefore, in all likelihood, Member States would favour the less suggestive notion of 'assistance' than the one of 'protection' even when their national legislation is using the latter one.[158]

Therefore, in order to conceptualise correctly the provision of assistance to unrepresented Union citizens in third countries under the provisions of Union law, it is necessary to distinguish furthermore between the notions 'consular protection' on the one side and 'consular assistance' on the other side. This is not a question of simple lexical formalism but rather the intention to delimit the scope of application of the relevant Union provisions against that of international and national legal rules contributing by this means to the legal certainty in this matter.

The question on the distinction between consular protection and consular assistance has been barely treated in the legal doctrine. JIMÉNEZ PIERNAS regards 'consular protection' as much more adjusted to the concept of diplomatic protection affirming that like in the case of diplomatic protection also the provision of consular protection requires an internationally wrongful act of a State. The difference to diplomatic protection is in his view in the fact that the State brings the claim not before the Government of the other State but directly before the authority that committed the wrongful action.[159] Besides, no previous exhaustion of all local remedies was required.

It can be agreed with this view as far as it seems, at least at the first sight, that both diplomatic and consular protection pursue, the same objective, which is to produce relief for the person affected in a certain

---

158 This seems to be the case of Germany for instance. Although the German Consular Act uses the notion "*Schutz*" [protection] e.g. in Article 6 para. 1 as well as the German version of the Treaty establishing the European Community and the Treaty on the Functioning of the European Union, the German Ministry of Foreign Affairs would prefer the general use of the notion "assistance" when the help provided to unrepresented Union citizens in third countries is concerned (Interview with a German official from the German Ministry of Foreign Affairs in 2010). See Article 6 para. 1 of the German Consular Act: "Consular officers shall, in the event of the consular district being struck or threatened by natural disasters, warlike or revolutionary complications or similar events, causing or likely to cause harm to the population or to any section thereof, take the necessary steps to give assistance and protection to the injured or threatened [...]".

The same position seems to be adopted by the Foreign and Common Wealth Office (Interview with an official from the Foreign and Common Wealth Office in 2011).

159 JIMÉNEZ PIERNAS, C., "La protección diplomática y consular del ciudadano de la Unión Europea", in *Revista de Instituciones Europeas*, 1993, Vol. 20, No. 1, p. 46.

situation of distress. However, this assumption is only relative taking into account that, as stated before, diplomatic protection seeks to redress a harm caused to the State by producing harm to a citizen of the nationality of that State. On the other side, JIMÉNEZ PIERNAS defines justifiably rather administrative functions of consular officers as 'consular assistance' facilitating the stay of their compatriots abroad.[160]

OKANO-HEIJMANS speaks in this context about 'consular diplomacy' acknowledging the recent developments in consular affairs and distinguishing between common consular affairs, constituting the large majority of issues and following standard procedures, and *ad hoc* consular diplomacy seeking to provide protection of citizens in distress in cases taking the limelight in the media and thus putting pressure on governments to improve the quality and intensity of consular service.[161]

A terminological differentiation according to the objective pursued by the different consular tasks is carried out also in the national legislation of some of the Member States. For instance, the prime example of national legislation on consular protection, the Consular Act of the Republic of Estonia[162] distinguishes between consular services on the one side and consular assistance on the other side. The Act subsumes under the heading "consular services" administrative consular tasks such as acts of attestation (Art. 30), provision of translation services (Art. 32), register of marriage, death and birth (Art. 33), issuance of driving licences (Art. 34), issue of certificates (Art. 39), authentications (Art. 40), legalisation of public documents (Art. 43) and issue of visas (Art. 45). In contrast, Article 52 of the Estonian Consular Act defines "consular assistance" as the provision of assistance to persons in distress in order for them to contact their families or other persons close to them or return to Estonia or in order for their rights to be protected or hospitalisation or other issues to be arranged for them.[163] A person in distress shall be a person who finds himself/herself in a temporary emergency situation as a result of an accident, an illness, falling victim to a crime or other circumstances and who is unable to resolve the

---

160 *Ibidem.*

161 OKANO-HEIJMANS, M., "Changes in Consular Assistance and the Emergence of Consular Diplomacy", pp. 21, 23, 24, *op. cit.*, footnote 54.

162 *Konsulaarseadus* RT I 2009, 29, 175 [Consular Act] of 20.05.2009 entered into force 01.07.2009, amended by Act RT I 2009, 62, 405 of 26.11.2009 and entered into force on 1.01.2010.

163 Article 52 para. 1 of the Consular Act of the Republic of Estonia: "A consular officer or honorary consul shall provide consultation and assistance to persons in distress in the consular district in order for them to contact their families or other persons close to them or return to Estonia or in order for their rights to be protected or hospitalisation or other issues to be arranged for them."

situation by him-/herself.[164] The Estonian legislation on consular protection distinguishes according to the objective pursued by the assistance provided by consular officers between administrative and other tasks aimed at facilitating the stay of the Estonian citizens abroad and those tasks pursuing to provide a remedy to citizens in distress comprising situations in which the fundamental rights of the persons concerned are at risk.

Besides, it is necessary to pay due attention to the multilevel context of the provision of assistance/protection to citizens abroad, taking into account the different legal frameworks operating at different levels, besides the national legislations on this matter. It should be therefore noted that according to the Vienna Convention on Consular Relations of 1963 as well as the national legislation and practices of each State, consular offices are vested with a wide range of functions reaching from furthering the development of commercial, economic, cultural and scientific relations between the sending State and the receiving State to acting as notary and civil registrar.[165]

Article 23 TFEU does not specify what kind of assistance should fall under the consular protection provided to unrepresented Union citizens in third countries. Given the mandate issued by former Article 8c of the Treaty of Maastricht,[166] the Member States adopted Decision 95/553/EC and Decision 96/409/CSFP[167] filling with content the Treaty provisions on consular protection.

Unlike the Vienna Convention on Consular Relations, Decision 95/553/EC and Decision 96/409/CSFP offer a considerably more limited catalogue of situations in which consular protection shall be provided. According to Article 5 para. 1 of Decision 95/553/EC, consular protection in terms of Article 23 TFEU shall comprise the assistance in case of death, serious accident or serious illness, arrest or detention, violent crime as well as the relief and repatriation of distressed citizens.[168] Moreover, Decision 96/409/

164 Article 52 para. 2 of the Consular Act of the Republic of Estonia: "For the purposes of this Act, a person in distress is a person who finds himself or herself in a temporary emergency situation as a result of an accident, an illness, falling victim to a crime or other circumstances and who is unable to resolve the situation by himself or herself."

165 Article 5 Vienna Convention on Consular Relations of 1963, *op. cit.*, footnote 115.

166 Article 8 c second sentence of the Treaty of Maastricht: "Before 31 December 1993, Member States shall establish the necessary rules among themselves and start the international negotiations required to secure this protection."

167 Decision 96/409/CSFP of the Representatives of the Governments of the Member States, meeting within the Council of 25 June 1996 on the establishment of an emergency travel document, Official Journal L 168 of 06.07.1996, pp. 0004-0011.

168 Article 5 para. 1 of Decision 95/553/EC: "1. The protection referred to in Article 1 shall comprise:

(a) assistance in cases of death;

(b) assistance in cases of serious accident or serious illness;

CSFP adds to this catalogue a sixth case in which consular protection should be provided – loss or theft of an identity document. In this case, the so called Emergency Travel Document shall be issued to the person affected.[169] The catalogue in Article 5 para. 1 of Decision 95/553/EC is not exhaustive, which is evidenced by the second paragraph establishing that consular protection may be provided also in other circumstances.[170] However, the "other circumstances" need to be "similar circumstances" to those listed in the first paragraph of Article 5 of Decision 95/553/EC and Decision 96/409/CSFP taking into account the spirit and purpose of the provisions in question and the exceptional character of the protection provided under the Union provisions to unrepresented Union citizens in third countries. All circumstances listed in Article 5 of Decision 95/553/EC and Article 1 of Decision 96/409/CSFP have in common the character of the situations described, being those situations of distress based on the violation of or threat for the undisturbed enjoying of their fundamental right, such as the right to life and to physical integrity, right to fair trial, right to property and freedom to movement. All these situations of limited or even impossible enjoyment of the rights of the persons concerned require relief granted by the competent authorities abroad different from any other type of consular acts pursuing other objectives, being those objectives the maintenance of cultural and commercial relationships between the host and the sending country or administrative tasks facilitating the stay of the own nationals in the host State. Accordingly, it could be said that consular assistance in general terms is governed by the Vienna Convention on Consular Relations as well as by national legislation and practices, but, however, it is not covered by Articles 20, 23 TFEU, Decision 95/553/EC and Decision 96/409/CSFP.

The category of consular assistance could be thus divided into two sub-categories: (a) those consular functions governed by the Vienna Convention on Consular Relations and by national legislation and practices without any direct or indirect link to the legal and political framework

(c) assistance in cases of arrest or detention;

(d) assistance to victims of violent crime;

(e) the relief and repatriation of distressed citizens of the Union."

169 Please see Preamble of Decision 96/409/CSFP: "Considering that the establishment of a common emergency travel document is likely to provide genuine help to the citizens of the Union in distress, […]". Moreover, Article 1 of Decision 96/409/CSFP provides for: "An emergency travel document shall be established, the uniform format of which is described in Annex I, which forms an integral part of this Decision."

170 Article 5 para. 2 of Decision 95/553/EC reads: "In addition, Member States' diplomatic representations or consular agents serving in a non-member State may, in so far as it is within their powers, also come to the assistance of any citizen of the Union who so requests in other circumstances."

of the European Union (e.g. furthering the development of commercial, economic, cultural and scientific relations between the sending State, ascertaining conditions and developments in the commercial, economic, cultural and scientific life of the receiving State, reporting thereon to the Government of the sending State and giving information to persons interested, etc.), and (b) consular functions relating to the Schengen regime but not falling under the scope of application of Article 23 TFEU.

Consular cooperation regarding the issue of visas for instance would fall under the Schengen agreements since it concerns the common set of rules applying to people crossing the external borders of the EU Member States as a consequence of the evolution of the external dimension of the Area of Freedom, Justice and Security[171] and not Union citizens staying in third countries outside the territory of the European Union.[172] The harmonisation of the conditions of entry into the Schengen area and of the rules on visas has facilitated the cooperation among the parties to the Schengen area allowing even the representation of a Member State by another Member State in a third country on permanent basis as regarding the issuance of the uniform format of Schengen visa according to Council Regulation (EC) No. 334/2002.[173] This type of assistance to non-Union citizens is, however, not covered by the protection offered to all Union citizens, and not only to those belonging to a country party to the Schengen area, under Article 23 TFEU, 46 of the Charter of Fundamental Rights of the European Union.

Consular protection in terms of the Treaties as well as of Decision 95/553/EC and Decision 96/409/CSFP concerns only a limited part of those consular functions, in particular those aimed at producing relief in situations of distress. The notion 'consular protection' has

---

[171] See Article 67 para. 2 TFEU: "It [the area of freedom, security and justice] shall ensure the absence of internal border controls for persons and shall frame a common policy on asylum, immigration and external border control, based on solidarity between Member States, which is fair towards third-country nationals." See to local consular cooperation as external dimension of the Area of Freedom, Security and Justice, FERNÁNDEZ, A.M., "La dimesión externa del Espacio de Libertad, Seguridad y Justicia. El caso de la cooperación consular local", in *Revista CIDOB d'Afers Internacionals*, No. 91, 2010, pp. 87-104.

[172] See to the cooperation among the EU Member States in the field of common visa policy FERNÁNDEZ, A.M., "Consular Affairs in an Integrated Europe", in *Consular Affairs and Diplomacy*, Leiden/ Boston 2011, pp. 97-114; "Local Consular Cooperation: Administering EU Internal Security Abroad", in *European Foreign Affairs Review*, Vol. 14 No. 4 (2009), pp. 591-606; "The Europeanisation of Consular Affairs: the Case of Visa Policy", in *Discussions Papers in Diplomacy*, The Hague 2006, pp. 1-21.

[173] Council Regulation (EC) No. 334/2002 of 18 February 2002 amending Regulation (EC) No. 1683/95 laying down a uniform format for visas, Official Journal L53/7 of 23.02.2002.

been used by the Member States in Decision 95/553/EC[174] as well as by the European Commission in its Action Plan 2007-2009 "Effective consular protection in third countries: the contribution of the European Union" of 05.12.2007.[175] The notion 'protection' reflects the spirit and purpose of the Union provisions: it suggests the existence of a situation of vulnerability that need immediate or at least a quick reaction by the competent authorities pursuing a determined goal: the rectification of a current situation of need, the prevention of further, imminent, threats for the life, health or important material goods of the person/s concerned. Any other consular act that does not in its essence pursue these objectives, is not covered by the EU provisions on consular protection and remains either pure national competence in the case of consular functions without any link to the European Union framework or a Schengen matter in case e.g. of visa issuing.

Thus, the notion 'consular protection' seems to be the most appropriate one to reflect the objective of the protection provided under EU law, as well as to contribute to the legal certainty by distinguishing between consular protection to unrepresented Union citizens and other consular functions governed by national law and practices and the Vienna Convention on Consular Relations on the one side and the Schengen *acquis* on the other side.

4. Conclusions

The multilevel context of consular protection poses great challenges before its conceptualisation as an institution of law operating within different legal orders. Article 23 TFEU integrates national law, international law and the law of the European Union — as only a few other legal norms do — and is a prime example of interaction and complementarity of legal rules stemming from different legal orders, contributing only in their interaction with each other to the correct conceptualision of a legal paradigm. In this sense the multilevel context of consular protection is not only a challenge to be overcome but also an opportunity to understand and define complex legal relationships as the one concerning the provision of protection to unrepresented Union citizens in countries outside the European Union.

The limitation of the scope of protection provided under European Union law on consular protection, distinguishing between diplomatic and consular protection, accounts for one the fundamental principles of Union law, the *effet utile* of Union provisions, as well as the conditions imposed

174 Please see Article 1 of Decision 95/553/EC: "Every citizen of the European Union is entitled to the *consular protection* of any Member State's diplomatic or consular representation [...]". (Emphasis added by author).

175 EUROPEAN COMMISSION, Action Plan 2007-2009, *op. cit.*, footnote 38.

by international law rules but also the practical circumstances and the environment in which the protection to be provided involves to some extent non-EU Member States.

The exceptional nature of the provisions of consular protection under EU law due to its extraterritorial character on the one side and its innovative approach aimed at filling the shortcomings and gaps in the protection of Union citizens in third countries on the other side needs to be reflected also in the delimitation of its concept against preceding consular functions governed by national and international legal rules and to reserve by this means an autonomous field of action for the EU legal framework.

Chapter III

Multilevel Citizenship as a Source of Fundamental Rights

1. Framing the Issue

The particularity of the EU provisions on consular protection is evidenced not only by its extraterritorial character producing effects beyond the borders of the European Union but also by its complex legal design that has been subjected to thorough discussions in the scholarship and by stakeholders. Not even the wording of Article 23 TFEU contains a clear and incontrovertible evidence of the legal character of the provision of consular protection to Union citizens abroad – namely, Article 23 TFEU does not mention the notion "right" but stipulates that EU citizens are "entitled" to consular protection. The look at other linguistic versions of the Article proves that apparently the Member States have consciously avoided to expressly stating that there is a "right" to consular protection. The French version of Article 23 TFEU for instance uses the notion "*bénéficie*":

> Tout citoyen de l'Union bénéficie, sur le territoire d'un pays tiers où l'État membre dont il est ressortissant n'est pas représenté, de la protection de la part des autorités diplomatiques et consulaires de tout État membre, dans les mêmes conditions que les nationaux de cet État.

Furthermore, and by way of example, neither the German nor the Spanish versions of Article 23 para. 1 contain the notion "right".[1]

The omission of the notion 'right' in Article 23 TFEU gains in importance with a view to the systematic context of Article 23 TFEU. The 'right' to consular protection is surrounded by the other citizens' rights and unlike

---

[1] German version of Article 23 para. 1 TFEU: "Jeder Unionsbürger genießt im Hoheitsgebiet eines dritten Landes, in dem der Mitgliedstaat, dessen Staatsangehörigkeit er besitzt, nicht vertreten ist, den diplomatischen und konsularischen Schutz eines jeden Mitgliedstaats unter denselben Bedingungen wie Staatsangehörige dieses Staates."

Spanish version of Article 23 para. 1 TFEU: "Todo ciudadano de la Unión podrá acogerse, en el territorio de un tercer país en el que no esté representado el Estado miembro del que sea nacional, a la protección de las autoridades diplomáticas y consulares de cualquier Estado miembro, en las mismas condiciones que los nacionales de dicho Estado."

consular protection, the Treaty applies the notion 'right' as regards the right to freely move and reside,[2] the right to vote and to stand as a candidate at municipal and European Parliament elections,[3] the right to petition.[4] Conversely, it could be assumed that the Member States intentionally chose not to use the notion 'right' regarding consular protection.

On the other side, the systematic position of the 'right' to consular protection among the citizens' rights according to Articles 20 et seq. TFEU speaks in favour of the 'right'-character of the provision of consular protection. Besides, the TFEU has overcome the reluctance of the Treaty establishing the European Community to expressly refer to consular protection as a right, establishing in Article 20 para. 2 TFEU that:

> Citizens of the Union shall enjoy the rights and be subject to the duties provided for in the Treaties. They shall have, inter alia:
>
> [...]
>
> (c) the *right*[5] to enjoy, in the territory of a third country in which the Member State of which they are nationals is not represented, the protection of the diplomatic and consular authorities of any Member State on the same conditions as the nationals of that State;

Moreover, the TEU (according to the Lisbon Treaty) issues a mandate to the diplomatic and consular missions of the Member States and the Union delegations in third countries to contribute to the implementation of:

> [...] the *right*[6] of citizens of the Union to protection in the territory of third countries as referred to in Article 20(2)(c) of the Treaty on the Functioning of the European Union.[7]

---

2 Article 21 TFEU (ex-Article 18 TEC): "Every citizen of the Union shall have the right to move and reside freely within the territory of the Member States, subject to the limitations and conditions laid down in the Treaties and by the measures adopted to give them effect."

3 Article 22 TFEU (ex-Article 19 TEC): "Every citizen of the Union residing in a Member State of which he is not a national shall have the right to vote and to stand as a candidate at municipal elections in the Member State, in which he resides, under the same conditions as nationals of that State."

"Without prejudice to Article 223(1) and to the provisions adopted for its implementation, every citizen of the Union residing in a Member State of which he is not a national shall have the right to vote and to stand as a candidate in elections to the European Parliament in the Member State in which he resides, under the same conditions as nationals of that State."

4 Article 24 para. 2 TFEU (ex-Article 21 TEC):

"Every citizen of the Union shall have the right to petition the European Parliament in accordance with Article 227."

5 Emphasis added by author.

6 Emphasis added by author.

7 Article 35 para. 3 of the TEU: "They [para. 1: The diplomatic and consular missions of the Member States and the Union delegations in third countries and international

Furthermore, consular protection has been included into the rights' catalogue of the Charter of Fundamental Rights of the European Union. Article 46 of the Charter establishes that:

> Every citizen of the Union shall, in the territory of a third country in which the Member State of which he or she is a national is not represented, be entitled to protection by the diplomatic or consular authorities of any Member State, on the same conditions as the nationals of that Member State.

In this regard, the Explanations Relating to The Charter of Fundamental Rights, prepared under the authority of the Presidium of the Convention which drafted the Charter of Fundamental Rights of the European Union and updated under the responsibility of the Presidium of the European Convention, should be taken into account since although they do not as such have the status of law, they are a tool of interpretation intended to clarify the provisions of the Charter, as stated in the Preamble of the Explanations.[8] According to the Explanation on Article 46:

> The right guaranteed in this Article is the right guaranteed by Article 20 of the Treaty on the Functioning of the European Union (cf. also the legal base in Article 23). In accordance with Article 52(2) of the Charter, it applies under the conditions defined in these two Articles.

Accordingly, the wording of the provisions on consular protection, both in the Treaties and in the Charter, is not (any more) opposed to the right-character of consular protection provided under Union law. Yet, the wording of the provisions on consular protection indicating, or at least not impeding, the existence of a legal right, is neither sufficient nor capable of offering a comprehensive analysis of its legal character.

So far, the provision of consular protection has been dealt with by scholars applying a rather pragmatic approach focused on its feasibility at international stage along with diplomatic protection and limited to the handling of selective questions related to the legal status of the right to consular protection, e.g. direct applicability and suability. Conversely, it has been barely analysed as a Union citizenship right taking into consideration the implications of an institution of law deriving from a specific, constitutional, status established by the Treaties themselves. The scientifically reasoned strike for pragmatism is indeed justified, particularly in a field like the one in question, where the practical relevance of the provisions on consular protection seems to be its greatest achievement

---

conferences, and their representations to international organisations] shall contribute to the implementation of the right of citizens of the Union to protection in the territory of third countries as referred to in Article 20(2)(c) of the Treaty on the Functioning of the European Union and of the measures adopted pursuant to Article 23 of that Treaty."

8 Explanations relating to the Charter of Fundamental Rights (2007/C 303/02), published in the Official Journal C303/17 of 14.12.2007.

and handicap at the same time. The pragmatic approach proves useful when interpreting and analysing the dogmatic features inherent to a legal institution but should, however, not replace them.

The existing analysis of the provisions on consular protection lacks a systematic examination of their structure and functions. According to KELSEN's theory on the structural analysis related to the understanding of the legal order as hierarchical system consisting of legal norms that should be examined in their relation to each other,[9] the consequences deriving from the normative character of the Treaties containing provisions on consular protection as well as the implications of possible referrals of the Treaty provisions to national legal norms of different legal ranking, such as national constitutions, parliamentary acts but also internal ministerial instructions and guidelines, need to be examined.

Particular attention should be paid to the legal character of the EU Treaties, which are not merely international agreements binding upon the Member States, but their provisions are directly applicable in the legal orders of the Member States and have under certain circumstances direct effect on the relationships between the Member States and the citizens. The direct effect of the Treaty provisions require on the other side instruments of control guaranteeing that the actions of the public power and of private persons are in line with those provisions. Based on its character as a source for secondary Union law, and in order to guarantee the uniformity of Union law, the Treaties constitute the essential criterion for the validity and interpretation of derived EU law.

The structural analysis of the provisions on consular protection needs to be complemented by an analysis of their functional elements since legal norms are an instrument to order social reality, and thus inseparable from their functions, as affirmed already by ROMANO.[10] In this regard, the functional analysis has to account for that rights, and in particular fundamental rights, can fulfil one or even multiple functions as for instance to guarantee the personal autonomy and/or to grant specific powers to the right holder, to guarantee other rights or constitutional values, taking into consideration their content and purpose.[11] By this means, and in the words of H. L. A. HART, the need for inter-relation between structural and functional elements of the analysis of institutions of law should be satisfied by interpreting the content of legal rules according to their different social functions

---

9 KELSEN, H., *Allgemeine Staatslehre*, Berlin 1925, pp. 32 et seq.

10 ROMANO, S., *Fragmentos de un diccionario jurídico*, Buenos Aires 1964, pp. 159, 160.

11 See for instance LUHMANN, N., *Rechtssoziologie*, Opladen 1987, pp. 24 et seq.; DENNINGER, E., *Staatsrecht: Einführung in die Grundprobleme des Verfassungsrechts der Bundesrepublik Deutschland*, Vol. 1, Reinbeck bei Hamburg 1973, pp. 48 et seq.

that could be coercive, imposing obligations or duties, or conferring powers.[12]

2. The Constitutional Relationship between Union Citizenship and Union Citizenship Rights

Union law detected early how to distinguish itself from traditional international law: already in the leading case *Van Gend & Loos*, the Court of Justice highlighted that the Member States have created a "new legal order". The distinctive feature of Union law in comparison with other international agreements was the fact that the Treaties did not merely create obligations among Member States but imposed obligations and conferred rights upon individuals.[13] Union law 'qualifies' by this means individuals as subjects of rights as a consequence of the decision of the Member States to limit their sovereign power to the benefit of the new legal order leading to the submission of the nationals of the Member States to a new public authority.

This juridification of the relationship between individuals and the Union sovereign power,[14] although apparently aimed at filling a gap in the democratic functioning of the European Union, was rather seeking to involve the nationals of the Member States in the European integration process. The Court made it utterly clear in the *Van Gend & Loos* case that raising individuals into subjects of the Treaties is directly linked to the concern of the Contracting Parties regarding the functioning of the common market which was the main objective of the EEC Treaty.[15]

The Court then progressively affirmed the subjective-right character of all four fundamental freedoms 'instrumentalising' the nationals of the Member States for the realisation of the integration goals set by the Treaties themselves.[16] However, the Court of Justice could not be blamed for its praetorian approach seeking to guarantee the effectiveness of the

---

12 HART, H.L.A., *The concept of Law*, 6. edition, Oxford/ New York 1975, pp. 39 et seq.

13 Judgment of the Court of Justice of 05.02.1963 in the case 26/62, *NV Algemene Transport- en Expeditie Onderneming van Gend & Loos v. Netherlands Inland Revenue Administration* (van Gend & Loos), ECR 1963, p. 00001.

14 NETTESHEIM, M., "Subjektive Rechte im Unionsrecht", in *Archiv des Öffentlichen Rechts*, Band 132 (2007), pp. 333, 334.

15 Judgment of the Court of Justice in the case van Gend & Loos, p. 00001, *op. cit.*, footnote 13: "The objective of the EEC Treaty, which is to establish a common market, the functioning of which is of direct concern to interested parties in the Community, implies that this Treaty is more than an agreement which merely creates mutual obligations between the Contracting States."

16 MASING, J., Die Mobilisierung des Bürgers für die Durchsetzung des Rechts-Europäische Impulse für eine Revision der Lehre vom subjektiv-öffentlichen Recht, 1997, pp. 23 et seq.

Treaty provisions, in particular by ensuring its uniform application in the Member States.[17] Rather, the Court was awarded with the mandate to interpret Union law, *inter alia*, by means of the procedure of reference for preliminary ruling according to ex-Article 234 TEC (now Article 267 TFEU) suggesting the creation of rights of the nationals of the Member State, that can be invoked before national courts. In this sense, the mobilisation of the individuals for the achievement of the integration process was surely not expressly stated in the Treaties but it is indeed invested in the whole system of judicial review established by them.

The criticism towards the advance of the individualising jurisprudence of the Court of Justice can be explained with the different functions of this subjectivisation in national and European context: whereas in a national context public subjective rights were historically directed towards the defence of individual autonomy against a powerful executive, individual entitlements were used during the first decades of the European Community as an instrument for the strengthening of a weak executive.[18]

In the meantime, the Union discovered the citizens of the Member States not only as 'instruments' to accomplish the mandates set by the Treaties but also as an object of Union action in order to consolidate the Union on a basis of a People's Union.[19] European integration extends now beyond the creation and deepening of an economic community and is aimed also at creating an "ever closer union among the peoples of Europe".[20] To this end, strengthening the protection of the rights and interests of the nationals of the EU Member States through the introduction of a citizenship of the Union became one of the objectives of the European Union.[21]

---

17 See to the principle of the uniform application of Union law NETTESHEIM, M., "Der Grundsatz der einheitlichen Wirkung des Gemeinschaftsrechts", in *Gedächtnisschrift für Grabitz*, 1995, pp. 447 et seq.

18 KINGREEN, T./ STÖRMER, R., "Die subjektiv-öffentlichen Rechte des primären Gemeinschaftsrechts", in *Europarecht* 1998, p. 264.

19 See on Union citizenship as a means of European integration REDDIG, M., *Bürger jenseits des Staates? Unionsbürgerschaft als Mittel europäischer Integration*, Baden-Baden 2005.

20 Article A section 2 of the Treaty of Maastricht (Article 1 para. 2 of the consolidated version of the Treaty on European Union):

"This Treaty marks a new stage in the process of creating an ever closer union among the peoples of Europe, in which decisions are taken as openly as possible and as closely as possible to the citizen."

21 Article B of the Treaty of Maastricht (Article 2 of the consolidated version of the Treaty on European Union:

"The Union shall set itself the following objectives:

...

– to strengthen the protection of the rights and interests of the nationals of its Member States through the introduction of a citizenship of the Union;"

Union citizenship – as a direct political link between the citizens of the Member States and the European Union – seeks to establish a new path of European integration: this time not by creating a Common Market and deepen economic relationships among citizens and among enterprises all over the European Union, but by fostering a sense of identity with the Union. It could be indeed proclaimed that the era of the fundamental freedoms has been replaced by the era of the Union citizenship rights.

The concern, or even hopes, that no individual rights may exist where individuals are not 'instrumentalised' within the process of integration according to the example of the fundamental freedoms, proved to be unfounded given the constitutional status of the Union citizenship rights and the correspondent case-law of the Court of Justice affirming the direct effect and the 'right character' of the freedom of residence and movement within the European Union, that is detached from 'market' freedom of workers and of service providers and receivers.[22]

2.1. Multilevel Design of Union Citizenship

Against this background, the objection that the new orientation of Union integration from a pure economic to an approach focused on people found no constitutional reflection since Union citizenship touched merely upon the position of the individuals in the legal orders of the Member States and not upon the relationship between Union citizens and the European Union itself[23] seems to be unsustainable. It is rather in the nature of the European Union, as a *sui-generis* union of States combining supranationality and intergovernamentalism in its framework reflected in a system of multilevel governance based on a complex distribution of competences, that rights of Union citizens can be created on the basis of Union law as against Member States.

In this sense, Union citizenship has a direct and an indirect dimension, being the direct dimension a summary of the legal relationships between Union citizens and the Union and the indirect dimension – a description of the relationships between Member States' nationals and the other Member States.[24] The direct dimension of Union citizenship consists of

22 See Judgment of the Court of Justice of 17.09.2002 in the case C-413/99, *Baumbast and R v. Secretary of State for the Home Department*, ECR 2002, p. I-07091.

23 See in this sense NETTESHEIM, M., "*Subjektive Rechte…*", *op. cit.*, footnote 14, pp. 333, 336.

24 SCHÖNBERGER uses the notions "vertical" and "horizontal" federal citizenship, See SCHÖNBERGER, C., *Unionsbürger. Europas Föderales Bürgerrecht in vergleichender Sicht*, Tübingen 2005, pp. 268-270. In our view, the notions "direct" and "indirect" citizenship account better for the role of Union citizenship as interface for the relationships between non-national Union citizens and Member States.

the right to petition the European Parliament, the right to call the European Ombudsman, the newly established right to launch and participate in a European Citizens Initiative as well as the right to elect the Members of the European Parliament and to stand as a candidate in the elections to the latter. In contrast, the right to freely move and reside, the right to vote and stand as a candidate in municipal elections as well as the right to consular protection establish obligations upon the authorities of the Member States and are thus part of the indirect dimension of Union citizenship.

A rather mixed case is the right to vote and stand as a candidate in European Parliament elections since the right is deemed to be exercised against the Member States, that are in charge of holding the elections to the European Parliament, although the right to elect and to stand as a candidate and thus under certain conditions to be elected as a Member of the European Parliament is directly related to an Union institution, namely the European Parliament.

The creation of rights, whose passive subjects are the Member State of a Union, is not new in federative units. For instance the privilege and immunities clause in Article IV of the U.S. Constitution establishes that "The Citizens of each State shall be entitled to all Privileges and Immunities of Citizens in the several States."[25]

In this sense, the concept promoted by SCHÖNBERGER of Union citizens as "federal" citizens[26] is thoroughly suitable to describe the relationships established by Union citizenship, involving a multilevel governance approach. Union citizenship brings indeed the "ever closer Union" nearer to a real federation.[27]

Although the Court of Justice has so far not referred in its case-law to the constitutional concept and dogmatic design of EU citizenship,[28] its constitutional status as a status regulated by the Union normative "Constitution",[29] consisting of the relationships between the Treaty as primary law, the Union legislative competences as secondary law as well as the exercise by Member States of their own powers in the field

25 Besides, the Fourteenth Amendment to the U.S. Constitution provides that "No State shall make or enforce any law which shall abridge the privileges or immunities of citizens of the United States."

26 SCHÖNBERGER, C., *Unionsbürger…*, *op. cit.*, footnote 24.

27 MAGNETTE, P., "European Citizenship from Maastricht to Amsterdam: The narrow Path of Legitimation", in *Journal of European Integration* No. 21 (1998), p. 49.

28 See OPERMANN, T. / CLASSEN, C. D./ NETTESHEIM, M., *Europarecht*, München 2009, p. 300.

29 See to the notion "normative Constitution": BALAGUER CALLEJÓN, F., "La construcción del lenguaje jurídico en la Unión Europea", in *Revista de Derecho Constitucional Europeo* 2004, No. 1, pp. 311, 312. See also SCHWARZE, J. (ed.), *The Birth of a European Constitutional Order*, Baden-Baden 2001.

concerned, has been repeatedly pointed out by the Court of Justice stating that Union citizenship is destined to be the fundamental status of nationals of the Member States.[30] The Court of Justice expressly referred in the case *Zhu and Chen* to the right to freely move and reside within the territory of the Member States (Art. 21 TFEU) as a "fundamental right".[31] The fundamental-right character of Union citizenship rights is evidenced also by its inclusion into the rights' catalogue of the Charter of Fundamental Rights of the European Union.

Nevertheless, some commentators argue that Union citizenship rights cannot be regarded as "Union fundamental rights" since their prime function is not to restrict the sovereign power of the Union itself, as classic fundamental rights do, but are instead directed against the Member States.[32] This view disregards, as stated before, the singularity of the sovereign power within the framework of the European Union exercised at different levels and shared among Member States and European Union in a complex system of multilevel governance. Thus, Union citizenship cannot be construed applying "unitary state-centred categories assuming that citizenship must be one and complete".[33] Rather, the constitutional dimension of Union citizenship needs to be conceived as a 'multilevel citizenship' governed by the national legislation of the Member States on national citizenship as well as the direct and indirect dimensions of Union citizenship.

In this regard, the multilevel design of Union citizenship is evidenced by its incursion into nationality rules bringing forward the constructive potential of Union citizenship reflected to some extent in its capacity to

30 See for instance Judgment of the Court of Justice of 20.09.2001 in the case C-184/99, *Rudy Grzelczyk v. Centre public d'aide sociale d'Ottignies-Louvain-la-Neuve*, ECR 2001, p. I-06193, para. 31.

31 Judgment of the Court of Justice of 19.10.2004 in the case C-200/02, *Kunqian Catherine Zhu and Man Lavette Chen v Secretary of State for the Home Department*, ECR 2004, p. I-09925, para. 33: "An interpretation of the condition concerning the sufficiency of resources within the meaning of Directive 90/364, in the terms suggested by the Irish and United Kingdom Governments would add to that condition, as formulated in that directive, a requirement as to the origin of the resources which, not being necessary for the attainment of the objective pursued, namely the protection of the public finances of the Member States, would constitute a disproportionate interference with the exercise of the fundamental right of freedom of movement and of residence upheld by Article 18 EC."

32 See e.g. KUBICKI, P., "Die subjektiv-rechtliche Komponente der Unionsbürgerschaft", in *Europarecht* 2006, No. 4, p. 498.

33 SCHÖNBERGER, C., "European Citizenship as Federal Citizenship. Some Citizenship Lessons of Comparative Federalism", in *Revue Européenne de Droit Public*, 2007, Vol. 19 (1), pp. 61, 76.

penetrate national citizenship.[34] This constitutional constructive potential of Union citizenship found expression *inter alia* in the *Rottmann* case[35] where the Court of Justice raised the objective dimension of Union citizenship to a routeing criterion to be observed by the Member States when deciding on the withdrawal of nationality of a Member State. Thus, the Union citizenship status gives rise not only to the establishment of rights of Union citizens (subjective dimension) but serves also as a constitutional principle or value for the entire multilevel legal order (objective dimension), the latter being inherent to fundamental rights established in national constitutions.[36]

This double-hatted constructive potential of Union citizenship as a source of fundamental rights and as a fundamental principle is not a side effect of certain policy choices but is the consequence of the epoch-making decision of Member States to constituonalise citizenship rights.[37] In this sense, the dogmatic approach, which in our opinion should be applied to the analysis of Union citizenship and citizenship rights, is necessarily a combination of the functionalist approach paying special attention to integration goals and the institutionalism and governance theories focusing on the decision-making process and the preference of the actors involved.[38]

2.2. Which Came First: the Citizenship or the Rights?

The 'fundamental' Union citizenship status is rather a process than a 'status' suggesting a static situation, that would not be suitable to describe the development that Union citizenship currently undergoes[39] in order to achieve its goal, as pinpointed by the European Commission in its Third Report on Union Citizenship: that of creating among citizens a sense of belonging to the European Union and of having a genuine

---

34 KOSTAKOPOULOU, T., "European Union Citizenship: Writing the Future", in *European Law Journal*, Vol. 13 (2007), No. 5, pp. 623, 629. See also WIENER, A., "Assessing the Constructive Potential of Union Citizenship – a Socio-Historical Perspective", in *European Integration On-line Papers*, Vol. 1, No. 17 (1997), pp. 2 et seq.

35 Judgment of the Court of Justice of the European Union of 02.03.2010 in the case C-135/08, *Janco Rottman v. Freistaat Bayern*, ECR 2010, p. I-01449.

36 See to the objective dimension of fundamental rights below, section 3.2.

37 SHAW, J., "The Interpretation of European Union Citizenship", in *The Modern Law Review*, Vol. 61, No. 3 (1998), p. 315.

38 *Ibidem*, pp. 313 et seq.

39 See in this sense also MAGNETTE, P., "European Citizenship from Maastricht...", *op. cit.*, footnote 27, p. 50, arguing that "When subjects become citizens, they may become conscious of the fact that they are given basic rights in relation to the public authority, but they may also consider themselves as the source of this authority, whose legitimacy derives from the fact that it acts on their behalf."

European identity.[40] Therefore, the demands for an abstract constitutional concept and a dogmatic approach explaining the "fundamental status" of Union citizenship cannot be expected to be satisfied by the interpretors of EU law, and in particular by the Court of Justice, since, in the words of PREUSS, "citizenship does not presuppose the community of which the citizen is a member, but creates this very community".[41]

Thus, no 'original' dogmatic approach could explain the constitutional concept of Union citizenship, but rather the constitutional dimension of Union citizenship is construed, and will be further developed, by exercising the Union citizenship status through enjoyment of the rights conferred upon Union citizens by the EU Treaties, filling out with content the "fundamental status" of Union citizens. SHAW rightfully remarks in this sense that 'it is significant that "citizenship becomes [...] not simply an object of study in itself, but also an instrument or even cypher within broader attempts to study the 'European condition'."[42]

This approach has been adopted by some social theorists, notably MARSHALL,[43] and adapted, *inter alia* by BOSNIAK and HABERMAS, to the realities of globalisation and citizenship in a non-state context. In this sense, BOSNIAK conceives citizenship through the rights implied by it but at the same time rejects the assumption that only the possession of certain rights is a condition for the belonging to the circle of persons forming the "citizenship class".[44]

This interplay between citizenship and rights is based on the assumption that there are two elements in citizenship: citizenship as a legal status and citizenship as the rights flowing from that status.[45] While

40 EUROPEAN COMMISSION, Third Report on Union Citizenship of 07.09.2001, Document COM (2001)506 final, p. 7: "Citizenship of the Union is both a source of legitimation of the process of European integration, by reinforcing the participation of citizens, and a fundamental factor in the creation among citizens of a sense of belonging to the European Union and of having a genuine European identity." Available at: <http://eur-lex.europa.eu/LexUriServ/LexUriServ.do?uri=COM:2001:0506:FIN:EN:PDF> (02.03.2009).

41 PREUSS, U., "Citizenship and Identity: Aspects of a Political Theory of Citizenship", in Bellamy (ed.), in *Democracy and Constitutional Culture in the Union of Europe*, London 1995, pp. 108, cited by KOSTAKOPOULOU, T., "European Union Citizenship...", *op. cit.*, footnote 34.

42 SHAW, J., "The Interpretation of European Union Citizenship", *op. cit.*, footnote 37, p. 310.

43 MARSHALL, T.H., Citizenship and Social Class and other essays, 1950; For further references see BOSNIAK, L. "Citizenship denationalized", in *Indiana Journal of Global Legal Studies*, Vol. 7 (2000), p. 464.

44 BOSNIAK, L., "Universal Citizenship and the Problem of Alianage", in *Northwestern Law Review*, Vol. 94 (2000), pp. 976 et seq.

45 BOSNIAK, L. "Citizenship denationalized", *op. cit.*, pp. 456 et seq. See also BOSNIAK, L., "Persons and Citizens in Constitutional Thought", in *International Journal of Constitutional Law* (I-CON) (2010), Vol. 8, No. 1, pp. 9-29.

the first is build upon a legal link between the State and its citizens, the "rights-citizenship" is established through the rights conferred upon citizens.[46] KOCHENOV rightfully describes in this context the citizenship status as a "formal" citizenship and the possibility to enjoy citizenship rights as an "informal" citizenship.[47] According to KOCHENOV, only those in possession both of "formal" and of "informal" citizenship are fully-fledged citizens,[48] although he affirms that there is a tendency of a decreasing importance of formal citizenship as to the possibility to enjoy citizenship rights.

In this context, the realisation of Union citizenship through the rights implied by it is again characteristic for federal citizenship that describes the legal status of citizens at federal level consisting of federal rights granted to the citizens in addition to the legal positions they continue to have at state level.[49] Those "federal rights" have been at the beginning of a federation typically free movement and equal-treatment rights, as for instance the "privilege and immunities clause" mentioned above, established first in the Articles of Confederation and later in Article IV of the U.S. Constitution.[50]

Admittedly, the citizenship of the Union does not operate within the boundaries of a federal State, even if the EU presents several traits of a federal architecture. In this sense the Union citizenship has a remarkable potential in becoming one of the pioneer elements of a federally constructed European Union. Therefore we can only agree with KOCHENOV's claim that the "EU is becoming the first polity where citizenship both as a legal status and as a bundle of rights has moved beyond the boundaries of a nation-state".[51] This 'federal' design of EU citizenship and EU citizenship rights as operating in a system of multi-level and multi-tier governance is all the more confirmed by the extension of the EU citizenship rights under certain conditions to non-EU citizens. This is for instance the case of the electoral rights in elections to the European Parliament granted also to third-country nationals if provided for in national electoral law.[52] This "openness" of

---

46 *Ibidem*, pp. 463 et seq.

47 KOCHENOV, D., "IUS Tractum of many faces. European Citizenship and the difficult relationship between status and rights", *Columbia Journal of European Law*, Vol. 15, p. 176.

48 *Ibidem*.

49 SCHÖNBERGER, C., "European Citizenship as Federal Citizenship. Some Citizenship Lessons of Comparative Federalism", *op. cit.*, footnote 33, pp. 67, 73.

50 *Ibidem*, pp. 67, 68.

51 KOCHENOV, D., "IUS Tractum of many faces", *op. cit.*, footnote 44, p. 181.

52 This is for instance the case of the United Kingdom.

the EU citizenship rights could be perceived as diluting the citizenship on which they are based, if we were in a nation-state context. However, in a quasi-federal architecture, as the one of the European Union, the interaction of EU and national rules within the structural and functional design of these rights is a direct consequence of its adaptation to a non-national context.[53] In this sense, Union citizenship rights, calling on Member States different from the one of nationality as well as on the European Union, weaken the link between nation-states and citizens,[54] without removing it, in order to strengthen the construction of a new, multilevel, citizenship operating in a supranational context.

This bottom-up approach, construing Union citizenship on the basis of the rights flowing from it, taking into account their structure and functions determined by the Union citizenship status as such, allows for to carry out a comprehensive analysis of the subjective dimension of Union citizenship as a source of individual rights conferred upon Union citizens, on the one side, and its objective dimension as a motor for further European integration on the basis of an Union citizens identity, on the other side. Framing the issue this way would allow for conducting an analysis of Union citizenship rights, amongst them also the right to consular protection, ensuring their effectiveness in order to achieve the constructive goals pursued by Union citizenship.

3. Subjective Rights in EU Law

3.1. **Invocabilité** *and Subjective Rights under Primary EU Law*

Against this background, it becomes clearer why although there seems to be no doubt that the rights deriving from Union citizenship are 'rights', technically speaking, with a subjective and a objective dimension, and no mere policy programmes, no EU law theory has been established so far in order to describe the characteristics of a subjective right under Union law, against which it would be examined whether a legal position has a right-character or not. The difficulties to identify a Union-wide dogmatic approach derive on the one side from the various legal cultures and traditions in the European Union, conceiving differently the legal relationships between the individual and the public power.[55]

---

[53] BOSNIAK, L. "Citizenship denationalized", *op. cit.*, p. 470.

[54] HABERMAS, J., "The European Nation State. Its Achievements and its Limitations. On the Past and Future of Sovereignty and Citizenship", *Ratio Juris*, Vol. 9, Issue 2 (1996), pp. 125-137.

[55] NETTESHEIM, M., "Subjektive Rechte im Unionsrecht", *op. cit.*, footnote 14, p. 339.

NETTESHEIM differentiates in this regard among three main patterns.[56] The majority of the national legal orders in the European Union, headed by the German legal tradition and assimilated to its great extent in Italy, Spain and a great part of the Eastern-European Member States, distinguish between substantive subjective rights and their judicial protection, being the judicial protection of a subjective right, for instance in the German legal doctrine, a procedural right to enforcement of the substantive right in question. Accordingly, in these legal traditions, the substantive right depends not on the existence of a jurisdictional guarantee; rather the right to enforce a substantive right is ancillary to the latter.[57]

Conversely, the common law, represented in the European Union by Great Britain, conceives rights as dependent on the "cause of action", i.e. on the possibility to enforce the right in the sense of a judicial review of the impossible or imperfect exercise of a right.[58]

Another approach offers the French legal tradition where individuals may initiate a procedure for an objective *contrôle de légalité*[59] based not necessarily on their subjective position as right-holders but rather on their entitlement in the sense of a legitimate interest to invoke an alleged objective illegality (*l'invocabilité d'exclusion*").[60]

The different concepts of individual legal positions against the public authority make it necessary to apply in the field of Union law a rather Union-law-own dogmatic approach to individual rights, taking into account the purpose and spirit of Union law and the dogmatic concepts developed by the Court of Justice, however, without disregarding the classical concepts of rights developed at national level, applying in the end a methodology inherent to the multilevel constitutionalism.[61] The dogmatic approach applied should be open enough to achieve a common European constitutional pattern[62] for individual rights accounting for the particularities of Union law.

---

56 *Ibidem*, pp. 340 et seq.

57 *Ibidem*, p. 340.

58 *Ibidem*, p. 341.

59 See GALMOT, Y./ BONICHOT, J. C., "La Cour de Justice des Communautés européennes et la transposition des directives en droit national", in *Revue Française de Droit Administratif*, Vol. 4 (1), 1988, pp. 1 et seq., cited by NETTESHEIM, M., "Subjektive Rechte…", *op. cit.*, footnote 14.

60 *Ibidem*.

61 PERNICE, I., "Multilevel Constitutionalism in the European Union", in *European Law Review*, No. 5 (2002), p. 513.

62 See in this sense also BALAGUER CALLEJÓN, F., "La construcción del lenguaje jurídico en la Unión Europea", *op. cit.*, footnote 29, p. 308.

At the first sight, it seems that the jurisprudence of the Court of Justice has blurred the boundaries between a substantive subjective right and its guarantee through a judicial review on the one side and a legitimate interest to initiate a judicial review of the objective legality of a norm on the other side. Some commentators argue that the Court of Justice has aligned the subjectivisation of the legal positions conferred by Union law with an interest of the individual to induce the judicial review of a legal norm in order to enforce not necessarily an individual legal position but rather integration goals related to the lack of direct effect of EU Directives, for instance.[63]

This approach seeks to establish a dogmatic concept of a subjective legal position under Union law in the context of the right of individuals to rely upon the provisions of a Directive. It becomes at this point evident that the attempt to establish criteria for the analysis of Union individual rights in general, regardless of their structure as deriving from primary or secondary Union law, is bound to fail.

In the field of EU directives, that have not been transposed by a Member State within the deadline set by the directive, the Court of Justice repeatedly held that individuals may, under certain circumstances, rely upon the provisions of a directive. The Court held in the judgment in the case *Becker* for instance that:

> [...] wherever the provisions of a Directive appear, as far as their subject matter is concerned to be unconditional and sufficiently precise, those provisions may, in the absence of implementing measures adopted within the prescribed period, be relied upon as against any national provision which is incompatible with the Directive or in so far as the provisions define rights which individuals are able to assert against the State.[64]

Some commentators point out that a merely procedural right is conferred upon individuals corresponding to no substantive right under the directive in question[65] and equate this procedural right with the direct effect of the directive. This poses the question of whether under Union law a distinction should be made between substantive right and judicial review and whether a mere interest of an individual to examine a Union provision from an objective-legality perspective should be sufficient to

---

63 See in this sense NETTESHEIM, M., "Subjektive Rechte...", *op. cit.*, footnote 14, pp. 342, 349; DOWNES, T.A./ HILSON, C., "Making Sense of Rights: Community Rights in E.C. Law", in *European Law Review*, 1999, pp. 7, 8.

64 Judgment of the Court of Justice of 19.01.1982 in the case C-8/81, *Ursula Becker v. Finanzamt Münster-Innenstadt*, ECR 1982, p. 00053, para. 25.

65 PRECHAL, S., *Directives in European Community Law*, Oxford/ New York, 2005, p. 125; DOWNES, T.A./ HILSON, C., "Making Sense of Rights...", *op. cit.*, footnote 55, pp. 8, 7.

constitute a 'subjective' legal position, according to the French model described above.[66]

The question whether as to the direct effect of directives a specific interest of the claimant suffices and no individual, substantive, right is necessary in order for the claimant to be able to invoke the directive before national courts,[67] can be left open here since no such distinction between rights, procedural rights and interests need to be made as regarding primary Union law. The jurisprudence of the Court of Justice concerning the direct effect of directives is narrowly linked with their lack of direct applicability and thus of practical effectiveness unless the Member States transpose them into national law within the term prescribed and according to the goals set by the Directives. Starting point is therefore the fact that directives address Member States and not individuals, so that this legislative instrument suffers, due to its own nature as addressing solely Member States, from gaps in its practical effectiveness. The Court of Justice, in order to close those gaps in the practical effectiveness of directives, has imposed sanctions on the Member States in the shape of direct effect of directives.[68] This construction may not be extended to provisions of primary Union law, which are, according to settled case-law of the Court of Justice, as a general rule, directly effective insofar as they are clear and unconditional.[69]

Accordingly, whereas directives are not directly applicable and their direct effect is exceptional under strict conditions, there is rather an assumption that primary Union law has direct effect since the Treaties are intended to address not only the Member States but also individuals and thus to confer individual rights and impose obligations.[70] In other words, Treaty provisions establishing a precise and unconditional obligation upon the Member States, Union institutions, etc., and intended to create individual rights, contain a substantive right, whereas directives create no substantive rights, at least until the national provisions transposing the directive concerned have been adopted and entered into force.[71] Thus, the question of whether the dogmatic approach to subjective rights in Union law should be based on the simple possibility to "rely" upon the provisions concerned in terms of a mere

66 See NETTESHEIM, M., "Subjektive Rechte…", *op. cit.*, footnote 14, pp. 379, 380.

67 DOWNES, T.A./ HILSON, C., "Making Sense of Rights…", *op. cit.*, footnote 55, p. 8.

68 According to RUFFERT, the idea of sanctioning the Member States replaces the invidualisation of the legal rule concerned. RUFFERT, M., "Dogmatik und Praxis des subjektiv-öffentlichen Rechts", in *Deutsches Verwaltungsblatt*, 1998, p. 71.

69 Since Judgment of the Court of Justice in the case *Van Gend & Loos*, *op. cit.*, footnote 15.

70 *Ibidem.*

71 RUFFERT, M., "Dogmatik und Praxis…", *op. cit.*, footnote 60, p. 72.

procedural right without substantive content (*invocabilité*) might play an important role as regarding the direct applicability of directives, but not in the context of rights conferred by Treaty provisions.

Rather, primary EU law provisions may be invoked and relied upon since they are capable of conferring substantive rights and not, as in the case of EU directives, despite of the lack of a substantive right. In other words, while the judicial review or the right to invoke Treaty provisions before the national authorities are ancillary to a substantive right conferred upon individuals by the provisions concerned, the procedural right to rely upon the provisions of a not duly transposed EU directive is granted instead of a substantive right, that still needs to be created by the transposing national legislation, or even when no substantive right shall be created at all but rather the individual use of the directive in question is necessary in order to prevent or remove any national obstacles to its goals.[72]

This exceptional *invocabilité*-construction of procedural rights regarding not duly transposed EU directives is thus not suitable to be applied to any Treaty provisions that have direct effect. In this case, it should be distinguished between the substantive right conferred upon individuals by the Treaty provisions concerned and the judicial review of an alleged violation of the subjective legal position.

3.2. Rights as Institutions of Law

The attempt to establish a common dogmatic approach to subjective rights regardless of their structure as rights established by primary or secondary Union law provisions reveals also another weak point in the theoretical approach: the indiscriminatory use of different legal concepts describing the content of the rights, their holders or (judicial) guarantees as to classify for instance the direct-effect problematic of directives.[73]

Singularities of Union law deriving from its character as based on international law rules and that has overcome in many fields the intergovernmentalism, cannot be squeezed into the national dogmatic framework of rights. However, Union law should not be denied the

[72] See in this sense the Judgment of the Court of Justice in the case Becker where the reason for the direct effect of the Directive is alternatively either the existence of conflicting national provisions or of subjective rights created by the Directive: "those provisions may, in the absence of implementing measures adopted within the prescribed period, be relied upon as against any national provision which is incompatible with the Directive or in so far as the provisions define rights which individuals are able to assert against the State" (Judgment of the Court of Justice in the case *Becker*, *op. cit.*, footnote 56, para. 25). See to the alternative legitimation to invoke an EU Directive also DOWNES, T.A./ HILSON, C., "Making Sense of Rights...", *op. cit.*, footnote 55, pp. 6, 7.

[73] See e.g. NETTESHEIM, M., "Subjektive Rechte...", *op. cit.*, footnote 14.

advantages brought by the evolution of the rights' dogmatic at national level. Rather the commonly recognised dogmatic features need to be adapted to the demands of Union law for respect for its autonomy and particularities.

The Court of Justice also accounts for the complex structure of rights and their function within the Union legal order[74] and does not limit itself to applying a mere liberalist approach to the analysis of rights limited to the scheme of scope of protection and interference in the scope of protection of the right concerned but indeed. Thus, in order to grasp the role and the scope of rights, taking into account both their structural features as well as their function, they should be analysed as institutions of law based on configuration elements that in their totality construe the institution in question.[75]

The concept of rights as institutions is based on HAURIOU's socio-institutional concept of rights[76] and Santi ROMANO's institutional theory of the legal order. Legal institutionalism assumes that the legal order is necessarily linked to the social reality leading to the juridification of pre-existent, already instituted, situations in the social life as rights,[77] detaching to a great extent the genesis of rights from the will of their subjects inherent to the "will" theories on subjective rights.[78] The legal order is thus conceived as formally consistent of legal norms and substantively based on institutions of law that fill in with content the legal norms.[79] According to MACCORMICK, legal ordering has shifted as a consequence of globalisation beyond the sovereign state and thus "law as an institutionalised normative order can be found in many contexts other than that of each

[74] Well-established case-law of the Court of Justice, see for instance Judgment of the Court of Justice of 13.12.1979 in the case C-44/79, *Liselotte Hauer v. Land Rheinland-Pfalz*, ECR 1979, p. 03727, p. 3734; Judgment of the Court of Justice of 13.07.1989 in the case C-5/88, *Hubert Wachauf v. Federal Republic of Germany, represented by the Bundesamt für Ernährung und Forstwirtschaft*, ECR 2000, p. 02609, para. 18.

[75] FREIXES SANJUÁN, T., *Constitución y derechos fundamentales, I – Estructura jurídica y función constitucional de los derechos, Introducción al sistema de derechos de la Constitución española de 1978*, Barcelona, 1992, pp. 43 et seq.

[76] HAURIOU, M., "La théorie de l'institution et de la fondation (Essai de vitalisme social)", in *Cahiers de la Nouvelle Journée*, Vol. IV, Paris, 1925.

[77] FREIXES SANJUÁN, T., "La Constitución y el sistema de derechos fundamentales y libertades públicas", in *Administraciones Públicas y Constitución. Reflexiones sobre el XX Aniversario de la Constitución Española de 1978*, Enrique Álvarez Conde (Coord.), Madrid, 1998, p. 144.

[78] HÄBERLE, P., *La garantía del contenido esencial de los derechos fundamentales*, Madrid, 2003, pp. 87 et seq.

[79] ROMANO, S., *El ordenamiento jurídico*, Madrid, 1963, pp. 135 et seq.; MACCORMICK, N., *Legal Reasoning and Legal Theory*, Oxford/ New York, 1978, pp. 82 et seq.

single state".[80] Accordingly, subjective rights, including those deriving from Union law, are also institutions of law, comprising an objective, institutional dimension, besides their subjective, individual dimension.[81]

The juridification of rights as fundamental rights in Europe and the United States reflected already most of the elements constituting the rights-institutions, such as right-holders, limits and guarantees.[82] In this regard it is worth noting that the Court of Justice has referred in its jurisprudence to these legal categories, although not always classifying dogmatically the concepts used. It has for instance frequently referred to the holders of the right conferred by Union law as individualising element of Union provisions.[83] Besides, the different possible types of right-holders may be observed for instance in the Charter of Fundamental Rights of the European Union where the right-holders are Union citizens (Title V on Citizens' rights), all citizens residing in the European Union (mainly Title I on Dignity and Title II on Freedoms), parents (art. 14 para. 3), employees (art. 27 to 32), children (art. 24), elderly (art. 25), persons with disabilities (art. 26), etc.

The role of the limits to the rights is treated in the jurisprudence of the Court of Justice on the one hand under consideration of the social function of fundamental rights leading to the conclusion that fundamental rights are not absolute but subject to limitations[84] and on the other hand imposing on restrictions limits in accordance with the principle of rule of law concretised in the first place by the principle of proportionality.[85] Moreover, the Court

---

80 MACCORMICK, N., Institutions of Law: An Essay in Legal Theory (Law, State, and Practical Reason), Oxford/ New York, 2007, p. 288.

81 See to the unitary approach to the two dimensions of rights in contrast to SCHMITT's separation between fundamental rights and institutional guarantees, HÄBERLE, P., *La garantía del contenido esencial de los derechos fundamentales*, pp. 74 et seq., *op. cit.*, footnote 70.

82 FREIXES SANJUÁN, T., "La Constitución y el sistema de derechos fundamentales y libertades públicas", p. 144, *op. cit.*, footnote 69.

83 See for instance Judgment of the Court of Justice of 19.10.2004 in the case C-200/02, *Kunqian Catherine Zhu and Man Lavette Chen v Secretary of State for the Home Department*, para. 20.

84 See for instance Judgment of the Court of Justice of 13.07.1989 in the case C-5/88, *Hubert Wachauf v. Federal Republic of Germany, represented by the Bundesamt für Ernährung und Forstwirtschaft*, ECR 1989, p. 02609, para. 18.

85 Judgment of the Court of Justice of 17.12.1970 in the case 11/70, *Internationale Handelsgesellschaft mbH v. Einfuhr- und Vorratsstelle für Getreide und Futtermittel*, ECR 1970, p. 1125, para. 10. The Court held in the case *Internationale Handelsgesellschaft* that no duties may be imposed on an individual that are not necessary in order to achieve the goal pursued by this obligation. In the case *Schmidberger* the Court went to conclude that a measure is deemed to be necessary when it is appropriate in order to achieve a legitimate objective and is proportionate to the legitimate aim pursued which means that there are no less-restrictive measures appropriate to achieve the aim. (See

has referred to the guarantees of the rights conferred by Union law pointing out *inter alia* the infringement procedures under Articles 258 and 259 TFEU (ex-Articles 226 and 227 TEC) as guarantees of individual rights.[86]

Besides, fundamental rights need to be analysed according to their content and exercise. The content of a right refers to a great extent to its objective dimension as a legal institution and to the legal value or object underlying this institution.[87] The Court of Justice has frequently linked the content of a right with the spirit and purpose of the provision concerned and has established a link between the scope of coverage of the right in question and its functions within the Union legal order.[88] The question of the exercise of a right is of a particular importance when analysing rights deriving from Union law due to the relevance of the direct effect of Union provisions on the relationships between individuals and Member States. Many commentators tend to consider the 'direct-effect' issue as a matter of jurisdictional guarantee to the right in question. Instead, the question of whether a Union legal provision has a direct effect refers to the capability of the provisions concerned to confer powers to individuals[89] to be exercised within the legal order of the Member States, which means the power to invoke the provisions concerned before all national public power[90] and not only the jurisdictional organs.[91] No other interpretation can be deduced from the jurisprudence of the Court of Justice

---

Judgment of the Court of Justice of 12.06.2003 in the case 112/00, *Eugen Schmidberger, Internationale Transporte und Planzüge v. Austria*, para. 59, 79, 82.). See to the concept of *Schranken-Schranken* also HÄBERLE, P., *La garantía del contenido esencial de los derechos fundamentales*, *op. cit.*, footnote 70, pp. 51 et seq.

86 See for instance Judgment of the Court of Justice in the case *Van Gend & Loos*, *op. cit.*, footnote 140: "A restriction of the guarantees against an infringement of article 12 by Member States to the procedures under article 169 and 170 would remove all direct legal protection of the individual rights of their nationals."

87 FREIXES SANJUÁN, T., "La Constitución y el sistema de derechos fundamentales y libertades públicas", p. 156, *op. cit.*, footnote 69.

88 So for instance the Judgment of the Court of Justice in the case *Van Gend & Loos*, *op. cit.*, footnote 15. See also Judgment of the Court of Justice in the case *Hauer*, *op. cit.*, footnote 66, p. 3733, where the Court held that the scope of the rights should be measured in relation to their social function. See also Judgment of the Court of Justice of 22.10.2002 in the case C-94/00, *Roquette Fréres SA v. Directeur général de la concurrence, de la consommation et de la répression des fraudes*, ECR 2002, p. I-09011, para. 29, as to the scope of fundamental rights as general principles of law.

89 See Judgment of the Court of Justice of 09.03.1978 in the case C-106/77, *Amministrazione delle Finanze pello Stato v. Simmenthal S.p.A.* (*Simmenthal II*), ECR 1978, pp. 00629, 00632.

90 And including sometimes with horizontal effect vis-à-vis other private persons.

91 See for instance Judgment of the Court of Justice of 09.03.1978 in the case C-106/77, *Amministrazione delle Finanze dello Stato v Simmenthal S.p.A.* [case *Simmenthal II*], ECR 1978, p. 00632.

on direct effect. The fact that the Court has dealt mainly with cases of the possibility to invoke Union provisions before national courts lies in the own nature of the procedure of reference for preliminary ruling that takes place within a national judicial procedure.

These configuration elements of the rights (right-holders, exercise, content, limits and guarantees) will serve as a starting point for the comprehensive rights' analysis under due consideration of their structural and functional aspects, in order to grasp the interaction among these elements and not only their strict distinction from each other.

4. Preliminary Considerations on the Right to Consular Protection as a Subjective Right

4.1. Consular Protection as a Positive Claim

A preliminary consideration is rather a formal one – on the different adjectives likely to be linked to the notion 'right'. The legal doctrine as well as legislation and jurisprudence denominate often indifferently rights as 'subjective', 'individual', 'fundamental', 'public freedoms', etc., reflecting, however, consistently considerable conceptual differences stemming from the historical evolution of the positivisation of rights with the construction of the classical Liberal State.[92]

It seems in this context to be at least problematic to insert consular protection among the individual rights or liberties contained in the most relevant texts of the liberal constitutionalism. A look at the iusnaturalist approach to the individual rights appearing in the Petition of Rights of 1628, the Habeas Corpus Amendment Act of 1679 as well as in the Bill of Rights of 1689 in Great Britain, such as right to life, liberty and property, suggests a conceptual difference between the right to consular protection and this kind of 'natural rights'.[93]

The right to consular protection seems in this context to feature a more complex structure as those rights that according to LOCKE are inherent and inalienable of the Men, identifying right-holders necessarily as owners, assuming that:

> [...] the preservation of property being the end of government, and that for which men enter into society, it necessarily supposes and requires, that the

[92] *Ibidem*, p. 14. Although first codification of rights can be observed already in the Magna Charta of 1215 and in the Golden Bull of 1222, it is not until the construction of the classical Liberal State when the process of positivisation of rights begins.

[93] See ROVIRA VIÑAS, A., *El abuso de los derechos fundamentales*, Barcelona, 1983, pp. 16 et seq.

> people should have property, without which they must be supposed to lose that, by entering into society, which was the end for which they entered into it [...].[94]

It was not until a century later, when the Declaration of Virginia of 1776, framing Virginia's first state constitution, interlinked individual rights, such as the right to life, to liberty, freedom of press and the freedom of worship, to a greater objective, that of "pursuing and obtaining happiness and safety".[95] The *Déclaration des Droits de l'Homme et du Citoyen* of 1789, based on the theory of ROUSSEAU of the law as result of liberty and formal equality of all citizens, contains also a rights' catalogue, although the majority of the rights included enjoyed no judicial guarantee. It was not until the Constitution of 1795 when liberty is defined according to a very individualist approach as liberty to do that which does not injure the rights of others.[96]

VON JHERING conceptualises subjective rights out of the process of positivisation of rights described above and refers to subjective rights as to rights that have been positivised by legal norms as the faculty to act recognised to the will of the individuals to do so.[97] He saw in the structure of the subjective right two elements: a substantial element defined by the practical interest or goal pursued by the holder of the right, and a formal element representing the means at the disposal of the individual to achieve the protection of the right in question. Accordingly, for VON JHERING, the subjective right represents a legally recognised and protected material interest.[98] Accordingly, liberal constitutionalism conceived subjective rights as an individual autonomy conferring the power to the person holder of that subjective right to act according to his will within this sphere of

94 LOCKE, J., *The Second Treatise of Civil Government*, London 1690, Chapter XI, Section 138.

95 THORPE, F. N. (ed.), *The Federal and State Constitutions, Colonial Charters and Other Organic Laws of the United States*, 1909, Vol. 7, 3812-14. The authorship of Jefferson is reflected also in the Declaration of Independence of 4th July of the same year pointing out just at the beginning of the Declaration that life, liberty and pursuit of happiness are rights unalienable to all Men. Only in 1791, when the first ten amendments to the Constitution of the United States of America of 1787 were adopted, known as the American Bill of Rights, the first declaration of rights with direct legal effects was constituted, including rights such as freedom of speech, freedom of religion, freedom of assembly and of petition, the prohibition of repeated trials and other rights of the accused (the so called Miranda rights) that enjoyed direct effect due to their inclusion into the supreme norm of the American legal order, the Federal Constitution.

96 La Constitution du 5 Fructidor an III du 22 Août 1795, Déclaration des droits et des devoirs de l'homme et du citoyen, Article 2: "*La liberté consiste à pouvoir faire ce qui ne nuit pas aux droits d'autrui.*"

97 VON JHERING, R., *Abreviatura de "El espíritu del derecho romano"*, Buenos Aires, 1947, pp. 32, 432.

98 *Ibidem*, pp. 31.

autonomy and implying as mirror picture the obligation of the State not to intervene within the sphere of autonomy created by the subjective right in question.[99] KELSEN even considered that there is no need to prohibit the acts of the State within the sphere of individual liberty due to the lack of an express mandate issued for the State to act in this field,[100] underlining by this means the "passive" role attributed to the State in times of liberalism, where the State was not allowed to act unless according to an express mandate. The role of the State was accordingly limited to the obligation to refrain from any intervention within the individual autonomy of the persons, and to providing jurisdictional guarantee against violations of this sphere of individual liberty when colliding with other spheres of individual autonomy,[101] being the jurisdictional post-review of violations of subjective rights the only known and reliable, i.e. effective means of protection of these subjective rights.

The Union provisions on consular protection, however, can be hardly conceived of as creating a mere defence right against Member States demanding from them nothing but abstention. Even if it was argued that consular protection is a mere right to equal treatment by the Member States, no equal treatment may be achieved by the mere negative obligation upon States not to treat equal cases differently. In this sense, the United States Supreme Court, in particular under the presidency of Judge WARREN, has repeatedly held in the civil rights cases regarding the Fourteenth Amendment to the U.S. Federal Constitution that the denial of equal protection includes not only state discrimination but also the states' failure to secure equality.[102]

The liberal rule-of-law[103] approach to subjective rights featuring the structure of a pure defence, or negative, right against the State is therefore uncapable to describe the constitutional concept of the provision of consular protection directed obviously towards a positive action in the

---

99 FREIXES SANJUAN, T., *Constitución y derechos fundamentales*, p. 30, *op. cit.*, footnote 67.

100 KELSEN, H., *Allgemeine Staatslehre*, p. 312, *op. cit.*, footnote 9.

101 FREIXES SANJUAN, T., *Constitución y derechos fundamentales*, p. 30, *op. cit.*, footnote 67.

102 SILARD, J., "A Constitutional Forecast: Demise of the "State Action" Limit on the Equal Protection Guarantee", in *Columbia Law Review* 1966, Vol. 66, No. 5, p. 855. See Judgment of the U.S. Federal Supreme Court in the case 79/81, No. 15, 282, *U.S. v. Hall*, cited by SILARD, J.: "Denying includes inaction as well as action and denying the equal protection of the laws includes the omission to protect."

103 A more active role of the State was ushered in by the emergence of the German concept of *Rechtsstaat* [State of Law], based on KANT's *reine Vernunft* philosophy [pure reason] and culminating in KELSEN's doctrine on the identification of Law and State, being a State nothing else than a legal order (KELSEN, H., *Reine Rechtslehre. Einleitung in die rechtswissenschaftliche Problematik*, Aalen, 1985, p. 117).

sense of a certain form of help actively provided by a Member State. Therefore, a rather institutional approach to the concept of the provision of consular protection is necessary that takes into account its objective dimension as ordering principle for a certain social reality.[104] The institutional approach to fundamental rights[105] allows for to conceive rights according to their "ordering" function for determined social issues, being the right then not a mere "right against" but rather a right oriented to the achievement of a specific goal, represented by the objective-institutional sense of the individual right.[106] This approach is akin to the concept of fundamental rights as objective values to be observed by the entire legal order (*Werttheorie*) as based on SMEND's doctrine on the integration of a cultural system of values by means of fundamental rights as objective legal norms.[107]

As stated already above, the *rationale* of the provision of consular protection cannot be achieved by a mere "negative" legal position against the Member States. Rather, the entitlement emanating from the fundamental status of Union citizens, Union citizenship, seeks to close any gap in the protection of the rights and interests of Union citizens abroad by deploying a solidarity network of protection by the Member States, aimed at the end at the creation of a real European identity and sense of belonging to the European Union. This added value of Union citizenship in comparison with national citizenship cannot be achieved by a mere abstention of the Member States but is rather conceived of as an entitlement to a positive action on the part of the Member States.

This kind of 'active'/'positive' right reminds of JELLINEK's *status civitatis*. Georg JELLINEK's definition of subjective rights combined WINDSHIELD's and GERBER's view of the individual, formal, "power of will" with VON JHERING'S doctrine of material "interests"[108] and sought to overcome the understanding inherent to liberal constitutionalism equating subjective rights with freedom suggesting above all absolute abstention of the State. JELLINEK distinguishes between *status subiectionis*, or passive status, where the person is merely subject of obligations imposed by the State; *status libertatis*, or negative status, according to the model of the natural rights of the liberal constitutionalism

---

104 HÄBERLE, P., *La garantía del contenido esencial de los derechos fundamentales*, pp. 104 et seq., *op. cit.*, footnote 70.

105 Fundamental rights are understood here as rights enshrined in a fundamental norm and not as in the jurisprudence of the U.S. Supreme Court as rights that are fundamentally important regardless of being included or not in a fundamental norm.

106 HÄBERLE, P., La garantía del contenido esencial de los derechos fundamentales, pp. 98 et seq., *op. cit.*, footnote 70.

107 SMEND, R., *Constitución y Derecho Constitucional*, Madrid 1985, pp. 54 et seq.

108 JELLINEK, G., System der subjektiven öffentlichen Rechte, Aalen 1979, p. 45.

creating an individual sphere of freedom impeding any interference on the part of the State; *status civitatis*, or positive status, conferring upon an individual a positive claim against the State and *status activae civitatis*, or active status, describing the power of the individual to act for the State exercising his political rights in the narrow sense.[109] Thus, only rights to a positive action of the State as well as rights to political participation constitute according to JELLINEK *Ansprüche* (claims) against the State and thus public subjective rights.[110]

The provision of consular protection may thus indeed be conceived as a positive claim against Member States in the sense of grating certain individuals a claim vis-à-vis Member States to undertake a positive action to the benefit of those individuals.

Nevertheless, some academics, as for instance already BÖCKENFÖRDE and MARTENS, have argued that granting positive claims to individuals would exceed the means at the disposal of the State and would condition the State in its policy-making[111] and are therefore per se *leges imperfectae.*[112] As for the case of consular protection it is worth noting that the entitlement conferred upon Union citizens is directed precisely to protection provided by already existing embassies or consulates in the third State and not to the creation of new facilities by the Member States in order to be able to provide help. BÖCKENFÖRDE relativises in this regard also the "factual impossibility" of positive claims against the State in so far as merely the active "participation" of the individuals in already existing facilities is concerned and not the creation of such facilities, which shall remain a policy option of the State.[113] However, it is in the meantime widely accepted to distinguish between the existence of a positive claim directed towards 'a' positive action by the State on the one side and the wide scope of discretion that may be granted to the State as to how to satisfy the claim of the individual taking into account

---

109 *Ibidem*, pp. 40, 41.

110 *Ibidem*, p. 87. In German, it is conceptually distinguished between "right" [*Recht*] and claim [*Anspruch*], assuming that the right gives rise to the claim, which is to some extent an "exercisable" right after having fulfilled any necessary conditions.

111 BÖCKENFÖRDE, E.-W., "Grundrechtstheorie und Grundrechtsinterpretation", in *Neue Juristische Wochenschrift* 1974, Heft 35, p. 1536; According to BÖCKENFÖRDE, social rights are thus typically denied to be capable of obliging the State to provide a positive action but are rather construed as participative rights in already established facilities.

112 MARTENS, W., Grundrechte im Leistungsstaaat. Die Dogmatik des Verwaltungsrechts vor den Gegenwartsaufgaben der Verwaltung by Martens/ Häberle/ Bachof/ Brohm (ed.), in *Veröffentlichungen der Vereinigung der Deutschen Staatsrechtler*, No. 30 (1972), p. 30.

113 BÖCKENFÖRDE, E.-W., "Grundrechtstheorie…", p. 1536, *op. cit.*, footnote 103.

any policy and financial considerations appropriate to constrain the scope of protection to be provided on the one side, and the limits to the right in question that could be justified on the other side. The following chapters will show that this kind of configuration of the positive claim conferred by the provisions on consular protection does not hinder its subjective-right character, provided that by this means it is not devoid of meaning, i.e. that despite this restriction of the scope of the right to consular protection and the limits applied to it, its core or essential content remains untangable.

The scope of the right to consular protection needs thus to be analysed in its interaction with one of its institutional guarantees,[114] that of the inviolability of the essential content of fundamental rights. The principle of the inviolability of the essential content of rights was recognised by the Court of Justice as one of the general principles of Union law emanating from the common constitutional traditions of the Member States for instance in the case *Wachauf*. The Court held that no restrictions may be imposed on the rights granted by the Treaties that represent, with regard to the aim pursued, disproportionate and intolerable interference, impairing the very substance of those rights.[115] The principle of the inviolability of the essential content of fundamental rights has been also codified in Article 52 para. 1 of the Charter of Fundamental Rights of the European Union stipulating that "any limitation on the exercise of the rights and freedoms recognised by this Charter must […] respect the essence of those rights and freedoms".

The characteristic of the right to consular protection as a right aimed at conferring a claim to a positive action suggests the use of the term 'subjective right' rather than more neutral notions as 'individual right', for instance, pretending to highlight differences to the concept of subjective public right. The notion 'right' is often used to describe claims, but also powers and permissions.[116] Powers authorise the performance of legal action, for instance the power or competence of an individual to acquire property[117] whereas permissions describe merely a freedom to do something without the capacity of this doing to produce changes in

[114] See for more details to institutional guarantees below, Chapter VIII.

[115] Well-established case-law of the Court of Justice, see for instance Judgment of the Court of Justice of 13.07.1989 in the case C-5/88, *Hubert Wachauf v. Federal Republic of Germany, represented by the Bundesamt für Ernährung und Forstwirtschaft*, ECR 1989, p. 02609, para. 18; Judgment of the Court of Justice of 13.04.2000 in the case C-292/97, *Kjell Karlsson and Others*, ECR 2000, p. I-02737, para. 45.

[116] HOHFELD, W. N., *Fundamental Legal Conceptions as Applied in Judicial Reasoning*, New Haven CT, 1964, pp. 36 et seq., 60; DOWNES, T. A./ HILSON, C., "Making Sense of Rights…", p. 2, *op. cit.*, footnote 55.

[117] ALEXY, R., *Teoría de los derechos fundamentales*, Madrid 1993, pp. 236 et seq.

the legal situation.[118] In this context, the notion 'subjective right' seems to describe best the claim-character of the right to consular protection, although the Court of Justice uses beside the term 'subjective right' also the notion 'individual right'[119] or merely 'right'[120] when describing subjective legal positions granted to individuals by the Treaty provisions.[121]

4.2. *Individualised Obligation to Provide Consular Protection*

Although the right to consular protection is directed to the provision of a positive action on the part of a Member State, the subjective-right character depends on whether the positive action described should be provided in an individualised form, i.e. to an individual or rather to a general public. The question is therefore whether the obligation established by the legal norms on consular protection concerned is deemed to be an individualised obligation owed to individuals.[122]

In this regard ROMANO's doctrine on obligations should be reminded. Santi ROMANO affirms that not every obligation upon the public authorities corresponds to a subjective right granted to an individual since constitutional texts may establish the obligation of an action by the public power in order to respond to existent public, general, interests.[123] The same approach can be found in JELLINEK's works, who points out that the objective of every State's action is the welfare of the general interest and that often this action benefits individuals, however, merely as a reflex and not aiming at the fulfilment of a subjective right.[124] Therefore, according to JELLINEK, the correlation between

118 ALEXY quotes the example of the permission to smoke respectively the not-prohibition to smoke. *Ibidem*, p. 229, 230.

119 Judgment of the Court of Justice of 07.07.1976 in the case C-118/75, *Lynne Watson and Alessandro Belmann*, ECR 1975, p. 01185.

120 See for instance Judgment of the Court of Justice of 04.12.1974 in the case C-41/74, *Yvonne Van Duyn v. Home Office*, ECR 1974, p. 01337.

121 According to DAVID, the English term "individual rights" is the equivalent of the "subjective right" commonly used in the civil law tradition in order to distinguish between "law" and "right", being the notion right used for both in German, French, Spanish, etc. (e.g. *Recht, droit, derecho*), so that "subjective right" would stay for right and "objective right" for law. See DAVID, R., "Sources of Law", in *International Encyclopedia of Comparative Law*, K. Zweigert and K. Drobnig (ed.), Vol. II-3, 1984, pp. 9 et seq.

122 See to the overcoming of the theory on the dualism between objective and subjective right KELSEN, H., *Reine Rechtslehre*, pp. 39 et seq., *op. cit.*, footnote 95.

123 ROMANO, S., *Fragmentos de un diccionario jurídico*, pp. 89 et seq., *op. cit.*, footnote 10.

124 JELLINEK, G., *System der subjektiven öffentlichen Rechte*, pp. 114, 115, *op. cit.*, footnote 89.

the right and a determined person constitutes the very foundation of the subjective right.[125] In this sense KELSEN regards the "person", holder of the subjective right, as identical with the subjective right itself, since no subjective right may exist without an addressee of the powers granted, who is as a consequence of his "holdership" entitled to exercise what is content of this right.[126] A right would indeed lose its "right"-character if the legal norm establishing this right does not appoint a subject of the right (*Rechtssubjekt*).[127]

At the first sight, the Court of Justice seems to apply a more extensive approach to the correlation between obligation and subjective rights, holding in the *Van Gend & Loos* case that rights under Union law arise as a counterpart to obligations imposed upon the Member States, *inter alia*. The Court went to conclude that:

> These rights arise not only where they are expressly granted by the Treaty, but also by reason of obligations which the Treaty imposes in a clearly defined way upon individuals as well as upon the Member States and upon the institutions of the Community.[128]

Nonetheless, it becomes clear, although not expressly stated by the Court, that mere reflex effects are not capable of producing subjective rights, but rather the intention of the norm, i.e. of the legislator, to create rights is central.[129] The Court held that:

> Independently of the legislation of Member States, Community law therefore not only imposes obligations on individuals but is also intended to confer upon them rights which become part of their legal heritage.[130]

Attention should be drawn to the fact that although the *Van Gend & Loos* case dealt with the question whether ex-Article 12 EEC[131] in

---

125 *Ibidem*, p. 44.

126 KELSEN, H., *Reine Rechtslehre*, pp. 41, 42, *op. cit.*, footnote 95.

127 *Ibidem*.

128 Judgment of the Court of Justice in the case *Van Gend & Loos*, para. 12, *op. cit.*, footnote 15.

129 Some German commentators have argued that the *Schutznormtheorie* (theory of the protective legal norm) is not applicable in Union law, since the Court would place the emphasis not on the interest of the citizen but rather on the underlying objective interest (See e.g. NETTESHEIM, M., "Subjektive Rechte…", p. 358, *op. cit.*, footnote 14, who at the end pleas for the application of a modified *Schutznotmtheorie*). This view falls short of the objective dimension of rights as institutions of law and their ordering function within the legal order. Besides, the question on the relationship between the individual and the general interest comes into consideration regarding direct effect of Directives, but not as regarding the right-holders of rights conferred under the Treaties.

130 Judgment of the Court of Justice in the case *Van Gend & Loos*, para. 12, *op. cit.*, footnote 15. Emphasis added by author.

131 European Economic Community.

concrete confers individual rights upon individuals, the Court interpreted the character of the concrete legal norm in the context of the spirit and purpose of the Treaties. The Court stated that:

> It follows from the foregoing considerations that, according to the spirit, the general scheme and the wording of the Treaty, Article 12 must be interpreted as producing direct effects and creating individual rights which national courts must protect.[132]

Accordingly, the Court does not limit itself to interpreting a specific legal provision in order to ascertain what was intended, but it interprets rather the Treaty as a constitutional document,[133] "laying down a general blueprint of what the place of individuals in the Community legal order was intended to be".[134] By this means the Court established something of a "presumption" in favour of the intention of Treaty provisions, whenever precise and unconditional, to create individual rights.[135] The provisions on consular protection, however, do not need to benefit from this presumption since the wording of Article 23 TFEU gives no rise for the establishment of (neutral) duties of the Member States that could be intended to satisfy general interests with a mere reflex-effect for the protection of unrepresented Union citizens abroad, but individualises rather a circle of right-holders.[136]

4.3. Enforceability as a Constitutive Element of a Right?

The concept of the right to consular protection as a positive claim inevitably poses the question of whether a substantive right needs to be judicially enforceable in order to be recognised as a fully-fledged legal right, i.e. whether the substantive right to consular protection depends on its possibility to be protected against violations by means of judicial review. Reference is made at this point to the remarks regarding the common-law principle on 'cause of action'.[137]

Taking up on VON JHERING's interest theory, the concept of right is constituted by two aspects: a substantive one, concerned with the practical purpose in the sense of the use, advantage and gain guaranteed by the right, and a formal aspect representing the means of achieving that purpose, namely legal

---

132 Judgment of the Court of Justice in the case *Van Gend & Loos*, para. 12, *op. cit.*, footnote 15, para. 12.

133 DOWNES, T. A./ HILSON, C., "Making sense of rights…", p. 6, *op. cit.*, footnote 55.

134 ELEFTHERIADIS, P., "The Direct Effect of Community Law: Conceptual Issues", in *Yearbook of European Law*, Vol. 16 (1997), p. 219, cited by DOWNES, T. A./ HILSON, C., "Making sense of rights…", p. 6, *op. cit.*, footnote 55.

135 See in this sense also DOWNES, T. A./ HILSON, C., "Making sense of rights…", *Ibidem.*

136 Please see details on the circle of right-holders, Chapter V below.

137 See previous section.

protection or the cause of action.[138] While for the representatives of the interest theory, such as VON JHERING, BENTHAM[139] and MACCORMICK,[140] the purpose or benefit play a central role in the concept of right, the will theories[141] focus rather on the control of the right-holder granted him by the norm, a control expressed above all in the ability to bring an action in protection of his rights.[142] KELSEN also refers to the legal capacity to enforce the substantive right as a condition of the existence of the substantive right at all, stating that a legal norm individualises to the degree of an entitlement only vis-à-vis the person affected by a legal wrong by making itself available in order for the right-holder to assert his interests and concludes that "the right …is the legal power to assert an existing duty".[143]

The concept of subjective rights with the legal structure described above, implying necessarily the existence of a legal 'action' facilitating the demand of the satisfaction of these rights, became problematical with the emergence of the constitutionalism of the social state denying the rights-character to social-economic rights due to their incapability to be claimed before the courts.[144] Rather, the concept of rights evolved at the time of the Weimar constitutionalism and began to conceive rights not only with the structure inherent to public subjective rights enjoying a jurisdictional guarantee but also of an institutional dimension of fundamental rights gathering effectiveness through institutional guarantees.[145] In the Weimar era, SCHMITT, in continuation of WOLFF's theory of the "guarantee of the institute", considered fundamental rights absolute in terms of limiting the State power to its role to guarantee the effectiveness of those rights and protect them against violations but denying its power to regulate the content of those rights, being the legislator bound by the institutional guarantees

[138] VON JHERING, R., *Geist des Römischen Rechts auf den verschieden Stufen seiner Entwicklung*, 5. edition, Wiesbaden/ Leipzig/ Paris, 1906, p. 339.

[139] See to BENTHAM's benefit theory HART, H.L.A., *Essays on Bentham: Studies in Jurisprudence and Political Theory*, Oxford/New York, 1982, Chapter 7.

[140] MACCORMICK, N., *Legal Rights and Social Democracy*, Oxford/New York 1982, pp. 62 et seq.

[141] See e.g. HART, H.L.A., *Essays on Bentham…*, *op. cit.*, footnote 131.

[142] ALEXY, R., *Teoría de los derechos fundamentales*, pp. 179, 180, *op. cit.*, footnote 109.

[143] KELSEN, H., *Reine Rechtslehre*, p. 48, *op. cit.*, footnote 95.

[144] FREIXES SANJUÁN, T., *Constitución y derechos fundamentales*, p. 40, *op. cit.*, footnote 67.

[145] *Ibidem*, pp. 37, 38. The Weimar Constitution of 1919 constitutes one of the prime examples of this period of positivisation of rights introducing for the first time the obligation of all public power to undertake a more active role than the one characteristic for the liberal constitutionalism in order to guarantee the practical effectiveness of the rights. From now on the rights are conferred a new function beside their concept as an individual autonomy – the power to require the public authorities to act in order to award the rights effectiveness creating *inter alia* institutional guarantees.

when limiting those rights.[146] Whereby, in the doctrine of SCHMITT the institutional guarantees where conceived, at least dogmatically, as institutes separated from fundamental rights and rather complementary to them,[147] such as for instance the freedom to teach as basis for the fundamental right of University,[148] later, institutional guarantees were regarded as a dimension of fundamental rights describing their "core nature"[149] giving rise for the development of the theory of the essential content (*Wesensgehalt*) of fundamental rights[150] mentioned above.

In this context, it is worth mentioning that Union law *a priori* cannot draw on a dependence of the Union substantive rights on their enforceability since the judicial review takes place in a different legal order, that of each Member State.[151] The Court of Justice recognised first the procedural autonomy of the Member States, stating that Union law seeks not to introduce new remedies into the Member States' national procedural systems,[152] and went later on to establish a general principle of law on effective judicial protection.[153]

Precisely the principle of effective judicial protection, codified in Article 47 of the Charter of Fundamental Rights of the European Union,[154] evidences that the capacity to enforce a right may not be implicit in the concept of a right since otherwise this principle would be deprived of any sense of such an automatic trigger-mechanism existed between right and

146 SCMITT, C., *Verfassungslehre*, 6. edition, Berlin, 1983, p. 46.

147 See insofar the famous slogan of SCHMITT: "Liberty is no Institute!" in SCHMITT, C., "Freiheitsrechte und institutionelle Garantien in der Reichsverfassung", in *Verfassungsrechtliche Aufsätze aus den Jahren 1924-1954. Materialien zu einer Verfassungslehre*, Berlin, 1985, p. 160.

148 *Ibidem*, pp. 140.

149 See CRUZ VILLALON, P., "Formación y evolución de los derechos fundamentales", in *Revista Española de Derecho Constitucional*, No. 25, 1989, pp. 35, 61.

150 HÄBERLE, P., *La garantía del contenido esencial de los derechos fundamentales*, Madrid 2003, *op. cit.*, footnote 70. See also GAVARA DE CARA, J. C., *Derechos fundamentales y desarrollo legislativo. La garantía del contenido esencial de los derechos fundamentales en la Ley Fundamental de Bonn*, Madrid, 1994.

151 RUFFERT, M., "Dogmatik und Praxis…", p. 73, *op. cit.*, footnote 60.

152 See for instance Judgment of the Court of Justice of 07.07.1981 in the case C-158/80, *Rewe-Handelsgesellschaft Nord mbH and Rewe-Markt Steffen v. Hauptzollamt Kiel*, ECR, 1981, p. 01805, para. 44.

153 See for instance Judgment of the Court of Justice of 15.05.1986 in the case 222/84, *Marguerite Johnston v. Chief Constable of the Royal Ulster Constabulary*, ECR, 1986 p. 01226, para. 18.

154 Article 47 para. 1 of the Charter of Fundamental Rights of the European Union: "Everyone whose rights and freedoms guaranteed by the law of the Union are violated has the right to an effective remedy before a tribunal in compliance with the conditions laid down in this Article."

judicial protection.[155] Rather, the effective judicial protection of the rights is construed as a guarantee to the rights granted under Union law and thus not as an imperative condition for a legal entitlement to be recognised as a subjective right. Yet, the obligation upon the passive addressees of a legal norm to ensure the effective judicial protection of the substantive right in question gives a valuable indication on the practical usefulness of the right in question.

5. Conclusions

The structural and functional traits of the provision of consular protection provide a comprehensive dogmatic framework for the definition of its legal character setting it in relation to the constitutional environment surrounding the provisions concerned and accounting for its function under due consideration of its capacity as a right deriving from the Union citizenship status. In this way, the singularities of the right to consular protection stemming from its extraterritorial character on the one side and its design as a positive claim against the Member States, lead to an alleged legal uncertainty regarding its dogmatic classification. This legal uncertainty is however not implicit in the concept of the provision of consular protection to unrepresented Union citizens abroad but is based on the lack of a systematic structural and functional analysis of the provisions concerned.

Precisely the particularity of the right to consular protection as a legal concept construed under consideration of the distribution of competences between the European Union and the Member States regarding consular protection of Union citizens abroad in a multilevel-governance environment needs to be reflected in the analysis to be carried out in the following chapters. Therefore, the constitutional dimension of the right to consular protection as a right deriving from the "fundamental status of Union citizens" should be taken into account from a structural and from a functional perspective.

On the one side, the structural traits of the right to consular protection as included in the Treaties themselves, including the Charter of Fundamental Rights of the European Union, shed light on the dogmatic features of the right to consular protection as a subjective right under distinction with individual legal positions conferred by secondary Union law. In this regard, a possible exceptional procedural reliance on the provisions of a non-transposed EU directive, find no justification within the framework of rights conferred upon individuals by the Treaties themselves. It should be therefore, as for the right to consular protection, distinguished between

[155] ALEXY, R., *Teoría de los derechos fundamentales*, p. 182, *op. cit.*, footnote 89.

the substantive right conferred by the Treaties, that need to create a subjective legal position conferred upon a determined or determinable circle of right-holders, and the judicial review of an alleged violation of the legal position granted as one of the guarantees effectively ensuring the enjoyment of the right-holders.

On the other side, the structural features of the right to consular protection give indication also about its functional environment as deriving from the Union citizenship status. Thus, the dogmatic concept of the right to consular protection may not disregard its functions as a Union citizenship right taking into account the spirit and purpose not only of Union citizenship as such but also again of its structural characteristics as a status embedded into the Union normative Constitution creating a real 'multilevel citizenship'.

In this regard, and analysing consular protection as an institution of law integrated in a complex hierarchical and interpretative interaction with other legal norms at European and national level, the social function of the right to consular protection, pre-determined by its structural particularities as Union citizenship right, should set the context for the analysis of the different elements configurating this right. Therefore, right-holders, exercise, scope, limits and guarantees of the right to consular protection should account for the oft-enunciated goal of Union citizenship to provide a new platform for European integration on a European identity created out of a qualitatively evolved Union of Rights as claimed by Walter HALLSTEIN.[156]

The demands of this ambitious aim for practical effectiveness designs on the other hand the right to consular protection as a positive claim directed towards a positive action to be provided by the Member States and rules out a liberalist approach to the right to consular protection conceiving it of as a mere defence right against the Member States. The positive-claim character of the right to consular protection represents on its part a challenge to its multilevel governance context involving action of Member States' national authorities according to national rules and practices.

Thus, the following chapters will seek to propose a possible coexistence of the necessary positive-claim character of the right to consular protection on the one side and the design of this positive claim in accordance to national rules on the other side, striking a balance between the effectiveness of the right to consular protection with regard to its underlying objective dimension, that of strengthening the identification with the European Union and creating a common European identity,

[156] HALLSTEIN, W., *Der unvollendete Bundesstaat. Europäische Erfahrungen und Erkenntnisse*, Düsseldorf/ Wien, 1969.

and the legitimate interest of the Member States to remain in control of the general political and financial decisions facilitating at the end the provision of protection to Union citizens abroad.

The structural and functional traits of the right to consular protection will therefore find expression in its configuration elements allowing for by this means to carry out a comprehensive legal analysis of the provisions concerned. To this end, first the enjoyment/exercise of the right to consular protection should be examined focusing on the question of the direct effect of the provisions on consular protection, taking into account the structural features of the right to consular protection but also its function in order to assert its unconditionality. Secondly, the right-holders of the right to consular protection should be defined as an obligatory subjectifying element. Moreover, the substantive scope of the right to consular protection will be examined in order to establish the 'rules of game' for consular protection provided by the Member States under Union law according to a complex system of interactions of national and Union rules, as well as the consequences for the limits to the right to consular protection. Thereafter, the guarantees ensuring the practical effectiveness of the right to consular protection should be examines, whereby not only jurisdictional but also other type of guarantees should be taken into account.

Chapter IV

Enjoyment of the Right to Consular Protection

1. Direct Effect of Union Citizenship

In European Union law, the possibility to enjoy, i.e. exercise, a legal right is narrowly linked to its 'direct effect' in the legal orders of the Member States. The enjoyment of their Union citizenship status will depend on the possibility for EU citizens to invoke the rights deriving from Union citizenship before national authorities, including national courts, of their own Member State but also of the other Member States. Whilst many commentators seem to favour a case-by-case approach to the direct applicability of the different Union citizenship rights, such as freedom of movement and residence, we suggest a more coherent dogmatic approach based on the functional and structural relationships between all Union citizenship rights and Union citizenship.

1.1. Direct Effect and Subjective Rights

The "new legal order" created by the Member States of the European Union features considerable differences in comparison to other international agreements. In contrast to many other international arrangements, the Treaties are binding not only upon the Member States – which is a characteristic inherent to any international treaty – but they are also binding in the Member States[1] upon any addressee of the provisions concerned, being those addressees the Member States themselves or even individuals. The applicability of EU provisions in the legal orders of the Member States, without the need of a specific implementation, is described by the principle of direct applicability.[2]

The 'direct effect' of Union provisions on the other side refers to the capability of Union provisions to produce effects within the relationship between Member States and individuals by creating rights for individuals. In this sense the Court of Justice went to conclude in the *Van Gend & Loos* case that "The very nature of this prohibition makes it ideally adapted to

---

1 OPERMANN, T./ CLASSEN, C. D./ NETTESHEIM, M., *Europarecht*, München, 2009, p. 163.

2 *Ibidem*.

produce direct effects in the legal relationship between Member States and their subjects."[3]

Notwithstanding, the notions of 'direct application' and 'direct effect' can be used synonymously when referring to primary Union law, being often used interchangeably by the Court of Justice.[4] In contrast, the distinction between direct applicability and direct effect gains in importance when dealing with secondary Union legislative acts. The direct applicability differentiates the Regulation from the EU directive being the Regulation according to Article 288 para. 2 TFEU "directly applicable *in* all Member States",[5] whereas the directive is "binding *upon* each Member State to which it is addressed".[6]

Therefore, both notions shall not be confused as regards a directive that could deploy direct effect within the relationship Member State – citizen, should the Member State concerned have failed to transpose the directive in due time,[7] but is never directly applicable since exactly the direct applicability differentiates the regulation from the directive.[8]

The direct effect of a Treaty provision should not, however, be equated with the existence of an individual right. Precisely the relevance of the 'direct effect' issue in the field of EU directives, that have not been duly transposed, shows that the existence of individual rights is no condition for the direct effect of a Union legal provision but rather according to well-established case-law of the Court of Justice, an individual may rely

---

3 Judgment of the Court of Justice of 05.02.1963 in the case 26/62, *NV Algemene Transport- en Expeditie Onderneming van Gend & Loos v. Netherlands Inland Revenue Administration* (van Gend & Loos), ECR, 1963, p. 0006.

4 BETHLEHEM, in contrast, argues that the notion "direct applicability" refers only to regulations, whereas "direct effect" describes the provisions of the Treaties and of Community secondary legislation, which, because certain conditions are satisfied, produce legal effects in the Member States due to the absence of national measures of implementation (See BETLEHEM, D., "International Law, European Community Law, National Law: Three Systems in Search of a Framework, Systematic Relativity in the Interaction of Law in the European Union", in *International Law Aspects of the European Union*, Martti Koskenniemi (editor), 1998, p. 184).

5 Emphasis added by author. Article 288 para. 2 TFEU: "A regulation shall have general application. It shall be binding in its entirety and directly applicable in all Member States."

6 Emphasis added by author. Article 288 para. 3 TFEU: "A directive shall be binding, as to the result to be achieved, upon each Member State to which it is addressed, but shall leave to the national authorities the choice of form and methods."

7 Judgment of the Court of 05.04.1979 in the case 148/79, *Pubblico Ministerio v. Tullio Ratti*, ECR 1979, p. 01629.

8 See opinion of the Advocate general Gerhardt REISCHL in the case *Ratti*, *Ibidem*, ECR 1979, p. 01650.

on the provisions of a directive for the purpose of having a contradictory national rule set aside.[9]

Although the distinction between 'direct effect' and the existence of an individual right is not as much important with regard to primary Union law as regarding EU directives, the direct effect of a Treaty provision is indeed implicit in the existence of individual rights.[10,11] Further conditions need to be fulfilled, however, in order for a legal position to be classified as subjective (individual) right. As mentioned above, the direct effect of a provision describes the capability of that provision to produce effects on the relationship between Member States and citizens enabling the individual concerned to invoke the provision in question before the national authorities. The question of whether the provision concerned creates individual rights refers additionally to the scope of the provision concerned, the right-holders, guarantees, etc.[12]

---

9 See for instance Judgment of the Court of Justice of 19.01.1982 in the case C-8/81, *Ursula Becker v. Finanzamt Münster-Innenstadt*, ECR 1982; Judgment of the Court of Justice of 26.09.2000 in the case C-443/98, *Unilever Italia SpA v Central Food SpA*, ECR 2000, p. I-07535, paras. 51, 52. See to the sufficiency of legitimate interests for the direct effect of EU directives also DOWNES, T. A./ HILSON, C., "Making Sense of Rights: Community Rights in E.C. Law", in *European Law Review*, 1999.

10 In contrast, PRECHAL argues that also provisions without direct effect may grant individual rights. He refers, however, rather to the capability of Union provisions to be relied on in the sense of a rather "procedural right" and not as granting substantive individual rights (See PRECHAL, S., *Directives in European Community Law*, Oxford/ New York, 2005, p. 105).

11 In this context, it seems contradictory when RODRÍGUEZ BARRIGÓN speaks about a "right" to diplomatic and consular protection denying at the same time the "*eficacia directa*" (direct effectiveness) of this "right" (RODRÍGUEZ BARRIGÓN, J. M., "La ciudadanía de la Unión Europea", in *Cuadernos y Debates*, No. 142, 2002, p. 559, 589). Most notably, the direct applicability of the right to consular protection involving the possibility of the individuals to invoke this right may not be declined arguing that the right to diplomatic protection was a "right" of the State and not of the individuals (OBWEXER, W., "Das Recht der Unionsbürger auf diplomatischen und konsularischen Schutz", in *ECOLEX* 1996, p. 323, 327; KAUFMANN-BÜHLER, W., "Kommentar zu Artikel 20 TEC", in *EU-und EG-Vertrag Kommentar*, Karl Otto Lenz/ Klaus Borhardt (Hrsg.) 4. edition, Wien 2006, Art. 20, para. 6) since, as stated above, consular protection in terms of EU Law should be distinguished from diplomatic protection in terms of international law. Otherwise, the autonomy and originality of the EU legal order as a "new legal order of international law" (See Judgment of the Court of Justice in the case *Van Gend & Loos*, *op. cit.*, footnote 2) and therefore its power to confer legal rights and to impose duties on its subjects as well as to use autonomous legal terms (See to the specific Community meaning of legal concepts for instance the Judgment of the Court of Justice of 03.07.1986 in the case C-66/85, *Deborah Lawrie-Blum v. Land Baden-Württember*, ECR 1986, p. 2121, paras. 16 et seq.), would become misconceived.

12 PRECHAL situates the "direct-effect"-issue as a question regarding only the scope of a legal provision, *op. cit.*, footnote 10.

In the following, the direct effect of the provisions on consular protection needs to be examined taking into account their structural traits, first as primary Union law provisions and second, as legal position stemming from the Union citizenship status, whereby the function of Union citizenship rights within the Union legal order will be accounted for.

As stated above, although the Treaties are binding upon the Member States, their provisions may also create rights and duties of individuals. According to the well-established jurisprudence of the Court of Justice since the *Van Gend & Loos* Judgement, in order to ascertain, whether the provisions of the Treaties are directly applicable in the national legal orders of the Member States and are capable of producing effects for individuals who may rely thereon before the national authorities, it is necessary to consider the spirit, the general scheme and the wording of those provisions.[13]

The Court held in the *Van Gend & Loos* case that, being the EEC Treaty more than an agreement which merely creates mutual obligations between the Contracting States, the Community constitutes a new legal order of international law whose subjects are not only Member States but also their nationals.[14] The Court then went to conclude that the Treaties addressing both Member States and individuals, affect those individuals not only by imposing obligations on them that are implemented by the Member States but also, as a counterpart to those obligations, confer upon them rights as "part of their legal heritage".[15]

Nonetheless, the Court clarified that the direct applicability/ effect of Treaty provisions is subject to certain conditions. The Court discussed for the first time in greater detail the requirements to be met by a provision of the Community primary law in order to apply directly in the Member States in the Judgement in the case *Alfons Lütticke GmBH v. Hauptzollamt Sarrelouis*. The Court held that a Member State's obligation under the EC Treaty, which is neither subject to any conditions nor, as regards its execution or effect, to the adoption of any measure either by the States or by the Community, is legally complete and consequently capable of producing direct effects on the

[13] Judgment of the Court of Justice in the case *Van Gend & Loos*, *op. cit.*, footnote 3.

[14] *Ibidem*.

[15] *Ibidem*: "Independently of the legislation of Member States, community law therefore not only imposes obligations on individuals but is also intended to confer upon them rights which become part of their legal heritage. These rights arise not only where they are expressly granted by the Treaty, but also by reason of obligations which the Treaty imposes in a clearly defined way upon individuals as well as upon the Member States and upon the institutions of the Community."

relations between Member States and individuals.[16] Such an obligation becomes an integral part of the legal orders of the Member States, and thus forms part of their own law, and directly concerns their nationals in whose favour it has created individual rights which national courts must protect.[17]

Thus, it should be examined whether the provision concerned has a "clear and unconditional character that is not qualified by any reservation on the part of States which would make its implementation conditional upon a positive legislative measure enacted under national law".[18]

The Court then detailed that the implementing measures in question prevent Union provisions not automatically from having direct effect but refers rather to such national measures to be adopted according to a wide discretion of the Member States. In this regard, the Court held for instance in the case *Hurd* that a provision produces direct effects when it is "clear and unconditional and not contingent on any discretionary implementing measures".[19] The Court later went to soften the requirements for direct effect with regard to possible scope of discretion granted to the Member States as to the implementation of the Union provisions in question. In this sense the Court held in the *Salgoil* case that the existence of discretion of the Member States to prevent the free movement of goods on grounds laid down in ex-Article 33 TEC did not preclude the direct effect of ex-Article 31 TEC since the cases established in ex-Article 33 were exceptional and did not undermine the force of the clear obligation contained in ex-Article 31 TEC.[20]

In summary, a Treaty provision is deemed to have direct effect on the relationships between Member States and citizens and thus to be invoked by the citizens concerned before the national authorities when it has a "self-executing character".

The capability of the Treaty provisions on consular protection, in particular Article 23 TFEU and Article 46 of the Charter of Fundamental Rights of the European Union, should be asserted taking into account its special character as a Union citizenship right.

---

16 Judgment of the Court of Justice of 16.06.1966 in the case C-57/65, *Alfons Lütticke GmBH v. Hauptzollamt Sarrelouis*, ECR 1966, pp. 00205, 00210.

17 *Ibidem*.

18 Judgment of the Court of Justice in the case *Van Gend & Loos*, *op. cit*., footnote 2.

19 Judgment of the Court of Justice of 15.01.1986 in the case C-44/84, *Derrick Guy Edmund Hurd v. Kenneth Jones (Her Majesty's Inspector of Taxes)*, ECR 1986, p. 00029 para. 47.

20 Judgment of the Court of Justice of 19.12.1968 in the case C-13/68, *SpA Salgoil v. Italian Ministry for Foreign Trade*, ECR 1968, pp. 00453, 00463.

1.2. Direct Effect of Union Citizenship Rights

Although the Court of Justice dealt already in the case *Grzelczyk* in detail with the right of Union citizens to freely reside within the territory of the Member States, the Court commented for the first time on whether a Union citizenship right deploys direct effects, namely that to freely reside and move within the territory of the Member States, in the *Baumbast and R.* case.[21] The Court held that the right to reside within the territory of the Member States under ex-Article 18 para. 1 TEC (Article 21 TFEU) is conferred directly on every citizen of the Union by a clear and precise provision of the TEC.[22] Moreover, the Court pointed out that the right of citizens of the Union to reside within the territory of another Member State is conferred subject to the limitations and conditions laid down by the EC Treaty and by the measures adopted to give it effect. Nonetheless, the Court reminded that the application of the limitations and conditions acknowledged in ex-Article 18 para. 1 EC in respect of the exercise of that right is subject to judicial review.[23] The Court went to conclude in the case *Van Duyn* that consequently any limitations and conditions imposed on that right do not prevent the provisions of ex-Article 18 para. 1 TEC from conferring on individuals rights which are enforceable by them and which the national courts must protect.[24] Those limitations and conditions must be applied in compliance with the limits imposed by Community law and in accordance with its general principles, in particular the principle of proportionality,[25] which means that relevant national measures must be necessary and appropriate to attain the objective pursued.

The Court confirmed this interpretation in the Judgment in the case *Trojani*[26] pointing out that the fact that the right to freely reside and move within the territory of the Member States is not unconditional, does not impede its direct applicability.[27] Although this jurisprudence of the Court of Justice refers expressly only to one of the citizens' rights, namely the right to freely move and reside within the territory of the EU Member States, this interpretation can be extended to all Union citizenship rights enshrined in Part Two of the TFEU.

---

21 Judgment of the Court of Justice of 17.09.2002 in the case C-413/99, *Baumbast, R v. Secretary of State for the Home Department*, ECR 2002, p. I-07091.

22 *Ibidem*, para. 84.

23 *Ibidem*, para. 86.

24 See, to that effect, also Judgment of the Court of Justice of 04.12.1974 in the Case 41/47, *Yvonne Van Duyn v. Home Office*, ECR 1974, p. 01337, para. 7.

25 Judgment of the Court of Justice in the case *Baumbast*, para. 91, *op. cit.*, footnote 21.

26 Judgment of the Court of Justice of 07.09.2004 in the case C-456/02, *Michel Trojani v. Centre public d'aide sociale de Bruxelles (CPAS)*, ECR 2004, p. I-07573, para. 30.

27 *Ibidem*, paras. 31, 32.

This conclusion is justified in the first place by the systematic context of the citizens' rights made visible by the new Article 20 para. 2 TFEU.[28] Whereas the Treaty establishing the European Community consecutively listed the different citizens' rights, without establishing a normative connection among them, Article 20 TFEU summarizes all citizens' rights in a general normative part. In this way the structural and functional homogeneity of those rights as deriving from the same legal status, Union citizenship, is accounted for. Article 20 para. 2, second clause TFEU subjects all citizens' rights to the same objective conditions – in particular, nationality of an EU Member State – as well as generally to the conditions and limits defined by the Treaties and by the measures adopted thereunder.[29]

Accordingly, taking into account the interpretation of the Court of Justice of the freedom of movement and residence, there could be no other reasoning as regards the other citizens' rights embraced by Article 20 TFEU, so that all citizens' rights should be deemed to be directly applicable and deploy direct effect in the Member States. The Court of Justice expressly ascribed the disengagement of the right of residence from the condition to carry out an economic activity to the introduction of the Union citizenship into the EC Treaty.[30] In this way the argument that this Union citizenship right is a special one due to its link to the fundamental freedoms – free movement of workers and freedom of establishment – was deprived of its base, contributing thereby to the consolidation of Union citizenship rights as rights deriving merely from the Union citizenship status and submitting the functional analysis of those rights to the sole objectives pursued by Union citizenship. In this sense, bearing in mind that according to the Court of Justice, Union

---

28 Article 20 para. 2 TFEU reads: "Citizens of the Union shall enjoy the rights and be subject to the duties provided for in the Treaties. They shall have, inter alia:

(a) the right to move and reside freely within the territory of the Member States;

(b) the right to vote and to stand as candidates in elections to the European Parliament and in municipal elections in their Member State of residence, under the same conditions as nationals of that State;

(c) the right to enjoy, in the territory of a third country in which the Member State of which they are nationals is not represented, the protection of the diplomatic and consular authorities of any Member State on the same conditions as the nationals of that State;

(d) the right to petition the European Parliament, to apply to the European Ombudsman, and to address the institutions and advisory bodies of the Union in any of the Treaty languages and to obtain a reply in the same language."

29 Article 20 para. 2, second clause TFEU: "These rights shall be exercised in accordance with the conditions and limits defined by the Treaties and by the measures adopted thereunder."

30 Judgment of the Court of Justice in the case *Baumbast*, para. 81, *op. cit.*, footnote 2.

citizenship is destined to be the fundamental status of nationals of the Member States,[31] no differentiating interpretation may be carried out as regards the direct application/effect of the various citizens' rights as all citizens' rights originate from this same fundamental status.

Thus, the direct effect/applicability of the right to consular protection shall be asserted according to the principles established by the case-law of the Court of Justice with regard to the "self-executing character" of the citizens' rights taking into account that the right to consular protection derives from the Union citizenship' status. Therefore, the conditions and limits imposed upon the exercise of the right to consular protection should be examined in order to ascertain whether these conditions are constitutive for the creation of the citizens' right as such or rather implementing measures that merely design the exercise of the right concerned without calling it into question.[32] Worth mentioning is that the Court of Justice held in the Judgement in the case *Defrenne II* as to the direct effect of ex-Article 141 TEC on equal pay for men and women that this is the case where the implementation measures are not indispensable for the application of the primary Union law provision in question that does not limit itself to merely refer the matter to the powers of the national legislative authorities.[33]

Thus, the possible "conditions" that could prevent the provisions on consular protection from deploying direct effect will be analysed taking into consideration their aims and systemic structure.

2. Conditionality of Consular Protection?

The great majority of the legal scholarship[34] on Article 8c of the Treaty of Maastricht had assumed that Article 8c was not directly applicable due to its second sentence establishing that:

---

[31] Judgment of the Court of Justice of 20.09.2001 in the case C-184/99, *Rudy Grzelczyk v. Centre public d'aide sociale d'Ottignies-Louvain-la-Neuve*, *op. cit.*, footnote 249, para. 31.

[32] See KLEINLEIN, T./ RABENSCHLAG, D., "Auslansschutz und Staatsangehörigkeit", in *Zeitschrift für ausländisches öffentliches Recht und Völkerrecht*, No. 67 (2007), p. 1313.

[33] Judgment of the Court of Justice of 08.04.1976 in the case C-43/75, *Gabrielle Defrenne v. Société anonyme belge de navigation aérienne Sabena*, ECR 1976, p. 455, paras. 25 et seq.

[34] ANDRÉS SÁENZ DE SANTA MARÍA, P., "La protección diplomática y consular de los ciudadanos de la Unión en el exterior", in *Revista de Derecho de la Unión Europea*, No. 11-2° semestre 2006, p. 11, 13; BLÁZQUEZ PEINADO, M. D., *La ciudadanía de la Unión (Los derechos reconocidos en los artículos 8.A a 8.D del T.C.E.)*, Valencia, 1998, p. 251, 276; OBWEXER, W., "Das Recht der Unionsbürger auf diplomatischen und konsularischen Schutz", *op. cit.*, footnote 11.

Before 31 December 1993, Member States shall establish the necessary rules among themselves and start the international negotiations required to secure this protection.

According to RODRÍGUEZ BARRIGÓN, the need for the Member States to establish rules among themselves refers to provisions that are necessary in order to apply in practice Article 8c. Otherwise, the right to consular protection was inoperative without those provisions as well as the international negotiations with third countries.[35] This twofold conditionality of the right to consular protection hinders, in the opinion of these authors, the direct applicability/ effect of the provisions on consular protection.

2.1. Implementing Rules

As for the first condition of the right to consular protection, the one relating to the necessary rules to be established by the Member States, according to BUSSE, already the fact that not the organs of the European Community but the Member States themselves are in charge of the adoption of more detailed rules, speaks in favour of a recognition of a right to consular protection according to Article 8c, first clause, only in compliance with the further requirements established by the Member States according to Article 8c second clause.[36] Accordingly, the right to consular protection was merely conditional and recognized under reservation and thus was not directly applicable.[37] However, this argument can be countered by pointing out that no decision of the Treaty between two options can be seen here but rather only the Member States could be assigned this task since the Community had no competence in this area.[38]

Similarly, BLÁZQUEZ PEINADO sees in this "mandate" for the Member States to establish the necessary rules among themselves a room for manoeuvre regarding the measures developing the right to consular protection hindering its direct effect.[39] Furthermore, JIMÉNEZ PIERNAS points out that the wide scope of assessment guaranteed to the public

---

35 RODRÍGUEZ BARRIGÓN, J. M., "La ciudadanía de la Unión Europea", p. 589, *op. cit.*, footnote 11.

36 BUSSE, C., "Enthält Artikel 20 S.1 EGV – Amsterdam einen unmittelbaren Anspruch auf diplomatischen und konsularischen Schutz?", in *Europablätter*, 1998 (Vol. 1), pp. 92, 93.

37 *Ibidem.*

38 In contrast, the Treaty of Lisbon added a second paragraph into Article 23 TFEU providing for the competence of the Council to enact directives.

39 BLÁZQUEZ PEINADO, M. D., *La ciudadanía de la Unión*, p. 276, *op. cit.*, footnote 34.

authorities impedes the affirmation of a clear, precise, complete and unconditional obligation.[40]

However, it should be pointed out that the time limit for the establishment of the rules among the Member States was removed from the wording of Article 20 TEC by the Treaty of Amsterdam[41] in consequence of the adoption of Decision 95/553/EC regarding protection for citizens of the European Union by diplomatic and consular representations on 19 December 1995 by the Representatives of the Governments of the Member States.[42] The preamble to Decision 95/553/EC of 19 December 1995 recalls that the Decision was adopted with a view to implementing the obligation set out in Article 20 of the EC Treaty (ex-Article 8c).[43]

Thus, it cannot be agreed with the allegation of BUSSE that the time limit was struck in order to disable the Court of Justice from declaring the provision directly applicable after the time limit has expired as in the case of the fundamental freedoms.[44] Rather, the time limit was removed since at the time of the drafting of the Treaty of Amsterdam, Decision 95/553/EC was already adopted and pending entry into force after the ratification by all Member States.[45]

Notwithstanding, the assignment to the Member States to agree upon detailed rules regarding the provision of consular protection (with or without a time limit) submitted the right to consular protection to a further-design reservation. Nevertheless, it could be argued that this

---

40 JIMÉNEZ PIERNAS, C., "La asistencia consular al ciudadano de la Unión: de Maastricht a Amsterdam" in *Acción exterior de la Unión Europea y Comunidad Internacional*, Fernando M. Mariño Menéndez (ed.), 1998, p. 219, 241.

41 Article 20 TEU-Amsterdam: "Member States shall establish the necessary rules among themselves and start the international negotiations required to secure this protection."

42 Published in the Official Journal L 314, 28/12/1995, pp. 0073-0076.

43 Preamble of Decision 95/553/EC: "Desirous of performing the obligation laid down in Article 8c of the Treaty establishing the European Community."

44 BUSSE, C., "Enthält Artikel 20 S.1 EGV – Amsterdam einen unmittelbaren Anspruch auf diplomatischen und konsularischen Schutz?", pp. 92, 93, *op. cit.*, footnote 36.

45 In this context it should be noted that according to the majority of the legal doctrine, Decision 95/553/EC is not a secondary community act but an intergovernmental agreement between the Member States taking into consideration that the Decision was not enacted by the Council as such but by the representatives of the Governments of the Member States. Thus the decision is not a sui generis community act but a joint legal action of the Member States (RUFFERT, M., "Diplomatischer und konsularischer Schutz zwischen Völker- und Europarecht", in *Archiv des Völkerrechts*, 35 (1997), p. 473; SZCZEKALLA, P., "Die Pflicht der Gemeinschaft und der Mitgliedstaaten zum diplomatischen und konsularischen Schutz", in *Europarecht*, Heft 3, 1999, p. 326) that needs to be ratified by all contract parties (the Member States) according to their internal legal order in order to entry into force.

conditionality of the right to consular protection does not contrast with the sufficiently clear and precise character of the provision itself.[46]

However, in the meanwhile this legal discussion has become less relevant since the Treaty of Lisbon has taken into account the entry into force of Decision 95/553/EC on 3 May 2002 and has amended the wording of Article 20 TEC establishing the new Article 23 TFEU that "Member States shall adopt the necessary provisions and start the international negotiations required to secure this protection."

Under this provision the Member States are not any more required to establish intergovernmental rules among themselves but to adopt the necessary provisions to secure this protection. The substitution of the notion "rules among themselves" by "adopt the necessary provisions" suggests a relocation of the consular protection from an intergovernmental into an EU context, from the establishment of common, basic arrangements among the Member States to the adoption of more precise implementation rules (e.g. better communication of the right to consular protection as pointed out in the Action Plan 2007-2009 of the European Commission)[47] as well as internal legal measures necessary to secure this protection under the national law of the Member States. Therefore, the "necessary provisions" shall strengthen the effectiveness of the citizens' right, instead of impeding its direct applicability and so diminishing its impact on the legal position of the Union citizens.

Besides, bearing in mind the case-law of the Court of Justice regarding the direct effect of citizens' rights requiring that the application of the limitations and conditions in respect of the exercise of those rights shall be subject to judicial review,[48] the necessary provisions adopted by the Member States are not exempted from the scope of jurisdiction of the Court of Justice. In this regard it should be stressed that the "necessary provisions" to be adopted by the Member States must not contradict primary EU law, i.e. shall be appropriate to attain the objective pursued which is to secure the provision of consular protection under Article 23 TFEU.

On the contrary, it is irrelevant whether Decision 95/553/EC (as an already adopted implementing regulation) can be subject of judicial

---

46 SZCZEKALLA, P., "Die Pflicht der Gemeinschaft und der Mitgliedstaaten zum diplomatischen und konsularischen Schutz", *Ibidem*, p. 327.

47 EUROPEAN COMMISSION, Action Plan 2007-2009 "Effective consular protection in third countries: the contribution of the European Union", Communication from the Commission to the European Parliament, the Council, the European Economic and Social Committee and the Committee of the Regions of 05 December 2007, COM(2007)767 final, p. 4. Available at: <http://eur-lex.europa.eu/LexUriServ/LexUriServ.do?uri=COM:2007:0767:FIN:EN:HTML> (15.08.2010).

48 Judgment of the Court of Justice in the case *Baumbast*, para. 91, *op. cit.*, footnote 21.

review by the Court of Justice. As mentioned above, the majority of the legal doctrine sees in the Decision no Community act *sui generis* but rather an intergovernmental agreement among the Member States. In this case the Court of Justice would have no jurisdiction over the Decision.[49]

On the other side, many Member States gave effect to Decision 95/553/EC within their internal legal order not by "ratifying" it as if it was an international agreement but rather by means of informal implementation into the internal legal order. Some of the Member States have applied the Decision directly, i.e. without issuing any implementing legal instrument (Cyprus, Ireland, Italy, the Netherlands, Poland, Slovakia and the United Kingdom). All these states consider Decision 95/553/EC as a Council Decision (and thus, as a secondary Community act) and thus have applied this Decision directly considering that Council Decisions are of direct application (except the United Kingdom which states that it applies the decision as a matter of policy). Other Member States have implemented Decision 95/553/EC by means of internal instructions, circulars and notifications, normally issued by the Ministry of Foreign Affairs and addressed to the diplomatic and consular representations of the respective states. This is the case of Bulgaria, the Czech Republic, Denmark, Finland, Germany and Malta.

However, in both cases actions undertaken on the basis of Decision 95/553/EC are subject to judicial review by the Court of Justice, either by means of an indirect examination by a preliminary ruling (art. 267 TFEU) or an infringement procedure (art. 258 TFEU), shall the Decision be an intergovernmental agreement, or, besides, by a direct review by means of an action for annulment (art. 263 TFEU), shall the Decision be considered as a Council Decision.

Accordingly, the first condition that could hinder the direct applicability/effect of the right to consular protection has ceased to exist with the entry into force of Decision 95/553/EC as well as the new wording of Article 23 TFEU.

2.2. International Negotiations

The extra-territorial character of the right to consular protection could also give rise for denying its direct effect, particularly when the cooperation of all third country in which some of the Member States is not represented would be necessary in order to provide consular protection to unrepresented Union citizens. As stated above, Article 23

49 RUFFERT, M., "Dogmatik und Praxis…", p. 473, *op. cit.*, footnote 45; SZCZEKALLA, P., "Die Pflicht der Gemeinschaft und der Mitgliedstaaten zum diplomatischen und konsularischen Schutz", p. 326, *op. cit.*, footnote 45.

para. 1 second clause TFEU makes reference to the effect of the right to consular protection beyond the borders of the European Union by stipulating that Member States shall "start the international negotiations required to secure this protection".

In this regard, the distinction between consular and diplomatic protection is of particular importance. According to Article 8 of the Vienna Convention on Consular Relations only a notification is necessary in order to provide consular protection to non-national citizens on behalf of their State of origin in third countries:

> Upon appropriate notification to the receiving State, a consular post of the sending State may, unless the receiving State objects, exercise consular functions in the receiving State on behalf of a third State.

In contrast, for the case of diplomatic protection of non-national citizens on behalf of their State of origin, Article 46 of the Vienna Convention on Diplomatic Relations (VCDR) stipulates that:

> A sending State may with the prior consent of a receiving State, and at the request of a third State not represented in the receiving State, undertake the temporary protection of the interests of the third State and of its nationals.

In this case, the provision of diplomatic protection to non-national EU citizens would be conditioned by the previous consent of the third State obtained in the course of international negotiations. However, even after obtaining the consent of the third State, Article 46 of the Vienna Convention on Diplomatic Relations allows for only a temporary protection. As stated above, this provision does not correspond to the intention underlying Article 23 TFEU to offer protection on a permanent basis to unrepresented Union citizens without the obligation of the Member States to establish own representations in each third country in order to prevent the extension of the temporary protection under Article 46 VCDR to a permanent protection of their nationals in those third states where the Member States concerned are not represented. As stated above, this is one of the reasons for the need to restrictively interpret Article 23 TFEU assuming that it refers only to consular protection and not to diplomatic protection in terms of international law as well.

In this context, attention is invited to the fact that the representatives of the legal doctrine on Article 8c-Maastricht, who throughout plead for a restrictive interpretation of Article 8c in accordance with the requirements of international law limiting this provision to consular protection only and excluding diplomatic protection from its scope of application, claim the need to conduct negotiations in order to obtain the consent of the third countries applicable to the provision of diplomatic protection to non-nationals only.[50] This approach seems to be inconsistent since the restriction of the scope of protection on the one side should consequently be reflected in the measures appropriate and necessary to secure this protection on the other side.

Moreover, it should be pointed out that the requirement to obtain the consent of all third countries where not all Member States are represented by an embassy or a consulate (all third countries except the United States, Canada and China) would render the putting into practice of the provisions on consular protection utterly impossible, not to mention that this situation would suppose the placing at the disposal of third countries of a leverage against the EU Member States.[51]

Accordingly, based on this premise, only a notification to the receiving State should be regarded as necessary and sufficient in order to guarantee the effective application of the consular protection provided to unrepresented non-national EU citizens.

The notion 'negotiations' in Article 23 TFEU is not at odds with the requirement of a simple notification since this notion is not used in terms of trade law, where negotiations are conducted towards an agreement by two or more parties, but rather in a more abstract-legal context allowing to subsume hereunder all kind of international actions of the Member States.[52] In this sense, 'negotiations' should not be confused with 'agreements' and do not have mandatorily to lead to the conclusion of agreements neither.[53]

In addition, the notion 'negotiations' shall reflect the particular EU-external dimension of the right to consular protection and presents a general term for all kind of actions to be undertaken by the Member

50 JIMÉNEZ PIERNAS, C., "La protección diplomática y consular del ciudadano de la Unión Europea", p. 241, *op. cit.*, footnote 40; BLÁZQUEZ PEINADO, M. D., *La ciudadanía de la Unión*, p. 278, *op. cit.*, footnote 34.

51 Besides, the existence of an explicitly indicated consent on the part of a third country to tolerate consular protection provided to unrepresented Union citizens by EU Member States of which the citizens concerned are not nationals does not prevent the third states from disregarding their previously issued consent in a concrete case, i.e. the risk that a "country of concern" could in practice hamper the provision of consular protection under Union law cannot be eliminated neither by obtaining the previous consent of the third state nor by notification.

52 KLUTH, W., "Kommentar zu Artikel 23 AEUV", in *EUV/EGV Kommentar*, Christian Calliess/Matthias Ruffert (ed.), 4. edition, München 2011, para. 8; Against this interpretation: STEIN, T., "Die Regelung des diplomatischen Schutzes im Vertrag über die Europäische Union", in *Der diplomatische Schutz im Völker- und Europarecht Aktuelle Probleme und Entwicklungstendenzen*, Georg Ress/Thorsten Stein (ed.), pp. 97, 99.

53 JIMÉNEZ PIERNAS, C., "La protección diplomática y consular del ciudadano de la Unión Europea", p. 33, *op. cit.*, footnote 40.

States on the international stage in order to secure this right. Article 23 TFEU pretends not to anticipate the Member States' decision on which actions will be the most appropriate and required in order to guarantee the *effet utile* of the right to consular protection, taking into account the wide range of possible actions, that can vary from negotiations seeking the consent of third countries, bilateral or multilateral agreements on humanitarian aid containing a clause on this subject, implied agreement, unilateral recognition by third states[54] to a simple notification to the third countries.

Furthermore, should the EU Member States establish the application of Article 23 TFEU within the international practice, an international custom with the content of the same provision could be created according to Article 38 of the Vienna Convention on the Law of Treaties of 1969[55] on Rules in a treaty becoming binding on third States:[56]

> Nothing in articles 34 to 37 precludes a rule set forth in a treaty from becoming binding upon a third State as a customary rule of international law, recognized as such.

Additionally, Article 23 para. 1, 2. clause TFEU issues a mandate to the Member States "to secure this protection" creating in this vein an obligation for the Member States to establish a special guarantee for the right to consular protection taking into account its impact outside the EU borders. Thus, being the mandate assigned by Article 23 TFEU to the Member States a guarantee of the consular protection of unrepresented Union citizens in third countries, international negotiations shall be considered as an instrument to achieve this goal and not the goal of this provision itself. But would the requirement of negotiations in the strictest sense condition the right to consular protection impeding its practical effectivity, this would contradict the objective set by Article 23 para. 1, second clause TFEU to secure the provision of consular protection to unrepresented non-national EU citizens.

Besides, it should be highlighted that Article 46 of the Charter of Fundamental Rights of the European Union, although referring abstractly to the limits and conditions established by the Treaty, does not even mention neither of both "conditions" which suggests the intention underlying the Treaties not to impose a mandatory pre-condition on the right to consular

54 SZCZEKALLA, P., "Die Pflicht der Gemeinschaft und der Mitgliedstaaten zum diplomatischen und konsularischen Schutz", p. 329, *op. cit.*, footnote 45.

55 Done at Vienna on 23 May 1969. Entered into force on 27 January 1980. *United Nations, Treaty Series*, Vol. 1155, p. 331.

56 RUFFERT, M., "Dogmatik und Praxis des subjektiv-öffentlichen rechts unter dem Einfluss des Gemeinschaftsrechts", p. 476, *op. cit.*, footnote 45; SZCZEKALLA, P., "Die Pflicht der Gemeinschaft und der Mitgliedstaaten zum diplomatischen und konsularischen Schutz", p. 329, *op. cit.*, footnote 45.

protection but rather to establish guarantees for its effectiveness inherent indeed to each subjective legal right.[57]

In this context it is worth mentioning that, according to the 1st Citizenship Report of the European Commission of 21 December 1993,[58] the authorities of all third countries were informed of Article 8c-Maastricht by the Presidency by *note verbale*.

Accordingly, the general framework for the practical application of Article 23 TFEU in third countries has been set so that also this alleged "condition" has been fulfilled and can be considered no longer as an obstacle to the direct effect of Article 23 TFEU.

2.3. Member States' Discretion

Another obstacle before the direct effect of the provisions on consular protection could result from the design of the right to consular protection as an equal-treatment right. According to Article 23 TFEU and Article 46 of the Charter, consular protection is provided by embassies and consulates of the Member States in third countries offering to unrepresented Union citizens the same protection as the one provided to their own nationals. As discussed below within the Chapter on the substantive scope of the right to consular protection, Member States provide protection to their nationals in distress abroad enjoying often a wide scope of discretion accorded by the national rules in question. This scope of discretion could deprive the provisions on consular protection from deploying direct effect taking into account the above-mentioned jurisprudence of the Court of Justice in the case *Hurd*, for instance, stating that a provision produces direct effect only if it is "clear and unconditional and not contingent on any discretionary implementing measure".[59]

The Court held that the differences between the practices of the Member States concerning the detailed rules and procedures for exempting teachers from domestic taxation show that the substance of the obligation, imposed by Article 5 of the EEC Treaty to refrain from any unilateral measure that would interfere with the system adopted for financing the Community and apportioning financial burdens between the Member States, is not sufficiently precise.[60]

---

57 Please see below for further details regarding guarantees as a configuration element of a subjective right, Chapter VII.

58 EUROPEAN COMMISSION, Report on the Citizenship of the Union of 21 December 1993, COM(93)702 final. Available at: <http://eur-lex.europa.eu/LexUriServ/LexUriServ.do?uri=COM:1993:0702:FIN:EN:PDF> (03.02.2009).

59 Judgment of the Court of Justice of 15.01.1986 in the case C-44/84, *Derrick Guy Edmund Hurd v. Kenneth Jones (Her Majesty's Inspector of Taxes)*, ECR 1986, p. 00029 para. 47.

60 *Ibidem*, para. 48.

The *rationale* behind this jurisprudence of the Court of Justice is obviously the consideration that a provision putting the Member States under the duty to act may not be capable of producing effects directly on the relationship between Member States and citizens if the Member States have been afforded a scope of discretion as to the implementation of the obligation established, in particular when Member States may chose from two or more options.

Notwithstanding, Article 23 TFEU imposes no obligation on the Member States that must be necessarily further implemented by them in order to become, in the words of Advocate General VAN GERVEN, "sufficiently operational".[61] Precisely the design of the right to consular protection as an equal-treatment right seems in this context to be no obstacle but rather an argument in favour of the direct effect of the provisions on consular protection: the equal treatment as such requires no further implementation by Member States in order to be achieved but is rather insured by mere application of the national rules concerned to Union citizens in the situations established by Decision 95/553/EC.

The Court of Justice thus confirmed already very early the direct effect of the rule on equal treatment stating that:

> The rule on equal treatment with nationals is one of the fundamental legal provisions of the Community. As a reference to a set of legislative provisions effectively applied by the country of establishment to its own nationals, this rule is, by its essence, capable of being directly invoked by nationals of all the other Member States.[62]

It is also well-established case-law of the Court of Justice that the general non-discrimination precept of Article 18 TFEU (ex-Article 12 TEC)[63] has direct effect and may thus be relied upon within the scope of application of the Treaties.[64]

In this sense, it should be noticed that the case-law of the Court of Justice on the lack of direct effect in case that further implementation is needed involving a margin of discretion refers to a scope of decision-making of the Member States at the level of implementation of the Union

---

61 Opinion of Advocate General VAN GERVEN of 27.10.1993 in the case C-128/92, H. J. *Banks & Co. Ltd v. British Coal Corporation*, ECR 1994, p. I-01209, para. 27.

62 Judgment of the Court of Justice of 21.06.1974 in the case C-2/74, *Jean Reyners v Belgian State*, ECR 1974, p. 00631, paras. 24, 25.

63 Article 18 para. 1 TFEU: "Within the scope of application of the Treaties, and without prejudice to any special provisions contained therein, any discrimination on grounds of nationality shall be prohibited."

64 See for instance Judgment of the Court of Justice in the case *Grzelczyk*, *op. cit.*, footnote 31 as well as Judgment of the Court of Justice of 02.10.2003 in the case C-148/02, *Carlos Garcia Avello v. Belgian State*, ECR 2003, p. I-11613.

provisions. In contrast, Article 23 TFEU accords no discretion as to any implementation of the provision of consular protection to unrepresented Union citizens abroad but affords rather a scope of discretion regarding the specific measures to be undertaken in each concrete case of consular protection provided to the citizens in distress, taking into consideration the circumstances in each particular situation.[65] The existence of a scope of discretion may not deprive a provision of its capability to produce effects on the relationship between State and citizens, e.g. by creating individual rights, unless it is not justiciable. In this sense the case-law of the Court of Justice regarding the direct effect of Union citizenship rights should be reminded pointing out that limits and conditions imposed on citizenship rights prevent them not from having direct effect provided they are subjects to judicial control.[66]

Therefore, Article 23 TFEU "can stand by itself"[67] so that it is capable of being applied by the national authorities of the Member States in concrete cases, which has been evidenced *inter alia* by the putting in practice of this provision through numerous requests for consular protection by unrepresented Union citizens abroad and the protection provided by the embassies and consulates of the Member States.

A question different from that regarding the need for further implementing measures is the question of whether further implementing measures would be recommendable in order to render EU legal provisions more effective. In this sense, the adoption of an EU directive on consular protection might be indeed advisable in order to improve the impact of Article 23 TFEU and Article 46 of the Charter, by, for instance, expanding the circle of right-holders or limiting the scope of discretion of the national authorities through the principle of proportionality, etc.;[68] however, it is not imperative in order for the provisions on consular protection to be capable of deploying direct effect.

2.4. Conditionality of Financial Advance

Under similar considerations regarding conditionality, one of the precepts of consular protection established by Decision 95/553/EC, that

---

65 Please see Chapter VI below on the distinction between discretion as to the question if consular protection is provided at all and the question of how consular protection is provided.

66 See Judgments of the Court of Justice in the cases *Baumbast, op. cit.*, footnote 21, and *Trojani, op. cit.*, footnote 26.

67 See Judgment of the Court of Justice of 23.04.1956 in the joined cases 7/54 and 9/54, *Groupement des Industries Sidérurgiques Luxembourgeoises v. High Authority of the European Coal and Steel Community*, ECR 1956, pp. 00175, 00181.

68 See Chapter VIII below.

of financial advance, stands out being conceived as conditional upon the consent of the Member State of origin. In this sense, according to Article 6 para. 1 of Decision 95/553/EC:

> Notwithstanding Article 3[69] and except in cases of extreme urgency, no financial advance or help may be given or expenditure incurred on behalf of a citizen of the Union without the permission of the competent authorities of the Member State of which that citizen is a national, given either by the Foreign Ministry or by the nearest diplomatic mission.

Remarkable is here first of all the conceptual difference between the financial advance in terms of Article 6 of Decision 95/553/EC and the rest of precepts: whereas Article 5 of the Decision enumerates mainly situations in which an unrepresented Union citizen shall be entitled to ask for consular protection, such as death, serious accident, serious illness, arrest or detention and falling victim to a violent crime, Article 5 para. 1 (e) and Article 6 stipulate the only concrete measures to be offered as consular protection to unrepresented Union citizens in distress: repatriation and financial advance.

Financial advance seems therefore to be a specific measure of consular protection applicable in the situations mentioned not exhaustively by Article 5 para. 1 (a)-(d) of Decision 95/553/EC.[70] However, while according to Article 5 para. 1 (e) the repatriation of distressed Union citizens is not subject to any conditions, the provision of financial advance is, as a general rule, dependant on the permission of the Member State of nationality granted either by the Ministry of Foreign Affairs or by the nearest diplomatic mission of that State. However, according to Article 6 para. 1, no permission of the Member State of nationality needs to be obtained in cases of extreme urgency.

Again, the question arises whether this conditionality of the provision of financial advance prevent the Union provisions concerned from deploying direct effect.

First, and as said beforehand, the provision of financial advance is merely one concrete measure that may be necessary to be provided as consular protection to unrepresented Union citizens in third countries in the situations stipulated in Article 5 para. 1 of Decision 95/553/EC or in any other similar situation of distress, so that the "conditionality" of this

---

69 Article 3 Decision 95/553/EC: "Diplomatic and consular representations which give protection shall treat a person seeking help as if he were a national of the Member State which they represent."

70 It should be noted that Decision 95/553/EC distinguishes between financial advance provided in the situations enumerated in Article 5 para. 1 (a)-(d) – death, serious accident or serious illness, arrest or detention, victim of violent crime – (Annex I to Decision 95/553/EC) and costs incurred on the occasion of repatriation, that may include also a small financial advance (Annex II to Decision 95/553/EC).

particular measure may not affect the direct effect of the right to consular protection as such.[71]

Without prejudice to these remarks, it should be again pointed out that the "conditionality" of the provision of financial advance is no conditionality in the sense of outstanding implementing measures on the part of the Member States. This alleged conditionality should not be confused with the condition of the previous adoption of necessary implementation measures by the Member States preventing the provision in question of being precise and clear and, therefore, capable of producing direct effect on the relationship between Member States and citizens by putting an intermediate step between the obligation established by Union provisions and the legal consequence for individuals.

Article 6 Decision 95/553/EC establishes rather a procedure for the exercise of the right to consular protection directed specifically to the provision of financial advance similar to the necessary previous notification and authorisation issued by the competent authority in order to be able to exercise the freedom of assembly. It has been well-established by the European Court of Human Rights as well as by many of the national Constitutional Courts that the freedom of assembly is a fundamental right conferred on individuals by the national constitutions and the European Convention of Human Rights establishing by law a special procedure for the exercise of that right with regard to public order and safety considerations.[72]

In this sense, the "condition" provided for in Article 6 Decision 95/553/EC is no condition regarding the (general) application of the provision of financial advance to unrepresented Union citizens but rather a procedure for the exercise of that right in each particular case, which by itself shows the capability of the provision concerned to produce effects on the relationship between Member States and citizens.

Remarkable is in this context also the fact that Decision 95/553/EC refers not to national rules of the Member States on recourse action of the Member State of origin towards the citizen who has been awarded financial advance.

---

[71] To the difference between the 'if' and 'how' of consular protection, please see Chapter VI below.

[72] Report of the European Human Rights Commission in the case *Rassemblement Jurassien and Unité Jurassienne v. Switzerland*, App. No. 8191/78, 17 DR 93; Judgment of the European Court of Human Rights of 17.07.2005 in the case *Bukta v. Hungary*, App. No. 25691/04, para. 36; Decision of the First Section of the German Federal Constitutional Court of 14.05.1985 in the case "*Brokdorf*", 1 BvR 233, 341/81, para. 73, BVerfGE 69, 315 making clear the difference between the requirement for an authorization of an assembly which refers to the exercise of the right and the ban on an assembly as a restriction of the freedom to assembly. See also Judgment of the Court of Justice of 12.06.2003 in the case C-112/00, *Eugen Schmidberger, Internationale Transporte und Planzüge v. Republik Österreich*, ECR 2003, p. I-05659.

Rather, Article 6 para. 3 Decision 95/553/EC establishes by itself a legal basis for the regress of the Member State of origin against its citizen[73] if the Member State has reimbursed the costs incurred to the assisting Member State.[74] Annex I to Decision 95/553/EC contains a form for the Undertaking to Repay (UTR) a financial advance[75] that need to be signed by the distressed citizen and establishing his/her obligation to repay the financial advance and any other costs or fees incurred to his/her own Member State, being the assisting Member State in this legal construction an agent of the home Member State of the unrepresented Union citizen acting on its behalf *inter alia* by keeping in custody the UTR document.

It should, however, be noted that albeit Article 6 Decision 95/553/EC makes no reference to any correspondent national rules, the common format for undertaking to repay financial advance in Annex I to the Decision reads "…undertake and promise to repay on demands to the Ministry of Foreign Affairs/ Government of … in accordance with the national law of that country the equivalent of the said sum…".

Nonetheless, the reference to the national rules on recourse refer rather to the possibility that the recourse of the State against its citizens may be waived according to national law underlining by this means that Decision 95/553/EC provides for the possibility of the Member State of origin to take recourse against its own citizens who have been granted financial

73 Article 6 para. 2 and 3 Decision 95/553/EC:

"2. Unless the authorities of the Member State of the applicant's nationality expressly waive this requirement, the applicant must undertake to repay the full value of any financial advance or help and expenditure incurred plus, where applicable, a consular fee notified by the competent authorities.

3. The undertaking to repay shall take the form of a document requiring the distressed national to repay to the Government of the Member State of which he is a national any costs incurred on his behalf or money paid to him, plus any applicable fee."

74 Article 6 para. 4 Decision 95/553/EC: "The Government of the Member State of which the applicant is a national shall reimburse all costs, on request, to the Government of the assisting Member State." Member States conclude often among each other payment arrangements on pro-rata basis as recommended in the 2006 Guidelines on Consular Protection of EU Citizens in Third Countries of 16.06.2006, Document 10109/2/06 Rev 2. Section 12.10 read: "Where EU nationals being evacuated are asked to pay the marginal costs of the evacuation as well as other expenses related thereto, payment arrangements should be made from Member State to Member State, on a pro-rata basis. It will then be the responsibility of the requesting Member State to pursue repayment from its nationals." Available at: <http://register.consilium.europa.eu/pdf/en/06/st10/st10109-re02.en06.pdf>. In some cases reimbursement can be waived according to reciprocity agreements between two Member States or when the costs incurred correspond to very small amounts (Interview with official from the German Ministry for Foreign Affairs, 2009).

75 See Annex I to Decision 95/553/EC, published in Official Journal L 314/73 of 28.12.1995.

advance but that it imposes no obligation on that Member State to do so, particularly when according to national law no such recourse is possible or can be waived, etc.

Accordingly, Decision 95/553/EC sets to a great extent the procedure for the granting of financial advance providing even a legal basis for the recourse that could be taken by the home Member State of nationality against the citizen who has been awarded a financial advance by another Member State in a third country and not limiting itself to the mere reference to national legal rules, that, if not already existent, would have needed to be first adopted by the Member States.

3. The Right to Consular Protection as a Fundamental Right under the EU Charter of Fundamental Rights

Since the Presidents of the European Parliament, the Council and the Commission signed and solemnly proclaimed the Charter at the European Council meeting in Nice on 7 December 2000, the Charter of Fundamental Rights of the European Union has been in numerous cases referred to by the Advocates General of the Court of Justice[76] and by the Court of First Instance,[77] endorsing in this vein the soft-law character of the Charter and underlining its function as an important interpretative instrument within the EU legal framework. For the first time, in its ruling of 27 June 2006 concerning the Directive on family reunification,[78] the Court of Justice relied on the Charter and stressed its importance.

While the conclusions of the Cologne European Council on 3/4 June 1999 left open the question of whether the Charter will be a proclamation or a legally binding text,[79] the Brussels June 2007 European Council

76 The Advocates General GEELHOED, STIX-HACKL, SIEGBERT ALBERT, LÉGER, JACOBS, TIZZANO, RUIZ-JARABO and MISCHO have repeatedly cited the Charter in their opinions stating that "the Charter has undeniably placed the rights which form its subject-matter at the highest level of values common to the Member States" (See Opinion of Advocate General GEELHOED of 5.07.2001 in the case C-413/99, *Baumbast and R.*; Opinion of Advocate General STIX-HACKL of 13.09.2001 in the case C-60/00, *Mary Carpenter/Secretary of State for the Home Department*).

77 See Judgment of the Court of First Instance of 15.01.2003 in joined cases T-377/00, T-379/00, T-380/00, T-260/01, T-272/01, Philip Morris International, Inc., R. J. Reynolds Tobacco Holdings, Inc., RJR Acquisition Corp., R. J. Reynolds Tobacco Company, R. J. Reynolds Tobacco International, Inc., Japan Tobacco, Inc. v. Commission, ECR 2003, p. II-00001.

78 Judgment of the Court of Justice of 27.06.2006 in the case C-540/03, *European Parliament v. Council of the European Union*, ECR 2006, p. I-05769.

79 "The European Council will propose to the European Parliament and the Commission that, together with the Council, they should solemnly proclaim on the basis of the draft document a European Charter of Fundamental Rights. It will then have to be considered

agreed in the mandate for the Intergovernmental Conference (IGC) on the Future of Europe to give the Charter legally binding force, whereupon Article 6 was included into the draft Reform Treaty.[80] Accordingly, Article 6 para. 1 of the Treaty on European Union (as modified by the Treaty of Lisbon) stipulates that the Charter shall have the same legal value as the Treaties.[81] Thus, the Charter has a mandatory legal effect and is not any more just a politically symbolical "solemn proclamation".

The fundamental rights contained in the Charter are conferred upon different groups of right-holders[82] – for instance, Union citizens in Title V on Citizens' rights, all citizens residing in the European Union in Title I on Dignity and Title II on Freedoms, parents in Article 14 para. 3, employees in Articles 27 to 32, children in Article 24, elderly in Article 25, persons with disabilities in Article 26. Accordingly, the rights contained in the Charter are directed towards individuals as active addressees of the provisions of the Charter. According to Article 51 para. 1 of the Charter, the passive subjects of the obligations imposed shall be the institutions, bodies, offices and agencies of the Union as well as the Member States.[83]

The Convention responsible for drafting the Charter of Fundamental Rights, chaired by Roman Herzog, had no difficulties to reach consent on the wording of Article 46 of the Charter on the right to diplomatic and consular protection and according to the draft on the Charter of the Presidium of 14 June 2000 the wording of Article 20 para. 1 TEC was adopted.[84]

---

whether and, if so, how the Charter should be integrated into the treaties." (European Council Conclusions, Cologne, 3-4 June 1999). Available at: <http://www.consilium.europa.eu/ueDocs/cms_ Data/docs/pressData/en/ec/kolnen.htm> (05.03.2010).

80 BRUSSELS EUROPEAN COUNCIL 21/22 June 2007, Presidency Conclusions, 11177/1/07 of 20 July 2007, Annex 1, Mandate 9. Available at: <http://www.consilium.europa.eu/ueDocs/cms_Data/docs/pressData/en/ec/94932.pdf> (05.03.2010).

81 Article 6 para. 1 TEU: "The Union recognises the rights, freedoms and principles set out in the Charter of Fundamental Rights of the European Union of 7 December 2000, as adapted at Strasbourg, on 12 December 2007, which shall have the same legal value as the Treaties."

82 RODRÍGUEZ, Á., *Integración Europea y Derechos Fundamentales*, Madrid, 2001, pp. 205, 207.

83 Article 51 of the Charter [Field of application]: "The provisions of this Charter are addressed to the institutions, bodies, offices and agencies of the Union with due regard for the principle of subsidiarity and to the Member States only when they are implementing Union law. They shall therefore respect the rights, observe the principles and promote the application thereof in accordance with their respective powers and respecting the limits of the powers of the Union as conferred on it in the Treaties."

84 Convention for a Charter of Fundamental Rights of the European Union, CHARTE 4360/00 of 14.06.2000, Proposal of the Presidium to Art. 26 a.

Article 46 of the Charter shall indeed not upgrade the extent of the right to consular protection provided under Article 20 in conjunction with Article 23 TFEU. This interpretation corresponds also to the conformity or congruence clause of Article 52 para. 2 of the Charter stating that the Charter shall not alter the system of rights conferred by the EC Treaty and taken over by the Treaties.[85]

This approach is confirmed also by the Explanation of the Praesidium of the Convention on the Draft Charter of Fundamental Rights of the European Union on Article 52. The Explanation on Article 52 para. 2 of the Charter clarifies that it refers to rights which were already expressly guaranteed in the Treaty establishing the European Community and which are now found in the Treaties, notably the rights derived from Union citizenship.[86] These rights shall remain subject to the conditions and limits provided by the Treaties.[87]

Thus, the question may be posed of whether the inclusion of the Union citizenship rights, and in particular, the right to consular protection, into the rights catalogue of the Charter may be put forward as an argument for the direct effect of the provisions on consular protection. To this end, the purpose of the Charter set out in its Preamble needs to be taken into account. According to the Preamble of the Charter, the Charter reaffirms already established rights resulting either from the common constitutional traditions of the Member States, the European Convention for the Protection of Human Rights and Fundamental Freedoms, the Social Charters adopted by the Union and by the Council of Europe and the case-law of the Court of Justice of the European Union and of the European Court of Human Rights. Accordingly the Charter does not pretend to create new individual rights but to consolidate existing rights making them above all more

---

85 Article 52 para. 2 of the Charter:

"Rights recognised by this Charter for which provision is made in the Treaties shall be exercised under the conditions and within the limits defined by those Treaties."

86 PRAESIDIUM of the Convention on the Draft Charter of Fundamental Rights of the European Union, Explanations Relating To The Charter Of Fundamental Rights, Document 2007/C 303/02, published in the Official Journal C 303/17 of 14.12.2007.

Explanation on Article 52 para. 2 of the Charter:

"Paragraph 2 refers to rights which were already expressly guaranteed in the Treaty establishing the European Community and have been recognised in the Charter, and which are now found in the Treaties (notably the rights derived from Union citizenship). It clarifies that such rights remain subject to the conditions and limits applicable to the Union law on which they are based, and for which provision is made in the Treaties. The Charter does not alter the system of rights conferred by the EC Treaty and taken over by the Treaties."

87 *Ibidem.*

visible for their right-holders. In this sense, the Preamble of the Charter reads:

> [...] it is necessary to strengthen the protection of fundamental rights in the light of changes in society, social progress and scientific and technological developments by making those rights more visible in a Charter.

The Charter is certainly not aimed only at making those rights visible for its active subjects, the right-holders, but also for those subjects of the Charter upon whom the provisions of the Charter establish/ reaffirm an obligation to a positive action or to an omission. But the Charter seeks not only to achieve a better visibility of the rights reaffirmed in its catalogue conceiving them as mere values to be observed by the Union institutions and by the Member States when implementing Union law: this approach would hardly be compatible with the character of the Treaties as European Union normative Constitution confirmed and strengthened in the tradition of liberal constitutionalism with a Bill of Rights in the shape of the Charter.[88] In this sense, the European Commission pointed out in its Communication on Strategy for the effective implementation of the Charter of Fundamental Rights by the European Union[89] that:

> The Charter is not a text setting out abstract values, it is an instrument to enable people to enjoy the rights enshrined within it when they are in a situation governed by Union law.[90]

This view is confirmed also by the Preamble of the Charter indicating that the rights contained therein are to be enjoyed and thus exercised by their right-holders. In this sense the Preamble of the Charter reads: "Enjoyment of these rights entails responsibilities and duties with regard to other persons, to the human community and to future generations." The Charter is no mere political declaration anymore limiting itself to launch legally unbinding programmes but is a real Bill of Rights having the status of a Treaty and thus primary Union law.[91] The new legal status of the Charter implies necessarily the direct effect of the rights contained therein and thus the possibility of the right-holders to enjoy those rights by exercising them vis-à-vis the Union institutions but also, when necessary, by invoking

---

88 DOUGLAS-SCOTT, S., "The Charter of Fundamental Rights as a Constitutional Document", in *European Human Rights Law Review*, Issue 1, 2004, p. 37.

89 EUROPEAN COMMISSION, Communication on Strategy for the effective implementation of the Charter of Fundamental Rights by the European Union of 19.10.2010, COM(2010)573 final, available at: <http://ec.europa.eu/justice/news/intro/doc/com_2010_573_en.pdf> (13.05.2011).

90 *Ibidem*, p. 3.

91 See in this sense LENAERTS, K./ DE SMIJTER, E. E., "A "Bill of Rights" for the European Union", in *Common Market Law Review*, 38 (2001), pp. 273-300.

them before the national authorities of the Member States when there is a link to Union law.[92] Otherwise, should the rights contained in the Charter, after the entry into force of the Lisbon Treaty, have still no direct effect, no difference would exist between the Charter as soft-law and the Charter as a legally binding Treaty, the legal status of the right-holders would not have experienced any improvement from the mere "visibility" concern leading to the solemn proclamation of the Charter in 2000 to the substance-concerns for the effectiveness of the Charter as a legal instrument.[93]

The fact that the Charter contains beside fundamental rights also fundamental principles, that need to be implemented by legislative and executive acts in order to produce direct effects, leads to no other conclusion here.

According to Article 52 para. 5 of the Charter titled "Scope and interpretation of rights and principles":

> The provisions of this Charter which contain principles may be implemented by legislative and executive acts taken by institutions, bodies, offices and agencies of the Union, and by acts of Member States when they are implementing Union law, in the exercise of their respective powers. They shall be judicially cognisable only in the interpretation of such acts and in the ruling on their legality.

Accordingly, principles established in the Charter will be invokable only if they have been implemented by legislative and executive acts of Union institutions and other bodies, offices, etc. or by the Member States and are thus not capable of having direct effect. The difference in the effects produced by rights and principles is clearly stated also in Article 51 para. 1 of the Charter establishing that whereas rights are respected, principles are observed.[94] The Charter adopts accordingly an approach similar to DWORKIN's theory on principles. DWORKIN differentiates between "rules" and "principles", assuming that:

> Rules are applicable in all-or-nothing fashion: If the facts a rule stipulates are given, then either the rule is valid, in which case the answer it supplies

[92] As for the right to consular protection, a link to Union law would exist when the right-holder invokes the right to consular protection under Union law and obviously not when a national challenges the decision of the national authority abroad not to provide consular protection in accordance with the national rules and practices.

[93] See MEEHAN, M., "(Un) Charted Waters: The Legal Background to Fundamental Rights Protection in the EU", in *An EU Charter of Fundamental Rights, Text and Commentaries*, Kim Feus (ed.), London, 2000, p. 94.

[94] Article 51 para. 1 of the Charter: "The provisions of this Charter are addressed to the institutions, bodies, offices and agencies of the Union with due regard for the principle of subsidiarity and to the Member States only when they are implementing Union law. They shall therefore respect the rights, observe the principles and promote the application thereof in accordance with their respective powers and respecting the limits of the powers of the Union as conferred on it in the Treaties."

must be accepted, or it is not, in which case it contributes nothing to the Decision.[95]

In contrast,

[...] a principle [...] states a reason that argues in one direction [...] Principles have a dimension that rules do not–the dimension of weight or importance. When principles intersect [...], one who must resolve the conflict has to take into account the relative weight of which.[96]

The text of the Charter, however, fails to clearly state which of the precepts are rights and which – mere principles, and uses often indiscriminatorily the notion "right".[97] Thus, some of the Members of the European Convention considered that Article 52 para. 5 of the Charter led to the restriction of the legal force of the Charter.[98] Paragraph 5 of Article 52 of the Charter was included upon the proposal of the Working Group on the Charter of Fundamental Rights of the European Union (Working Group II) within the European Convention[99] and under the pressure of the UK Government. According to DE BÚRCA, the main aim behind this provision was to prevent many of the so called economic and social rights from being justiciable reclassifying them as "principles".[100] Regard being had of the conceptual similarity between social rights and the right to consular protection insofar as the right to consular protection is likewise directed towards a positive act, the question arises whether the right to consular protection could be conceived as a mere principle under the Charter and thus without direct effect.[101]

95 DWORKIN, R., *Taking Rights Seriously*, 8. edition, 1996, p. 24.

96 *Ibidem*, p. 26.

97 For instance "rights of the elderly" in Article 25 of the Charter although this provision is obviously to general and abstract to be capable of conferring subjective rights.

98 EUROPEAN CONVENTION for the Future of Europe, CONV 378/02, Plenary of the Convention on 28 and 29 October 2002, p. 10. Available at: <http://register.consilium.europa.eu/pdf/en/02/cv00/cv00378.en02.pdf> (14.03.2010).

99 Final report of Working Group II of the European Convention for the Future of Europe of 22.10.2002, CONV 354/02. Available at: <http://register.consilium.europa.eu/pdf/en/02/cv00/cv00354.en02.pdf> (27.11.2009).

100 DE BÚRCA, G., "Fundamental Rights and Citizenship", in *Ten Reflections on the Constitutional Treaty for Europe, Study by the European University Institute*, Bruno de Witte (ed.), presented by Vice-President Amato to the European Convention, CONV 703/03 of 28.04.2003, p. 23. Available at: <http://register.consilium.europa.eu/pdf/en/03/cv00/cv00703.en03.pdf> (14.03.2009).

101 Such a concept of "principles" in the Charter would then present significant differences with DWORKIN's understanding of principles as conditioning the decision of the judges in the sense of just one possible response to a conflict. The so called social and

Nonetheless, as DE BÚRCA rightly remarks, there is no indication that the Charter would label as subjective rights enjoying direct effect only negative, defence rights according to the model of the liberal constitutionalism and deny the direct effect of all rights directed to a positive act, at least since "the division between social/economic rights and civil/political rights does not map onto a distinction between rights requiring positive action and defence rights requiring mere non-interference for their protection".[102]

According to the Explanation to Article 52 para. 5 of the Charter, this distinction between rights and principles is consistent both with the case-law of the Court of Justice[103] and with the approach of the Member States' constitutional "principles", particularly in the field of social law. The Explanation cites as examples for principles recognised in the Charter Articles 25 (The rights of the elderly), 26 (Integration of persons with disabilities) and 37 (Environmental protection).

The clear programmatic character of those precepts presupposing the implementation by means of further Union legislative acts and acts of the Member States, preserving them from having "self-executing character", is to be distinguished with Article 46 on consular protection inserted into the Chapter of Citizens' Rights and capable of producing by itself effects on the relationship between Member States and distressed unrepresented Union citizens.[104] This conclusion is supported also by the expressed intention of the European Council of Cologne to include into the rights' catalogue of the Charter "the fundamental rights that pertain only to the Union's citizens".[105]

In summary, the function of the Charter to make fundamental rights in the European Union more visible and to achieve their effective enjoyment as well as the structure of the right to consular protection as citizens' right,

---

economic rights may not be squeezed into DWORKIN's understanding of "principles" as part of the law regardless of their positivisation. See DWORKIN, R., *Taking Rights Seriously*, p. 71, *op. cit.*, footnote 95.

102 *Ibidem*.

103 See for instance on the "precautionary principle" in Article 191(2) of the Treaty on the Functioning of the European Union Judgment of the Court of First Instance of 11.09.2002 in the case T-13/99, *Pfizer Animal Health SA v. Council of the European Union*, ECR 2002, p. II-03305.

104 See above to the direct effect of the right to consular protection under Article 23 TFEU, Chapter IV.

105 EUROPEAN COUNCIL, Conclusions of the Presidency at the occasion of the European Council of Cologne of 3 and 4 June 1999 on the drawing up of a Charter of Fundamental Rights of the European Union, Annex IV on European Council Decision on the drawing up of a Charter of Fundamental Rights of the European Union. Available at: <http://www.consilium.europa.eu/ueDocs/cms_Data/docs/pressData/en/ec/kolnen.htm>.

which direct effect is reaffirmed by the Charter, overcomes any debate on the direct effect of the provisions relating to consular protection[106] enabling the right-holders to invoke the right to consular protection contained in the Charter before the national authorities including the courts of the Member States within the scope of application of EU Law by the Member States, which is the case when a Member State denies providing consular protection to unrepresented non-national EU citizens, respectively providing insufficient protection.

4. Conclusions

The functional and structural analysis of the Union provisions on consular protection leads to the conclusion that they deploy direct effect on the relationship between Member States and citizens. Starting from the intention of those provisions as provisions of primary Union law to address not only Member States but also individuals, as held by the Court of Justice already in the *Van Gend & Loos* case, and taking into account the structure of the right to consular protection as deriving from the fundamental status of Union citizens, their Union citizenship, as well as its function to fill with content that Union citizenship providing an added value for the protection of Union citizens abroad by establishing a real solidarity-relationship between Member States as regarding consular protection in third countries, the direct effect of the right to consular protection is inherent to its effectiveness and to the pursuit of greater accomplishments to the benefice of Union citizens in distress beyond the borders of the European Union.

There could be no doubt that the right to consular protection is regarding its legal concept as well as its practicability the most challenging of the Union citizens rights. This complexity is based mainly on its extra-territorial character on the one side and on its design as an equal-treatment right on the other side.

The complex legal design of the right to consular protection may indeed lead to certain confusion about its direct effect, in particular when the structure and function of this right are disregarded. Precisely, as a citizens' right deriving from Union citizenship, which according to the Court of Justice is the fundamental status of nationals of the Member States, the same criteria are to be applied to this right as established by the Court of Justice with regard to the right to freely reside and move within the territory of the member States (Article 21 para. 1 TFEU). Therefore, the conditionality of a citizens' right in the sense of necessary

[106] See in this since also MAGIERA, S., "Kommentar zu Artikel 46 der Charta der Grundrechte der Europäischen Union" in *Kommentar zur Charta der Grundrechte der Europäischen Union*, Jürgen Meyer (ed.), Baden-Baden, 2003, para. 11.

implementing measures, limits and conditions imposed thereon do not hinder the direct effect of the citizens' right in question provided that these "conditions" are subject to judicial review by the Court of Justice.[107]

It can be concluded that Article 23 TFEU establishes no constitutive conditions on the right to consular protection which as a start shall "create" this right but rather mere implementing regulations as well as guarantees in order to secure the effectiveness of the right to consular protection as a citizens' right established by the Treaty. In this regard it should be mentioned that neither the adoption of "necessary measures" by the Member States nor the international negotiations required to secure consular protection are dedicated to hinder the direct effect of the right to consular protection but rather shall guarantee its practical effectiveness and secure its unobstructed exercise.

The design of the right to consular protection as an equal-treatment right, that at the first sight seems to hinder the direct effect of that provision due to the scope of discretion that may be granted to national authorities by the national rules on consular protection as well as due to the procedural requirements of the provision of financial advance as a form of consular protection, emerged as being indispensable for the direct effect of the provisions concerned avoiding the need for Union law to establish more detailed substantive conditions for the provision of consular protection to unrepresented Union citizens in third countries.

Besides, the lack of the capability of the right to consular protection to be exercised would not be compatible with its capacity as a fundamental right contained in the catalogue of the Charter of Fundamental Rights of the European Union. The aim of the now legally binding Charter to make the rights contained therein more visible by means of their effective enjoyment could not be achieved otherwise than by reaffirming the right to consular protection as a Union citizens' right that can be invoked by its right-holders before the national authorities of the Member States.

[107] Judgments of the Court in the cases *Baumbast* and *Trojani*, *op. cit.*, footnote 21 and footnote 26.

Chapter V

Holders of the Right to Consular Protection

1. 'Unrepresented' European Union Citizens

1.1. Holders of Union Citizenship

The holders of the right to consular protection are, according to the definition contained in the Treaties, the European Union citizens who are those having the nationality of one of the EU Member States.[1] According to Article 20 para. 1 second sentence TFEU:

> Every person holding the nationality of a Member State shall be a citizen of the Union. Citizenship of the Union shall be additional to and not replace national citizenship.

Article 20 TFEU does not make the enjoyment of the rights deriving from Union citizenship dependent upon the attainment of a minimum age. Worth mentioning is in this regard the judgment of the Court of Justice in the case *Zhu and Chen* where the Court concluded that a young child can take advantage of the rights of free movement and residence guaranteed by Community law since the capacity of a national of a Member State to be the holder of rights guaranteed by the Treaty and by secondary law on free movement of persons cannot depend on legal capacity to exercise those rights personally.[2]

Accordingly, the only requirement in order to be a Union citizen is to hold the nationality of a Member State,[3] whereby being a national of a Member State is accordingly a condition *sine qua non* for acquiring EU citizenship, and therefore enjoying the rights linked to it, so that acquisition and loss of Union citizenship depend automatically on acquisition and loss of national citizenship of a Member State[4] and cannot be regarded detached from the national context of citizenship.

---

1 Article 20 para. 1, first sentence TFEU: "Citizenship of the Union is hereby established. Every person holding the nationality of a Member State shall be a citizen of the Union."

2 Judgment of the Court of Justice of 19.10.2004 in the case C-200/02, *Kunqian Catherine Zhu and Man Lavette Chen v Secretary of State for the Home Department*, para. 20.

3 The Treaties do not contain a distinction as regarding gender neither.

4 See Opinion of Mr Advocate General POIARES MADURO delivered on 30.09.2009 in the case C-135/08, *Janco Rottmann v. Freistaat Bayern*, ECR 2009, p. I-01449, para. 15.

It is to be noted that while nationality refers to the relationship between a State and its nationals, Union citizenship grants rights beyond the borders of the State of nationality, vis-à-vis the other EU Member States and the European Union itself. Therefore, Union citizenship has been construed in contrast to national citizenship as an "interstate citizenship"[5] on the one side but also as a citizenship reflecting the Union's sovereign powers on the other side.

Like nationality, that in terms of international law is "a legal bond having as its basis a social fact of attachment, a genuine connection of existence, interests and sentiments, together with the existence of reciprocal rights and duties",[6] Union citizenship describes the political and legal status of the citizens of the European Union, however, regardless of the social reality in the sense of the need of an effective bond between the Union citizen and the European Union and the Member States since Union citizenship, unlike nationality in terms of international law, is not aimed at resolving jurisdictional conflicts between States.[7]

The dependence of Union citizenship on a nationality of a Member State does not however preclude it from being 'autonomous'. Both, national and Union citizenship exist side by side and the character of Union citizenship as "secondary" in relation to national citizenship pales steadily beside the increasing quality of Union citizenship to be measured by advantages in the shape of individual rights and political participation in the democratic functioning of the European Union and the Member States establishing an autonomous political relationship between Union citizens and the European Union reflecting and creating at the same time a new type of identity, that of Union citizens.

The Court of Justice has accounted for the complex relationship between nationality and Union citizenship in several cases and in particular in the judgment in the case *Micheletti*. Recalling Declaration number 2 on Nationality of a Member State annexed by the Member States to the Final Act of the Treaty on European Union,[8] the Court of Justice held

---

5 SCHÖNBERGER, C., "European Citizenship as Federal Citizenship. Some Citizenship Lessons of Comparative Federalism", in *Revue Européenne de Droit Public* 2007, Vol. 19 (1), pp. 61-82.

6 Judgment of the International Court of Justice in the case *Nottebohm, Liechtenstein v. Guatemala*, ICJ Reports 1955, 4 (23).

7 *Ibidem*.

8 Declaration No. 2 on Nationality of a Member State, Official Journal C 191 of 29.07.1992: "The Conference declares that, wherever in the Treaty establishing the European Community reference is made to nationals of the Member States, the question whether an individual possesses the nationality of a Member State shall be settled solely by reference to the national law of the Member State concerned. Member States may declare, for information, who are to be considered their nationals for Community

that nationality is governed by the national rules of the Member State concerned so that matters of nationality remain within the exclusive competence of the Member States.[9] However, the Court highlighted that this competence must be exercised with due regard to Community law and that a Member State may not restrict the effects of the grant of the nationality of another Member State by imposing an additional condition for recognition of that nationality with a view to the exercise of the fundamental freedoms provided for in the Treaty.[10]

Whilst the Court of Justice invoked in the judgement in the case *Micheletti* the need to preserve the uniformity of the application of the Community rules on freedom of establishment in all Member State, there was no such a link to the fundamental freedoms in the *Rottmann* case.[11] The applicant in the case before the *Bundesverwaltungsgericht*,[12] that referred a question for preliminary ruling to the Court of Justice, Mr Janco Rottmann, had the Austrian nationality until he applied for and was granted the German nationality after he had spent four years in Munich, Germany. By becoming a German national, he lost the Austrian nationality according to the relevant Austrian legislation. However, shortly after the Freistaat Bayern withdrew Rottmann's German nationality with retroactive effect since he had failed to mention the fact that he was accused by the Austrian authorities to have committed a fraud in Austria and that a warrant for his arrest had been issued in Graz (Austria). As a consequence, Mr Rottmann became a stateless person. The Court of Justice confirmed in its judgment first that the acquisition and loss of nationality is indeed a matter of the Member States.[13] Nevertheless, the Court pointed out that even in matters falling into the exclusive competences of the Member States, the national rules concerned must comply with Union law as regarding situations covered by the latter. The Court recalled in this regard its case-law regarding national rules governing the persons' name (*García Avello* case)[14] or direct taxation

purposes by way of a declaration lodged with the Presidency and may amend any such declaration when necessary."

9 Judgment of the Court of Justice of 07.07.1992 in the case C-369/90, *Mario Vicente Micheletti and others v. Delegación del Gobierno de Cantabria*, European Court reports 1992, p. 04239, para. 10.

10 *Ibidem*. The Court held in particular that Spain could not prevent the plaintiff establishing himself on Spanish territory by refusing to recognise his Italian nationality, on the grounds that his primary nationality was his Argentinean nationality due to the fact that he habitually resided in Argentina. (*Ibidem*, para. 11).

11 Judgment of the Court of Justice of the European Communities of 02.03.2010 in the case C-135/08, *Janco Rottman v. Freistaat Bayern*, ECR 2010, p. I-01449.

12 Federal Administrative Court.

13 Judgment in the case *Rottmann*, para. 39, *op. cit.*, footnote 11.

14 Judgment of the Court of Justice of the European Communities of 02.10.2003 in the case C-148/02, *Carlos García Avello v. Belgian State*, ECR 2003, p. I-11613.

(*Schempp* case).[15] Against the view of the European Commission and of the Advocate General,[16] the Court of Justice held that the loss of Union citizenship as a consequence of the loss of the nationality of a Member State does fall within the ambit of European Union law since the loss of Union citizenship leads automatically to the loss of the rights linked to it.[17]

The Court, however, acknowledged the legitimate interest of the Member States to revoke in certain situation nationality, protecting by this means "the special relationship of solidarity and good faith between it [the Member State] and its nationals and also the reciprocity of rights and duties, which form the bedrock of the bond of nationality".[18] Notwithstanding, in order for a withdrawal decision to comply with Union law, the principle of proportionality should be observed so far as concerns the consequences that this decision entails for the situation of the person concerned in the light of European Union law, taking into account the specific circumstances of the case.[19]

It is worth mentioning that the Court clearly distinguished the situation of a third country national, who had never had the nationality of a Member State, from that of a Union citizen, who held the nationality of a Member State but whose nationality has been withdrawn.[20] In the judgment in the case *Kaur*,[21] the Court of Justice had concluded that the United Kingdom rules on nationality and residence

> […] did not have the effect of depriving any person who did not satisfy the definition of a national of the United Kingdom of rights to which that person might be entitled under Community law. The consequence was rather that such rights never arose in the first place for such a person.[22]

15 Judgment of the Court of Justice of the European Communities of 12.07.2005 in the case C-403/03, *Egon Schempp v. Finanzamnt München V*, ECR 2005, p. I-06421.

16 See Opinion of Mr Advocate General POIARES MADURO delivered on 30.09.2009 in the case C-135/08, *Janco Rottmann v. Freistaat Bayern*, ECR 2009, p. I-01449.

17 Judgment of the Court of Justice of the European Communities in the case *Rottmann*, para. 42: "It is clear that the situation of a citizen of the Union who, like the applicant in the main proceedings, is faced with a decision withdrawing his naturalisation, adopted by the authorities of one Member State, and placing him, after he has lost the nationality of another Member State that he originally possessed, in a position capable of causing him to lose the status conferred by Article 17 EC and the rights attaching thereto falls, by reason of its nature and its consequences, within the ambit of European Union law", *op. cit.*, footnote 11.

18 *Ibidem*, para. 51.

19 *Ibidem*, para. 55.

20 *Ibidem*, para. 49.

21 Judgment of the Court of Justice of the European Communities of 20.02.2001 in the case C-192/99, *The Queen v Secretary of State for the Home Department, ex parte: Manjit Kaur*, ECR 2001, p. I-01237.

22 *Ibidem*, para. 25.

In this way the Court attributes a particular importance to the rights attached to Union citizenship for the possibility to enjoy this status.[23] Moreover, the case-law of the Court of Justice shows unmistakably the irremovable connection, and even dependence, between Union citizenship on the one side and the rights deriving from Union citizenship on the other side as legal content filling out the political and legal framework created by the Union citizenship as such. Thus, Union citizenship describes on the one side the rights stemming from it, while the citizenship rights upgrade on the other side the citizenship of the Union making it in fact "additional" to the nationality of the Member States in the sense of presenting an "added value" to it for Union citizens.

As a consequence, the original dependence of Union citizenship on the nationality of a Member State has evolved to a circumstance conditioning the decisions of the Member States in matters concerning nationality. Therefore, the loss of the nationality of a Member State would not lead merely to the loss of the status as an Union citizen but would deprive the citizen concerned of the substance of this status, which are the rights deriving therefrom.

1.2. Lack of a Diplomatic or Consular Representation of the Member State of Nationality

According to Article 23 TFEU, a Union citizen is entitled to protection by the diplomatic or consular missions of a Member State different from his State of nationality when the latter is not represented in the territory of a third country.[24] However, Article 23 TFEU provides no further explanation on what the notion "not represented" shall mean. The Member States filled this notion with content by means of Decision 95/553/EC regarding Protection for Citizens of the European Union by Diplomatic and Consular Representations. Article 1 of Decision 95/553/EC reads:

> Every citizen of the European Union is entitled to the consular protection of any Member State's diplomatic or consular representation if, in the place in which he is located, his own Member State or another State representing it on a permanent basis has no:
>
> – accessible permanent representation, or – accessible Honorary Consul competent for such matters.

[23] See Judgment of the Court of Justice in the case *Rottmann*, para. 49, *op. cit.*, footnote 11.

[24] Article 23 para. 1 TFEU: "Every citizen of the Union shall, in the territory of a third country in which the Member State of which he is a national is not represented, be entitled to protection by the diplomatic or consular authorities of any Member State, on the same conditions as the nationals of that State. Member States shall adopt the necessary provisions and start the international negotiations required to secure this protection."

Furthermore, Rule 2 (b) of Annex II of Decision 96/409/CSFP on the Establishment of an Emergency Travel Document stipulates that ETDs may be issued when the recipient

> […] is in the territory of a country where the person's Member State of origin has no accessible diplomatic or consular representation with the capacity to issue a travel document or, where that State is not otherwise represented […].

Accordingly, the Member State of nationality of the Union citizen in situation of distress must not have any accessible permanent representation or competent Honorary Consul on the territory of the third country where the situation of distress takes place.

1.2.1. Representation by another State on a Permanent Basis

Article 1 of Decision 95/553/EC refers not only to the Member State of nationality of the Union citizen concerned but also to any other State representing the State of nationality of the Union citizen on a permanent basis. The prime example of such a representation on a permanent basis is the representation of Luxembourg by Belgian diplomatic and consular representations abroad according to the Agreement between the Grand Duchy of Luxembourg and the Kingdom of Belgium on Consular Cooperation of 30 September 1965.[25] This is a general agreement on consular cooperation concluded between Luxembourg and Belgium after the signature of the *Union économique belgo-luxembourgeoise* on 29 January 1963. The agreement is aimed at compensating the fact that Luxembourg, being a very small country with approximately 502,066 habitants,[26] has a barely developed network of consular and diplomatic missions.[27] Therefore, the agreement stipulates the provision of assistance to the citizens of Luxembourg by Belgian representations abroad where there are no diplomatic or consular missions of the Grand Duchy of

[25] Convention entre le Grand-Duché de Luxembourg et le Royaume de Belgique relative à la coopération dans le domaine consulaire. Act of sanctioning of the abovementioned agreement of 16 August 1966, Doc. Parl. No. 1197, Sess. Ord. 1965-1966 (Loi du 16 août 1966 portant approbation de la Convention entre le Grand-Duché de Luxembourg et le Royaume de Belgique relative à la coopération dans le domaine consulaire, signée à Bruxelles le 30 septembre 1965), published in Journal Officiel du Grand-Duché de Luxembourg (Amtsblatt des Großherzogtums Luxemburg), Recueil de Legislation A-No. 51 of 21.09.1966.

[26] Information available at: <http://www.luxembourg.public.lu/fr/societe/population/index.html> (14.08.2011).

[27] It should be noted that Luxembourg is the Member State with the fewest number of representations abroad: 7. See EUROPEAN COMMISSION, Impact Assessment, on "Effective consular protection in third countries: the contribution of the European Union. Action Plan 2007-2009", 05 February 2008, SEC(2007) 1600, p. 87. Available at: <http://eur-lex.europa.eu/LexUriServ/LexUriServ.do?uri=CELEX:52007SC1601:EN:HTML> (13.05.2010).

Luxembourg.[28] Article 1 para. 2 of the Agreement establishes that the Government of Luxembourg may request the services of the Belgian officials in order to provide consular protection.[29] It should be pointed out that according to information provided by the Ministry of Foreign Affairs of Luxembourg, consular protection is provided to nationals of Luxembourg primarily by the Belgian representations abroad and merely subsidiarily by the representations of other Member States.[30]

Another similar agreement is the Agreement on Consular Cooperation between Estonia, Latvia and Lithuania from February 1999,[31] whereby all citizens of the Baltic States are guaranteed consular aid and representation in countries where not all of those States have consular facilities.[32] Worth mentioning are also the Agreements between Poland and Lithuania, whereby Poland represents Lithuania in consular matters in Morocco, Tunisia and Algeria.[33] Moreover, the agreement "Protocol

---

28 See Article 1, para. 1 of the Agreement between the Grand Duchy of Luxembourg and the Kingdom of Belgium on Consular Cooperation of 30 September 1965: "*Les Hautes Parties Contractantes coopèrent, conformément aux dispositions de la présente Convention, en vue de faire assurer la protection et la défense des intérêts consulaires luxembourgeois par les fonctionnaires consulaires belges établis dans les circonscriptions où le Grand-Duché de Luxembourg ne possède pas de service consulaire.*"

29 Article 1, para. 2 of Agreement between the Grand Duchy of Luxembourg and the Kingdom of Belgium on Consular Cooperation of 30 September 1965: "*Le Gouvernement luxembourgeois peut avoir recours aux bons offices d'un fonctionnaire consulaire belge lorsque, notamment pour des raisons de distance, le fonctionnaire consulaire luxembourgeois qualifié n'est pas en mesure d'intervenir d'une manière adéquate.*"

30 Information available at the official web site of the Ministry of Foreign Affairs of Luxembourg: <http://www.mae.lu/fr/Site-MAE/VISAS-Passeports/Conseils-aux-voyageurs-Documents-de-voyage-Visas/Voyager-a-l-etranger/Assistance-consulaire>.

31 Agreement on Consular Assistance and Co-operation between the Government of the Republic of Estonia, the Government of the Republic of Latvia and the Government of the Republic of Lithuania, Vilnius, 5.02.1999, in force since 23.09.1999, published e.g. in Estonian Official Gazette RT II 1999, 25, 147 (*Latvijas Republikas valdības, Igaunijas Republikas valdības un Lietuvas Republikas valdības līgums par konsulāro sadarbību un palīdzību* of 05.02.1999, published e.g. in the Latvian Official Gazette No. 302 on 15.09.1999, entry into force on 23.09.1999).

32 Article 2 of the Agreement on Consular Assistance and Cooperation establishes that, when necessary, a citizen whose home country does not have a representation in a third country may ask one of the parties of the agreement permanently providing consular services in the third country for consular assistance.

33 Agreement the Government of the Republic of Lithuania and the Government of the Republic of Poland on Consular Assistance in the Kingdom of Morocco concluded on 14.12.1999, published in *Valstybės žinios* (Lithuanian Official Gazette), 2000, No. 71-2091; Agreement the Government of the Republic of Lithuania and the Government of the Republic of Poland on consular assistance in the Republic of Tunisia concluded on 09.09.2002, published in *Valstybės žinios* 2000, No. 71-2092; Agreement the Government of the Republic of Lithuania and the Government of the Republic

of the Ministry of Foreign Affairs of the Slovak Republic and Ministry of Foreign Affairs of the Czech Republic on Cooperation and Mutual Assistance in Case of Extraordinary Incidents and Emergency Crisis Abroad" should be mentioned.[34] Article 1 of that Agreement establishes a mutual obligation to provide in situations of accidents, emergency and distress to the nationals of the other State assistance in third countries, where only one of the States is represented.

It is at least doubtful whether Article 1 of Decision 95/553/EC in conjunction with the above-mentioned agreements may, if they are conceived as a primary instrument of consular protection by States different from the own State of the Union citizen in distress, effectively prevent Union citizens of asking "any" Member State for help in a third country where their Member State of nationality has no representation, as established by Article 23 TFEU.

However, this approach seems to be pragmatic and undermines not the right to consular protection, provided that the "primary" consular protection is offered by another EU Member State, as the case is in all agreements cited above. In that case protection would be provided by a specific Member State with priority to assistance provided by any other Member State represented in the third country, which limits the possibility of the Union citizen in distress to choose among all Member States represented there, though it must not necessarily mean a limitation of the scope of protection provided.[35] Besides, it is to be noted that this kind of bilateral or multilateral agreements are likely to be concluded between countries with similar linguistic and cultural characteristics, so that, from a pragmatic point of view, it can be assumed that the citizens of the "unrepresented" country would anyway prefer to approach the country of agreement.

It seems, in contrast, to be problematic when a Member State is represented on a permanent basis by a non-Member State in a third country. This would be the case of the Nordic Cooperation Treaty of 23 March 1962 between Sweden, Denmark, Finland, Norway and Iceland[36] Article 34 of this agreement establishes that public officials

---

of Poland on consular assistance in the Democratic and Popular Republic of Algeria concluded on 09.09.2000, published in *Valstybės žinios* 2000, No. 71-2090.

34 Sdělení Ministerstva zahraničních věcí o sjednání Ujednání mezi Ministerstvem zahraničních věcí České republiky a Ministerstvem zahraničních věcí Slovenské republiky o spolupráci v oblasti konzulárních služeb of 04.02.1993, done in Bratislava. Translation by Ms Katharina Getlik.

35 See to the scope of the right to consular protection and the differences in the protection offered by the Member States, Chapter VI.

36 Nordic Cooperation Treaty of 23.03.1962, most recently amended on 29.09.1995, published e.g. in Swedish Treaty Series 28/1962. Available also at: <http://www.norden.

in the Foreign Services of any of the High Contracting Parties who are serving outside the Nordic countries shall, to the extent that it is compatible with their duties and when no objection is lodged by the country in which they are serving, also be of assistance to citizens of the other Nordic countries, should the latter not be represented in the territory concerned.[37] Another example is the Agreement on Consular Protection approved in July 2008 at the XIII extraordinary meeting of the Council of Ministers of the Community of Portuguese Speaking Countries (*Comunidade de Países de Língua Portuguesa, CPLP*),[38] whose members are Portugal, Angola, Brazil, Cape Verde, Guinea Bissau, Mozambique, Sao Tomé and East Timor. Both Treaties establish no priority of the consular protection provided by the parties to those agreements over protection provided by other countries. However, this kind of priority over consular protection provided under European Union law would restrict the scope of the right to consular protection under Union law, which would violate the loyalty-obligation of the Member States according to Article 4 para. 3 TEU.[39] Accordingly, Member States shall abstain from adopting measures or concluding agreements that could jeopardize the attainment of the objectives of the Treaties[40] and are thus obliged to ensure the material scope of Union provisions.[41]

For the case of international agreements concluded with third countries before the inclusion of the provisions on consular protection into the Treaties, Article 351 para. 2 TFEU requires the Member State concerned to eliminate the obstruction of the Union's objectives.[42] Thus, should

org/en/about-nordic-co-operation/agreements/treaties-and-agreements/basic-agreement/the-helsinki-treaty> (08.09.2010).

37 Translation by Mr Caspar Visser.

38 Acordo de Cooperação Consular entre os Estados Membros da Comunidade dos Países de Língua Portuguesa (CPLP) of 24.07.2008. Available at: <http://www.cplp.org/Default.aspx?ID=445> (12.09.2011).

39 Article 4 para. 3 TEU: "Pursuant to the principle of sincere cooperation, the Union and the Member States shall, in full mutual respect, assist each other in carrying out tasks which flow from the Treaties. The Member States shall take any appropriate measure, general or particular, to ensure fulfilment of the obligations arising out of the Treaties or resulting from the acts of the institutions of the Union. The Member States shall facilitate the achievement of the Union's tasks and refrain from any measure which could jeopardise the attainment of the Union's objectives."

40 See also already Judgment of the Court of Justice of 23.01.1975 in the case C-31/74, *Filippo Galli v. Pretore di Roma*, ECR 1975, p. 00047, para. 29/30.

41 HATJE, A., "Kommentar zu Artikel 4 EUV", in *EU-Kommentar*, Jürgen Schwarze (ed.), 3. edition, Baden-Baden 2012, para. 72.

42 Article 351 para. 2 TFEU: "To the extent that such agreements [agreements concluded before 1 January 1958 or analogically before the inclusion of a provision into the

any agreements with third countries establish the provision of consular protection by the third State as prior to consular protection provided by a Member State under Article 23 TFEU, the agreement should be interpreted in line with Union law so that an unrepresented Union citizen may not be deprived of his/her right to approach a Member State for consular protection instead of the third country that concluded an agreement with the Member State of nationality of the Union citizen concerned.

1.2.2. Consular Protection by Honorary Consuls

States are represented by diplomatic and consular missions in third countries according, in the first place, to the Vienna Convention on Diplomatic Relations and the Vienna Convention on Consular Relations. Seeking to adopt a pragmatic approach securing the purpose of the Union provisions on consular protection, the Member States linked the condition of lack of a representation of the Member State of nationality of the Union citizen concerned to the authorisation of the authorities of the Member State of nationality present in the third country to provide the protection in the situations described by Decision 95/553/EC and Decision 96/409/CSFP.

Whereas diplomatic and consular missions are, in compliance with the rule established by the Vienna Convention on Diplomatic Relations and the Vienna Convention on Consular Relations, always competent to provide the protection necessary in the situations listed in Decision 95/553/EC and Decision 96/409/CSFP, the question arises whether a Honorary Consul would be competent to provide such kind of protection.

Both, Decision 95/553/EC as well as Decision 96/409/CSFP, establish that a Union citizen is not deemed to be "unrepresented" in terms of Article 23 TFEU if there is a Honorary Consul competent to provide consular protection. According to the Vienna Convention on Consular Relations, honorary consular officers fall under the category of consular officers in terms of the Convention,[43] and each State is free to decide whether it will appoint or receive honorary consular officers.[44]

Treaties] are not compatible with the Treaties, the Member State or States concerned shall take all appropriate steps to eliminate the incompatibilities established. Member States shall, where necessary, assist each other to this end and shall, where appropriate, adopt a common attitude."

43 See Article 1 para. 2 of the Vienna Convention on Consular Relations of 1963: "Consular officers are of two categories, namely career consular officers and honorary consular officers. The provisions of Chapter II of the present Convention apply to consular posts headed by career consular officers, the provisions of Chapter III govern consular posts headed by honorary consular officers."

44 Article 68 of the Vienna Convention on Consular Relations: "Each State is free to decide whether it will appoint or receive honorary consular officers."

Nonetheless, the Vienna Convention on Consular Relations provides no definition of the institution of the Honorary Consul. Rather, the concept of this institution is governed by traditional assumptions.[45] According to LEE and QUIGLEY, honorary consuls are private citizens, and not public officials, normally of the nationality of the receiving State, and usually occupying a distinguished position in business, industry or financial services of the receiving State.[46] Honorary consuls are known for their good knowledge of the local habits, culture and language. As a general rule, honorary consuls are not paid for their services by the sending State but rather directly by the citizens approaching them for assistance.[47]

However, the functions of consular officers are not governed by the Vienna Convention but rather by the national legislation of each State, whereby the functions assigned to honorary consuls by national law/rules may not exceed the scope of the functions of ordinary consular officers according to Article 5 of the Vienna Convention on Consular Relations.[48] Therefore, the question whether honorary consuls are authorized or not to offer protection to the nationals of the sending Member State in the cases described by Decision 95/553/EC and Decision 96/409/CSFP, is governed by the rules and practices of the Member States,[49] which differ considerably from each other.

Whereas in some Member States, like for instance Estonia, honorary consuls have the power to provide the same consular protection as consular officers, though after a general authorisation issued by the Ministry of Foreign Affairs,[50] the functions of honorary consuls of other Member States,

---

45 STRINGER, K.D., "Honorary Consuls in an Era of Globalization, Trade, and Investment", in *Consular Affairs and Diplomacy*, 2011, pp. 63, 65.

46 LUKE, T. L./ QUIGLEY, J., *Consular Law and Practice*, Oxford/ New York, 2008, pp. 514.

47 *Ibidem*.

48 Article 58 paras. 1 and 2 of the Vienna Convention on Consular Relations stipulate which of the provisions regarding ordinary consular officers apply also to honorary consuls, excluding from those provisions Article 5 of the Vienna Convention on functions of consular officers.

49 See also COUNCIL OF THE EUROPEAN UNION, Guidelines for further implementing a number of provisions under Decision 95/553/EC of 24.06.2008 (COCON), approved by COREPER on 25.06.2008 and adopted by the Council of the European Union on 8.07.2008, Document 11113/08, PESC 833, COCON 10. Available at: <http://register.consilium.europa.eu/pdf/en/08/st11/st11113.en08.pdf> (21.12.2009).

50 According to Article 15 para. 1 of the Estonian Consular Act (*Konsulaarseadus*), the competence of each honorary consul shall be established by a directive of the Minister of Foreign Affairs. Article 58 para. 1 of the same Act reads: "A consular officer or an honorary consul shall provide consultation and assistance to persons in distress in the consular district in order for them to contact their families or other persons close to

e.g. Spain and France, are decided by the Ministry of Foreign Affairs of the sending State on a case-by-case basis for every honorary consul, limiting their competences often in comparison to those of ordinary consular officers. "German" honorary consuls, for instance, are not empowered to issue Emergency Travel Documents.[51] Moreover, the Spanish Royal Decree 1390/2007 on the Statutory Regulation of Honorary Consuls of Spain Abroad[52] states that honorary consuls will be specially authorised to provide, in connection with the correspondent consular office or diplomatic mission, support and consular protection.[53] French legislation contains a similar provision: according to Decree No. 76-548 of 16.06.1976 on General Consuls, Consuls, Vice-Consuls and Honorary Consuls[54] a Decree of the Ministry of Foreign Affairs establishes the functions for each of the "French" honorary consuls abroad.

Accordingly, a Union citizen would have first to approach a Honorary Consul of his/her Member State of nationality for consular protection and, if the latter is not competent to provide the protection sought, the Union citizen would be deemed to be "unrepresented" in the third country in terms of Article 23 TFEU, Decision 95/553/EC and Decision 96/409/CSFP.

This legal situation bears two main issues. First, it is at least problematic to expose a citizen in distress to a scenario in which they would have first to approach a honorary consul, wait until the Honorary Consul concerned has asked for instructions the Ministry of Foreign Affairs or the nearest diplomatic mission of the sending State and, in case of a negative response, approach only then the diplomatic or consular office of another Member State. However, this issue could be solved at least partially by making public the authorisation of each honorary consul in every third country or by providing relevant information under the emergency telephone number of the Ministries of Foreign Affairs of the Member States.

---

them or return to Estonia or in order for their rights to be protected or hospitalisation or other issues to be arranged for them." Available in English at: <http://www.careproject.eu/database/upload/ETlaw001/ETlaw001TransEng.pdf> (02.04.2011).

51 Instructions of the Ministry of Foreign Affairs to the German Representations abroad: "Aid for Germans abroad" as of 31.03.2005, p. 63, not published.

52 Real Decreto 1390/2007, de 29 de octubre, por el que se aprueba el Reglamento de los Agentes Consulares Honorarios de España en el extranjero, published in BOE 272 of 13.11.2007. Article 14, para. 2.

53 Article 14 para. 2 of Royal Decree 1390/2007: "En el ejercicio de sus funciones estarán especialmente facultados para prestar, en conexión con la Oficina consular de carrera o, en su caso, de la Misión Diplomàtica de la que dependa, la asistencia y protección consular debida a los nacionales españoles."

54 Décret No. 76-548 du 16 juin 1976 relatif aux consuls généraux, consuls et vice-consuls honoraires et aux agents consulaires, published in Journal officiel of 25.06.1976.

Furthermore, the diplomatic and consular missions in third countries where not every Member State is represented should be informed of the powers of the honorary consuls of those Member States not having further representations in the third country in order for the officials approached for consular protection under Union law to be able to assess whether the Union citizen concerned is in fact "unrepresented" or not.[55]

1.2.3. Accessibility of the Representation

According to Decision 95/553/EC and Decision 96/409/CSFP Union citizens are "unrepresented" in a third country and thus entitled to request consular protection from the competent authorities of another Member State, if their own Member State has no "accessible permanent representation", as well as accessible honorary consuls competent for the matters in question. There is indeed no "accessible representation" of the Member State of nationality of the Union citizen seeking consular protection in a third country where the Member State of origin has no representation within the territory of the third country concerned.

However, taking into account the utmost emergency of some of the situations described by Decision 95/553/EC, in which Union citizens could suffer a violation of their fundamental rights, such as life or physical integrity, e.g. in case of natural disasters, warlike conflicts but also in case of serious accidents or illness, and regard being had of the specific circumstances in many third countries such as big territories, poor infrastructure, lack of transport facilities, etc., the question arises whether a Union citizen in distress could be deemed to be "unrepresented" in terms of Article 23 TFEU, Decision 95/553/EC and Decision 96/409/CSFP although his/her own Member State has a representation on the territory of the third country.

---

[55] A different question from the one regarding the competence of honorary consuls to provide consular protection to nationals of the sending Member State is the question of whether honorary consuls are empowered to provide consular protection under Union law to unrepresented Union citizens. Many of the Member States make the provision of protection under Article 23 TFEU and Decision 95/553/EC by their honorary consuls dependent on the authorisation by the Ministry of Foreign Affairs. According to the Instructions of the Ministry of Foreign Affairs to the German Representations abroad, honorary consuls may provide such kind of protection after having requested timely instruction by the German Ministry of Foreign Affairs (Instructions of the Ministry of Foreign Affairs to the German Representations abroad: "Aid for Germans abroad" as of 31.03.2005, p. 63, not published). The Handbook of the Dutch missions abroad contains a similar rule establishing that honorary consuls are not obliged to offer assistance to unrepresented Union citizens in third countries (The Handbook contains instructions on consular matters of the Dutch Ministry of Foreign Affairs. Not published.) As a general rule, honorary consuls are not competent to issue Emergency Travel Documents in terms of Decision 96/409/CSFP.

The purpose of the Union provisions on consular protection to fill the gaps in the protection of Union citizens abroad could be indeed undermined if the Union citizen concerned is not able to physically reach the representation of his/her own Member State or if he/she would not be able to reach the representation of his/her own Member State timely in order to prevent e.g. the occurrence of a damage. Therefore, seeking to guarantee the effectiveness of the provision of consular protection to Union citizens in third countries, the Council of the European Union adopted in 2008 the Guidelines for further implementing a number of provisions under Decision 95/553/EC.[56]

The Guidelines stipulate that the notion "accessible permanent representation" should be interpreted as a representation "that is safely reachable by an EU citizen by land (road or rail), within convenient distance and reasonable time, depending upon specific circumstances in the third country concerned".[57] The same criterion can be applied also to competent honorary consuls.[58]

Furthermore, the Guidelines point out that the person concerned must also be able to pay for the relevant transportation to the representation of his/her own Member State in order for that to be considered as "accessible".[59]

The interpretation of the notion "accessible representation" adopted by the Guidelines is aimed at applying a pragmatic and flexible approach to the practical challenges to the provision of effective consular protection to Union citizens in third countries. Although this interpretation is far from being precise using abstract legal concepts, which need to be further specified and interpreted on a case-by-case basis, it is not recommendable to narrow this term further down since the circumstances in each third country and of each case of distress can vary considerably.

Within the Consular Cooperation Working Group of the Council of the European Union (COCON)[60] the proposal was submitted to revise

56 COUNCIL OF THE EUROPEAN UNION, Guidelines for further implementing a number of provisions under Decision 95/553/EC of 24.06.2008 (COCON), approved by COREPER on 25.06.2008 and adopted by the Council of the European Union on 8.07.2008, Document 11113/08, PESC 833, COCON 10. Available at: <http://register.consilium.europa.eu/pdf/en/08/st11/st11113.en08.pdf> (06.08.2010).

57 *Ibidem*, Section II "Accessible permanent representation" and "accessible competent honorary consuls", point 4, p. 3.

58 *Ibidem*.

59 *Ibidem*.

60 The COCON was set up in 2006 in order to organise exchanges of information on best national practices. See EUROPEAN COMMISSION, Green Paper on Diplomatic and Consular Protection, *op. cit.*, footnote 29.

the Guidelines for further implementing a number of provisions under Decision 95/553/EC and specify the notion of "considerable geographical distance" as distance requiring a journey of more than four hours.[61] It should be, however, noted that whereas in big countries disposing of well developed infrastructure, such as Australia, Canada, etc., a journey of 4 hours would normally represent no burden for a citizen in distress, in less developed countries even a shorter journey could be unbearable in the specific circumstances of the case in question. Thus, the flexibility of the interpretation of "accessible representation" adopted in the 2008 Guidelines seems to respond best both to the need to adapt to each particular case and the circumstances of each third country concerned, and the demand of effective and practical consular protection.

Besides, the 2008 Guidelines stipulate that the diplomatic and consular representations in third countries may agree on practical arrangements in terms of Article 4 of Decision 95/553/EC establishing that although a Member State has a representation in a third country, its nationals may be assisted by the diplomatic and consular missions of another Member State, if lack of resources or expertise by that person's diplomatic or consular representation make it advisable.[62] In this way the "accessibility" of Member States' representations abroad is asserted not only according to their physical availability taking into account the risk for the occurrence of damage but also according to the quality of the protection that can be offered to Union citizens, emphasising the underlying idea of the provisions regarding consular protection – strengthening European solidarity as an instrument to create an Union citizenship' identity.

This kind of practical arrangements play a significant role within the framework of the Lead State concept, where Member States agree on the leadership of one of the Member States represented in a third country in situations of major crises.[63] The Lead State concept allows for acting of the Lead State involving not only "unrepresented" Union citizens but also nationals of Member States represented in the third country,[64] accounting for by this means the capability of the Lead State to handle better local

---

61 Consular Cooperation Working Group of the Council of the European Union (COCON), Document CFSP/ SEC/ 1267/ 08, Note 2: "reasonable time means for example a travel period of not over four hours in a third country but of course it may vary from country to country depending on local circumstances."

62 *Ibidem*, Section II, point 2, p. 3. Article 4 of Decision 95/553/EC reads: "Without prejudice to Article 1, diplomatic and consular representations may agree on practical arrangements for the effective management of applications for protection."

63 See European Union guidelines on the implementation of the consular Lead State concept, OJ 2008, C 317, p. 06.

64 Please see for details on the Lead State concept Chapter VIII Section 1 below.

circumstances due to, as a general rule, its longstanding traditional relationships with the third country.

Moreover, providing consular protection to "represented" Union citizens has gained in importance particularly as regarding evacuation from third countries in case of natural disasters, warlike conflicts, etc. For instance, Hungary evacuated in the eve of the Libyan crisis 29 Romanians, 27 Hungarians, 20 Bulgarians, 8 Germans, 6 Czechs and 6 other EU and non-EU nationals, as well as later a few British nationals,[65] from Tripoli, although Bulgaria, Germany, the Czech Republic, Romania and the United Kingdom have embassies in Tripoli.[66] Besides, according to information provided by the European Business Council for Africa and the Mediterranean (EBCAM), a Spanish armed forces plane carrying 124 people evacuated from Tripoli 40 Spaniards as well as, *inter alia*, British and Portuguese nationals,[67] although Portugal is also represented in Libya. Moreover, a Greek passenger ship evacuated Portuguese, Dutch and Britons having embassies in Libya.

All these examples show that in large-scale crisis, where immediate evacuation is required in order to prevent bodily harm of Union citizens, the representations of the Member States in third countries stick not to the requirement established by Article 23 TFEU and Decision 95/553/EC of lack of an accessible representation of the person's own Member State. Rather, Member States are adopting a very pragmatic approach, driven by humanitarian reasons, aimed at guaranteeing the physical integrity of all Union citizens exposed to a situation bearing considerable risks.

This differentiation between large-scale crises requiring the repatriation of Union citizens on the one side and the other circumstances requiring consular protection according to Article 5 of Decision 95/553/EC (death, serious accident or illness, arrest or detention, etc.) and Decision 96/409/CSFP (loss or theft of travel documents) on the other side, becomes evident also in the Council Conclusions on Common practices in Consular Assistance outside the EU of 14 June 2010,[68] where

---

65 See article on BBC of 23.08.2011, available at: <http://www.bbc.co.uk/news/uk-14635477> (25.08.2011).

66 See information on EU Member States' representations in third countries: <http://ec.europa.eu/consularprotection/index.action;jsessionid=BCtHTP1fzrTQVTqVLQmsghw9vNhtbJCpRj019nYyT5xTDQszJSDh!1556677622> (25.10.2011).

67 European Business Council for Africa and the Mediterranean (EBCAM), Memorandum No. 34/2011 Special on Libya 04.03.2011. Available at: <http://www.nabc.nl/Portals/0/docs/EBCAM%2034%20-%20MEMORANDUM%20N%C2%BA%2034%20-%202011.txt.pdf> (25.10.2011).

68 COUNCIL OF THE EUROPEAN UNION, Common practices in consular assistance outside the EU, adopted by COCON on 09.06.2010 and by the Council of the European

assistance to distressed citizens in a crisis situation is treated separately from the common practices in the rest of circumstances.[69]

2. Family Members who are not Union Citizens

Bearing in mind the social context of travels and residence of Union citizens abroad, it is likely that the situations of distress described by Article 5 of Decision 95/553/EC and Article 1 of Decision 96/409/CSFP, such as death, serious accident or illness, arrest or detention, violent crime, loss/theft of travel documents, warlike conflicts, natural disasters, etc. could affect not only the Union citizens themselves but also persons accompanying them on their business trip, tourist visit or during their stay in the third country.

While there is no need, and besides, it would not be feasible, to extend the protection provided to Union citizens to every person accompanying him/her in third countries despites the lack of a legally recognised relationship of affection between the Union citizen and his/her companion, the question arises whether the protection offered under European Union law to unrepresented Union citizens in third countries should be extended to family members of the Union citizen who are affected by the same situation of distress concerning the Union citizen in question.

The protection provided to unrepresented Union citizens certainly does not need to be extended to family members who are nationals of a Member State that has no diplomatic or consular representation in the third country concerned since those citizens are "unrepresented" Union citizens in terms of Article 23 TFEU, Decision 95/553/EC and Decision 96/409/CSFP and dispose of their own entitlement to ask for help the representation of any other of the Member States in the third country and thus also the Member State of nationality of their ("represented") family member.[70]

This question would neither arise, at least not with the same intensity, in those cases where family members, who are not Union citizens, have a diplomatic or consular representation of their country of nationality so that they could be referred in the first place to the help provided by their own country. This does not exclude the possibility of EU Member

Union on 14.06.2010, Document 10698/10, COCON 28, PESC 745. Available at: <http://register.consilium.europa.eu/pdf/en/10/st10/st10698.en10.pdf> (25.10.2011).

69 *Ibidem*, pp. 2 and 6, Annex II on Crisis Coordination.

70 A different question is the one of whether family members of an Union citizen who are unrepresented Union citizens should in the first place ask for help the representation of his/her Member State of nationality (under the rules established by national law, if such) before asking for protection a the representation of a Member State under Union law. Although such approach is most likely to be followed in practice, there is no need to establish this kind of subsidiarity of protection under Union law.

States to provide help to this kind of family members of unrepresented Union citizens if the competent authorities consider it to be indicated, for instance in order to provide effective remedy to the unrepresented Union citizen in question. This kind of assistance would, however, not correspond to an obligation upon the Member State concerned and would not constitute a claim in favour of such family members who are, at the end, not reliant on the help provided by a country different from their home country.

Accordingly, the possible extension of the circle of holders of the right to consular protection to family members of Union citizens, who are themselves not nationals of an EU Member State and whose home country is not represented in the third country in question, should be considered.

The European Commission argued in its Green Paper "Diplomatic and consular protection of Union citizens in third countries" for the need to extend consular protection also to family members of unrepresented EU citizens who are not EU nationals[71] taking into account that for instance approximately six million Union citizens are married to third country nationals.[72] In this regard the European Commission recalled the need of joint protection emerged in the Lebanon conflict in 2006, with the procedures for evacuating and repatriating via Cyprus family members of citizens whose Member State was not represented.[73]

The extension of the circle of right holders to certain family members as regarding the right to consular protection can be observed in the national rules of some of the Member States; however, the great majority of Member States is reluctant in recognising this kind of legal position.

For instance, the German Act on Consular Officers, their Functions and Powers (hereinafter: German Consular Act)[74] of 11.09.1974 establishes in Article 5 para. 2 that, if it is deemed just and proper in the particular circumstances, consular officers may ("*können*") also render assistance to distressed non-nationals which are members of the family of a German citizen, if they share same household with him or have done so for considerable period of time. The notion "may" implies a scope of

---

[71] EUROPEAN COMMISSION, Green Paper "Diplomatic and consular protection of Union citizens in third countries", COM(2006)712 of 28 November 2006. Official Journal C 30 of 10.02.2007, p. 8.

[72] EUROPEAN COMMISSION, Impact Assessment on "Effective consular protection in third countries: the contribution of the European Union. Action Plan 2007-2009", p. 27, *op. cit.*, footnote 27.

[73] EUROPEAN COMMISSION, Green Paper, *op. cit.*, footnote 71.

[74] *Gesetz über die Konsularbeamten, ihre Aufgaben und Befugnisse* of 11 September 1974, published in the State Official Gazette (*Bundesgesetzblatt*) I 1974, 2317. The Act was lastly amended on 27.12.2003.

discretion conferred on the competent authorities so that under German law the family member in a situation of distress would have the right to a decision by the competent authorities free of discretion' mistakes but not the right to a concrete action/remedy. Family members would indeed have the right to a concrete action by the consular or diplomatic authorities provided the scope of discretion has reduced to "zero". This would be the case when in the particular situation, taking into account the circumstances of the case, there was only one possible action capable of providing a remedy to the situation in question.[75]

In contrast, in cases of natural disasters, warlike or revolutionary complications or like events, causing or likely to cause harm to the population or to any section thereof, non-national family members have the right to receive the same assistance as German citizens, whereby no discretion is conferred to the consular officers.[76]

The national rules of many Member States address not specifically non-national family members of its citizens, but contain rather provisions regarding foreigners in general, so that family members who are third country nationals could be provided with consular protection if they feature a particular link with the Member State in question, such as permanent residence, residence or work permit, etc. Denmark, for instance, provides consular protection under the Foreign Service Act No. 150 of 13 April 1983[77] to aliens holding a valid Danish residence permit. The same provision can be found in the Directive of the Ministry of Foreign Affairs on Consular Assistance to Czech Citizens in Case of Emergency No. 301366/2000-KO/5.[78] Moreover, according to Section 2 para. 1 of the Finnish Consular Services Act No. 498 of 22.04.1999,[79] consular protection may be provided also to foreign citizens in a crisis

---

75 To the reduction of the scope of discretion to "zero", see IPSEN, J., *Allgemeines Verwaltungsrecht*, 6. edition, Köln/ München, 2009, paras. 527 et seq.; MAURER, H., *Allgemeines Verwaltungsrecht*, 17. edition, München, 2008, pp. 135 et seq.

76 Article 6 para. 1 of the German Consular Act: "Consular officers shall, in the event of the consular district being struck or threatened by natural disasters, warlike or revolutionary complications or like events, causing or likely to cause harm to the population or to any section thereof, take the necessary steps to give assistance and protection to the injured or threatened insofar as they are Germans. This provision shall apply equally to descendants of Germans and to non-German members of their families if they share the same household with them or have done so for a considerable period of time."

77 *Lov om Udenrigstjenesten* of 13.04.1983, as amended by Acts No. 331 of 14.05.1997 and No. 410 of 06.06.2002.

78 Directive of the Ministry of Foreign Affairs on Consular Assistance to Czech Citizens in Case of Emergency No. 301366/2000-KO/5.

79 *Konsulipalvelulaki* No. 498 of 22.04.1999, available at: <http://www.finlex.fi/fi/laki/kaannokset/1999/en19990498.pdf> (30.05.2010).

situation residing permanently in Finland and having a permit to reside or work.[80] Under special circumstances assistance is provided also to other foreigners, not complying with the aforementioned requirements.[81] Worth mentioning is Article 52 para. 2 of the Estonian Consular Act that requires no link between the alien in distress and the Estonian State.[82]

Nonetheless, it should be highlighted that the great majority of the Member States consider the provision of consular protection to non-national family members who are not EU citizens on a case-by-case basis[83] or even deny such kind of protection generally.[84]

Accordingly, there is no uniform practice of the Member States with regard to the provision of consular protection to family members who are not Union citizens.[85] The lack of protection for third-country nationals who are members of a Union citizen's family can cause great difficulties and distress when citizens and their families are in trouble. Moreover, this

---

80 Section 2 para. 2 of the Finnish Consular Act: "Unless a consular service is subject to other provisions, consular services referred to in Chapters 3 to 10 of this Act may be provided for a Finnish legal person or a Finnish citizen or for a foreign citizen residing permanently in Finland, who is in possession of or has been granted a permit to reside or work in Finland either permanently or in a comparable manner."

81 Section 2 para. 3 of the Finnish Consular Service Act: "Under special circumstances consular services referred to in Chapters 4 and 10 of this Act may also be provided for other foreign citizens."

82 Article 52 para. 2 of the Estonian Consular Act: "For the purposes of this Act, a person in distress is an Estonian citizen or alien who finds himself or herself in a temporary emergency situation as a result of an accident, an illness, falling victim to a crime or other circumstances and who is unable to resolve the situation by himself or herself."

83 See for instance the Comments delivered by the Government of Ireland on the European Commission' Green Paper "Diplomatic and Consular Protection of union citizens in third countries", p. 2: "In emergency situations, we will assist other EU nationals but could not agree to a blanket requirement to assist members of their families who are not EU citizens. We would of course look at each case individually." Document available at: <http://ec.europa.eu/justice_home/news/consulting_public/consular_protection/contributions/contribution_ireland_en.pdf> (30.05.2010).

84 See e.g. the United Kingdom response to the Commission's Green Paper on Diplomatic and consular protection of Union citizens in third countries from March 2007, p. 4, where the UK government justifies its reluctance to provide consular protection to family members both of British and of unrepresented Union citizens with the lack of financial resources, putting forward that UK consular assistance is funded exclusively through passport fees. The UK government seems, however, to relativise this reluctance in case of evacuation pointing out its policy of avoiding splitting families, however, provided the family member concerned possess visa for the destination country. Document available at: <http://ec.europa.eu/justice_home/news/consulting_public/consular_protection/news_contributions_consular_protection_en.htm> (30.05.2010).

85 Some Member States provide consular protection to recognized refugees (e.g. Austria, Belgium, Bulgaria, the Czech Republic, Spain, Finland, Lithuania, the Netherlands, Portugal, Romania, Sweden), and/or to stateless persons (e.g. Belgium, the Czech Republic, Lithuania, Portugal, Romania and Sweden) mainly in emergency situations.

situation could difficult the exercise of the right to consular protection by unrepresented Union citizens or even render its exercise impossible, obliging unrepresented Union citizens to make a difficult (or even impossible) decision on whether to leave behind their family members in a third country affected for instance by an war conflict or natural disaster and enjoy the protection offered by a Member State under EU law.[86]

Thus, the question on the extension of the protection provided under Union law to unrepresented Union citizens abroad to family members of unrepresented Union citizens who are third-country nationals and whose home country has no representation in the country concerned, concerns the effectiveness of the provision of consular protection to unrepresented Union citizens and therefore, one of the general principles of interpretation of European Union law, that on the practical effectiveness (*effet utile*) of Union provisions.[87]

The *effet utile* of Union law is in this sense not only guaranteed through the principle of primacy of Union law over national law[88] leading to interpretation of national rules in conformity with Union law[89] and if not possible, to the inapplicability of conflicting national law,[90] but also through a purposeful interpretation of the Union provisions themselves seeking to achieve their best possible unfolding.[91]

A comparison with other Union citizenship rights, as for instance the right to freely move and reside, shows that the extension of the right holders' circle to Union citizens' family members is aimed at guaranteeing the effective exercise of the Union citizenship right in question by the Union citizens themselves, i.e. it seeks to establish a

---

86 It is hardly to imagine that an unrepresented Union citizen would accept to be repatriated back to the European Union without e.g. his wife, who is a third-country national, leaving her behind in a situation of distress, such as for instance a natural disaster or a terrorist attack.

87 SCHWARZE, J., "Kommentar zu Artikel 19 EUV", in *EU-Kommentar*, para. 38, *op. cit.*, footnote 41.

88 See LANAERTS, K./ VAN NUFFEL, P., *Constitutional Law of the European Union*, London, 2005, pp. 666, 667.

89 See e.g. Judgment of the Court of Justice of 13.11.1990 in the case C-106/89, *Marleasing SA v La Comercial Internacional de Alimentacion SA*, ECR 1990, p. I-04135, para. 8.

90 See e.g. Judgment of the Court of Justice of 09.03.1978 in the case C-106/77, *Amministrazione delle Finanze dello Stato v Simmenthal SpA* [case *Simmenthal II*], ECR 1978, p. 00629, paras. 16, 21.

91 Settled case-law of the Court of Justice, see e.g. Judgment of the Court of Justice of 06.10.1970 in the case C-9/70, *Franz Grad v. Finanzamt Tarunstein* [case "*Leberpfennig*"], ECR 1970, p. 825, para. 25; Judgment of the Court of Justice of 04.12.1974 in the case C-41/74, *Yvonne van Duyn v. Home Office*, ECR 1974, p. 1337, para. 12; Judgment of the Court of Justice of 06.10.1981 in the case C-246/80, *C. Broekmeulen v. Huisarts Registratie Commissie*, ECR 1981, p. 2311, para. 16.

"derived right" for certain persons in order not to factually deprive Union citizens from the enjoyment of their rights flowing from their status as Union citizens.

Worth mentioning is in this regard Directive 2004/38/EC of the European Parliament and of the Council of 29 April 2004 on the right of citizens of the Union and their family members to move and reside freely within the territory of the Member States.[92] Directive 2004/38/EC grants to family members of Union citizens, who have exercised their right to freely move and reside within the territory of the European Union, the right to entry the territory of the host Member State, as well as the right to reside there temporary or permanently under certain conditions.[93]

Furthermore, the Court of Justice has repeatedly highlighted the importance of the extension of the right to freely move and reside within the territory of the European Union to family members of Union citizens in order to guarantee the practical effectiveness of this Union citizenship right. This approach of the Court of Justice finds its best expression in the judgment in the case *Zhu and Chen.*[94] Catherine Zhu was the child

---

92 Directive 2004/38/EC of the European Parliament and of the Council of 29 April 2004 on the right of citizens of the Union and their family members to move and reside freely within the territory of the Member States amending Regulation (EEC) No. 1612/68 and repealing Directives 64/221/EEC, 68/360/EEC, 72/194/EEC, 73/148/EEC, 75/34/EEC, 75/35/EEC, 90/364/EEC, 90/365/EEC and 93/96/EEC, Official Journal L 158 of 30.4.2004, p. 77. See in this sense also EUROPEAN COMMISSION, Action Plan 2007-2009 "Effective consular protection in third countries: the contribution of the European Union", Communication from the Commission to the European Parliament, the Council, the European Economic and Social Committee and the Committee of the Regions of 05 December 2007, COM(2007)767 final, p. 8. Available at: <http://eur-lex.europa.eu/LexUriServ/LexUriServ.do?uri=COM:2007:0767:FIN:EN:HTML> (15.08.2010).

93 Article 5 para. 1 (Right of entry) of Directive 2004/58/EC: "Without prejudice to the provisions on travel documents applicable to national border controls, Member States shall grant Union citizens leave to enter their territory with a valid identity card or passport and shall grant family members who are not nationals of a Member State leave to enter their territory with a valid passport"; Article 6 para. 2 (Right of residence for up to three months): "The provisions of paragraph 1 shall also apply to family members in possession of a valid passport who are not nationals of a Member State, accompanying or joining the Union citizen"; Article 6 para. 2 (Right of residence for more than three months): "The right of residence provided for in paragraph 1 shall extend to family members who are not nationals of a Member State, accompanying or joining the Union citizen in the host Member State, provided that such Union citizen satisfies the conditions referred to in paragraph 1(a), (b) or (c)"; Article 16 para. 2 (Right of permanent residence): "Paragraph 1 shall apply also to family members who are not nationals of a Member State and have legally resided with the Union citizen in the host Member State for a continuous period of five years."

94 Judgment of the Court of Justice of 19.10.2004 in the case C-200/02, *Kunqian Catherine Zhu and Man Lavette Chen v Secretary of State for the Home Department*, ECR 2004, p. I-09925.

of a Chinese couple working and living in the United Kingdom. She was born in Ireland and received automatically Irish citizenship due to the *jus soli* rule applied at this time in Ireland.[95] Her mother, Mrs Chen, moved with her to Wales, where she worked and catered for Catherine. However, she was refused by the competent national authorities to be granted a permanent residence permit arguing that Catherine, a child of eight months of age, was not exercising any rights arising from the EC Treaty and the fact that Mrs Chen was not entitled to reside in the United Kingdom under primary and secondary EU law. The Court of Justice recalled the *effet utile* of Union provisions and held that the circle of holders of the right to freely move and reside within the territory of the European Union need to be extended to family members facilitating the enjoyment of this Union citizenship by the Union citizen in question in order to guarantee the useful effect of that right and not emptying it from its content. The Court held that:

> A refusal to allow the parent, whether a national of a Member State or a national of a non-member country, who is the carer of a child to whom Article 18 EC grants a right of residence, to reside with that child in the host MS would deprive the child's right of residence of any useful effect.

The Court therefore went to conclude that:

> It is clear that enjoyment by a young child of a right of residence necessarily implies that the child is entitled to be accompanied by the person who is his/her primary carer and accordingly that the carer must be in a position to reside with the child in the host MS.

It is worth mentioning that while the Court of Justice based its decision in the case *Baumbast* to extend the circle of right-holders to family members of Union citizens yet additionally on the fundamental right of family reunification recognised by the European Convention for the Protection of Human Rights and Fundamental Freedoms and the settled case-law of the Court,[96] it refrained from referring to this fundamental right in the subsequent judgements in the cases *Zhu and Chen*,[97] *Zambrano*,[98] etc., drawing merely on the need for effectiveness of Union citizenship

[95] This rule has been abandoned in the meantime.

[96] Judgment of the Court of Justice of 17.09.2002 in the case C-413/99, *Baumbast and R v. Secretary of State for the Home Department Baumbast*, ECR 2002, p. I-07091 para. 72: "Moreover, in accordance with the case-law of the Court, Regulation No. 1612/68 must be interpreted in the light of the requirement of respect for family life laid down in Article 8 of the European Convention. That requirement is one of the fundamental rights which, according to settled case-law, are recognised by Community law."

[97] Judgment in the case *Zhu and Chen, op. cit.*, footnote 94.

[98] Judgment of the Court of Justice of the European Union of 08.03.2011 in the case C-34/09, *Ruiz Zambrano v Office national de l'emploi (ONEm)*, ECR 2011, p. 00000.

rights. The Court of Justice upheld this approach in the judgements in the cases *Ibrahim*[99] and *Teixeira.*[100]

But the Court went even further and emphasised the importance of the Union status as such, without the need to draw on the exercise of a concrete citizenship right but rather on the importance of the mere possibility to exercise the rights deriving from the Union citizenship status. The applicants in the case *Zambrano*[101] were refused by the Belgian authorities to be granted asylum. However, during the asylum procedure, Mr Zambrano signed an employment contract for an unlimited period, although he had no work permit, and Mrs Zambrano gave birth to two children who acquired Belgian nationality. Mr Ruiz Zambrano then had a number of periods of unemployment. The Belgian authorities refused to authorise Mr and Mrs Zambrano to reside in Belgium in their capacity as ascendants of a Belgian national arguing that they had intentionally omitted to take the necessary steps with the Columbian authorities to have their children recognised as Columbian nationals, precisely in order to regularise their own residence in Belgium. The *Tribunal du travail de Bruxelles,*[102] before which the proceedings challenging the rejection decisions were brought, asked the Court of Justice whether Mr Zambrano may rely on European Union law to reside and work in Belgium even though Mr Zambrano's children have never exercised their right of free movement within the territory of the Member States. The Court of Justice argued for the first time that the extension of the right to freely move and reside within the European Union to family members renders effectiveness not only to the right of residence of the Union citizen of question but guarantees in general the genuine enjoyment of all rights conferred by virtue of their status as citizens of the Union.[103] The Court concluded that:

99 Judgment of the Court of Justice of 23.02.2010 in the case C-310/08, *London Borough of Harrow v Nimco Hassan Ibrahim and Secretary of State for the Home Department*, ECR 2020, p. I-01065, paras. 55, 57.

100 Judgment of the Court of Justice of 23.02.2010 in the case C-480/08, *Maria Teixeira v London Borough of Lambeth and Secretary of State for the Home Department*, ECR 2010, p. I-01107, paras. 66 et seq.

101 Judgment of the Court of Justice of the European Union in the case *Zambrano*, *op. cit.*, footnote 98.

102 Employment Tribunal of Brussels.

103 Judgment of the Court of Justice in the case *Zambrano*, para. 45, *op. cit.*, footnote 98. The Court held that: "Citizenship of the Union requires a Member State to allow third country nationals who are parents of a child who is a national of that Member State to reside and work there, where a refusal to do so would deprive that child of the genuine enjoyment of the substance of the rights attaching to the status of citizen of the Union. This requirement applies even when the child has never exercised his right to free movement within the territory of the Member States."

Article 20 TFEU precludes national measures which have the effect of depriving citizens of the Union of the genuine enjoyment of the substance of the rights conferred by virtue of their status as citizens of the Union.[104]

The Court confirmed the right of Union citizens to "genuine enjoyment of the substance of the rights" conferred by the Union citizenship status in the case *Shirley McCarthy.*[105] The Court relied by this means for the first time on the general clause of the new Article 20 TFEU introduced by the Treaty of Lisbon, paving the way for the extension of the circle of right-holders whenever necessary in order to guarantee the practical, useful effect of all Union citizenship rights.

Accordingly, in order to render the provision of consular protection to unrepresented Union citizens effective, the protection provided for under Article 23 TFEU and Decision 95/553/EC should be extended to third-country family members, at least in situations affecting both the unrepresented citizen and his/her family members, e.g. natural disaster, armed conflict, etc.

Besides, being the purpose pursued the effectiveness of the assistance provided to unrepresented Union citizens, a conditionality between the effective enjoyment of consular protection by the Union citizen concerned and the extension of that protection to his/her family members is necessary. In other words, protection should be provided only if consular protection of the Union citizen concerned would not be effective without extending the protection to his/her family members. This means that in either case the character of the right of family members as a "derived right" should be emphasised in the sense that family members would not be authorised to claim this right autonomously, i.e. without the request of the Union citizen vis-à-vis the competent authorities of the Member State providing help.

Thus, consular protection should be extended to family members who are not Union citizens as regarding the situations of distress described by Article 5 of Decision 95/553/EC, however, provided that the unrepresented Union citizen as well as his/her family members are affected by the same circumstances, i.e. share the same situation of distress.[106]

Regard being had of the fact that the notion 'family members' in terms of the extension of consular protection under the national rules of some of the Member States, is interpreted differently, as for instance requiring that the family member concerned shares or have shared same household

---

104 *Ibidem*, para. 42.

105 Judgment of the Court of Justice of 05.05.2011 in the case C-434/09, *Shirley McCarthy v Secretary of State for the Home Department*, ECR 2011, p. 00000, para. 47.

106 To the proposal of a Directive on consular protection, see Chapter IX below.

with the national[107] or subsuming under the notion 'family members' merely the spouse and children of the national in distress,[108] the notion 'family members' in terms of consular protection provided under Union law should be interpreted autonomously.

In this regard, the purpose and spirit of the provisions regarding consular protection should be taken into consideration. Therefore, although it could be indeed drawn on the definition provided by Article 2 para. 2 of Directive 2004/38/EC on the right of citizens of the Union and their family members to move and reside freely within the territory of the Member States,[109] Union legislation should account for the different objectives pursued by the right to freely move and reside in the Member States on the one side and the right to consular protection on the other side.[110]

Accordingly, the current legal situation leaving the extension of the circle of the holders of the right to consular protection to the discretion of the Member States in accordance to their national legislations and practices is not capable of guaranteeing the useful effect of the provision of consular protection to Union citizens in third countries, contributing at the same time to the legal certainty on this matter, so that this obstacle to the effectiveness of the provisions on consular protection need to be removed by a legislative instrument.[111]

In this context, the inclusion of an obligation to provide consular protection to third-country family members of 'unrepresented' Union

---

107 See German Consular Act, Article 5 para. 2 and Article 6 para. 1. Published in *Bundesgesetzblatt* (State Official Gazette) I 1974, 2317.

108 See draft bill 2002/03:69 on the Swedish Consular Financial Assistance Act (Chapter 9, Section 6, p. 49) suggesting that accompanying spouses and children under the age of 18, as well as persons living together with the applicant if they have been married or have (or have had) common children, are included into the circle of right-holders. Available at: <http://www.riksdagen.se/webbnav/index.aspx?nid=37&dok_id=GQ0369> (16.01.2011).

109 Article 2, para. 2, Directive: "'family member' means:

(a) the spouse;

(b) the partner with whom the Union citizen has contracted a registered partnership, on the basis of the legislation of a Member State, if the legislation of the host Member State treats registered partnerships as equivalent to marriage and in accordance with the conditions laid down in the relevant legislation of the host Member State;

(c) the direct descendants who are under the age of 21 or are dependants and those of the spouse or partner as defined in point (b);

(d) the dependent direct relatives in the ascending line and those of the spouse or partner as defined in point (b)".

110 To the proposal of a Directive on consular protection, see Chapter IX.

111 *Ibidem*.

citizens is likely to entail an amendment of the national rules on consular protection provided to family members of nationals, unless the Member States are keen to accept a discrimination of their own nationals in comparison with 'unrepresented' Union citizens.

3. Third Country Nationals Enjoying Consular Protection by a Member State

Some Member States have undertaken according to bilateral or multilateral agreements with third countries the obligation to provide consular protection to the citizens of that country where there is no representation of the country concerned.[112] Accordingly, the question should be posed whether those third country nationals, who are not Union citizens and who are entitled to consular protection by an (unrepresented) EU member state according to an international agreement, should be included into the circle of holders of the right to consular protection under Union law, so that such citizens would be authorised to ask for help in situations of distress any of the Member States represented in a third country where neither its State of nationality nor the EU member state obliged to provide protection have a diplomatic or consular representation.[113]

It is worth mentioning that without any previous discussion in the Green Paper on Diplomatic and Consular Protection or in the Action Plan 2007-2009, the Council of the European Union included into the Guidelines on Consular Protection of EU Citizens in Third Countries issued on 05 November 2010 and approved by the Council on 17 November[114] a new category of persons to be provided with consular protection, referred to as

112 See e.g. the Cooperation agreement between the Ministry of Foreign Affairs of the Republic of Bulgaria and the Ministry of Foreign Affairs of Montenegro on visa and consular protection. By virtue of this agreement the Bulgarian diplomatic missions in Azerbaijan, Armenia and Georgia will provide consular protections to the nationals of Montenegro within the territories of those States in cases of: detention or arrest; visit to prisoners serving a prison sentence, issuance of a provisional pass for the purpose of return of Montenegrin nationals to their country; provision of financial assistance, after the development of a mechanism for its reimbursement on the part of Montenegro.

113 Besides, many of the Member States provide consular protection under their national rules or practices to third country nationals possessing permanent residence permit in the Member State concerned, recognised refugees or stateless persons residing their.

114 COUNCIL OF THE EUROPEAN UNION, Guidelines on Consular Protection of EU Citizens in Third Countries, of 05.11.2010, Document 15613/10, COCON 40 PESC 1371, available at: <http://register.consilium.europa.eu/pdf/en/10/st15/st15613.en10.pdf> (02.02.2011). Approval by the Council of the European Union at its 3045th meeting on 17.11.2010, Document 16369/10, p. 20, available at: <http://www.consilium.europa.eu/uedocs/cms_data/docs/pressdata/en/ecofin/117790.pdf> (02.02.2011).

"entitled persons".[115] According to the Guidelines, third countries citizens falling under the responsibility of an EU Member State as a consequence of a bilateral agreement may be evacuated by another Member State upon request of the Member State concerned.[116] It should be, however, mentioned that the Guidelines extend consular protection to those third country nationals only regarding evacuation in crisis situations and not regarding the other types of protection offered under Decision 95/553/EC and Decision 96/409/CSFP.[117]

Besides, it is to be noted that the Guidelines, which are not legally binding,[118] seem not to seek to establish a direct claim of those "entitled persons" according to bilateral agreement against a Member State. Rather, the Member State, under whose responsibility the third country nationals fall, may request another Member State, represented in the country at question, to evacuate any "entitled persons".

Thus, an "entitled person" could address the Ministry of Foreign Affairs of the Member State with a bilateral agreement with his/her home country with the petition to ask the authorities of another Member State represented in the third country to provide help in evacuating the person concerned, but those persons are not included as such into the circle of the right-holders as regarding the provision of consular protection under Union law.[119]

The same applies to other third-country nationals who might be entitled to consular protection by a Member State abroad, such as long-term residents and recognised refugees.[120] The right of those citizens to

---

115 *Ibidem*, p. 3.

116 *Ibidem*, p. 7.

117 *Ibidem*, pp. 6, 7.

118 *Ibidem*, p. 2.

119 See COUNCIL OF THE EUROPEAN UNION, Guidelines, section 12.11: "Member States requesting the inclusion of their nationals and entitled persons will:

(a) notify the evacuating state (both locally and centrally) of the details of the entitled persons they wish to have evacuated;

(b) if possible, ensure that the entitled persons reach the embarkation point;

(c) provide consular verification at the point of embarkation if they are represented locally (or send staff from the nearest local mission if requested by the evacuating state); and

(d) take responsibility for their entitled persons from the point of disembarkation."

120 Under the 1951 UN Convention relating to the Status of Refugees and its Protocol of 1967, refugees are entitled to the issue of passports by the authorities of the country in which they have the status of a refugee. However, according to Article 16 of the Protocol, there is no obligation of the State concerned to provide consular and diplomatic protection to a refugee abroad: "The issue of the document does not in any way entitle the holder to the protection of the diplomatic or consular authorities of

seek protection abroad under national law may not be transferred to other Member States on the basis of the Union provisions on consular protection of Union citizens. Nonetheless, Member States are not deprived from approaching each other with the request to provide assistance also to this kind of persons. Union provisions on consular protection may not however be called upon in order for a third-country national, who is not a family member of a Union citizen, to seek help from another Member State in a situation of distress.

4. Conclusions

The Union provisions on consular protection identify as holders of the right to consular protection all Union citizens, being Union citizens all nationals of the EU Member States according to their national legislation and regardless age and gender, whose Member State of origin is not represented in the third country concerned.

The requirement of the "accessibility" of the representation of the Member State of nationality is thereby narrowly related to the extend of the circle of the right-holders, being those Union citizen having an accessible representation of their own Member State in the third country not entitled to ask for help the representation of another Member State. The extensive interpretation of the "accessibility" of the representation of the Member State of nationality of the person concerned facilitates a flexible and practical approach in each concrete case, accounting for the specific circumstances prevailing in the third country in question.

This pragmatic approach leads in certain types of consular protection, as evacuation in crisis situations or actions carried out by a so called Lead State, to an alleged contradiction *in termini* assuming that Union citizens are 'unrepresented' even if there are indeed 'represented' by a diplomatic or consular mission of their own Member State. Rather than a contradiction, it is an implied exception from the requirement for a Union citizen in order to be entitled to consular protection to have no representation of his/her own Member State in the third country. As any exception from a rule, this exception should be interpreted restrictively and applied only in cases of utmost urgency and taking into account the gravity of the harm that the Union citizen in need could suffer.

This prudence is indicated *inter alia* in order to comply with the international practice as well as by the Vienna Convention on Consular Relations and Vienna Convention on Diplomatic Relations whereupon an embassy or consulate is in charge of a determined territory, in general the

---

the country of issue, and does not confer on these authorities a right of protection." Available at: <http://www.unhcr.org/3b66c2aa10.html> (02.02.2011).

whole third country in the case of an embassy. The provision of consular protection to an Union citizen under Union law although his/her own Member State has a representation in the third country, constitutes a double responsibility, one under the Vienna Convention on Consular Relations incumbent upon the representation of the citizens' own Member State and one under Union law upon the consulate or embassy of another Member State in the remote area of the third country in question. Nonetheless, those responsibilities are alternative and each of both responsibilities ceases to exist when the Union citizen concerned is effectively provided with consular protection.

Besides, in order to guarantee the effective enjoyment of the right to consular protection by 'unrepresented' Union citizens, the creation of a second group of 'secondary' right-holders is necessary, extending the circle of right-holders to non-national family members of 'unrepresented' Union citizens in third countries. This extension of the circle of right-holders responds to the claim of the Union citizenship status to be the fundamental status of Union citizens and not only to provide Union citizens with rights additional to those stemming from their capacity as nationals of a State, but also to ensure the effectiveness of this fundamental status by means of guaranteeing the effective enjoyment of all rights deriving therefrom. The circle of right-holders should therefore be defined taking into consideration the need to ensure the useful effect of the provisions concerned for the Union citizens as subjects of the legal norms concerned, so that family members should be provided with consular protection under Union law merely in situations of "complicity" affecting both the Union citizen in distress as well as his/her family members, being the protection of the family members conditional for the effective enjoyment of the right to consular protection by the Union citizen concerned.

Chapter VI

Substantive Scope of the Right to Consular Protection

1. A Mere Right to Equal Treatment?

The function of the right to consular protection – to fill out with legal power the political status of Union citizens in particular situations requiring action by a Member State – faces a challenge in the structure of the right to consular protection that suggests indeed a claim to a positive action but fails to identify what the positive action shall consist of. Rather, the wording of Article 23 TFEU and Article 46 EU Charter seems to limit the positive obligation imposed upon the Member States to the obligation to secure the equal treatment of unrepresented Union citizens in third countries when providing them with consular protection. The Treaties therefore set up the right to consular protection as an equal-treatment right.

The design as an equal-treatment right is not unusual for a citizens' right and its equal-treatment character deprives it not from being a subjective right, as the look at the rights to vote and stand as a candidate at municipal elections as well as in elections to the European Parliament shows.[1] Besides, the Court of Justice has repeatedly confirmed the subjective-right character of the general principle of non-discrimination on the grounds of nationality enshrined in Article 18 TFEU (ex-Article 12 TEC). The Court went to conclude in the case *Bickel* for instance that the nationals of the Member States had a "right to equal treatment"[2] conferred directly by Community law[3] and held in the *Phil Collins* case that:

---

1 Article 22 para. 1, first clause TFEU: "Every citizen of the Union residing in a Member State of which he is not a national shall have the right to vote and to stand as a candidate at municipal elections in the Member State in which he resides, under the same conditions as nationals of that State."; Article 22 para. 2, first clause TFEU: "Without prejudice to Article 223(1) and to the provisions adopted for its implementation, every citizen of the Union residing in a Member State of which he is not a national shall have the right to vote and to stand as a candidate in elections to the European Parliament in the Member State in which he resides, under the same conditions as nationals of that State."

2 Judgment of the Court of Justice of 24.11.1998 in the case C-274/96, *Criminal proceedings against Horst Otto Bickel and Ulrich Franz*, ECR 1998, p. I-07637, paras. 16, 18.

3 Judgment of the Court of Justice of 02.02.1989 in the case C-186/87, *Ian William Covan v. Trésor Public*, ECR 1989, p. 000195, para. 11.

> [...] that right may, therefore, be relied upon before a national court as the basis for a request that it disapply the discriminatory provisions of a national law which denies to nationals of other Member States the protection which they accord to nationals of the State concerned.[4]

Thus, the special equal-treatment right enshrined in Article 23 TFEU is *a fortiori* capable of being a subjective right in analogy to the general equal-treatment right established by Article 18 TFEU.

But what refers the equal treatment to?

According to Article 23 TFEU, unrepresented EU citizens shall be entitled to protection by the diplomatic or consular authorities of any Member State "on the same conditions as the nationals of that State". This equal-treatment clause raises two main questions that are interrelated with each other: first, whether the "conditions" are conditions established by Union law or rather by national law and practices, and second, does the notion "conditions" refer only to the question of 'how' consular protection is provided or also to the question 'if' consular protection is provided.

With reference to the first problem area, IANNIELLO SALICETI suggests that the clause "on the same conditions" has to be referred to "the conditions of EU law" meaning the standards established by Decision 95/553/EC.[5] This seems at the first sight to be problematic with regard to the uncertain legal character of both, Decision 95/553/EC and Decision 96/409/CFSP that might not be regarded as EU law technically speaking. As stated above under Chapter IV, the majority of the legal commentators consider both Decisions as intergovernmental treaties and not as *sui generis* Community acts adopted in the former first and second pillars. This view is supported by the lack of a legal basis for the adoption of a legal act on consular protection by the Council under ex-Article 20 TEC that issued rather a mandate to the Member States to "establish the necessary rules *among* themselves".[6] Besides, both Decisions are entitled "Decision of the Representatives of the Governments of the Member States *meeting within* the Council of [...]"[7] and not Decision of the Council as institution of the European Communities. On the other hand, the Decisions have not been ratified by the great majority of Member States as the case would be in

4 Judgment of the Court of Justice of 20.10.1993 in joined cases C-92/92 and C-326/92, Phil Collins v. Imtrat Handelsgesellschaft mbH and Patricia Im- und Export Verwaltungsgesellschaft mbH and Leif Emanuel Kraul v. EMI Electrola GmbH, ECR 1993, p. I-05145, para. 34.

5 IANNIELLO SALICETI, A., "The Protection of EU Citizens Abroad: Accountability, Rule of Law, Role of Consular and Diplomatic Services", in *European Public Law*, 17, No. 1 (2011), p. 98.

6 Emphasis added by author.

7 Emphasis added by author.

case of international agreements. Moreover, both Decisions have been published in the Official Journal of the European Communities under the section "legislation".

In any case, Decision 95/553/EC establishes in fact no measures of consular protection that should be applied equally to nationals and to unrepresented Union citizens. Decision 95/553/EC sets up rather the situations[8] in which unrepresented Union citizens in third countries are entitled to consular protection: death, serious accident, serious illness, falling victim of violent crime, other situations of distress requiring relief and repatriation[9] as well as, in Decision 96/409/CFSP, loss or theft of travel document. In addition, Decision 95/553/EC and Decision 96/409/CFSP establish two concrete measures to be provided as consular protection in the situations mentioned before: repatriation, financial advance and issue of ETDs. Neither of both Decisions stipulates what kind of assistance should be provided to unrepresented Union nationals in case of death, serious illness, serious accident, crime, etc.

The different possible types of assistance have been in contrast established by means of the Common Practices in Consular Assistance and Crisis Coordination, adopted by the Council of the European Union on 14 June 2010.[10] The common practices on consular protection shared by the Member States have been compiled by COCON on the basis of a study prepared by the Instituto Europeo de Derecho.

According to this document, in case of death a common practice is to provide assistance in obtaining death and medical certificates as

---

8 Already before the adoption of Decision 95/553/EC, the Council of the European Union agreed on 29/30 March 1993 upon (legally unbinding) Guidelines for the protection of unrepresented EU citizens by missions of the Member States in third countries, COUNCIL OF THE EUROPEAN UNION, Doc 7124/94 CFSP 161 COCON 2. (Entry into force of the Guidelines as of 1 July 1993.)

9 Article 5 of Decision 95/553/EC reads:

1. The protection referred to in Article 1 shall comprise:

(a) assistance in cases of death;

(b) assistance in cases of serious accident or serious illness;

(c) assistance in cases of arrest or detention;

(d) assistance to victims of violent crime;

(e) the relief and repatriation of distressed citizens of the Union.

2. In addition, Member States' diplomatic representations or consular agents serving in a non-member State may, in so far as it is within their powers, also come to the assistance of any citizen of the Union who so requests in other circumstances.

10 COUNCIL OF THE EUROPEAN UNION, Common Practices in Consular Assistance and Crisis Coordination, Document of 09.06.2010, 10698/10 (COCON), adopted as Conclusions of the Council within its meeting of 14.06.2010. Available at: <http://register.consilium.europa.eu/pdf/en/10/st10/st10698.en10.pdf> (17.04.2011).

well as laissez-passer and to notify family members. In case of serious accident or illness, consular and diplomatic authorities offer assistance regarding medical care and legal advice and provide other non-economic advice. In the case of arrest or detention, visits to the detainee are paid, detainees are informed on their rights and the minimum standards of treatment in prisons are monitored. Member States inform relatives, provide information on legal assistance and health care in case of a citizen being a victim of violent crime. Worth noting is that according to the Common Practices document, financial assistance is provided only in case of extreme emergency or destitution, though such requirements have not been established by Article 6 Decision 95/553/EC.

However, the Common Practices are not a legally binding act but mere recommendations and are thus no EU law establishing the conditions according to which unrepresented Union citizens and nationals of the assisting Member State should be treated equally. Moreover, not all of the "conditions" in terms of Article 23 TFEU may be "conditions of EU law" as proposed by IANNIELLO SALICETI: Article 23 points to "the same conditions as the nationals" of the Member State approached for help and no EU law conditions are applicable to the right to consular protection of the nationals of a Member State vis-à-vis that Member State, which would be a pure national case.

Accordingly, Article 23 TFEU refers at least partly to national rules and practices on consular protection. In this regard, the question arises whether the relevant national rules should be applied only as to the way in which consular protection is provided to unrepresented Union citizens or also to the question whether consular protection should be provided at all.

2. The 'If' and 'How' of Consular Protection

The lack of precise Union provisions on the kind of measures that could be claimed by 'unrepresented' Union citizens in situation of distress in a third country lead to a legal uncertainty that could have a particularly adverse impact on unrepresented Union citizens bearing in mind their vulnerability due to the situation of distress that they have to deal with as well as the lack of national authorities *in loco*.[11] In this context it is worth mentioning that according to a 2012 Flash Eurobarometer, 55% of EU citizens think that all embassies abroad should provide exactly the same type of help as they would receive from

[11] See in this sense also EUROPEAN COMMISSION, Impact Assessment accompanying the Proposal for a Directive of the Council on coordination and cooperation measures regarding consular protection for unrepresented EU citizens, COM(2011)881 final, p. 12.

their own embassy,[12] which shows how far the wishes of the citizens are from the reality.

The lack of concrete consular protection measures, besides the issue of ETDs, repatriation and the provision of financial advance, could indeed deter unrepresented Union citizens from approaching the consulate or embassy of a Member State different from the one of nationality and thus could encumber the exercise of the right to consular protection.

Nonetheless, the lack of precise Union provisions regarding the particular actions to be undertaken within the provision of assistance in the cases mentioned in Article 5 of Decision 95/553/EC can be justified with the need of flexible reaction by the consular officers providing consular protection taking into account the great range of unforeseeable circumstances in each individual case. In order to meet the challenges presented by this diversity of individual circumstances, consular protection is characterised by a wide scope of discretion conferred to the consular officers by the respective national rules as to the question how consular protection is provided. Any further "common practices" in this field are welcome due to their visibility for the citizens but need to leave the consular officers the scope of discretion that they need in order to provide consular protection most efficiently taking into account the specific circumstances of the case as well as the local conditions.

Accordingly, being the discretion regarding the way consular protection is provided reasonable ('how' consular protection is provided), it seems to be more problematical with regard to legal-certainty aspects whether the decision to provide or not consular protection at all is at the discretion of the consular officers ('if' consular protection is provided at all). Governed national rules also the question 'if' consular protection is provided, the existence (or not) of a legal right to consular protection would depend on the existence of such a right under national law.

Therefore, in the following, it will be examined whether the national rules of the 28 EU Member States conceive of the provision of consular protection to their nationals abroad as an individual right.

3. National Rules on Consular Protection

3.1. Austria

In Austria, there is no law codifying the rules concerning consular assistance abroad. The Federal Act on the Duties and Organization of

---

[12] EUROPEAN COMMISSION, Flash Eurobarometer 365, November 2012, p. 46. Available at <http://ec.europa.eu/public_opinion/flash/fl_365_en.pdf> (12.05.2013).

the Foreign Office Statute (*Bundesgesetz: Aufgaben und Organisation des auswärtigen Dienstes – Statut*)[13] establishes in Article 18, para. 1 the obligation of the Foreign Service officials to provide consular protection to Austrian and other EU citizens even outside working hours. However, the Federal Act on the Duties and Organization of the Foreign Office – Statute regulates merely the (internal) employment relationship between the officials and the Foreign Service (e.g. mobility, rotation, relocation, employment of the family members of the official abroad etc.). The addressees of the duties and rights established by the Act are not the citizens but the Foreign Service officials.

The provision of consular protection to unrepresented Union citizens was implemented by circulars of the Ministry of Foreign Affairs to the Austrian representations abroad.

Accordingly, Austria provides consular protection as a matter of policy and not under law. Consular protection is considered as a power of the State to provide a service to its nationals and not as a subjective right conferred upon individuals.[14] As mentioned above, the Federal Act on the Duties and Organization of the Foreign Office – Statute concerns the relationships between the officials and the Foreign Service and does not establish any rights of the citizens abroad. The Guidelines on consular assistance laid down in the Manual for Foreign Service as well as the information provided on the website of the Federal Ministry for Foreign Affairs (<www.bmeia.gv.at>) outline extent and coverage of the Austrian policy on consular protection.

3.2. Belgium

Belgium does not have legislation regulating the provision of consular protection to its nationals. Specific aspects of consular protection are regulated in a statutory law, as for instance the consular fees to be paid by citizens provided with consular protection.[15] There is no right to consular protection under Belgian law or practice, but rather a discretionary privilege. This is confirmed by the *Tribunal de Première Instance* of

---

[13] Entry into force on 1.07.1999, last amendment in 2008. Published in the State Official Gazette (*Bundesgesetzblatt, BGBl.*) BGBl. I No. 129/1999. Available also at: <http://www.ris.bka.gv.at/GeltendeFassung.wxe?Abfrage=Bundesnormen&Gesetzesnummer=10001572> (23.09.2010).

[14] See also official web site of the Austrian Ministry for Foreign Affairs (*Bundesministerium für Auswärtige Aneglegenheiten*), <http://www.bmeia.gv.at/aussenministerium/buergerservice/notfaelle-im-ausland.html> (23.09.2010).

[15] *Loi portant le tarif des taxes consulaires et des droits de chancellerie* of 30.06.1999. Available at: <http://www.careproject.eu/database/scheda.php?caseother=137> (22.04.2011).

Brussels in a judgment of 16 November 2005.[16] The Court held that consular protection cannot be demanded, but can only be requested as there is no substantive right to consular protection. It is worth mentioning that the judgment was circulated to the consular services with an explanatory note on the Judgement.[17]

3.3. Bulgaria

Article 25 para. 5 of the Bulgarian Constitution stipulates that Bulgarian citizens, residing abroad, are under the protection of the Republic of Bulgaria.[18] Furthermore, Article 5 para. 1 of the Act on Bulgarians Residing Abroad (*Закон за българите, живеещи извън Република България*)[19] contains a special provision regarding persons of Bulgarian parentage (but without Bulgarian nationality) and considering themselves as Bulgarians establishing that these citizens, although they are not Bulgarian nationals, enjoy the protection of the Bulgarian State which shall protect their interests abroad.[20] Besides, Article 44 para. 2 of the Statute of the Ministry of Foreign Affairs (*Устройствен Правилник на Министерството на външните работи*)[21] the Directorate of Consular Relations at the Ministry of Foreign Affairs provides consular services to Bulgarian and foreign natural and legal persons. However, all these legal provisions establish merely the right to consular protection without to determine its scope of protection.[22] There are no national rules on the concrete configuration of this right as there is no specific Act on consular protection.

As mentioned above, the Bulgarian Constitution establishes the right of Bulgarian citizens to consular protection so that consular protection is provided under law. However, there are no legal provisions establishing

---

16 Judgment of the Tribunal de Première Instance de Bruxelles of 16.11.2005 in the case *Charles Thijs v. L'Etat Belge*, Ref. 162/76/05. Available at: <http://www.careproject.eu/database/upload/BEcaselaw1/BEcaselaw1Text.pdf> (22.04.2011).

17 *Note à la Direction Générale des Affaires Consulaires* (13.01.2006). Ref: JL/80/SG/2003/13642. Information provided by the Ministry of Foreign Affairs of Belgium, June 2010).

18 Constitution of the Republic of Bulgaria, available at: <http://www.parliament.bg/en/const> (14.10.2010).

19 Published in State Official Gazette (*Държавен вестник*) No. 30 of 11.04.2000.

20 It is about Bulgarian minorities abroad, e.g. in Moldavia, Former Yugoslav Republic of Macedonia, Serbia etc. See BORISOV, O., *Diplomatichesko i konsulsko pravo*, Sofia, 2011, pp. 83 et seq.

21 Published in the State Official Gazette No. 64 of 18.07.2008. Last amendment of 21.12.2011. Available also at: <http://www.mfa.bg/bg/pages/view/5283>.

22 See VLADIMIROV, I., *Дипломатическо и консулско право*, 3. edition, Sofia, 2007, pp. 62 et seq.: BORISOV, O., *Дипломатическо и консулско право*, *op. cit.*, footnote 607, pp. 54 et seq.

the circumstances requiring consular protection as well as the type of protection provided by the consular officers in these cases. Therefore, it could be said that the question of "whether" there is generally a right to consular protection is stipulated by law, while the question of 'how' consular protection is provided is a matter of policy and depends basically on the discretion of the competent authorities (Ministry of Foreign Affairs and representations abroad).[23]

3.4. Croatia

Article 10 para. 1 of the Croatian Constitution establishes that the Republic of Croatia shall safeguard the rights and interests of its citizens living or residing abroad.[24] In 2013, the Croatian 1996 Foreign Service Act was amended to include the provisions on the protection of Croatian citizens abroad by the diplomatic and consular representations of other Member States as well as the protection of unrepresented Union citizens by Croatian authorities.[25]

3.5. Cyprus

In Cyprus there are no statutory laws on consular protection. Rather consular protection is provided as a matter of policy according to the Vienna Convention on Consular Relations ratified by Act 7/76 on the Vienna Convention on Consular Relations.[26] Accordingly, there is no legal right to consular protection under Cypriot law.[27]

3.6. Czech Republic

The relevant national legislation on consular protection consists of the Directive of the Ministry of Foreign Affairs on Consular Assistance to Czech Citizens in Case of Emergency No. 301366/2000-KO/5 ("Emergency Directive") as well as the Guidelines on consular protection of nationals of the EU Member States No. 00574/2004-KO/5.[28] The Czech

---

23 Interview with a representative of the Bulgarian Ministry of Foreign Affairs, July 2011.

24 Constitution of the Republic of Croatia of 22.12.1990, consolidated version of 6.07.2010 available at <http://www.sabor.hr/Default.aspx?art=2405> (12.08.2013).

25 *Zakon o vanima vanjskim poslovima*, available at <http://www.zakon.hr/z/602/Zakon-o-vanjskim-poslovima> (12.08.2013).

26 See official web site of the Cypriot Ministry of Foreign Affairs: <http://www.mfa.gov.cy/mfa/mfa2006.nsf/All/32AD3A4258FE8801C22571C400389107?OpenDocument> (12.12.2010). Act not available.

27 See information available at the official web site of the Cyprus Ministry of Foreign Affairs on the national practices on consular protection, <http://www.mfa.gov.cy/mfa/mfa2006.nsf/consular05_en/consular05_en?OpenDocument> (12.12.2010).

28 Směrnice o poskytování pomoci občanům CR, kteri se v zahranici ocitli v nouzi and Směrnice o konzulární ochraně občanů členských států EU. Available in the

Republic has no comprehensive legislation on consular protection such as a general consular Act. Consular protection is rather provided on the basis of administrative circulars issued by the Ministry of Foreign Affairs. In cases of emergency the Ministry of Foreign Affairs applies the above-mentioned Emergency Directive. Accordingly, the provision of consular protection to citizens abroad is regulated as a matter of policy ant there is no subjective right to consular protection. Instead, consular protection is regarded as a "service" offered to citizens abroad.

3.7. Denmark

Denmark provides consular protection to Danish citizens abroad under the Foreign Service Act (*Lov om Udenrigstjenesten*) No. 150 of 13 April 1983,[29] complemented by non-statutory regulations such the Instructions for the Danish Foreign Service (*Instruks for Udenrigstjenesten*) and the Executive Order on payment for services provided by the Danish foreign service.[30] Accordingly, consular assistance is provided under law and not as a matter of policy, and is considered a legal right.

3.8. Estonia

The Constitution of the Republic of Estonia stipulates that "everyone has the right to the protection of the State and of the law" and that "the Estonian State shall also protect its citizens abroad" so that the right to consular protection is a fundamental right in Estonia.[31] Besides, the Consular Act of 2009 (*Konsulaarseadus*)[32] establishes detailed rules on consular protection provided to nationals and Union citizens.[33] Consular

CARE project database, <http://www.careproject.eu/database/upload/CZguidelines/CZguidelinesTransEng.pdf> (21.03.2011).

29 Article 1 para. 3 of the Foreign Service Act: "The Foreign Service provides assistance to Danish citizens as well as assistance to Danish businesses in their commercial relations with foreign countries." Foreign Service Act available at: <https://www.retsinformation.dk/Forms/R0710.aspx?id=72039> (17.12.2010). Translation by Mr Caspar Visser.

30 *Bekendtgørelse om betaling for tjenestehandlinger i udenrigstjenesten*, Ministry of Foreign Affairs, Executive Order No. 1228 of 10.12.2009. Available at: <http://www.careproject.eu/database/upload/DAfees/DAfeesTransEng.pdf> (12.01.2011).

31 Section 13 para. 1 of the Estonian Constitution. Available at: <http://www.president.ee/en/republic-of-estonia/the-constitution/index.html> (13.01.2011).

32 Consular Act adopted on 20.05.2009, published in *Riigi Teataja* (Official State Gazette, hereinafter RT) RT I 2009, 29, 175. Available at: <https://www.riigiteataja.ee/akt/13186034> (02.04.2011). In English: <http://www.careproject.eu/database/upload/ETlaw001/ETlaw001TransEng.pdf> (02.04.2011). The Consular Act of 2009 replaced the former Consular Act of 2004, RT I 2003, 78, 527; 2004, 14, 92; 30, 208; 2005, 33, 243; 39, 308; 2006, 14, 111; 58, 439.

33 Chapter 5 of the Estonian Consular Act.

protection is thus provided under law and the right to consular protection is a fundamental right.

3.9. Finland

Consular protection is provided in Finland on the basis of the Consular Services Act No. 498 of 22 April 1999 (*Konsulipalvelulaki*).[34] Articles 1 and 2 of the Consular Act establish the right to consular protection as a right conferred upon individuals.[35]

3.10. France

There are no statutory provisions in France addressing the provision of consular protection. There are indeed some Government Decrees on the internal organisation, etc. of the French representations abroad;[36] however, these legal norms establish no legal right to consular protection. As a consequence, consular protection is provided as a matter of policy and there is no legal right thereto.

3.11. Germany

The right to consular protection is regulated by the Act on Consular Officers, their Functions and Powers (Consular Act) (*Gesetz über die Konsularbeamten, ihre Aufgaben und Befugnisse*) of 11 September

[34] Finnish Consular Services Act available at: <http://www.finlex.fi/en/laki/kaannokset/1999/en19990498.pdf> (21.11.2010). In English: <http://www.careproject.eu/database/upload/FIkonsulipalvelulaki/FIkonsulipalvelulakiTransEng.pdf> (16.03.2011).

[35] Article 1 Finnish Consular Services Act: "For the purposes of this Act, consular services mean such consular functions set forth in Article 5 of the Vienna Convention on Consular Relations (FTS 50/1980) as may be exercised by a diplomatic mission or consular post that is part of the Finnish foreign service (hereafter referred to as mission), for the purpose of providing assistance to individual persons or legal persons or to protect their interests, and the provision of which under this Act fall within the functions of the foreign affairs administration, unless the service in question is subject to other provisions or orders."

Article 2 of the Finnish Consular Services Act: "Unless a consular service is subject to other provisions, consular services referred to in Chapters 3 to 10 of this Act may be provided for a Finnish legal person or a Finnish citizen or for a foreign citizen residing permanently in Finland, who is in possession of or has been granted a permit to reside or work in Finland either permanently or in a comparable manner."

[36] Le Décret No. 69-222 du 6 mars 1969 relatif au statut particulier des agents diplomatiques et consulaires (version consolidée le 23 février 2008) [Decree on statute of diplomatic and consular officers], Le Décret No. 76-548 du 16 juin 1976 relatif aux consuls généraux, aux consuls et vice-consuls honoraires et aux agents consulaires [Decree on general consuls, honorary consuls and vice-consuls and consular officers]. Available at: <http://admi.net/jo/20020503/MAEF0210016D.html> (18.02.2011).

1974.[37] Furthermore, the Instructions of the Ministry of Foreign Affairs to the German Representations abroad: "Aid for Germans abroad" (hereafter: Consular Instructions) as of 31 March 2005,[38] as well as the Act on Fees for Public Services Abroad of 1978 (*Auslandskostengesetz*) are worth mentioning.[39]

The German Consular Act of 1974 establishes a subjective right to consular protection, which has been confirmed also by the German Federal Constitutional Court holding that an obligation is imposed upon the State to protect its citizens abroad.[40] However, the Consular Act grants to the consular officers a certain scope of discretion.[41] This discretion is regulated by the Consular Instructions of the Ministry of Foreign Affairs to the German representations abroad. Due to this scope of discretion of the consular officers, there is only a right to a decision free of abuse of discretion and no subjective right to a determined action of the public administration. In particular circumstances, a diminution of the administrative discretion to "zero" is possible, when just one single decision is the appropriate/right one. In this case, the right holder has the right to claim a determined action/ decision (administrative act etc.) of the public administration.

The Consular Instructions, which regulate the scope of discretion conceded to the consular officers, are internal directives without external effects for citizens. This means that they cannot be cause of action. However, internal instructions obtain indirectly external effects when the administration, acting in accordance with those instructions, establishes a correspondent administrative practice. In this case, the established administrative practice in conjunction with the prohibition of discrimination according to Article 3 of the German Basic Law may constitute a cause of action of the right holder (Self Commitment of the Public Administration).

---

37 Published in the State Official Gazette (*Bundesgesetzblatt*) I 1974, 2317. The Act was lastly amended on 27.12.2003. Available also at: <https://www.juris.de/purl/gesetze/_ges/KonsG> (13.12.2009).

38 Not published.

39 Published in the State Official Gazette 1978 Part I No. 11, Page 301 ff., from 28.02.1978. The Act was lastly modified in 2004. Available also at: <http://www.gesetze-im-internet.de/bundesrecht/akostg/gesamt.pdf> (31.05.2010).

40 See Judgment of the German Federal Constitutional Court 37, 217 (p. 241), available at: <http://www.servat.unibe.ch/dfr/bv037217.html> (23.02.2010); 40, 141 (pp. 177 ff.), available at: <http://www.servat.unibe.ch/dfr/bv040141.html> (23.02.2010); 55, 349 (364 ff.), available at: <http://dejure.org/dienste/vernetzung/rechtsprechung?Text=BVerfGE%2055,%20349> (23.02.2010).

41 The general clause of Article 5 para. 1 of the Consular Act reads: Consular officers *should* provide German citizens with the *necessary* aid" (emphasis added by author.)

3.12. Greece

Article 52, para. 1, sub b) of Act No. 3566/2007[42] stipulates that the consular authorities "provide every possible assistance to Greek citizens and persons of Greek origin, protect their rights and interests […]". Consular protection is thus provided under law as a subjective right.

3.13. Hungary

Pursuant to Article 69 of the Hungarian Constitution "all Hungarian nationals are entitled to enjoy the protection of the Republic of Hungary while legally residing or staying abroad".[43] In addition, Act XLVI of 2001 on consular protection[44] establishes that "The Republic of Hungary performs the protection of the interests of Hungarian citizens abroad by way of consular protection".[45] Accordingly, the right to consular protection is established as a fundamental right by the Hungarian Constitution, whereby the substance of this right is further developed by Act XLVI on consular protection as well as by several Ministry Decrees. Accordingly, consular protection is granted under law as a legal right to Hungarian nationals and not as a matter of policy.

3.14. Ireland

In Ireland, there is no national legislation dealing specifically with consular protection. The Diplomatic Relations and Immunities Act of 1967 incorporates into Irish law the provisions of the 1967 Vienna Convention on Consular Relations, but limits itself to regulate issues such as immunities and privileges of consular officers.[46] Accordingly, there is no right to consular protection under Irish law, but consular protection is provided as a matter of policy.

---

42 Οργανισμός του Υπουργείου Εξωτερικών της Ελληνικής Δημοκρατίας, Organization of the Hellenic Ministry of Foreign Affairs [Act on the Organisation of the Ministry of Foreign Affairs] published in the Official Gazette of the Government of the Hellenic Republic, Vol. I, No. 117, 5.06.2007. Available also at: <http://www1.mfa.gr/organismos-ypex/> (06.02.2011).

43 Constitution of the Republic of Hungary, available at: <http://www.mkogy.hu/parl_en.htm> (26.12.2011).

44 2001. évi XLVI. törvény a konzuli védelemről, available at: <http://www.mfa.gov.hu/kum/hu/bal/Konzuli_informaciok/Kulfoldiek_beutazasa/Jogszabalyok/2001_evi.htm> (17.11.2010).

45 Article 1 para. 1 of Act XLVI of 2001, available at: <http://www.mfa.gov.hu/kum/en/bal/consular_services/consularservices.htm> (17.11.2010).

46 Diplomatic Relations and Immunities Act of 1967 available at: <http://www.irishstatutebook.ie/1967/en/act/pub/0008/index.html> (14.11.2010).

3.15. Italy

Consular protection is provided by the Italian authorities on the basis of several legal provisions. Worth mention are the Circular of Ministries of Foreign Affairs of 8 June 1993, "European cooperation policy: consular protection of EU citizens in third countries" as well as Decree of the President of the Republic, 5/1/1967, No. 18, "Organization of Administration of Foreign Affairs".[47] Recently, the Decree of the President of the Republic, 5/1/1967, No. 200, "Provisions on consular functions and powers" has been replaced by a legislative decree on organisation and functions of consular services.[48] Consular protection is accordingly provided under law as a right conferred upon individuals.

3.16. Latvia

Article 98 of the Constitution of the Republic of Latvia (*Satversme*) stipulates that everyone having a Latvian passport shall be protected by the State when abroad.[49] Besides, the 1994 Act on Consular Regulations (*Konsulārais reglaments*) contains detailed arrangements regarding consular protection of Latvian citizens abroad.[50] Therefore, it could be concluded that consular protection is a fundamental right under Latvian law granted to individuals.

3.17. Lithuania

National rules on consular protection are provided by a number of legal acts. First and foremost, it should be highlighted that Article 13 para. 1 of the Constitution provides that the State of Lithuania shall protect its citizens abroad.[51] The same notion, although, with a different wording, is reiterated by

---

47 Ordinamento dell'amministrazione degli affari esteri d.p.r. 5 gennaio 1967, No. 18 e successive modificazioni e integrazioni. Available at: <http://www.esteri.it/mae/normative/Normativa_Consolare/ParteGenerale/DPR_18_1967.pdf> (15.11.2010).

48 Decreto Legislativo of 03.12.2011, No. 7, Ordinamento e funzioni degli uffici consolari, ai sensi dell'articolo 14, comma 18, della legge 28 novembre 2005, No. 246 (GU No. 110 del 13-5-2011). Available at: <http://www.careproject.eu/database/upload/ITdpr200/ITdpr200Text.pdf> (15.06.2011).

49 Constitution of the Republic of Latvia, available at: <http://www.saeima.lv/en/legislation/constitution> (03.02.2011).

50 Act on Consular Regulations of 03.07.1994, published in *Latvijas Vēstnesis* (Official gazette) on 06.11.1996. Available also at: <http://www.likumi.lv/doc.php?id=57318&menu_body=KDOC>.

Worth mentioning is also Regulations on Return Certificates of 25.08.2008, published in *Latvijas Vēstnesis* on 29.08.2008.

51 Constitution of the Republic of Lithuania, available at: <http://www3.lrs.lt/home/Konstitucija/Constitution.htm> (04.01.2011).

the Citizenship Act[52] which provides that the State of Lithuania shall protect and take care of its citizens beyond the borders of the Republic of Lithuania (Art. 5). These provisions set up the basic principles of consular protection while more details are included in the Act on Consular Statute (*Konsulinis Statutas*) (hereinafter Consular Statute).[53] The Consular Statute establishes that consular assistance are consular functions performed upon request (or also without it) of citizens of the Republic of Lithuania. Accordingly, the right to consular protection is a fundamental right enshrined in the Lithuanian Constitution. More detailed arrangements regarding the question of how consular protection is provided are set by the Consular Statute.

3.18. Luxembourg

Luxembourg authorities provide consular protection as a matter of policy since there is no statutory regulation addressing this issue.[54] Therefore, consular protection is not a legal right in Luxembourg but rather a discretional State power which is exercised by the State taking into consideration the circumstances of each individual case and also within the framework of the abovementioned agreement with Belgium.

---

[52] Lithuanian Citizenship Act of 17.09.2002, No. IX-1078. Last amendment: 15 July 2008, No. X-1709. Available at: <http://www.coe.int/t/dghl/standardsetting/nationality/National%20legislation/Lithuania-Law%20on%20Citizenship%202003.pdf> (04.01.2011).

[53] Act on Consular Statute, 9.05.1995, No. I-886, published in *Valstybės Žinios*, 1995, No. 43-1047. Last amendment: Act of the Republic of Lithuania modifying the Consular Statute, 25 May 2006, No. X-169, published in *Valstybės Žinios*, 17 June 2006, No. 68-2492. Available also at: <http://www3.lrs.lt/pls/inter3/dokpaieska.showdoc_l?p_id=17774> (04.01.2011).

[54] It should be noted that there is an Agreement between the Grand Duchy of Luxembourg and the Kingdom of Belgium on consular cooperation of 30.09.1965 (*Convention entre le Grand-Duché de Luxembourg et le Royaume de Belgique relative à la coopération dans le domaine consulaire*). Act of sanctioning of the abovementioned agreement of 16 August 1966, Doc. Parl. No. 1197, Sess. Ord. 1965-1966 (*Loi du 16 août 1966 portant approbation de la Convention entre le Grand-Duché de Luxembourg et le Royaume de Belgique relative à la coopération dans le domaine consulaire, signée à Bruxelles le 30 septembre 1965*). Available at: <http://www.legilux.public.lu/rgl/1966/A/0954/1.pdf>. This is a general agreement on consular cooperation establishing the provision of certain assistance to the citizens of Luxembourg covered also by the scope of protection stipulate by Article 20 TEC. However, the Act contains no special provisions on consular protection. The Act of 16.08.1966 incorporates the text of the agreement with Belgium establishing that the Luxembourg Government may request the services of the Belgian officials in order to provide consular protection (Article 1 para. 2 of the Agreement). Neither the Law nor the Agreement grant a right to consular protection to the citizens but rather establish cooperation in order to make effective the consular protection to be provided to the citizens of a small country by means of the consular service of another country.

3.19. Malta

Consular protection is not provided under law in Malta. The Consular Conventions Act contains no provisions on consular protection but only provisions regarding immunities and privileges of consular officers.[55] According to information provided by the Ministry of Foreign Affairs,[56] Malta offers consular protection as a matter of policy on the basis of respect for fundamental rights, such as the protection of a person's life, health, personal freedom and security. Accordingly, there is no legal right to consular protection in Malta.

3.20. The Netherlands

Neither the Dutch Consular Act (*Consulaire Wet*) of 25 July 1871[57] relating to consular functions in a similar way as the Vienna Convention on Consular Relations nor the Consular Decree (*Consulair Besluit*) of 23 November 1981[58] establish a subjective right to consular protection. The fact that under Dutch law there is no right to consular protection was confirmed by the Court of Appeal of The Hague in the case The State of The Netherlands v. Van Dam of 25 November 2004.[59] It is worth mentioning that under the Consular Act and the Consular Decree the decision whether or not to assist a national and if so in which way is left to the discretion of the Ministry of Foreign Affairs, respectively to the representations abroad. Accordingly, consular protection is provided as a matter of policy under Dutch law leaving the competent authorities a wide scope of discretion.

[55] Consular Conventions Act, Chapter 144 of the Laws of Malta (enacted by Act XXXI of 1955, as amended by Emergency Ordinance XV of 1958; Ordinance XXV of 1962; Legal Notice 46 of 1965 and Act I of 1966). Available at: <http://www.imldb.iom.int/viewDocument.do?id=%7BD6DC23DD-EFBD-4D91-A42A-E34D1D88286A%7D> (10.12.2010).

[56] See official web site of the Maltese Ministry of Foreign Affairs: <http://www.mfa.gov.mt/default.aspx?MDIS=13> (03.02.2011).

[57] Wet van 25 juli 1871, houdende regeling van de bevoegdheid der consulaire ambtenaren tot het opmaken van burgerlijke akten, en van de consulaire regtsmagt (Consular Act of 25.07.1871 governing the powers of consular officers to establish civil status records and the consular jurisdiction), available at: <http://www.wetboek-online.nl/wet/Consulaire%20Wet.html> (23.11.2010).

[58] *Besluit van 23 november 1981, tot vaststelling van een nieuw Consulair besluit* (Royal Decree of 23.11.1981 on the adoption of a new consular decree. Available at: <http://lexius.nl/consulair-besluit> (23.11.2010).

[59] Judgment of the Court of Appeal of The Hague in the case The State of The Netherlands v. Van Dam of 25 November 2004, LJN: AR7484, Gerechtshof 's-Gravenhage, 02/43.

3.21. Poland

The right to consular protection is enshrined in the Polish Constitution as a fundamental right. Article 36 of the Constitution establishes that "Polish citizens shall, during a stay abroad, have the right to protection by the Polish State".[60] In addition, Article 37 stipulates that "anyone, being under the authority of the Polish State, shall enjoy the freedoms and rights ensured by the Constitution". Worth mentioning is also the Act on the Functions of Consular Officers of 13 February 1984 (*Ustawa o funkcjach konsulów Rzeczypospolitej Polskiej z dnia 13 lutego 1984, Dz. U. No. 9 poz. 34*), with further amendments.[61] According to Article 10 of this Act, consuls shall protect the rights and interests of Polish nationals. Besides, the Act establishes the concrete duties of the consular officers in different situations of distress. In summary, Polish nationals enjoy a fundamental right to consular protection enshrined in the national Constitution and further regulated by the Act on the Functions of the Consul of 1984.

3.22. Portugal

The right to consular protection is a fundamental right also in Portugal. Article 14 of the Portuguese Constitution states that "Portuguese citizens who find themselves or reside abroad enjoy the State's protection for the exercise of rights and are subjected to the duties that are not incompatible with their absence from the country."[62] Further details on the right to consular protection are regulated by the Consular Regulation (*Regulamento Consular*), approved by Decree-Law 381/97, of 30 December 1997, and amended by Decree-Law 162/2006 of 08 August 2006[63] and Decree-Law 71/2009 of 31 March 2009.[64] The

---

60 Constitution of the Republic of Poland, available at: <http://www.sejm.gov.pl/prawo/konst/angielski/kon1.htm> (01.12.2010).

61 The consolidated version of the Statute on the functions of consuls is published in the Journal of Laws (Dz. U. No. 215 poz 1823, 2002), including further amendments. Available at: <http://isap.sejm.gov.pl/DetailsServlet?id=WDU20022151823> (01.12.2010). In English: <http://www.careproject.eu/database/upload/PLfunctionsofconsuls/PLfunctionsofconsulsTransEng.pdf>.

62 Constitution of the Republic of Portugal, available at: <http://app.parlamento.pt/site_antigo/ingles/cons_leg/Constitution_VII_revisao_definitive.pdf> (23.11.2010).

63 *Ministério dos Negócios Estrangeiros Decreto-Lei No. 162/2006 de 8 de Agosto* [Decree-Law 162/2006], published in *Diário da República* (State Official Gazette), 1.a série – No. 152 – 8 de Agosto de 2006, p. 5658. Available also at: <http://www.dre.pt/pdf1s/2006/08/15200/56585670.pdf> (12.11.2010).

64 *Ministério dos Negócios Estrangeiros Decreto-Lei No. 71/2009 de 31 de Março* [Decree-Act 71/2009], published in *Diário da República*, 1.ª série – No. 63 – 31 de Março de 2009, p. 1961. Available also at: <http://dre.pt/pdf1s/2009/03/06300/0196101973.pdf> (12.11.2010).

Act defines the objectives and competences of consular services and the legal principles which their actions must observe. Among other functions, the consulates shall protect the rights and legitimate interests of the Portuguese, defend their rights as citizens of the European Union and provide them with social support (article 2, b), c) and d)) of the Consular Regulation).

Also relevant is Decree-Law 53/94, of 24 February 1994, modified by Decree-Law 430/99, of 22 October 1999, which establishes a national administrative authority (*Direcção-Geral dos Assuntos Consulares e Comunidades Portuguesas*) that coordinates the action of the Portuguese consulates, and defines, promotes and executes measures of protection and support to the Portuguese communities abroad.[65]

By way of conclusion it can be said that in Portugal the right to consular protection has the status of a fundamental right conferred upon individuals.

3.23. Romania

The Constitution of Romania establishes in Article 17 that "Romanian citizens abroad shall enjoy the protection of the Romanian State and they are required to perform their duties, except those that are not compatible with their absence from the country".[66] There is no statutory provision in Romania stipulating more detailed rules regarding the provision of consular protection. Rather, further details are established by the Consular Guidance Book issued by the Ministry of Foreign Affairs.[67] Accordingly, in Romania consular protection is conceived of as a fundamental right granted to Romanian citizens.

3.24. Slovakia

According to Article 14 para. 2 a) Act No. 575/2001 of 12 December 2001 on Powers of the Ministries (*Zákon o organizácií činnosti vlády a organizácií ústrednej štátnej správy*),[68] the Ministry of Foreign Affairs of the Slovak Republic provides protection of rights and interests of Slovak citizens abroad. On the basis of the obligation imposed upon the Ministry of Foreign Affairs, the provision of consular protection is considered to

65 See official web site of the General Directorate, <http://www.secomunidades.pt/web/guest/PostosConsulares> (24.10.2011).

66 Constitution of the Republic of Romania, available at: <http://www.cdep.ro/pls/dic/site.page?id=371> (13.11.2010).

67 Consular Guide for Support of Romanian Citizens Abroad, available at: <http://www.careproject.eu/database/scheda.php?trans=_en&caseother=106> (12.05.2011).

68 The Act was lastly amended on 02.11.2010. Available at: <http://www.vyvlastnenie.sk/predpisy/zakon-o-organizacii-cinnosti-vlady-a-organizacii ustrednej-statnej-spravy/> (12.04.2011).

be a legal right conferred upon individuals whereby since there is no further statutory regulation as to the configuration of the right to consular protection, the question of what kind of assistance is covered by the right to consular protection is governed by the Vienna Convention on Consular Relations and the discretion of the competent State authorities.[69] Hence, the question on "whether" consular protection shall be provided or not is stipulated by Act 575/2001, while the question on 'how' consular protection is provided depends basically on the discretion of the competent authorities.

3.25. Slovenia

Slovenian consular and diplomatic authorities provide consular protection to Slovenian nationals abroad under the Foreign Affairs Act.[70] Worth mention are also the Instructions for Honorary Consular Officers of the Republic of Slovenia[71] as well as the Act on Travel Documents.[72]

Consular protection is provided to Slovenian nationals abroad as a legal right under Article 24 of the Foreign Affairs Act, which establishes that consular officers shall protect the interests of its citizens and legal entities when abroad, and conduct consular-legal affairs. The Foreign Affairs Act was amended *inter alia* by the Act on Amendments and Modifications of the Foreign Affairs Act introducing a new Article 24 a into the Foreign Affairs Act.[73] According to Article 24a of the Foreign Affairs Act "The Republic of Slovenia ensures protection to citizens of the European Union, as envisaged by the Decision of the Representatives of the Governments of the Member States meeting within the Council of 19 December 1995 regarding protection for citizens of the European Union by diplomatic and consular representations (95/553/EC), [...]".

---

69 See Report on Slovak legislation and practices in the field of consular protection by Katharina Getlik, Instituto Europeo de Derecho, not published yet.

70 Zakon o zunanjih zadevah – 7.6.2001 (spremembe in dopolnitve: 8.8.2003, 25.7.2008, 28.12.2009); neuradno prečiščeno besedilo objavljeno: 12.1.2010 – ZZZ-1-NPB3, published in the Official Journal of the Republic of Slovenia No. 113/03 (20.11.2003). Available in English at: <http://www.careproject.eu/database/upload/SLforeignaffairsact/SLforeignaffairsactTransEng.pdf> (21.06.2011).

71 Navodilo za častne konzularne funkcionarje Republike Slovenije – of 21.03.2007 – ZKD-1154/07. Available at: <http://www.mzz.gov.si/fileadmin/pageuploads/Zakonodaja_in_dokumenti/INSTRUCTION_Honorary_Consular_Officers_2007.pdf> (13.11.2010).

72 *Zakono potnih listinah uradno prečiščeno besedilo (ZPLD-1-UPB3)*. Consolidated text, published in the Official Journal No. 3/06 (10.01.2006). Available also at: <http://www.uradni-list.si/1/objava.jsp?urlid=200962&stevilka=2959> (13.11.2010).

73 Published in the State Official Journal, No. 76/08 of 25.07.2008.

Accordingly, consular protection is conferred as a legal right both to nationals and non-national EU citizens.

3.26. Spain

In Spain, consular protection is subject to regulation by diverse statutory norms. Spanish citizens abroad enjoy protection by diplomatic and consular protection under Act 40/2006 of 14 December 2006 on the Statute of Spanish Citizens Abroad (*Ley del Estatuto de la ciudadanía española en el exterior*).[74] The Act confers the right to consular protection upon individuals[75] conceiving it of as a right guaranteeing on its part the fundamental rights of the citizens abroad. In this sense, Article 2 a) of the Act stipulates as the first of the objectives of the Act, "the regulation of the rights of citizens abroad in order to guarantee their exercise by means of the commitment of the public authorities to promote the conditions necessary to make those rights real and effective". Article 5 of Act 40/2006 refers to "assistance and protection of Spanish nationals abroad" and is included into Chapter 1 on participative rights.

Moreover, Order AEX/1059/2002 of 25 April of the Ministry of Foreign Affairs on basic regulation of financial aid for consular protection and assistance abroad (*Orden AEX/1059/2002 de bases reguladoras de las ayudas de protección y asistencia consulares en el extranjero*)[76] establishes the requirements for Spanish nationals to receive financial aid in a situation of distress.

In addition, it should be mentioned that Article 1 c) of Royal Decree 1748/2010 on basic organizational structure of the Ministry of Foreign Affairs and Cooperation[77] establishes that the competences of the Ministry of Foreign Affairs are, *inter alia*, to implement an

---

74 *Ley 40/2006 de 14 de diciembre, del Estatuto de la ciudadanía española en el exterior*, published in Boletín Oficial del Estado (BOE) (Spanish State Official Gazette) of 15.12.2006, No. 299. Available at: <http://www.boe.es/boe/dias/2006/12/15/pdfs/A44156-44166.pdf> (30.10.2010).

75 Article 2 of Act 40/2006 refers to the subjective field of application of the Act establishing the beneficiaries of the rights abroad.

76 *Orden AEX/1059/2002 de bases reguladoras de las ayudas de protección y asistencia consulares en el extranjero*, published in BOE of 14.05.2002, No. 115. Available at: <http://www.boe.es/boe/dias/2002/05/14/pdfs/A17475-17477.pdf> (30.10.2010). Order AEX/1059/2002 was amended by Order AEC/3119/2005, of 26 September, published in BOE of 10.10.2005, No. 242. Available at: <http://www.boe.es/boe/dias/2005/10/10/pdfs/A33180-33180.pdf> (30.10.2010).

77 Real Decreto 1748/2010, de 23 de diciembre, por el que se desarrolla la estructura orgánica básica del Ministerio de Asuntos Exteriores y de Cooperación, published in BOE of 14.01.2011, No. 12. Available at: <http://www.boe.es/boe/dias/2011/01/14/pdfs/BOE-A-2011-696.pdf> (24.01.2011).

appropriate end effective policy for the protection of Spanish citizens abroad. Accordingly, consular protection is provided under law in Spain and has the legal character of a subjective right.[78]

3.27. Sweden

In Sweden, only one of the types of consular assistance is regulated by a comprehensive statutory provision – that is the provision of financial aid to Swedish citizens in distress abroad. According to Article 6 para. 1 of the Act on Consular Financial Assistance of 26 June 2003 (*Lag om konsulärt ekonomiskt bistånd*, 2003:491),[79] a distressed person or a person who has experienced difficulty abroad and therefore is in need of financial assistance has the right to consular financial assistance if the need cannot be met in another way and if it is considered reasonable to provide consular financial assistance. The Act on Consular Financial Assistance has been complemented by the Regulation containing Instructions for the Foreign Representations (*Förordning med instruktion för utrikesrepresentationen*, 1992:247, amended on various occasions, most recently on 1 July 2009),[80] that contains references to other types of consular protection, as well as by the Decree on Consular Financial Assistance (*Regeringskansliets föreskrifter om konsulärt ekonomiskt bistånd m.m.*, *UF* 2003:10).[81] Besides, a number of explanatory statements concerning the content of the Act on Consular Financial Assistance are to be found in the so-called *travaux préparatoires* of the governmental bill (proposition) 2002/03:69.[82]

Accordingly, Swedish authorities provide consular protection to Swedish citizens abroad under the Act on Consular Financial Assistance, complemented by lower ranking regulations. Consequently, at least the right to receive financial aid in a situation of distress abroad is considered to be a subjective right.

---

78 See also NUÑEZ HERNÁNDEZ, J./ MARTÍ MARTÍ, X., *La función consular en el derecho español*, 3. edition, Madrid 2009; JIMÉNEZ-UGARTE, J., *Práctica consular e Inmigración*, Valencia, 2008.

79 Lag om konsulärt ekonomiskt bistånd, available at: <http://62.95.69.3/SFSdoc/03/030491.PDF> (14.10.2011). In English: <http://www.careproject.eu/database/upload/SV2003_491/SV2003_491TransEng.pdf> (14.10.2011).

80 Förordning med instruktion för utrikesrepresentationen, available at: <http://se.vlex.com/vid/ouml-1992-utrikesrepresentationen-50448809> (14.10.2011).

81 Regeringskansliets föreskrifter om konsulärt ekonomiskt bistånd, available at: <http://beta.riksdagen.se/sv/Dokument-Lagar/Utredningar/Statens-offentliga-utredningar/Utrikesforvaltning-i-varldskla_GZB321/> (14.10.2011).

82 *Proposition 2002/03:69 En ny lag om konsulärt ekonomiskt bistånd* [Draft bill on the Swedish Consular Financial Assistance Act]. Available at: <http://www.riksdagen.se/webbnav/index.aspx?nid=37&dok_id=GQ0369>. Preparatory works on proposed laws are subsidiary sources of law. They are used as a supporting means in interpreting the law.

3.28. The United Kingdom

There are no statutory provisions under UK law dealing with consular protection. According to the statement of the UK Government within the consultation on the European Commission's Green Paper on Consular Protection of March 2007, consular assistance is provided to British nationals abroad as a matter of policy, so that there is no statutory obligation to provide consular assistance and, thus, no legal right to consular protection.[83] It is therefore all the more surprising that the UK government argued in the *Gibraltar* case before the Court of Justice that consular protection is like freedom of movement and residence a legal right.[84] This seems to be rather the unofficial position of the UK government since according to Mr Shehzad CHARANIA of the Foreign & Commonwealth Office, the official position of the government is still not to recognise a legal subjective right to consular protection conferred upon British nationals.[85]

4. Scope of Coverage and Limits to the Right to Consular Protection

4.1. A Multilevel Right

The analysis of the national legal rules and practices shows that eighteen of the twenty-eight Member States provide consular protection as a legal right. These are Bulgaria, Croatia, Denmark, Germany, Estonia, Finland, Greece, Hungary, Italy, Latvia, Lithuania, Poland, Portugal, Romania, Slovenia, Slovakia, Spain and Sweden. In nine of those Member States the right to consular protection is enshrined in the national constitution (Bulgaria, Croatia, Estonia, Hungary, Latvia, Lithuania, Poland, Portugal and Romania).

---

83 Letter of the Minister for Europe of the United Kingdom in response to the Commission's Green Paper on Diplomatic and consular protection of Union citizens in third countries of 21.03.2007, section 1.7: "British nationals do not have a legal right to consular assistance overseas. The UK Government is under no general obligation under domestic or international law to provide consular assistance (or exercise diplomatic protection). Consular assistance is provided as a matter of policy, which is set out in the public guide, 'Support for British Nationals Abroad: A Guide'." Available at: <http://www.publications.parliament.uk/pa/cm200607/cmselect/cmeuleg/41-xvi/4104.htm>.

84 See Judgment of the Court of Justice of 12.09.2006 in the case 145/04, *Kingdom of Spain v United Kingdom of Great Britain and Northern Ireland*, ECR 2006, p. I-7917, para. 54: "The United Kingdom also argues that some rights which under the Treaty are conferred only on citizens can be extended by Member States to such persons, such as the **right** to the protection of the diplomatic or consular authorities." (Emphasis added by author).

85 Speech of Mr Shehzad CHARANIA at the conference "Diplomatic and Consular Protection in the 21st Century" on 3 May 2011, held at the British Institute of International and Comparative Law in London.

However, there are ten Member States that provide consular protection merely as a matter of policy and do not recognise under national law an individual right to consular protection. These are Austria, Belgium, Cyprus, the Czech Republic, France, Ireland, Luxembourg, Malta, the Netherlands and the United Kingdom.

This outcome leads to the conclusion that would Article 23 TFEU refer to national rules not only as regarding the question which type of assistance is provided but also to the question of whether consular protection is provided at all, the legal position conferred under Article 23 TFEU would not be the same for all unrepresented Union citizens in third countries but would be contingent on the choice of Member State to be approached for consular protection.

As a consequence, it can be assumed that were the citizens aware of which Member States provide consular protection as a legal right, unrepresented EU citizens would prefer to approach for help the diplomatic or consular mission of a Member State, whose national rules establish a legal right to consular protection, due to the stronger legal position conferred by a legal right (judicial, institutional and other guarantees). This could lead to a "protection shopping"[86] by unrepresented Union citizens choosing preferably among those Member States recognising a legal right to consular protection. In this case, Member States that provide consular protection as a legal right would be more heavily burdened as those denying generally the existence of such a right.[87]

Besides, disconnecting the right to consular protection from Union law could deprive the equal-treatment right from any practicability in those cases where pursuant to national law or practices the consular officers may due to their wide scope of discretion decide not to provide consular protection to an unrepresented Union citizen in distress. This would mean that the right to equal treatment as to how consular protection is provided would be of no avail if consular officers were free to decline to provide consular protection at all, without any possibility for the unrepresented Union citizen concerned to seek redress.[88]

---

86 See also in this sense DOLZER, R., "Diplomatic protection of Foreign Nationals" in *Encyclopedia of Public International Law (EPIL)*, Vol. 10 (1987), p. 121. and STEIN, T., "Die Regelung des diplomatischen Schutzes im Vertrag über die Europäische Union", in *Der diplomatische Schutz im Völker- und Europarecht. Aktuelle Probleme und Entwicklungstendenzen*, Georg Ress/Thorsten Stein (ed.), Baden-Baden, 1996, p. 105.

87 HATJE, A., "Kommentar zu Artikel 23 AEUV", in *EU Kommentar*, J. Schwarze (ed.), Baden-Baden, 2012, para. 14.

88 For instance, an unrepresented citizen A in a third country asks the consulate of Member State B for help after falling victim of a robbery whereby his passport, credit

A comparison with other citizens' rights as the right to vote and stand as a candidate at municipal elections and in elections to the European Parliament, show that those rights refer to equal treatment under the conditions established by national law[89] as regarding the design of voting and standing as a candidate whereas there could be no doubt that a Union citizen residing in a Member State different from his/her Member State of nationality has a subjective right to vote and stand as a candidate regardless of whether the Member State of residence confers such a subjective right under national law to its own nationals or even has no statutory rules on this matter.[90] The functional and structural similarities between the rights to vote and stand as a candidate in municipal and European Parliament elections, on the one side, and the right to consular protection, on the other side, as citizens' rights stemming from the Union citizenship status suggest that in analogical interpretation the existence of a right to consular protection may not be contingent on the existence of such a right under national law and that the "conditions" referred to in Article 23 TFEU and Article 46 of the Charter correspond to the question of how consular protection is provided in terms of procedures, types of assistance, etc.

Picking up on IANNIELLO SALICETI's proposal to link the conditions in terms of Article 23 TFEU to the consular protection standards stipulated in Decision 95/553/EC, it should be pointed out that in fact, although Decision 95/553/EC lacks specific provisions on the concrete protection measures to be offered to unrepresented Union citizens ('how' of consular protection), it precisely stipulates together with Article 23 TFEU the "conditions" for the right-holders in order to be entitled to consular protection by a Member State: an unrepresented Union citizen in a third country who suffers at least one of the situations of distress established by Decision 95/553/EC and Decision 96/409/CFSP.

---

cards and cash have been stolen and he suffered bodily harms. He has been refused to be provided medical care in the local hospitals since he has no travel insurance and no financial means to pay for the treatment. Besides, he doesn't know how he should proceed in order to report the offence. The consular officers in the consulate of Member State B refuse to provide any help due to work overload.

89 Article 22 para. 1, first clause TFEU: "Every citizen of the Union residing in a Member State of which he is not a national shall have the right to vote and to stand as a candidate at municipal elections in the Member State in which he resides, under the same conditions as nationals of that State.", Article 22 para. 2, second clause TFEU: "[…] every citizen of the Union residing in a Member State of which he is not a national shall have the right to vote and to stand as a candidate in elections to the European Parliament in the Member State, in which he resides, under the same conditions as nationals of that State."

90 IANNIELLO SALICETI, A., "The Protection of EU Citizens Abroad…", p. 96, *op. cit.*, footnote 5.

Thus, it should be distinguished between the requirements to be complied with in order for an individual to be entitled to consular protection, stipulated by Article 23 TFEU in conjunction with Decision 95/553/EC and Decision 96/409/CFSP, and the legal consequences of the compliance with these requirements which are the actions that are (concretely) performed in order to provide protection, established by national rules on consular protection.[91]

Member States may not alter by means of national legislation the first block of requirements, i.e. those established by Article 23 TFEU in conjunction with Decision 95/553/EC and Decision 96/409/CFSP, adding for instance further conditions to be fulfilled by unrepresented Union citizens in order to be entitled to ask for help. In a similar vein, consular officers may not be awarded a scope of discretion as to the assessment of the existence of those conditions.[92] In contrast, the equal-treatment character of the right to consular protection admits indeed a wide scope of discretion of the Member States as to the measures to be employed in situations of distress as well as on the part of national authorities as to the choice among several possible remedies capable of providing relief.

This approach is confirmed also by the very existence of Decision 95/553/EC: if Article 23 TFEU was referring in all aspects to the national rules of the Member States on consular protection, then it would not have been necessary to establish situations in which consular protection is provided; rather, the national provisions on consular protection could have been applied in order to determine in which situations unrepresented Union citizens would be entitled to consular protection.

The structure of the right to consular protection as involving in its context not only the interaction with international law rules due to its extraterritorial character but also Union law provisions as well as national provisions and even practices on consular protection, allows

---

91 In this sense, a distinction is made in German law between *Tatbestand* (elements, conditions) and *Rechtsfolge* (legal consequences). KELSEN speaks in this context about *Bedingung* (condition) and *Folge* (consequence), KELSEN, H., *Reine Rechtslehre: Einleitung in die rechtswissenschaftliche Problematik*, Aalen, 1985, pp. 80, 85, 103.

See to the thesis that the 'if'-elements (*Tatbestand*) are rooted in the constitutional principle of rule-of-law whereas the legal consequences are constitutionally based in the principle of Social State, KRAHL, M., *Tatbestand und Rechtsfolgen: Untersuchungen zu ihrem dogmatisch-methodologischen Verhältnis im Strafrecht*, Frankfurt a.M., 1999, pp. 302 et seq.

92 Consular officers may not be authorized to decide that a Union citizen whose Member State of nationality has no diplomatic or consular representation in the third country in question is not entitled to consular protection although he/she has been victim of a violent crime.

for to approach the challenges posed by the complex legal framework of consular protection conceiving of the right to consular protection as a 'multilevel right'.

4.2. Reverse Discrimination

Admittedly, this approach could lead to the creation of a better legal position of unrepresented Union citizens compared to nationals of those Member States not recognising a legal obligation to provide consular protection vis-à-vis their own nationals. This consequence, however, is not capable of constituting a violation of the equality principle at national level since the rule of equality is each binding upon one and the same legislator. In contrast, in the case of consular protection of unrepresented Union citizens Union law (primary and, in the future, also secondary Union law) is involved, besides the relevant national rules, in cases with link with Union law, while merely national law is applied in cases unrelated to Union law, i.e. where a national of a Member State asks for help the diplomatic or consular representations abroad of that same Member State.[93]

With regard to the Union law principle of equal treatment, the Court of Justice has repeatedly approved discrimination against own nationals as a consequence of the application of stricter rules to nationals than to other EU citizens within the framework of the fundamental freedoms.[94]

Nonetheless, it is doubtful whether the considerations regarding the realisation of the Single European Market by means of the Community fundamental freedoms[95] could be applied to Union citizenship' rights. While better treatment of non-national EU citizens might be necessary in order to secure the effective functioning of the Single Market, the nature of citizens' rights as "uncoupled" from any economic activities hinders the attempt to squeeze them into the same interrelation pattern.[96] The

---

93 See OPPERMANN, T./ CLASSEN, C. D./ NETTESHEIM, M., *Europarecht*, p. 419, para. 16.

94 Judgment of the Court of Justice of 16.02.1995 in the joined cases C-29/94, C-30/94, C-31/94, C-32/94, C-33/94, C-34/94 and C-35/94, *Criminal proceedings against Jean-Louis Aubertin, Bernard Collignon, Guy Creusot, Isabelle Diblanc, Gilles Josse, Jacqueline Martin and Claudie Normand*, ECR 1995, p. 00301, para. 13.

95 *Ibidem*; See also Judgment of the Court of Justice of 27.10.1982 in the joined cases 35 and 36/82, Elestina Esselina Christina Morson v. State of the Netherlands and Head of the Plaatselijke Politie within the meaning of the Vreemdelingenwet; Sweradjie Jhanjan v State of the Netherlands, ECR 1982, p. 03723, paras. 12 et seq.; Judgment of the Court of Justice of 7.02.1979 in the case 115/78, *J. Knoors v. Secretary of State for Economic Affairs*, ECR 1979, p. 00399, paras. 9 et seq.

96 See KOCHENOV, D., "IUS Tractum of many faces. European Citizenship and the difficult relationship netween status and rights", in *Columbia Journal of European Law*, Vol. 15, p. 213.

question arises therefore whether by granting a better legal position to unrepresented Union citizens as compared to nationals in a simple national case of consular protection, the goal of Union citizenship to foster a sense of identity with the Union and to strengthen solidarity among Member States would be undermined.[97]

On the other side, it should be pointed out that Union citizenship by its nature requires the existence of a case with a link with Union law and thus according to the Court of Justice:

> Citizenship of the Union, established by Article 17 EC, is not, however, intended to extend the scope *ratione materiae* of the Treaty also to internal situations which have no link with Community law.[98]

In this regard, it should be highlighted that the Court of Justice endorsed in the case *Garcia Avello* the possibility to grant Union citizens a better legal position as nationals in the context of Union citizenship rights where the situations of both groups are not identical.[99]

The situation of an unrepresented Union citizen in a third country is not the same as the one of a national asking for consular protection: an unrepresented Union citizen is exposed to a greater distress since he/she must deal not only with the difficult circumstances such as serious accident, illness or natural disaster but also with the fact that there is no representation of his/her Member State of origin in the third country concerned and that he/she is forced to approach for help the authorities of a different Member State. It is settled case-law of the Court of Justice that different situations must not be treated in the same way.[100]

4.3. The Right to Consular Protection in a Process of Juridification

The difficulties in the structure of the right to consular protection as an equal-treatment right derive from the different state of juridification of the right to consular protection in the Member States: as the analysis of the Member States' rules on consular protection shows, whereas the majority of the Member State recognise under law a legal individual right to consular protection,

97 See in this sense BESSON and UTZINGER who see European citizenship as an equal status for all. BESSON, S./UTZINGER, A., Introduction: Future Challenges of European Citizenship-Facing a Wide-Open Pandora's Box, 13 EUR. L.J., Vol. 13 (2007), p. 573, 583 et seq.

98 Judgment of the Court of Justice of 02.10.2003 in the case C-148/02, *Carlos Garcia Avello v. Belgian State*, para. 26.

99 *Ibidem*, para. 31.

100 See inter alia, Judgment of the Court of Justice in the case *Garcia Avello*, *ibidem*, para. 31.

enshrined often even in the national constitution, some of the Member State provide consular protection as a matter of policy and thus consider this kind of protection to be a power of the State and not an individual right.

The right to consular protection corresponds thus to certain social pretensions that have been juridified in the majority of the Member States as well as at EU level but not in some of the other Member States. In those countries, the right to consular protection is still in the process of legal construction passing from a more soft-law to a rather hard-law character. The lack of juridification in some countries could be explained by the vast transformation of the social realities due to globalisation bringing more and more people to remote places in the world so that the legal construction has not been able to catch up with the social necessities.

This legal construction in the Member States, whose legal order considers consular protection to be a State' power, is likely to become driven by the social pretensions of their own nationals that is expected to arise in the light of the better legal position of unrepresented Union citizens. The juridification of a right to consular protection could thus induce the power that according to Santi ROMANO is necessary for a social pretension in order to be juridified.[101]

4.4. Positive Claim under the Right to Consular Protection: an 'Umbrella Right'

The comparison between the right to consular protection on the one side and the rights to vote and stand as a candidate in municipal and European Parliament' elections on the other side sheds light on the reasons for the reluctance to recognise a substantive aspect of the right to consular protection besides its equal-treatment perspective whereas no such doubts arise as regarding the electoral rights. The right to consular protection is in the end directed to the provision of a positive action on the part of a State which could indeed strain the means at the disposal of that State and condition the State in its policy-making.[102]

Therefore, and as stated under Chapter III above, the right to consular protection may not be directed towards the creation of facilities, i.e. Member States' representations abroad, in order to provide consular protection – this approach would contradict the very purpose of Article 23 TFEU and Article 46 of the Charter to close the gaps in the protection of Union citizens in third countries establishing a solidarity network of existing Member States' representations. Rather, some of the smaller

---

[101] ROMANO, S., *El ordenamiento jurídico*, Madrid, 1963, pp. 122 et seq.

[102] BÖCKENFÖRDE, E. W., *Staat, Verfassung, Demokratie: Studien zur Verfassungstheorie und zum Verfassungsrecht*, 2. edition, Frankfurt a.M., 1992, pp. 154 et seq.

Member States could even close existing representations in third countries, which have not the infrastructure and expertise that could be offered by representations of the bigger Member States, and some Member States could refrain from establishing a representation in a third country with view of the traditional presence there of other Member States. The right to consular protection under Union law is precisely no right directed to one concrete Member States but the obligation to secure its practical effectiveness is imposed on all Member States represented in the third country in question.

This approach deprives unrepresented Union citizens not from their right to choose among the Member States represented in a third country and to approach the Member State of their choice but for the sake of effective protection, particularly in major crisis situations, the right to consular protection is equipped with mechanisms for collaboration and coordination among the Member States, such as Lead State concept, burden-sharing arrangements and pooling of resources.[103] All these mechanisms are aimed at guaranteeing the efficient provision of consular protection to unrepresented Union citizens by bridging shortcomings for instance in the infrastructural capacities of individual Member States. The right to consular protection under Union law is therefore not directed to the creation of new facilities enabling Member States to provide this kind of assistance but consists rather of the active "participation" of the individuals in already existing facilities while the creation of such facilities remains a policy option of the State.[104]

But what is then the substantive content of the right to consular protection? Whereas the scope of coverage of negative, defence rights, is easily to be construed as imposing an obligation upon its passive subject to forbear any interference in the sphere of autonomy protected by the scope of coverage of the right in question, the structure of a positive right, such as the right to consular protection, makes it more difficult to determine the power conferred upon individuals that correlates with an obligation of the State. The scope of coverage of positive rights is therefore all the more linked to their function as institutions ordering a determined social reality, being the violation of the positive right concerned the failure to avoid the violation, respectively the failure to secure the inviolability, of the legal interests underlying the right in question.

This institutional approach is particularly suitable in the case of the right to consular protection due to its character as an 'umbrella right': the legal values

103 See to the non-judicial guarantees of the right to consular protection next Chapter VII.

104 See to the practicability of participative positive claims, BÖCKENFÖRDE, E.-W., "Grundrechtstheorie und Grundrechtsinterpretation", in *Neue Juristische Wochenschrift*, 1974, Heft 35, p. 1536.

underlying the right to consular protection are not only superior fundamental values integrating the constitutional order such as democracy or equality[105] but are themselves fundamental rights. The right to consular protection is not an end in itself but is aimed at the protection of other fundamental rights, such as the right to life, physical integrity, property, liberty, human dignity enshrined in the Charter of Fundamental Rights of the European Union.[106] The functional embodiment of the right to consular protection as a right guaranteeing other fundamental rights is not unusual in European constitutionalism. In a similar vein, the right to privacy is deemed to be a guarantee of the right to personal liberty while the right to inviolability of one's home is aimed at guaranteeing the right to privacy.[107] The most evident example of a right-guarantee is the right to effective judicial protection construed as a right-guarantee of all other fundamental rights.[108]

It is established case-law of the Court of Justice that the scope of the rights should be interpreted according to their social function.[109] This institutional, functional approach allows us for to conceive of the scope of coverage of the right to consular protection without forfeiting its practical effectiveness against RAWLS' thesis on the need to limit the recognition of rights to the so called "basic goods".[110]

The obligation imposed on the Member States as counterpart to the subjective right to claim consular protection is thus the obligation to secure those underlying fundamental rights. Therefore, what is required to fulfil the obligation under the right to consular protection corresponds to what has to be done to avoid the violation of the right to life, physical integrity, human dignity, property, etc. of the unrepresented Union citizen in a situation of distress.[111]

The substantive scope of coverage of the right to consular protection, interpreted in conjunction with its underlying fundamental rights

105 See to the superior constitutional values in Spain and in the European constitutionalism, PECES-BARBA, G., *Los valores superiores*, Madrid, 1986.

106 The fundamental rights enshrined in the Charter of Fundamental Rights are applicable within the framework of consular protection provided to unrepresented Union citizens abroad since such cases are obviously connected with Union law. Unclear in so far the position of KLEINLEIN, T./ RABENSCHLAG, D., "Auslandsschutz und Staatsangehörigkeit", in *Zeitschrift für ausländisches öffentliches Recht und Völkerrecht*, (67) 2007, p. 1311.

107 GÓMEZ SÁNCHEZ, Y., *Derecho Constitucional Europeo: derechos y libertades*, Madrid, 2008, p. 445.

108 *Ibidem*.

109 See inter alia Judgment of the Court of Justice in the case *Hauer*, *op. cit.*, footnote 280, p. 3733.

110 RAWLS, J., *A Theory of Justice*, 2. edition, Oxford/London/New York, 1993, pp. 78 et seq.

111 In this sense also IANIELLO SALICETI, A., "The Protection of EU Citizens Abroad...", p. 100, *op. cit.*, footnote 1.

converting it into an 'umbrella right', is in the following to be analysed as a starting point for the definition of the limits to the right to consular protection as well as the restrictions imposed on these limits.

4.5. **'Schranken-Schranken'** *to the Right to Consular Protection*

The inclusion into the scope of coverage of the right to consular protection under Union law of a substantive aspect related to the question if consular protection shall be provided at all, does not lead to the creation of an absolute right imposing on the Member States the heavy burden of an unconditional obligation to provide consular protection. Rather, the right to consular protection is subject to limitations.

Notwithstanding, these limitations must on their part comply with certain standards inherent to a "Community based on the rule of law",[112] in the first place with the principle of proportionality. The principle of proportionality is rooted in the German legal doctrine as a *Schranken-Schranke*[113] (limits to the limits) and has found reflection in the case-law of the European Court of Human Rights, although in a less strict interpretation awarding States a "margin of appreciation" as to the proportionality of a restrictive measure.[114]

The Court of Justice first applied the principle of proportionality as a limitation on the restrictions of fundamental rights in the leading case *Internationale Handelsgesellschaft*[115] affirming that the principle of proportionality is one of the general principles of Community law.[116] The Court went to conclude that no restrictions may be imposed on a fundamental right that are not necessary in order to achieve the goal pursued by them.[117] According to the Court, a measure is deemed to be necessary when it is appropriate in order to achieve a legitimate objective

---

[112] Judgment of the Court of Justice of 23.04.1986 in the case C-294/83, *Parti écologiste "Les Verts" v. European Parliament*, ECR 1986, p. 1339, para. 23.

[113] See LERCHE, P., *Übermass und Verfassungsrecht: zur Bindung des Gesetzgebers an die Grundsätze der Verhältnismässigkeit und der Erforderlichkeit*, Köln, 1961.

[114] Well-established case-law of the European Court of Human Rights, see for instance Judgment of the ECHR of 07.12.1976 in Case of *Handyside v. The United Kingdom*, application No. 5493/72, Series A, Vol. 24, paras. 48, 49.

[115] Judgment of the Court of Justice of 17.12.1970 in the case 11/70, *Internationale Handelsgesellschaft mbH v. Einfuhr- und Vorratsstelle für Getreide und Futtermittel*, ECR 1970, p. 1125.

[116] See e.g. Judgment of the Court of Justice of 11.07.1989 in the case 265/87, *Hermann Schräder HS Kraftfutter GmbH & Co. KG v. Hauptzollamt Gronau*, ECR 1989, p. 2237, para. 21.

[117] Judgment in the case *Internationale Handelsgesellschaft*, para. 10 et seq., *op. cit.*, footnote 115.

and is proportionate to the legitimate aim pursued which means that there are no less-restrictive measures appropriate to achieve the aim.[118]

The *Schranken-Schranke* principle has been codified at EU level in Article 52 para. 1, 2. clause of the Charter of Fundamental Rights of the European Union stating that:

> Subject to the principle of proportionality, limitations may be made only if they are necessary and genuinely meet objectives of general interest recognised by the Union or the need to protect the rights and freedoms of others.

The Court has frequently applied the principle of proportionality as a limitation to the limitations imposed by the Member States on citizenship' rights. As for the right to equal treatment regarding the right to freely move and reside within the territory of the Member States (Article 18 in conjunction with Article 20 TFEU), the Court of Justice held in the cases *de Cyper* and *Morgan* that a restriction of the right to freely move and reside can be justified in the light of Community law only if it is based on objective considerations of public interest independent of the nationality of the persons concerned and proportionate to the legitimate objective of the national provisions.[119] The Court pointed out that a measure is proportionate when, while appropriate for securing the attainment of the objective pursued, it does not go beyond what is necessary in order to attain it.[120]

The two-level scope of the right to consular protection distinguishing between the question of whether consular protection shall be provided and how it is provided leads necessarily to a similar distinction regarding the restrictions that could be imposed on that right. On the one side, the right to consular protection of unrepresented Union citizens may be restricted by denying to provide the right-holder with consular protection, and, on the other side, the provision of concrete measures might violate the right to consular protection if the measures chosen were not appropriate to avoid or atone for a harm and other, more effective, measures were at the disposal of the competent authorities.

A refusal to provide consular protection to an unrepresented EU citizen by a Member State approached for protection should be based on objective considerations of public interests and be necessary in order to

---

118 See e.g. Judgment of the Court of Justice of 12.06.2003 in the case 112/00, *Eugen Schmidberger, Internationale Transporte und Planzüge v. Austria, op. cit.*, footnote 291, paras. 59, 79, 82.

119 Judgment of the Court of Justice of 18.07.2006 in the case 406/04, *Gérald De Cuyper v. Office national de l'emploi*, ECR 2006, p. I-06947, paras. 40, 42.; Judgment of the Court of Justice of 23.10.2007 in the joined cases 11/06 and 12/06, *Rhiannon Morgan* (C-11/06) *v. Bezirksregierung Köln*, and *Iris Bucher* (C-12/06) *v. Landrat des Kreises Düren*, ECR 2007, p. I-09161, para. 33.

120 *Ibidem*.

attain this legitimate objective. In doing so, allowance should be made of the particular importance of the right to consular protection as a right deriving from the fundamental status of all EU citizens, Union citizenship.

Accordingly, a denial to provide consular protection would be justified only in very extreme cases, where the provision of consular protection shall take a back seat to other considerable interests which would be the case of an imminent danger for the life of the consular officers if they would be supposed to pay a visit to an unrepresented Union citizens arrested in a third country suffering a violent street turmoil, being the protection of the life and physical integrity of the State officials a legitimate objective lying in the public interest. The denial of consular protection would be justified also when the Member State approached for help disposes not (or not any more) of an airplane in order to evacuate an unrepresented Union citizen from a third country in a situation of a natural disaster.

Nonetheless, the question arises whether the denial of consular protection by the diplomatic or consular representation of a Member State would not violate the essential content of the right to consular protection. According to the Court of Justice in the case *Wachauf*, no restrictions may be imposed on the rights granted by the Treaties that represent, with regard to the aim pursued, disproportionate and intolerable interference, impairing the very substance of those rights.[121] The principle of the inviolability of the essential content of fundamental rights is enshrined also in the Charter of Fundamental Rights of the European Union stating in Article 52 para. 1 that "any limitation on the exercise of the rights and freedoms recognised by this Charter must [...] respect the essence of those rights and freedoms".

The substance[122] of the right to consular protection needs to be analysed again in light of the structure of the right to consular protection as an 'umbrella right' and its underlying fundamental rights. Thus, the substance of the right to consular protection would not be violated if the substance of the underlying fundamental rights has been preserved.

In this context, the structure of the right to consular protection aimed at bridging the gaps in the protection of certain fundamental rights of unrepresented Union citizens in third countries by means of

---

[121] Judgment of the Court of Justice of 13.07.1989 in the case C-5/88, *Hubert Wachauf v. Federal Republic of Germany, represented by the Bundesamt für Ernährung und Forstwirtschaft*, ECR 2000, p. 02609, para. 18.

[122] To the concept of relative or absolute essential content, see PIEROTH, B./ SCHLINK, B., *Grundrechte, Staatsrecht II*, 16. edition, Heidelberg, 2000, paras. 300, 301. The German Federal Constitutional Court left the question open whether the essential content of a fundamental right shall remain to its concrete right-holder or to the society.

a solidarity network of Member States' representations abroad should be taken into account. Being the effectiveness of this protection the cornerstone of the Union provisions on consular protection reflected in the mandate issued by Article 23 TFEU to the Member States to "secure this protection", the right to consular protection has been, as stated above, equipped with extra-judicial guarantees in the shape of collaboration and cooperation mechanisms among the Member States. Instruments such as Lead State concept, burden-sharing arrangements and pooling of resources allow for the distribution of the obligation imposed by Article 23 TFEU as a counterpart to the subjective right to consular protection among all Member States represented in the third country where the unrepresented Union citizen concerned has suffered a situation of distress.

As stated above, this distribution of the obligation to provide consular protection among the Member States deprives unrepresented Union citizens not from their right to approach for help the authorities of any Member Sate as stipulated in Article 23 para. 1 TFEU[123] and may not be used by the Member States as a simple referral from one Member State to another in order to evade their obligation to provide consular protection. Rather, effective consular protection may be provided in the circumstances of limited capacities, inherent to the context of consular protection in countries where not all Member States are represented, only by means of collaboration among the Member States.

Thus, for instance, in a situation where Member States have agreed on a Lead State, the refusal to provide consular protection to an unrepresented Union citizen by the authorities of a Member State, that is not the Lead State, would be proportional and would not violate the very substance of the right to consular protection if the citizen concerned can be evacuated by the Lead State.

In this context, the question could be posed why the substantive scope of the right to consular protection could not be limited from the outset in a manner that the Member States are awarded a wide scope of discretion also as to whether consular protection should be provided and not only as to the question how protection is provided. The difference lies in the fact that in the approach proposed here the scope of coverage of the right to consular protection is conceived of widely as covering both the 'if' and 'how' of consular protection. The limits to the right to consular protection are themselves subject to limits such as the principle of proportionality

[123] Article 23, para. 1, first clause TFEU: "Every citizen of the Union shall, in the territory of a third country in which the Member State of which he is a national is not represented, be entitled to protection by the diplomatic or consular authorities of any Member State [...]."

and the essential content of the scope of coverage of that right cannot be violated so that at least the very substance of the right to consular protection will need to be protected.

This means that if a Member State, even after application of the principle of proportionality, is not capable of providing consular protection, this denial may be justified if the guarantees of the right to consular protection are suitable for effectively protecting its very substance. This would be the case when for instance in case of evacuation in a major crisis the Member State approached for help may not repatriate the unrepresented Union citizen concerned since after applying the principle of proportionality there is no more place in the evacuating aircraft, the right to consular protection of the Union citizen may be guaranteed by the mechanisms of cooperation and coordination in crisis situations so that the citizen concerned will be entitled to obtain protection by another Member State.

As to the choice of the measure to be adopted in order to provide consular protection ('how'), the scope of discretion, awarded often by the national rules on consular protection to the consular officers, would also need to be assessed in light of the principle of proportionality.

That the scope of discretion conferred upon national authorities by national law needs to be limited by the constitutional principle of proportionality where the decision at stake affects Union citizenship, has been affirmed by the Court of Justice in the *Rottmann* case. The Court first confirmed the *Micheletti* case-law[124] holding that Member States' nationality is governed by national rules. In that case, the relevant German legal provisions placed the decision to withdraw the nationality of a naturalised citizen at the disposal of the competent authorities.[125]

Nonetheless, the Court went to conclude that the national authorities shall use their discretion by observing the principle of proportionality "so far as concerns the consequences it entails for the situation of the person concerned in the light of European Union law".[126] Moreover, the Court held that applying the principle of proportionality, the importance which primary law attaches to the status of citizen of the Union should be taken

124 Judgment of the Court of Justice in the case C-369/90, *Micheletti v. Delegación de Gobierno en Cantabria*, ECR 1990, p. 4239.

125 Article 48, para. 1 of the Code of Administrative Procedure of the Land of Bavaria (*Bayerisches Verwaltungsverfahrensgesetz*) is worded as follows:

"(1) Even when it is no longer open to challenge, an unlawful administrative act may be withdrawn in whole or in part, […]". Emphasis added by author.

126 Judgment of the Court of Justice of the European Communities of 02.03.2010 in the case C-135/08, *Janco Rottman v. Freistaat Bayern*, ECR 2010, p. I-01449, para. 55.

into account. Therefore, national authorities shall use their discretion under due consideration of the consequences that their decision entails for the Union citizen concerned.[127]

Since the right-holder has no right to be provided with a determinated type of consular protection, the refusal to adopt a concrete action requested by the right-holder is not *per se* a violation of the right to consular protection. This should be the case only if in the circumstances of the case there is only one measure appropriate to achieve the objective pursued, i.e. avoid or atone for any harm on the fundamental rights underlying the right to consular protection. In this case the application of the principle of proportionality would result in the reduction of the scope of discretion of the consular officers to zero.[128] Thus, the unrepresented Union citizen concerned would be entitled to request the only measure appropriate to provide relief, so that the refusal to provide this type of consular protection would constitute a violation of the right to consular protection.

5. Conclusions

The right to consular protection under Article 23 TFEU and Article 46 of the Charter of Fundamental Rights of the European Union involve in its legal framework, as just a few other legal provisions, the interaction between Union law and national rules. The character of the right to consular protection as an equal-treatment right poses a challenge before its legal construction as well as before its practical effectiveness due to the different state of juridification of this right in the Member States. The systematic and structure of the right to consular protection as deriving from Union citizenship and the comparison with the rest of citizens' rights comprising a substantive claim beside their equal-treatment aspect, leads to the conclusion that it needs to be distinguished between the question of 'if' consular protection shall be provided and which type of assistance shall/ may be provided in the situations of distress stipulated.

Whereas the first question is governed by Article 23 TFEU in conjunction with Decision 95/553/EC and Decision 96/409/CFSP and is not dependent on the recognition of a subjective right to consular protection in the legal orders of the Member States, the question of how consular protection shall be provided is regulated by the national rules

127 *Ibidem*, para. 56.

128 In this context, the principle of "*Ermesensreduktion auf Null*" (reduction of the discretion to zero) applicable in the German Public Law (See Judgment of the Federal Administration Court of 23.04.1998, 3 C 15.97, BVerwGE 106, 328) seems to be an appropriate instrument in order to make allowance on the one side for the legitimate demand of the Member State to retain their discretion and on the other side for the legitimate interests of the individuals concerned.

and practices and shall be applied to unrepresented Union citizens in situations of distress in the same manner as to nationals of the assisting Member State. This approach prevent the right to consular protection under Union law to be deprived of any sense when unrepresented Union citizens ask for help Member States not conferring under its national rules a subjective right to consular protection so that a treatment equal to that of nationals would be of no avail for unrepresented Union citizens abroad.

Furthermore, the scope of coverage of the right to consular protection needs to be determined taking to account the structure of the right to consular protection as a positive right on the one side and its function as a legal institution aimed at ordering a certain social reality on the other side. The right to consular protection may not be conceived of as a right to the creation of new facilities but is aimed at the participation in already existing facilities in order for the Member States to remain Masters of the political decision on the deployment of a network of diplomatic and consular representations abroad. The obligation on the part of the Member States corresponding to the subjective right to consular protection should be determined under due consideration of the function of the right to consular protection as a right aimed at guaranteeing the exercise of other fundamental rights such as the right to life, to physical integrity, property and human dignity. Thus, the violation of the obligation to protect those fundamental rights in a situation of distress as stipulated by Decision 95-553/EC and Decision 96/409/CFSP would constitute a violation of the right to consular protection.

Nonetheless, the existence of a substantive scope of the right to consular protection beside its equal-treatment aspect does not lead to an absolute obligation imposed upon the Member States to provide consular protection. Rather, the refusal to provide consular protection may be justified as complying with the principle of proportionality when the fundamental rights underlying the right to consular protection could be secured by means of the mechanisms of collaboration and coordination with regard to consular protection, such as Lead State concept, burden-sharing arrangements and pooling of resources.

Thus, the obligation to provide consular protection to unrepresented Union citizens is not deemed to be violated by the refusal by the consular authorities of a Member State to provide protection with view to existent arrangements among the Member States' representations in the third country concerned aimed at guaranteeing effective consular protection under consideration of available capacities and infrastructures, provided the protection of the underlying fundamental rights is secured effectively.

In contrast, the scope of the right to consular protection as for the question how consular protection is provided, the national rules of the

Member States apply. National legislation and practices are likely to award consular officers a wide scope of discretion regarding the decision which type of measures should be provided taking into consideration the specific circumstances of each case.

This discretion awarded by national legal norms needs to be exercised with regard to the principle of proportionality as a general principle of Union law deriving from the principle of rule-of-law and recognized as a constitutional principle limiting the restrictions of fundamental rights in the constitutional traditions of all Member States. Thus, although the decision, which type of assistance should be provided in each case, may be placed at the discretion of consular officers, an unrepresented Union citizen should be entitled to claim the provision of a specific measure, provided that that measure is the only one capable of providing efficiently relief. This would be the case if otherwise the fundamental rights of the citizen concerned underlying the right to consular protection may not be protected and the interest to prevent a threatening damage prevails over any conflicting public interests.

Accordingly, the scope of coverage of the right to consular protection should be interpreted widely in order to guarantee its practical effectiveness as comprising a substantive aspect concerning the question if consular protection is provided as well as an equal-treatment aspect concerning the question of how consular protection is provided. This distinction should find an expression also in the requirements on the limits that could be imposed on the right to consular protection.

CHAPTER VII

Guarantees of the Right to Consular Protection

1. Judicial Guarantees of the Right to Consular Protection

Although neither the Treaty on European Union nor the Treaty on Functioning of the European Union mention expressly that rights are guaranteed by the system of judicial remedies established, the Court of Justice pointed out already in the case *Van Gend & Loos* that for instance the infringement procedures according to Articles 258 and 259 TFEU,[1] that can be brought by the European Commission or by a Member State before the Court of Justice, are guarantees against the violation of individual rights conferred upon the Treaties.[2]

Since the pillar structure introduced by the Maastricht Treaty was overcome with the entry into force of the Treaty of Lisbon, the jurisdiction of the Court of Justice of the European Union was extended to the law of the European Union, unless the Treaties provide otherwise.[3] According to Article 19 para. 1 TEU, the Court shall ensure that in the interpretation and application of the Treaties the law is observed. Hence, the Court has full jurisdiction over any judicial dispute relating to Article 23 TFEU.

Therefore, should a Member State approached by an unrepresented Union citizen refuse to provide consular protection without this decision being justified by the existence of cooperation measures such as an agreement of the Member States on a Lead State in the third country concerned or of burden-sharing arrangements aimed at the distribution of the protection-burden among the representations of the Member States in a manner appropriate to ensure the effective provision of consular protection to unrepresented Union citizens, or should the choice of the

1 Ex-Articles 226 and 227 TEC.

2 The Court held that "A restriction of the guarantees against an infringement of article 12 by Member States to the procedures under article 169 and 170 would remove all direct legal protection of the individual rights of their nationals."

3 Please note Article 10 of Protocol No. 36 to the Lisbon Treaty on transitional provisions. It is provided that, as a transitional measure, the powers of the Court of Justice are to remain the same with respect to acts in the field of police cooperation and judicial cooperation in criminal matters which have been adopted before the entry into force of the Treaty of Lisbon. This transitional measure is to cease to have effect five years after the date of entry into force of the Treaty of Lisbon.

concrete measure of consular protection not observe the principle of proportionality being not appropriate to prevent or atone for the violation of fundamental rights protected by the right to consular protection or unproportional with view to the harm suffered or threatening, the Commission or another Member State (e.g. the Member State of origin of the person seeking help) could initiate an infringement procedure according to Articles 258, 259 TFEU.

Furthermore, according to Article 267 para. 1 (ex-Article 234 TEC), the Court of Justice has jurisdiction to give preliminary rulings concerning the interpretation of the Treaties and, thus, also of Article 23 TFEU.[4] Article 267 TFEU establishes to this end the possibility or obligation of a national court before which such a question has been raised, to request the Court of Justice to give a ruling thereon.[5]

Accordingly, a precondition for the possibility to request the Court of Justice for a preliminary ruling is a pending judicial proceeding before a national court. This on its turn would presuppose the possibility of an individual person concerned to lodge an appeal with a national court against the denial of consular protection or its insufficiency, respectively against the non-equal treatment regarding the provision of consular protection.

This precondition of a preliminary ruling of the Court of Justice according to Article 267 TFEU could be problematical account being taken of the fact that not all Member States provide for under their legal orders the possibility of a judicial review of the denial or unsatisfactory provision of consular protection. In this regard, it should be mentioned that all seventeen Member States recognizing a subjective right to consular protection provide for as a consequence also a judicial appeal falling under the jurisdiction of the administrative courts in order to provide redress in case of violation of the right concerned.[6]

Problematical is in contrast the judicial review in those ten Member States that provide consular protection as a matter of policy. Since these

---

4 Article 267, para. 1 TFEU: "The Court of Justice of the European Union shall have jurisdiction to give preliminary rulings concerning:

(a) the interpretation of the Treaties."

5 Article 267 para. 2 and 3 TFEU:

"Where such a question is raised before any court or tribunal of a Member State, that court or tribunal may, if it considers that a decision on the question is necessary to enable it to give Judgment, request the Court to give a ruling thereon.

Where any such question is raised in a case pending before a court or tribunal of a Member State against whose decisions there is no judicial remedy under national law, that court or tribunal shall bring the matter before the Court."

6 Instituto Europeo de Derecho, Study on Member States' Practices and Legislations in the Field of Consular Protection, 2009, available from DG Justice at the European Commission.

Member States do not consider consular protection as a legal, subjective right, they consequently are not "required" from a legal point of view to offer a judicial review of decisions on this issue of the competent State authorities. However, as regards Austria and the United Kingdom it is worth mentioning that although these Member State provide consular protection as a matter of policy and there is no statutory obligation to provide such kind of protection, judicial review of the refusal to provide consular protection may be sought by the person affected. According to the Austrian Federal Constitution, the Austrian Administrative Court is "competent to secure the legality of all acts of the public administration ...",[7] and "renders judgments on complaints which allege a) the illegality of decisions of administrative authorities".[8] Thus, any refusal or abuse of rights by Austrian authorities (in this sense also rights guaranteed under EU law), can be – ultimately – brought before the High Administrative Court. In the United Kingdom individuals who are refused consular assistance may also seek judicial review of the decision in accordance with the Civil Procedure Rules, Part 54.[9]

Besides, it should be pointed out that Member States not recognizing consular protection as a legal right, and thus not providing a formal administrative and judicial appeal, usually establish some sorts of an internal, informal complaint to the superior authority which is mostly the Ministry of Foreign Affairs (e.g. Belgium: Council of State – Department for Administrative Disputes). These informal complaints are usually of institutional nature and do not form part of an administrative procedure ruled by law. The result of such informal complaints is not subjected to any judicial review.

However, regardless the question of whether the Member States provide for or not judicial remedies in case of refusal, insufficient and non-equal provision of consular protection, it should be stressed that Member States are obliged under Union law to enable right-holders to seek judicial review of State acts relating to their Union rights. In this regard, Article 19 para. 1, second clause TEU is worth mentioning: "Member States shall provide remedies sufficient to ensure effective legal protection in the fields covered by Union law." Article 19 TEU materialises the right to effective judicial remedy established by the Court of Justice already in its Judgment in the case *Johnston* as a general principle of Community law. The Court held that the right to effective judicial control is a principle which underlies the constitutional traditions common to the Member States and which is laid down in Articles 6 and

7 Article 129 of the Austrian Federal Constitution.

8 Article 130 para. 1 of the Austrian Federal Constitution.

9 See <http://www.justice.gov.uk/civil/procrules_fin/contents/parts/part54.htm> (23.03.2010).

13 of the European Convention for the Protection of Human Rights and Fundamental Freedoms.[10]

Moreover, the right to an effective remedy is also enshrined in the Charter of Fundamental Rights of the European Union. According to Article 47 para. 1 of the Charter:

> Everyone whose rights and freedoms guaranteed by the law of the Union are violated has the right to an effective remedy before a tribunal in compliance with the conditions laid down in this Article.

Hence, the exclusion of any judicial review by the national courts of a Member State of a denial, insufficient or non-equal provision of consular protection would violate the fundamental right to an effective judicial remedy. As a consequence, those Member States not providing any possibility of a judicial review of a denial, etc. of consular protection under national law, are obliged under the Treaties (Article 19 TEU and Article 47 of the Charter) to enable unrepresented EU citizens who have approached the Member State concerned for consular protection under EU Law to submit the decision of the consular officers to a judicial review. Member States may not elude the efficacy of subjective rights that they agreed to be granted under EU law by refusing providing suitable instruments for judicial review of possible violations of these rights under national law.

It is settled case-law of the Court of Justice that the Union right to effective judicial remedy shall not deprive Member States of their autonomy as regarding the detailed procedural rules governing actions at law intended to safeguard the rights which individuals derive from the direct effect of Community law.[11] The Court, however, made it clear that those rules cannot be less favourable than those governing rights which originate in domestic law (principle of equivalence) and that they cannot render virtually impossible or excessively difficult the exercise of rights conferred by Community law (principle of effectiveness).[12] The Court held that particularly the principle of effectiveness must lead the national court to apply the detailed procedural rules laid down by domestic law only in so far as they do not compromise the *raison d'être* and objective of the Union law provision in question.[13]

---

[10] Judgment of the Court of Justice of 15.05.1986 in the case 222/84, *Marguerite Johnston v. Chief Constable of the Royal Ulster Constabulary*, ECR 1986, p. 01226, para. 18.

[11] Settled case-law, see for instance Judgment of the Court of Justice of 08.11.2005 in the case C-443/03, *Götz Leffler v. Berlin Chemie AG*, ECR 2005, p. I-09611, para. 49.

[12] Judgment of the Court of Justice of 16.12.1976 in the case C-33/76, *Rewe-Zentralfinanz eG and Rewe-Zentral AG v Landwirtschaftskammer für das Saarland*, ECR 1976, p. 01989, para. 5.

[13] Settled case-law of the Court of Justice, see Judgment in the case *Rewe*, *Ibidem*.

Accordingly, Member States not providing any judicial remedy under national law as to the violation of an individual right stemming from Union law, may not receive a more advantageous treatment than Member States providing judicial remedies that need to be measured against the principles of effectiveness and equivalence. Therefore, even before the inclusion of Article 19 into the TEU imposing upon Member States the obligation to establish judicial remedies in the field covered by Union law, the Court of First Instance[14] held in the case *Ayadi* that national courts shall refrain from applying national rules excluding from judicial review a refusal of national authorities to take action with a view to guaranteeing rights deriving from Union law.[15]

Worth mentioning is that a Member State, in particular the Member State of nationality of the unrepresented Union citizen concerned, may intervene within the trial initiated by the citizen against the approached Member State by means of pierce intervention.[16]

In addition to the so called primary judicial remedies, EU citizens who have been denied to be provided with consular protection, have received insufficient protection or who have not been treated equally to nationals may claim compensation for damages caused by the refusal, etc. of consular protection. In this regard, it should be pointed out that the principle of state liability for non-compliance with EC law has been established by the Court of Justice as a general principle of law. State liability derives from the fact that EU Member States are responsible for the creation and above all for the implementation and enforcement of EC law. The Court went to conclude in the leading case *Francovich* that the full effectiveness of Community rules would be impaired and the protection of the rights which they grant would be weakened if individuals were unable to obtain reparation when their rights are infringed by a breach of Community law for which a Member State can be held responsible. The Court held that such a possibility of reparation by the Member State is particularly indispensable where the full effectiveness of Community rules is subject to prior action on the part of the State and where, consequently, in the absence of such action, individuals cannot enforce before the national courts the rights conferred upon them by Community law.[17] It follows that

---

14 After of the entry into force of the Lisbon Treaty, General Court.

15 Judgment of the Court of First Instance of 12.07.2006 in the case T-253/02, *Chafiq Ayadi v. Council of the European Union*, ECR 2006, p. II-02139, para. 152.

16 IANNIELLO SALICETI, A., "The Protection of EU Citizens Abroad: Accountability, Rule of Law, Role of Consular and Diplomatic Services", in *European Public Law*, 17, No. 1 (2011), p. 104.

17 Judgment of the Court of Justice of 19.11.1991 in the joined cases C-6/90 and C-9/90, *Andrea Francovich and Danila Bonifaci and others v. Italian Republic*, ECR 1991, p. 05357, paras. 33, 34.

the principle whereby a State must be liable for loss and damage caused to individuals by breaches of Community law for which the State can be held responsible is inherent in the system of the Treaty.[18]

In this context, it should be highlighted that in accordance with the case-law of the Court of Justice even in the case of liability for breach of Community Law (in the event that the refusal of consular protection concerns an EU citizen), "it is in principle for the national courts to assess whether a breach of Community law is sufficiently serious for a Member State to incur non-contractual liability vis-à-vis an individual in accordance with the guidelines laid down by the Court for the application of those criteria".[19] According to the criteria established in the *Francovich* case, in order to claim compensation from a Member State a breach of EC law is necessary that is attributable to the Member State, which causes damage to an individual.[20] If these elements are established, compensation may be claimed in a legal action before a national court.

2. Non-Judicial Guarantees

Beside the jurisdictional guarantees described above, the same Article 23 TFEU induces the establishment of further guarantees in order to secure the provision of consular protection.[21] To this end the Member States have agreed on different instruments securing the provision of consular protection to all EU citizens in crisis situations occurring in third countries.

2.1. Burden-Sharing

The Council of the European Union issued in 2006 Guidelines on consular protection of EU citizens in third countries.[22] The Guidelines

---

18 *Ibidem*, para. 35.

19 Judgment of the Court of Justice of 05.03.1996 in the joined cases C-46/93 and C-48/93, *Brasserie du Pêcheur and Factortame*, European Court reports 1996, p. 1029, paras. 55 to 57; Judgment of 26.03.1996 in the case C-392/93, *The Queen v. H.M. Treasury, ex parte British Telecommunications*, ECR 1996, p. 1631, paras. 38, 39; Judgment of 08.10.1996 in the joined cases C-178/94, C-179/94, C-188/94, C-189/94 and C-190/94, *Dillenkofer and Others v. Federal Republic of Germany*, ECR 1996, p. 4845, paras. 20, 21; Judgment of 17.10.1996 in the joined cases C-283/94, C-291/94 and C-292/94, *Denkavit Internationaal and Others v. Bundesamt für Finanzen*, ECR 1996, p. 5063, paras. 47 et seq.

20 Judgment of the Court of Justice in the case *Francovich*, paras. 33 et seq., *op. cit.*, footnote 17.

21 Article 23 para. 1, second clause TFEU reads: "Member States shall adopt the necessary provisions and start the international negotiations required to secure this protection."

22 COUNCIL OF THE EUROPEAN UNION, Guidelines on consular protection of EU citizens in third countries, Document of the Council 10109/2/06 REV 2 of 16.06.2006.

are designed to provide a framework for consular cooperation, especially in situations in which the safety of EU citizens is endangered in a third country. They have been drawn up as part of the implementation of the mutual protection obligation provided for in Article 20 of the Treaty establishing the European Community[23] and of the cooperation tasks, as stipulated under Article 20 of the Treaty of the EU.[24]

According to the Guidelines in countries at risk of a crisis where not all Member States are represented, Heads of Mission should decide amongst themselves how they will share responsibilities for ensuring that nationals of all Member States are covered by contingency plans. Their decision should be based on pragmatism, flexibility and a fair division of the consular burden. This may extend to deciding that nationals of particular unrepresented Member States who seek assistance should be directed to particular EU Member States' representations as agreed by Heads of Mission locally.[25] Furthermore, the Guidelines provide for that in areas where distance and transport are a problem, visits to prisons and hospitals can be co-ordinated through advance planning, allowing EU missions to share the burden of visiting their nationals, or increasing the number of visits their nationals receive.

Although these Guidelines are non-binding legally and their implementation is left to the discretion of the heads of missions or posts in the light of local circumstances,[26] the provisions regarding sharing of the burden of the Member States represented in third countries where not all Member States are represented aim to guarantee a better and effective protection of unrepresented EU citizens seeking a just distribution of the tasks under Article 23 TFEU among the Member States. Hence, the sharing of burden seems to be an appropriate instrument to secure and render more effectiveness to the right to consular protection under Article 23 TFEU.

These updated consular guidelines were drafted following the Indian Ocean tsunami of December 2004. Available at: <http://register.consilium.europa.eu/pdf/en/06/st10/st10109-re02.en06.pdf> (12.03.2012).

23 *Ibidem*, p. 3.

24 Article 35 TEU (ex-Article 20 TEU) reads: "The diplomatic and consular missions of the Member States and the Union delegations in third countries and international conferences, and their representations to international organisations, shall cooperate in ensuring that decisions defining Union positions and actions adopted pursuant to this Chapter are complied with and implemented. They shall step up cooperation by exchanging information and carrying out joint assessments. They shall contribute to the implementation of the right of citizens of the Union to protection in the territory of third countries as referred to in Article 20(2)(c) of the Treaty on the Functioning of the European Union and of the measures adopted pursuant to Article 23 of that Treaty."

25 COUNCIL OF THE EUROPEAN UNION, Guidelines on consular protection of EU citizens in third countries, p. 4, *op. cit.*, footnote 22.

26 *Ibidem*, p. 2, 3.

2.2. Lead State Concept

The Council of the European Union on General Affairs and External Relations concluded in its meeting on 18 June 2007 that "in the event of a major consular crisis and without prejudice to the primary responsibility of Member States to protect their nationals, the Lead State will endeavour to ensure that all European Union citizens are assisted and will coordinate between Member States on the ground".[27] In order to implement this so called "Lead State concept" the Council drew up in 2008 the "European Union guidelines on the implementation of the consular Lead State concept".[28] According to these Guidelines, a Member State would take on the role of Lead State on a voluntary basis, with the active support and participation of all Member States. In all cases, other Member States will continue to monitor the situation of their nationals on the ground, share intelligence and situation assessments and provide reinforcements and additional resources as required.[29]

In the event of a major consular crisis, the Lead State will implement assistance measures for all persons who would be given consular assistance by their Member State. The Lead State will inform the Member States concerned by the crisis of developments in the situation. Locally, it will be the responsibility of the head of mission or post of the Lead State to facilitate cooperation on the ground between Member States which have sent additional personnel, financial resources, equipment, and medical assistance teams, in accordance with point. The head of mission or post of the Lead State will also be in charge of coordinating and leading assistance and assembly operations, and if necessary, evacuation to a place of safety, with the support of the other Member States concerned.[30]

If the Lead State deems necessary to evacuate persons affected, it will inform the Member States concerned at local level and in the capitals. The Member States concerned will inform the Lead State in return regarding their national position on the evacuation, and regarding their wish to benefit or not from the assistance of the Lead State in the matter. If a Member State declines the assistance of the Lead State, it

---

27 COUNCIL OF THE EUROPEAN UNION, General Affairs, Conclusions of the Luxembourg Council of 17-18 June 2007, Press Release 10654/07, p. 2. Available at: <http://www.consilium.europa.eu/ueDocs/cms_Data/docs/pressData/en/gena/94803.pdf> (12.11.2012).

28 COUNCIL OF THE EUROPEAN UNION, European Union guidelines on the implementation of the consular Lead State concept Document 2008/C 317/06, published in the Official Journal of the European Union of 12.12.2008.

29 *Ibidem*, Introduction Section 2.

30 *Ibidem*, Section 2, subsections 2.1 and 2.2.

will be in charge of providing assistance to its nationals and to other potential beneficiaries of its consular assistance. Its nationals and other potential beneficiaries of its consular assistance remain, in accordance with the principle of non-discrimination, eligible to receive assistance from the Lead State.[31]

As set up in the Guidelines, the Member States will reimburse the Lead State for expenses incurred in protecting their nationals in a pragmatic way.[32] It will then be the responsibility of the requesting Member State to pursue repayment from its nationals.

Although also these Guidelines are not legally binding,[33] they already have been applied in practice. The Lead State concept in crisis situations, adopted by the EU Council on 18 June 2007, was put into practice for the first time in Chad, with a very successful outcome. It has proven to be an effective method of providing consular protection to EU citizens in crisis situations in third countries. As Lead State in Chad, France efficiently coordinated and carried out activities to ensure the necessary protection of EU citizens. It evacuated more than 1,200 citizens from 12 Member States and third countries. It is worth mentioning that in Chad only France and Germany have embassies.[34]

Thus, the consular Lead State concept qualifies as another practical instrument to guarantee the provision of consular protection and to contribute significantly to its effectiveness.

2.3. Pooling of Resources

For most Member States it is economically not viable to maintain representations in every third country. The number of nationals residing in, or travelling to certain countries stands in no proportion to the expenses of operating an embassy or consulate on a permanent basis. For this reason, smaller Member States have often opted for only opening representations in key countries, complemented with a network of (relatively cheap) honorary consuls. But also major countries with a traditionally extensive diplomatic and consular network, such as France, the United Kingdom and Germany, are increasingly aware of the costs involved, and are willing to undertake a new, post-imperial, attitude in this regard.

---

31 *Ibidem*, Subsection 2.2.

32 *Ibidem*, Section 5, subsection 5.5.

33 *Ibidem*, Introduction section 5.

34 Slovenian Presidency of the EU (2008), Press release: Evacuation of EU citizens from Chad and application of the consular Lead State concept, Press releases 11.02.2008. Available at: <http://www.eu2008.si/en/News_and_Documents/Press_Releases/February/0211MZZ_Chad.html>.

As a general rule, these costs tend to increase year after year as the number of Europeans travelling to third countries shows a steadily upwards trend. As a result, more and more Member States have started to pool their resources by creating co-locations (concentration of two or more diplomatic and/or consular missions in one building or facility), Common Visa Application Centres (CVAC: mutual accreditation of an external service provider at a joint visa application centre) or Common Administrative Centres (CAC: issuance of Schengen visa by several Member States in the same building or by one Schengen member in full representation of all Schengen partners in visa matters). Especially the Schengen area has given a boost to the creation of CVAC/CAC, due to the fact that, contrary to traditional consular services (including visa) which were applied differently according to the national legislations of the Member States, the issuing of Schengen visa is done on the basis of unified criteria, thus paving the way for joint handling of visa applications.

There is for instance a co-location (providing consular protection) in Kabul (Afghanistan) where at the German Embassy are co-located also the Danish and Hungarian representations; furthermore, in Abuja (Nigeria) there is a consular co-location of Germany, Italy and the Netherlands.

The pooling of resources is another method designed to secure the effectiveness of consular protection in third country and can therefore be considered as a further guarantee of the right to consular protection under Article 23 TFEU.

2.4. Cooperation Arrangements: Guarantees of or Restrictions upon the Right to Consular Protection?

The concepts of Lead State, burden-sharing and pooling of recourses have been presented in the sections above as non-judicial guarantees of the right to consular protection.[35] Nonetheless, looking into the content of the right to consular protection determined above under Chapter F, the question arises of whether all these alleged guarantees could be instead limits to the right to consular protection, that need to be justified and to this end to comply with the requirements of a justified limit to a fundamental right.

At first sight, the Lead State concept, burden-sharing agreements and pooling of resources seem rather to limit the right to consular protection directed to the provision of protection in certain situations of distress of "any" Member State represented in the third country concerned.[36]

[35] See Chapter VII, section 2.

[36] According to Article 23 para. 1 TFEU, "Every citizen of the Union shall, [...], be entitled to protection by the diplomatic or consular authorities of *any* Member State, [...]" (Emphasis added by author).

Articles 23 TFEU and 46 of the Charter seem to confer within the right to consular protection also a "sub-right" to choose which of the Member States disposing of a representation should be approached. In contrast, the above-mentioned concepts limit the choice of the right-holder born by his will to exercise the powers granted to him by the right to consular protection.

In the first place, it is questionable whether the right to consular protection confers to the right-holders the power to choose among the representations of the Member Sates in the third country where their own Member State is not represented. An argument against this view would be the assumption that Articles 23 TFEU, 46 of the Charter aim at achieving a qualitative and not a quantitative protection of unrepresented Union citizens abroad in the sense that at the end only one Member State should provide protection under Union law and its own legislation and practices. The mere possibility of choice among all represented Member States in third countries contributes as such not to the relief of the citizen concerned.

Besides, the mere possibility to choose to approach a Member State whose official language is the same or similar to the own language cannot be considered as a legal position created by the Union provisions on consular protection. The language issue is rather a matter of comfort but it does not affect the quality of the protection provided as such. No intention may be deduced from the provisions on consular protection that unrepresented Union citizens should have the right to be attended by the authorities of the Member State approached for help in their own language or in a language similar to their own language. Otherwise, Union citizens whose mother tongue is Greek or Hungarian for instance, would be discriminated against.

Nevertheless, the choice among the representations of the Member States could indeed represent a qualitative difference for the citizens affected taking into consideration the existing discrepancies among the concrete protection measures provided by each Member State under its national legislation and according to its national practices. Against this background, the possibility to choose among the representations of the Member States and to select the one providing the highest protection standard,[37] would indeed represent an added value within the right to consular protection.

Would the possibility of choice among all represented Member States represent an independent legal position that need to be legally protected, the collaboration and cooperation concepts described above would represent a limit to this right of choice and would need to be submitted

[37] To the danger of "protection shopping", please see Chapter VI above.

to the test to be applied to limits of fundamental rights. The limits must have observed the guarantee of statutory reservation for instance. Thus, according to Article 52 para. 1 of the Charter of Fundamental Rights of the European Union, the right could not be limited by a provision that is not established by law.[38]

Irrespective of whether the possibility of choice among all represented Member States shall represent or not an independent legal position, the above-mentioned collaboration and cooperation measures are aimed at ensuring the effective exercise of the right to consular protection.[39] In this sense, regard being had of the fact that, as stated above, the right to consular protection confers no right to the creation of new facilities but guarantees rather the participation in those already existing, those arrangements seek to coordinate the existing facilities of the Member States in a manner ensuring their availability for the citizens in distress. While the Lead State concept is aimed at ensuring the best possible quality through effectiveness of the protection provided, the burden-sharing agreements seek above all to guarantee the reasonable distribution of the existing capacities.

Precisely in view of the danger of protection shopping that could amount to a break-down of the capacities of the representation of a Member State providing a particularly high standard of consular protection, burden-sharing agreements are a capable means to distribute in a fair manner the burden over all Member States represented in a third country, ensuring at the same time the effective enjoyment of the right to consular protection by the persons affected. Thus, the collaboration arrangements in question strengthen the right to consular protection by adjusting it to the social reality.

To this end, and in order to achieve the objectives of those arrangements as guarantees to the effective exercise of the right to consular protection, the information of the Union citizens, above all, on existing burden-sharing agreements is obligatory in order to prevent Union citizens from approaching in vain the representation of a Member State, that is according to a burden-sharing agreement not responsible for the protection of Union citizens of the nationality concerned.

Notwithstanding, these collaboration arrangements cannot be invoked by the representations of the Member States beyond what is

[38] Article 52, para. 1 of the Charter of Fundamental Rights of the European Union: "Any limitation on the exercise of the rights and freedoms recognised by this Charter must be provided for by law…".

[39] See to the limits to fundamental Rights aimed at safeguarding the fundamental rights as institutes HÄBERLE, P., *La garantía del contenido esencial de los derechos fundamentales*, p. 116.

appropriate and necessary in order to guarantee the effective protection of unrepresented Union citizens. Thus, such agreements may not be cited against a Union citizen in distress, when otherwise his/her rights could suffer harm. For instance, should an unrepresented Union citizen approach the representation of a Member State with the request for help in an urgent situation, the citizens may not be referred to the representation of the Member State in charge of citizens of the nationality of the distressed citizen. Only in this way the collaboration and cooperation arrangements are capable of being conceived as guarantees of the right to consular protection and not as restrictions.

3. Conclusions

The right to consular protection is efficiently guaranteed by means of judicial and non-judicial guarantees. As for the judicial guarantees of the right to consular protection it should be stressed that the Court of Justice has full jurisdiction over any judicial dispute relating to Article 23 TFEU. Therefore, should a Member State approached by an unrepresented EU citizen refuse to provide consular protection or provides it in the view of the person concerned in an unsatisfactory manner, the European Commission or another Member State (e.g. the Member State of origin of the person seeking help) could initiate an infringement procedure according to Articles 258, 259 TFEU.

Furthermore, according to Article 267 para. 1 (ex-Article 234 TEC), the Court of Justice has jurisdiction to give preliminary rulings concerning the interpretation of the Treaties and thus, also of Article 23 TFEU. Although not all Member States provide for the possibility of judicial review regarding consular protection (particularly those not recognising a subjective right to consular protection), Union citizens have according to Articles 19 TEU and Article 47 of the Charter of Fundamental Rights of the European Union the right to be provided with the possibility to lodge a judicial remedy in a case of violation of their right to consular protection.

Besides, should a Member State violate the right to consular protection of an unrepresented Union citizens or entitled family members, the individuals affected may claim compensation for damages caused by the refusal, etc. of consular protection from that Member State.

In addition, it should be stressed that the practices related to burden-sharing arrangements, Lead State concept and pooling of resources in the field of consular protection could be also considered as guarantees of consular protection insofar as they offer a major number of centres where consular protection may be requested or lead to a better efficiency of the protection measures.

However, the utility of such arrangements in the practice as guarantees, although limiting the possibility of unrepresented Union citizens to choose among all Member States represented in the third country, need to be measured on their capability to ensure the effective consular protection of the citizens concerned. Therefore, such arrangements would miss their own target, which is not the cooperation among Member States as an end in itself, but rather the effective protection of Union citizens, when representations of Member States abroad would invoke them in situations bearing an unreasonable risk for the physical integrity of the person concerned or the inviolability of his/her fundamental rights.

Chapter VIII

Consular Protection by the European Union

1. Political and Legal Background of the Consolidation of the EU Action Abroad

The fact that the right to consular protection addresses not directly the Union institutions but the Member States has been put forward criticising the lack of a direct link with the Union institutions themselves. In this regard it should be mentioned that a new concept of consular protection provided directly by the European Union has become relevant with the entry into force of the Lisbon Treaty and in particular with the creation of a European External Action Service (EEAS).

The EEAS was created to assist the new High Representative for Foreign Affairs and Security Policy and is under his authority.[1] Under the Lisbon Treaty, the EEAS should be constituted from "relevant departments" of the Commission and the Council's General Secretariat, plus staff seconded from the diplomatic services of the Member States.[2] In bringing together staff from the Commission and the Council, the EEAS – like the new High Representative – connects the EU's "Community" and intergovernmental elements.

The idea of a Union service undertaking consular functions is not new and can be traced back to the BARNIER' report pleading for the creation of so called "Euro-consulates".[3]

---

1 Article 27, para. 3 TEU: "In fulfilling his mandate, the High Representative shall be assisted by a European External Action Service."

2 Article 27, para. 3 TEU: "This service shall work in cooperation with the diplomatic services of the Member States and shall comprise officials from relevant departments of the General Secretariat of the Council and of the Commission as well as staff seconded from national diplomatic services of the Member States. The organisation and functioning of the European External Action Service shall be established by a decision of the Council. The Council shall act on a proposal from the High Representative after consulting the European Parliament and after obtaining the consent of the Commission."

3 BARNIER, M., *For a European Civil Protection Force: europe aid*, 2006, p. 24. Available at: <http://ec.europa.eu/archives/commission_2004-2009/president/pdf/rapport_barnier_en.pdf> (14.09.2012).

The creation of a European External Action Service has been the subject of political controversy, along the lines of the debate over the new High Representative post. For some, the EEAS is seen as marking the birth of a European foreign service that could foster the development of a more distinctive and coherent EU external policy and international presence. For others, the EEAS is likely to impinge on the intergovernmental Common Foreign and Security Policy and represents therefore a threat to national foreign ministries and policies.

The provisions dealing with the EEAS in the Lisbon Treaty remained unchanged from those in the Constitutional Treaty (Article III-296 425). In March 2005, High Representative SOLANA and Commission President BARROSO circulated a joint "Issues Paper" which was discussed with Member States. This was followed up in June of the same year by a Joint Progress Report presented to the European Council on the basis of those discussions.[4] In the June 2005 Progress Report on the EEAS, it was suggested that the new Union delegations might themselves take on consular tasks – "although it was recognised that this was a complex issue which would require some detailed examination".[5] However, in the aftermath of the French and Dutch "no" votes in the referendums on the Constitutional Treaty, the work on the EEAS was suspended. In the wake of the agreement on the Lisbon Treaty in 2007, the 2005 documents were revisited.

According to Article 35 para. 3 TEU (ex-Article 20), the diplomatic and consular missions of the Member States and the Union delegations in third countries and international conferences, and their representations to international organizations

> [...] shall contribute to the implementation of the right of citizens of the Union to protection in the territory of third countries as referred to in Article 20(2)(c) of the Treaty on the Functioning of the European Union and of the measures adopted pursuant to Article 23 of that Treaty.[6]

Before the amendments brought by the Lisbon Treaty, the European Commission was maintaining delegations in third countries and at a number of international organisations. These were delegations of the

4 Joint Progress Report by the High Representative and the Commission to the European Council on the European External Action Service, 9956/05, 9 June 2005. The Progress Report includes the March 2005 "issues paper". Both documents are reproduced in "The EU Foreign service: how to build a more effective common policy", European Policy Centre Working Paper No. 28, November 2007. Available at: <http://www.epc.eu/pub_details.php?pub_id=424&cat_id=1> (21.03.2011).

5 *Ibidem*.

6 Article 35 para. 3: "They shall contribute to the implementation of the right of citizens of the Union to protection in the territory of third countries as referred to in Article 20(2)(c) of the Treaty on the Functioning of the European Union and of the measures adopted pursuant to Article 23 of that Treaty."

Commission, not the EU as a whole. The development of this network of international delegations was driven primarily by the Commission's responsibilities for trade and for the disbursement of development aid and other forms of financial assistance. However, like the Commission itself, the delegations became increasingly active and visible in other areas of external responsibility, such as enlargement and Neighbourhood Policy.

Under the Lisbon Treaty, the delegations of the European Commission in third countries and at international organisations have been converted into European Union delegations.[7] In January 2010, 54 of the European Commission's 136[8] offices abroad became new EU delegations, including Afghanistan, China, India and 33 African states. Under the Lisbon Treaty, the new EU delegations are placed under the authority of the new High Representative. The Lisbon Treaty does not explicitly state that the EU delegations in third countries and at international organisations would form part of the EEAS. However, the June 2005 Commission/High Representative progress report on the EEAS stipulated that "there is broad consensus that the […] future Union Delegations […] should be an integral part of the EEAS."[9]

On 25 March 2010, the High Representative of the Union for Foreign Affairs and Security Policy, Ms Catherine Ashton, appointed by European Council Decision 2009/880/EU,[10] submitted a Proposal for a Council Decision establishing the Organisation and Functioning of the European External Action Service. The proposal clarifies that the EU delegations shall form part of the EEAS.[11]

Thus, since the EU delegations have been integrated into the EEAS and bearing in mind that according to Article 35 para. 3 TEU, cited above,

7 Article 35 para. 1 TEU: "The diplomatic and consular missions of the Member States and the Union delegations in third countries and international conferences, and their representations to international organisations, shall cooperate in ensuring that decisions defining Union positions and actions adopted pursuant to this Chapter are complied with and implemented."

8 According to the Report by the High Representative to the European Parliament, the Council and the Commission of 22.12.2011, in 2011, there were 140 Union delegations abroad. Available at: <http://www.eeas.europa.eu/images/top_stories/2011_eeas_report_cor.pdf> (21.03.2012).

9 Joint Progress Report by the High Representative and the Commission to the European Council on the European External Action Service, 9956/05, 9 June 2005, *op. cit.*, footnote 4.

10 European Council Decision 2009/880/EU taken with the agreement of the President of the Commission of 1 December 2009 appointing the High Representative of the Union for Foreign Affairs and Security Policy, published in Official Journal L 315 of 2.12.2009, p. 49.

11 Article 1, para. 4 of the Proposal: "The EEAS shall be made up of a central administration and of the Union delegations to third countries and to international organisations."

Union delegations shall contribute to the implementation of the right of citizens of the Union to protection in the territory of third countries, the question arises whether the EEAS will be in charge of provision of consular protection under Articles 20, 23 TFEU and how would be the competences between the EU (EEAS) and the Member States shared in this field. The legal basis for the creation of the EEAS is Article 27 para. 3 TFEU reading:

> In fulfilling his mandate, the High Representative shall be assisted by a European External Action Service. This service shall work in cooperation with the diplomatic services of the Member States and shall comprise officials from relevant departments of the General Secretariat of the Council and of the Commission as well as staff seconded from national diplomatic services of the Member States. The organisation and functioning of the European External Action Service shall be established by a decision of the Council. The Council shall act on a proposal from the High Representative after consulting the European Parliament and after obtaining the consent of the Commission.

The legal status of the EEAS was largely controversial. The European Parliament had since the beginnings advocated for including the EEAS within the European Commission and thus to "communitarise" the service in terms of the former three pillars of the European Union, ensuring by this means its tight control over the new service. This intention was clearly stated in the Resolution adopted by the European Parliament on the Institutional Aspects of the EEAS in 2005, pleading that the service should be "incorporated, in organizational and budgetary term, in the Commission's staff structure".[12] In contrast, Mr SOLANA and Mr BARROSO described in their 2005 Joint Progress Report the EEAS as *sui generis* in nature[13] and not located within the framework of the European Commission. By this means duplication of functions should be avoided and costs should be saved, while at the same time the EEAS would be facilitated the use of support by both Commission and Council.[14]

In spite of the formally limited role of the European Parliament within the legislative process of the adoption of the Council Decision on the creation of EEAS restricted to the mere consultation of the Parliament,[15]

---

12 EUROPEAN PARLIAMENT, Resolution on the Institutional Aspects of the European External Action Service of 26.05.2005, para. 2, published in the Official Journal C 117 E, 18.5.2006, p. 232.

13 Joint Progress Report, para. 6, *op. cit.*, footnote 4.

14 DUKE, S., "Providing for European-Level Diplomacy after Lisbon: The Case of the European External Action Service", in *The Hague Journal of Diplomacy*, No. 4 (2009), p. 218.

15 Article 27, para. 3, forth clause TEU: "The Council shall act on a proposal from the High Representative after consulting the European Parliament and after obtaining the consent of the Commission."

the European Parliament used as leverage its power as regarding the amendment of the staff regulation to adapt it to the EEAS staff as well as regarding the budget of the EEAS and could take considerable influence on the final outcome of the negotiations on the shaping of the new service. The Parliament pleaded *inter alia* for the participation in the EEAS leadership of the Commissioners for Neighbourhood Policy, for Development Aid and Humanitarian Aid, as well as for the appointees to senior EEAS posts to be auditioned by the relevant parliamentary Committee.

A compromise with the European Parliament was found at the end of June 2010 and the Council adopted the decision creating the EEAS on 26 July. According to Article 1 Council Decision 2010/427/EU of 26 July 2010 establishing the Organisation and Functioning of the European External Action Service,[16] the EEAS is an autonomous body in relation with the European Commission and the Council General Secretariat and not as a *sui generis* service.[17] The EEAS is treated as a Union "institution" due to the status of its staff.[18] The autonomy of the EEAS finds an expression also in the fact that it has its own budget within that of the Union over which the Parliament can exercise budgetary control.

The European Parliament managed to push through its concept of the EEAS as linked at least by means of personal expertise to the European Commission by establishing Council Decision 2010/427/EU that permanent officials of the Union should represent at least 60% of all EEAS staff while personnel from the diplomatic services of the Member States should represent at least one third of all EEAS staff at administrator level.[19] Therefore, should the EEAS through the

16 Council Decision of 26.07.2010 establishing the organisation and functioning of the European External Action Service (2010/427/EU), published in the Official Journal L 201/30 of 03.08.2010.

17 Article 1, para. 2 Decision…: "The EEAS, which has its headquarters in Brussels, shall be a functionally autonomous body of the European Union, separate from the General Secretariat of the Council and from the Commission with the legal capacity necessary to perform its tasks and attain its objectives."

18 See consideration (8) of Council Decision 2010/427/EU: "For matters relating to its staff, the EEAS should be treated as an institution within the meaning of the Staff Regulations and the CEOS."

19 Article 6, para. 9 of Council Decision 2010/427/EU: "When the EEAS has reached its full capacity, staff from Member States, as referred to in the first subparagraph of paragraph 2, should represent at least one third of all EEAS staff at AD level. Likewise, permanent officials of the Union should represent at least 60% of all EEAS staff at AD level, including staff coming from the diplomatic services of the Member States who have become permanent officials of the Union in accordance with the provisions of the Staff Regulations."

Union delegations be in charge of providing consular protection, this assistance would be provided effectively by the Union and not by the Member States gathered within the framework of the EEAS, that would be the case if the EEAS staff was composed by national diplomats only. Against this background, the role of the EEAS in providing consular protection under Union law should be asserted, taking into account both legal as well as policy considerations.

2. Consular Protection or Consular Coordination by EEAS?

As mentioned before, Article 35 para. 3 TEU suggests the possibility for the Union delegations as part of the EEAS to provide by themselves, beside the Member States' representation abroad, consular protection under Article 23 TFEU by establishing that they "shall contribute to the implementation of the right of citizens of the Union to protection in the territory of third countries".

It has been put forward that the provision of consular protection to unrepresented Union citizens abroad would suppose a measurable benefit for smaller Member States not disposing of a spread net of diplomatic and consular representations by allowing them to strengthen their external representation by reducing at the same time costs.[20] In contrast, large Member States, as for instance France and Great Britain, are reluctant of giving up their own embassies and consulates,[21] which might be seen as a post-imperial attitude.

Another rather pragmatic than a legal consideration is the one regarding the capacity of the Union delegations to provide consular protection in situations of distress. While the Member States maintain approx. 3,000 diplomatic and consular mission abroad manned with some 30,000 diplomats,[22] the EEAS has 3,611 staff, including 1,551 working in Brussels and 2,060 in the 140 delegations in third countries.[23] Worth mentioning is also in this context the lack of expertise on the part of the Union delegation as regarding the provision of consular protection, whereas the Member States can reflect upon a large tradition of protection of their nationals abroad.

---

[20] MAURER, A./ REICHEL, S., "The European External Action Service, Elements of a Three-Phase Plan", in *Stiftung Wissenschaft und Politik (SWP) Comments*, No. 36, 2004, p. 5.

[21] *Ibidem.*

[22] DUKE, S., "Providing for European-level Diplomacy after Lisbon", p. 224, *op. cit.*, footnote 4.

[23] Report of the High Representative of 22.12.2011, p. 8, *op. cit.*, footnote 8.

These pragmatic considerations but also the reluctance to see its own embassies and consulates by Union representations abroad prompted the Government of the United Kingdom to insist on the inclusion of two declarations to the Final Act of the Lisbon Treaty.

Declaration number 13 concerning the Common Foreign and Security Policy underlines that Treaty provisions on Common Foreign and Security Policy, including the creation of the office of High Representative and the establishment of an External Action Service, do not affect the responsibilities of the Member States for the formulation and conduct of their foreign policy nor of their national representation in third countries and international organization.[24] Furthermore, Declaration number 14 adds that provisions covering the Common Foreign and Security Policy including in relation to the High Representative and the External Action Service will not affect the existing legal basis, responsibilities, and powers of each Member State in relation to the formulation and conduct of its foreign policy, its national diplomatic service, relations with third countries, etc.[25]

As a result of these misgivings regarding the role of the EEAS, the Member States, the European Commission and the Parliament agreed on Article 5 para. 10 of Council Decision 2010/427/EU establishing the Organisation and Functioning of the European External Action Service, which stipulates that:

> The Union delegations shall have the capacity to, upon request by Member States, support the Member States in their diplomatic relations and in their role of providing consular protection to Union citizens in third countries.

24 Declaration 13 concerning the Common Foreign and Security Policy to the Final Act of the Lisbon Treaty 2007/C 306/02, published in the Official Journal C 306/231 of 17.12.2007: "The Conference underlines that the provisions in the Treaty on European Union covering the Common Foreign and Security Policy, including the creation of the office of High Representative of the Union for Foreign Affairs and Security Policy and the establishment of an External Action Service, do not affect the responsibilities of the Member States, as they currently exist, for the formulation and conduct of their foreign policy nor of their national representation in third countries and international organisations."

25 Declaration number 14 concerning the Common Foreign and Security Policy to the Final Act of the Lisbon Treaty 2007/C 306/02, published in the Official Journal C 306/231 of 17.12.2007: "In addition to the specific rules and procedures referred to in paragraph 1 of Article 11 of the Treaty on European Union, the Conference underlines that the provisions covering the Common Foreign and Security Policy including in relation to the High Representative of the Union for Foreign Affairs and Security Policy and the External Action Service will not affect the existing legal basis, responsibilities, and powers of each Member State in relation to the formulation and conduct of its foreign policy, its national diplomatic service, relations with third countries and participation in international organisations, including a Member State's membership of the Security Council of the United Nations."

Accordingly, the EU delegations as part of the EEAS will merely support the provision of consular protection by the Member States and will not be considered as a possible "debtor" of the provision of consular protection under Article 23 TFEU. That the obligation established by Article 23 TFEU to provide consular protection to unrepresented Union citizens falls into the scope of competence of the Member States and not of the Union delegations within the EEAS has been underpinned by stating that the Union delegation shall support the Member States in "their role" of providing consular protection.

However, it can be assumed that unrepresented Union citizens in distress would in case of doubt tend to ask a present EU delegation for consular protection rather than the representation of a Member State, all the most bearing in mind that in visa matters there are some collocations of Member States with the participation of the European Commission (e.g. in Kazakhstan).

In these cases, the structures of the EU delegations may be used as a contact point referring unrepresented EU citizens asking for consular protection to the appropriate Member State according to the burden-sharing agreements concluded among the Member States. By this means, the support of the EU delegations would represent an added value to the protection offered by the Member States in compliance with Article 23 TFEU and become a further instrument promoting the practical effectiveness of the right to consular protection.

A more active role for the EEAS in major crisis situations seems to be envisaged in the European Commission's Proposal of a Directive on Consular Protection of EU Citizens Abroad referring to a possible evacuation by the Union itself. Article 15 para. 2 reads:

> In the event of a crisis Member States and the Union shall closely cooperate to ensure efficient assistance of unrepresented citizens. Member States and the Union shall inform each other about available evacuation capacities in a timely manner.

Moreover, coordination at Union level may include support provided by consular experts, in particular from the unrepresented Member States.[26] This approach seems to be accepted also by the High Representative, who points out in her Report to the European Parliament and the Council of 22 December 2011 that:

> It would certainly not be responsible to raise citizens' expectations about the services to be provided by EU delegations, beyond their capacity to deliver in

[26] Article 15 para. 2 second clause of Proposal of a Directive on Consular Protection of EU Citizens Abroad: "Upon request Member States may be supported by existing intervention teams at Union level including consular experts, in particular from the unrepresented Member States."

such a sensitive area. And the existing expertise within the EEAS in this area is extremely limited. However, over the past year we have also seen that the EU Delegations can play an important role in the coordination of evacuations of citizens and that pragmatic solutions can be found on the ground.[27]

Thus, no consular protection will be provided directly by the Union itself, except evacuation in crisis situation, but rather the Union delegations could undertake an important coordination role with regard to the cooperation agreements concluded among the Member States seeking to distribute the burden of the provision of consular protection to unrepresented Union citizens (burden-sharing agreements) and to ensure the effectiveness of consular protection by means of Lead-State arrangements in crisis situations, for instance. The shortcomings of these mechanisms pointed out above, such as their possible disadvantage for Union citizens in distress due to the lack of information about those arrangements, could be bridged by the Union delegations providing coordination and information support.

As a middle way, some propose that the EEAS as at least partly entrusted with consular protection tasks for smaller Member States lacking the wide-spread net of diplomatic and consular representations of the bigger Member States. Currently, it is being discussed within the Council of the European Union whether those Member States willing to see their unrepresented citizens abroad assisted by the Union delegations shall also fund the EEAS in a higher proportion than those Member States not benefitting from its new competences.[28]

3. Conclusions

The difficult negotiations surrounding the creation and the design of the new EEAS led to a solution on the least common denominator, limiting the competences of the Union delegations to functions deployed

[27] Report of the High Representative of 22.12.2011, p. 8, *op. cit.*, footnote 8. It should be noted that although the Report was presented under Article 13 para. 2 of the EEAS Decision ("The High Representative shall submit a report to the European Parliament, the Council and the Commission on the functioning of the EEAS by the end of 2011. That report shall, in particular, cover the implementation of Article 5(3) and (10) and Article 9"), the Report replied also to a memorandum signed by the Ministers of Foreign Affairs of 12 Member States (Belgium, Estonia, Finland, France, Germany, Italy, Latvia, Lithuania, Luxembourg, the Netherlands, Poland and Sweden) and presented on 08.12.2011 complaining about bureaucracy and bad management hampering the effectiveness of the EU's new diplomatic service (Information provided by EUobserver in an article published on 06.01.2012, available at: <http://euobserver.com/24/114783> (06.01.2012).

[28] See KRISTI, R. "Serving the citizens? Consular role of the EEAS grows in small steps", in *European Policy Center Policy Brief*, 30.04.2013. Available at: <http://www.epc.eu/documents/uploads/pub_3488_consular_role_of_the_eeas.pdf> (12.08.2013).

already by some of the Commission's Directorate Generals and the Council General Secretariat, reshuffling therefore the Union competences for external action under the new institutions created under the Lisbon Treaty, thus beside the EEAS also the High Representative and the President of the European Council, and not relocating new competences from the Member States' domain to the Union domain.

What could have be desirable from the citizens' point of view – in particular the simplification of the exercise of the right to consular protection by unrepresented Union citizens in the light of the complex design of the right to consular protection as a multilevel right as well as the burden-sharing and other arrangements among the Member States – seems not to be recommendable for practicability and efficiency reasons due to the yet lacking expertise and personnel capacity of the Union delegations to provide effective consular protection.

The infrastructure of the new EEAS could be, however, indeed used for coordination and information proposals, avoiding *inter alia* the pitfalls of the consular coordination in major crisis situations but also in day-to-day consular business where complex burden-sharing arrangements among the Member States concluded in order to guarantee the effectiveness of consular protection under Union law in third countries raise concerns over their practicability in distress situations requiring rapid response in order to prevent or repair damages.

This role of the EEAS within the provision of consular protection, on the side of providing a further guarantee for the effectiveness of that right, suits in a particularly appropriate manner to the concept of the right to consular protection as a multilevel fundamental right implying the involvement of both Union and Member States' institutions under due consideration of the distribution of competences in this field and observing the subsidiarity principle requiring action on the level that can most effectively achieve the objectives pursuit.

Chapter IX

Proposal for a Directive on Consular Protection

1. Legal Basis and Procedure for the Adoption of a Directive on Consular Protection

OKANO-HEIJMANNS described the European Commission's intention to "raise the European profile" of consular protection provided to unrepresented Union citizens abroad, outlined in the Commission's Green Paper in 2006,[1] as "a bold and somewhat premature conclusion that may be more representative of the Commission's aspirations than of EU citizens' wishes".[2] Admittedly, the lack of awareness of Union citizens in 2006 of the existence of a right to consular protection for unrepresented Union citizens does not by itself lead to a legislative legitimation on the part of the Union in this field. Nonetheless, the efforts made both by the European Commission and the Member States to inform Union citizens on the possibilities offered by Article 23 TFEU, seem to have borne fruits so that in the meanwhile an average of 79% of the Union citizens is deemed to be aware of the existence of the right to consular protection under Union of that right.[3] Remarkable is also in this context that Union citizens express their understanding of the right to consular protection as a right to obtain the same level of help regardless of which Member State's consulate they turn to (62% of the inquired Union citizens).[4] These high expectations of the Union citizens with regard to the right to consular protection do justify a certain urge on the part of the European Commission to push forward new legislative measure in order to clarify the scope and further implementation of the right to consular protection.

Yet, with the entry into force of the Lisbon Treaty, the possibility for the Council has been created to adopt a Directive by including in Article 23 TFEU a new, second paragraph stating that:

---

1 EUROPEAN COMMISSION, EUROPEAN COMMISSION, Green Paper "Diplomatic and consular protection of Union citizens in third countries", COM(2006)712 of 28.11.2006, p. 4. Official Journal C 30 of 10.02.2007.

2 OKANO-HEIJMANNS, M., "Changes in Consular Assistance and the Emergence of Consular Diplomacy", in *Consular Affairs and Diplomacy*, Leiden/Boston, 2011, p. 37.

3 EUROPEAN COMMISSION, Flash Eurobarometer No. 294 on European Union Citizenship, *op. cit.*, footnote 27, p. 26.

4 *Ibidem*, p. 33.

The Council, acting in accordance with a special legislative procedure and after consulting the European Parliament, may adopt directives establishing the coordination and cooperation measures necessary to facilitate such protection.

The special legislative procedure, prescribed by the TFEU for the adoption of legislative measures in the field of Union citizenship' rights,[5] is regulated partly in Article 289 TFEU. According to Article 289 para. 2 TFEU, the special legislative procedure has been established by the Treaty in two variations: adoption of the legislative act in question by the European Parliament with participation of the Council or adoption by the Council with participation of the European Parliament. In the case of consular protection, Article 23 para. 2 TFEU prescribes the adoption of directives by the Council of the European Union after consulting the European Parliament.

Pursuant to Article 289 para. 3 TFEU, acts adopted according to the ordinary or special legislative procedures constitute legislative acts.[6] The distinction between legislative and non-legislative acts has some important practical implications: according to the TFEU, the Council must meet in public when adopting or discussing legislative acts, but is not under an obligation to do so when discussing non-legislative acts.[7]

Unlike the ordinary legislative procedure, the Treaty on the Functioning of the EU does not give a precise description of special legislative procedures. The rules of special legislative procedures are therefore defined on an *ad hoc* basis by the provisions of the TEU and the TFEU. In the case of consular protection, Article 23 para. 2 TFEU prescribes the adoption of legislative acts according to a special legislative procedure, however, without mentioning whether the Council shall adopt those acts by a simple or qualified majority or unanimously. According to Article 16 para. 3 TEU, "the Council shall act by a qualified majority except where the Treaties provide otherwise". Therefore, a directive under Article 23 para. 2 TFEU needs to be adopted by a qualified majority of the Members of the Council[8] and not unanimously as the case is for the majority of the

---

5 Only exception is Article 21 para. 2 TFEU prescribing the adoption of provisions facilitating the exercise of the right to freely move and reside within the European Union according to the ordinary legislative procedure, while according to Article 21, para. 3 TFEU, the special legislative procedure applies in case of measures concerning social security and protection.

6 Article 289, para. 3 TFEU: "Legal acts adopted by legislative procedure shall constitute legislative acts."

7 Article 15, para. 2 TFEU: "The European Parliament shall meet in public, as shall the Council when considering and voting on a draft legislative act."

8 According to Article 16, para. 4 TEU, the former definition for qualified majority should apply transitionally until 31 October 2014 (Article 16, para. 4 TEU: "As from 1

Union citizenship' rights. The Directive needed to be proposed by the European Commission according to Article 17 para. 2 TEU since nothing else has been established by Article 23 TFEU.[9]

Taking up the invitation of the European Council in the Stockholm Programme to "consider appropriate measures establishing coordination and cooperation necessary to facilitate consular protection in accordance with Article 23 TFEU",[10] the European Commission committed itself in its Working Programme for 2011[11] to present a proposal for a directive until the end of 2011 and submitted on 14 December 2011 a proposal for a Council directive on consular protection for citizens of the Union abroad.[12]

2. Is a Directive on Consular Protection Necessary?

So far, the *acquis* in the field of consular protection are limited to the *sui generis* Decisions 95/553/EC and 96/409/CFSP as well as to legally non-binding recommendations issued by the Council of the European Union scattered over several Guidelines, failing to comply with any considerations of systematic.[13] This situation makes it not only impossible

November 2014, a qualified majority shall be defined as at least 55% of the members of the Council, comprising at least fifteen of them and representing Member States comprising at least 65% of the population of the Union"). According to Article 3, para. 3 of the Protocol No. 36 to the Treaty of Lisbon on transitional provisions (published in the OJ C83/322 of 30.03.2010), and after the weighting of votes, "Acts shall be adopted if there are at least 255 votes in favour representing a majority of the members where, under the Treaties, they must be adopted on a proposal from the Commission. In other cases decisions shall be adopted if there are at least 255 votes in favour representing at least two thirds of the members." Since directives under Article 23, para. 2 TFEU need to be adopted upon proposal of the European Commission (Article 17, para. 2 TEU), it would be sufficient if the "weighted" majority corresponds to the majority of the members of the Council.

9 Article 17, para. 2 TEU: "Union legislative acts may only be adopted on the basis of a Commission proposal, except where the Treaties provide otherwise."

10 The Stockholm Programme – An open and secure Europe serving and protecting the citizens, Council document 17024/09 of 2 December 2009, *op. cit.*, footnote 30.

11 EUROPEAN COMMISSION, Communication to the European Parliament, the Council, the European Economic and Social Committee and the Committee of the Regions, Commission Work Programme 2011, Annex II: Indicative list of possible initiatives under consideration, 27.10.2010, COM(2010)623 final. Available at: <http://ec.europa.eu/atwork/programmes/docs/cwp2011_annex_en.pdf> (14.07.2011).

12 EUROPEAN COMMISSION, Proposal for a Council Directive on consular protection for citizens of the Union abroad of 14.12.2011, COM(2011)881 final. Available at: <http://ec.europa.eu/justice/citizen/files/consular-protection_en.pdf> (14.07.2011).

13 Guidelines on consular protection of EU citizens in third countries of 05.11.2010, Document 15613/10 (updated version of the 2006 Guidelines, Document 10109/2/06); Common practices in consular assistance and crisis coordination of 09.06.2010,

for the Union citizens to keep track of the developments in the field of consular protection and contributes to a considerable legal uncertainty, but falls also short of an appropriate legal design of one of the rights deriving from the fundamental status of Union citizens, their Union citizenship.

All these considerations lead to the conclusion that a directive on consular protection could significantly improve the legal position of Union citizens. This improvement could be achieved formally, under legislative-technique aspects, by recasting all existing *acquis* in the field of consular protection into one legislative act, as well as substantively, under legal-certainty aspects, by clarifying the scope of protection provided under Union law, etc. Thus, although Article 23 para. 2 TFEU issues no imperative mandate for the adoption of a directive on consular protection,[14] the adoption of such a directive appears to be in order.

A directive on consular protection would comply also with the principle of subsidiarity according to Article 5 para. 3 TEU. Pursuant to Article 5 para. 1 second clause TEU, "the use of Union competences is governed by the principles of subsidiarity and proportionality", whereby the principle of subsidiarity has been observed:

> [...] if and in so far as the objectives of the proposed action cannot be sufficiently achieved by the Member States, either at central level or at regional and local level, but can rather, by reason of the scale or effects of the proposed action, be better achieved at Union level.[15]

Document 10698/10; Guidelines for further implementing a number of provisions under Decision 95/553/EC of 24.06.2008, Document 11113/08; European Union guidelines on the implementation of the consular Lead State concept of 01.12.2008, Document 2008/C 317/06.

14 Remarkable is in this context that while Member States "shall" adopt the necessary measures required to secure consular protection of unrepresented Union citizens in third countries, according to Article 23, para. 2 TFEU, the Council "may" adopt directives. IANNIELLO SALICETI sees in this wording a logical order of priority between paragraph 2 and 3 of Article 23 TFEU in the sense that "directives adopted by the Council oblige the Member States, which, in turn adopt the necessary provisions". (IANNIELLO SALICETI, A., "The Protection of EU Citizens Abroad: Accountability, Rule of Law, Role of Consular and Diplomatic Services", in *European Public Law* 17, No. 1 (2011), pp. 94, 95).

15 Article 5, para. 3 TEU: "Under the principle of subsidiarity, in areas which do not fall within its exclusive competence, the Union shall act only if and in so far as the objectives of the proposed action cannot be sufficiently achieved by the Member States, either at central level or at regional and local level, but can rather, by reason of the scale or effects of the proposed action, be better achieved at Union level."

The principle of subsidiarity precedes conceptually the principle of proportionality since whereas the principle of proportionality refers to the question of 'how' a Union competence should be exercised (e.g. which legislative act is appropriate and sufficient), the principle of subsidiarity refers to the question of whether an existing Union competence (according to the principle of conferral) should be exercised at all in the case concerned.

As the European Commission rightly points out in its proposal for a directive on consular protection, the cross-border dimension of consular protection provided to unrepresented Union citizens in third countries as well as the design of the right to consular protection as an equal-treatment right make legislative measures on the part of individual Member States inadequate to strengthen the effectiveness of this right.[16] The two-level character of the right to consular protection as involving a claim under Union law itself ('if') as well as under the national provisions of the Member States ('how') suggests the need for coordination of those two legal-order levels by means of Union legislative acts in order to guarantee the equal treatment of Union citizens as well as the effectiveness of the provisions on consular protection. In this context, the adoption of Union legislative measures would also account for the link between Union citizens and the European Union, their Union citizenship, as giving rise for the right to consular protection as a citizens' right.[17]

3. Possible Content of a Directive on Consular Protection

3.1. What Subject according to Article 23 para. 2 TFEU?

Article 23 para. 2 TFEU links the adoption of directives to a particular goal that should be pursuit thereby: that of facilitating consular protection of unrepresented Union citizens in third countries.[18] The notion "facilitate" has been employed by the Treaty also as regards the right to freely move and reside within the European Union, establishing Article 21 para. 2 TFEU that the Council and the European Parliament may adopt provisions

---

See e.g. CALLIES, C., *Schriftliche Stellungnahme zum öffentlichen Expertengespäch des Unterausschusses Europarecht des Rechtsausschusses des Deutschen Bundestages zum Thema "Prüfung des unionsrechtlichen Subsidiaritätsprinzips"* of 16.06.2010, p. 4. Available at: <http://www.bundestag.de/bundestag/ausschuesse17/a06/ua_europarecht/anhoerungen/01_Subsidiaritaet/02_Stellungnahmen/Stellungnahme_Calliess.pdf> (13.03.2011).

16 EUROPEAN COMMISSION, Proposal for a Council Directive on consular protection for citizens of the Union abroad, *op. cit.*, footnote 12.

17 In this regard, it should be noted that the argument put forward by the European Commission in the proposal for a Directive on Consular Protection that by adopting a Union Directive, the possibility for national courts will be opened to request guidance on interpretation from the European Court of Justice, is misleading, since it fails to acknowledge that the right to consular protection under Article 23 TFEU and 46 of the Charter is already directly effective and can thus be invoked before national authorities, including national courts, and that it is subject to the jurisdiction of the European Court of Justice.

18 Article 23, para. 2 TFEU: "The Council [...] may adopt directives establishing the coordination and cooperation measures necessary to facilitate such protection."

with a view to "facilitating the exercise" of that right.[19] Moreover, Article 77 para. 3 TFEU, relating also to the freedom of movement within the European Union, refers to the facilitation of the exercise of that right as well.[20] Therefore, in analogical interpretation, the directive to be adopted under Article 23 para. 2 TFEU shall be aimed at facilitating the exercise of the right to consular protection by its right-holders. This, however, does not mean that any other provisions related to the content of the right to consular protection or its guarantees, for instance, would be excluded. Rather, taking into account the interaction among the different configuration elements of a right, it can be assumed that provisions relating to the circle of right-holders or to the guarantees or scope of the right to consular protection will necessarily have a considerable bearing on the exercise of this right.

Nonetheless, Article 23 para. 2 TFEU authorises the Council to adopt merely directives establishing "coordination and cooperation measures", so that this restriction carries over into the question of whether the Council may adopt a directive on consular protection or rather merely a directive on consular cooperation. As stated above, cooperation and collaboration arrangements aim at ensuring the practical effectiveness of the provision of consular protection and have thus the function of non-judicial guarantees of the right to consular protection. In this context, a directive limited to the establishment and respectively the strengthening of cooperation and collaboration measures among the Member States could fall short of providing a comprehensive legal framework since the guarantees to a right are hardly separable of the other configuration elements of that right, such as right-holders, exercise and content.

Moreover, as stated before, the Member States already established numerous cooperation arrangements amongst themselves aimed at ensuring the practicability and thus the efficiency of the provision of consular protection of unrepresented Union citizens abroad, such as the Lead State concept, burden-sharing agreements and the pooling

---

19 Article 21, para. 2 TFEU: "If action by the Union should prove necessary to attain this objective and the Treaties have not provided the necessary powers, the European Parliament and the Council, acting in accordance with the ordinary legislative procedure, may adopt provisions with a view to facilitating the exercise of the rights referred to in paragraph 1."

20 Article 77, para. 3 TFEU: "If action by the Union should prove necessary to facilitate the exercise of the right referred to in Article 20(2)(a), and if the Treaties have not provided the necessary powers, the Council, acting in accordance with a special legislative procedure, may adopt provisions concerning passports, identity cards, residence permits or any other such document." See also IANNIELLO SALICETI, A., "The Protection of EU Citizens Abroad…", p. 95, *op. cit.*, footnote 14.

of resources on the basis of ex-Article 20 second clause TEC.[21] The cooperation arrangements are, however, not legally binding having the form of informal guidelines issued by the Council of the European Union and the compliance with some of them has been placed at the discretion of the Member States' representations in third countries.[22] In this sense, the new regulation of Article 23 para. 2 TFEU allows for improving the legal status of such arrangements converting them into legally binding Union law.

Irrespective of these considerations, Article 23 para. 2 TFEU needs to be analysed taking into account also the structure of the right to consular protection as an equal-treatment right. The two-level character of the right to consular protection involving the national rules of the 28 Member States that differ from each other, requires a certain degree of coordination among the different national standards regarding the shaping of the right to consular protection, dodging by this means the pitfalls of the right to consular protection stemming from its equal-treatment-right character. Such coordination measures may not, however, seek to achieve the identical application of the right to consular protection in all Member States[23] since Article 23 para. 2 TFEU allows for no harmonisation of national rules on consular protection. This approach would also conflict with the equal-treatment character of the right to consular protection that by its nature tolerates the existence of divergent national rules, provided non-national Union citizens are treated as nationals and are not prevented by means of implicit discrimination from enjoying their rights under Union law.

Thus, a Directive under Article 23 para. 2 TFEU may indeed address any issues related with the need to coordinate national standards on consular protection and not only collaboration and cooperation measures as specific guarantees to the right to consular protection.

The European Commission, though without mentioning this problematic neither in the proposal for a directive on coordination and cooperation measures nor in the correspondent Impact Assessment,[24]

---

21 Ex-Article 20 second clause TEC: "Member States shall establish the necessary rules among themselves [...] required to secure this protection."

22 See for instance COUNCIL OF THE EUROPEAN UNION, Guidelines on consular protection of EU citizens in third countries of 05.11.2010 (15613/10) relating to consular contingency plannings, etc. state that "Implementation is left to the discretion of the heads of missions or posts in the light of local circumstances" (p. 3). Available at: <http://register.consilium.europa.eu/pdf/en/10/st15/st15613.en10.pdf> (08.12.2010).

23 See IANNIELLO SALICETI, A., "The Protection of EU Citizens Abroad...", p. 98, *op. cit.*, footnote 14.

24 EUROPEAN COMMISSION, Impact Assessment accompanying the document Proposal for a Directive of the Council on coordination and cooperation measures

seems to follow the same approach and address for instance an issue belonging to the matter of right-holders of the right to consular protection, extending the circle of right-holders to non-EU family members.[25]

3.2. Assessment of the European Commission's Proposal

The European Commission presented on 14 December 2011 a proposal for a Council directive on consular protection for citizens of the Union abroad. This legislative initiative was announced just shortly before in the Communication of the Commission to the European Parliament and the Council of March 2011[26] and raised high expectations that unfortunately have not been met with the Proposal.

In its Communication of March 2011, the Commission bemoaned the lack of legal and practical certainty with regard to the scope of consular protection for EU citizens due to discrepancies among the national rules and practices on consular protection. It stated that "legal certainty and predictability for EU citizens abroad should be a primary concern"[27] and proclaimed that "the Union has a mandate to further turn this right into practice".[28]

The proposal for a directive of 14 December 2011 falls, however, short of these ambitious goals but also of the targets exposed in the own explanatory memorandum of the Proposal. For instance, while the explanatory memorandum states that "it should be clarified to which extent also third country family members of unrepresented EU citizens are beneficiaries of consular protection", the Proposal limits itself to a mere subparagraph on family members of unrepresented Union citizens stipulating that they should be provided consular protection if family members of own nationals would be entitled to consular protection, and failing thus to clarify to which extent family members are right-holders of the right to consular protection under Union law.

In the following, a proposal will be made on the provisions that should be included into a directive under Article 23 para. 2 TFEU,

regarding consular protection for unrepresented EU citizens, 14.12.2011, Document SEC(2011)1556 final, not published.

25 See Article 2 para. 3 Proposal for a Directive on consular protection for citizens of the Union abroad, *op. cit.*, footnote 12.

26 EUROPEAN COMMISSION, Communication to the European Parliament and the Council on Consular protection for EU citizens in third countries: State of play and way forward, 23.03.2011, Document COM(2011)149/2, p. 11. Available at: <http://ec.europa.eu/justice/policies/citizenship/diplomatic/docs/communication_consular_protection.pdf> (04.03.2012).

27 *Ibidem*.

28 *Ibidem*, p. 13.

offering an examination of the Proposal presented by the European Commission in 2011.

3.2.1. Right-Holders

The Proposal of the European Commission dedicates a considerable part of the draft legislative act to the personal scope of the right to consular protection. It should be, however, noted that the Commission uses the notion "beneficiaries" instead of "right-holders". Although there is no substantive difference between the two notions and the notion "beneficiaries" can be found also in Directive 2004/38/EC on the freedom of movement and residence, the notion "right-holders" would have pointed much better the way, setting an end to any controversy on the legal character of the right to consular protection.

The Commission's proposal addresses in a satisfactory way the definition of the accessibility of the permanent representation of the own Member States stipulating in draft Article 2 para. 2 that:

> Citizens of the Union at least need to be able to reach the embassy or consulate and return to their place of departure the same day, via means of transport commonly used in the third country, unless the urgency of the matter requires swifter assistance. The embassy or consulate is not accessible if it is temporarily not in a position to effectively provide protection, in particular if it is temporarily closed in case of crisis.

The Proposal addresses also the situations in which a Member State is represented on a permanent basis by another Member State stating in Article 4 para. 2 that "A Member State may represent another Member State on a permanent basis […]". As stated above, the directive should besides clarify that where a Member State is represented on a permanent basis by a non-EU country, such agreements are not capable of depriving a Union citizen from his/her right to consular protection under Union law.

Furthermore, as mentioned before, the European Commission failed to effectively address the issue on the extension of the circle of right-holders of the right to consular protection to family members of unrepresented Union citizens. Article 2 para. 3 of the Commission's proposal establishes:

> Family members of unrepresented citizens who themselves are not citizens of the Union are entitled to consular protection under the same conditions as the family members of nationals of the assisting Member State who themselves are not nationals.

First of all, the draft provision lacks a distinction between family members, who are themselves not represented by an embassy or a consulate of their country of origin in the third State, and those, who dispose of such a representation. Besides, the Proposal delivers no definition of the notion 'family members' and refers allegedly also insofar to the national rules that differ considerably from each other. As stated before, a definition similar to the one employed in Directive 2004/38/EC could be used, taking, however, into account the different objectives pursued by the right to freely move and reside in the Member States on the one side and the right to consular protection on the other side.

Moreover, the Proposal falls short of its stated goal to clarify to which extent family members of unrepresented Union citizens may enjoy consular protection: the establishment of a principle of equal treatment of family members of unrepresented Union citizens and those of nationals of the Member State concerned is not suitable for shedding light on the capacity of family members to be entitled to consular protection since the rules of the Member States thereon differ considerably from each other. As a consequence of the provision in Article 2 para. 3 of the Proposal, the equal treatment of family members of an unrepresented Union citizen by a Member State not providing such kind of protection under national rules and practices[29] would mean that these family members would not receive any kind of protection.

Therefore, the directive should contain a provision limiting the discretion of the Member States to provide or not consular protection to family members of unrepresented Union citizens to the concrete measures to be applied ('how'), clarifying that family members would have the right to consular protection ('if') under Union law provided that otherwise the protection of the unrepresented Union citizen would not be effective. This is above all the case when both unrepresented Union citizen and family members are affected by the same situation of distress. By this means the character of the right to consular protection of family members as a 'derived right' would be emphasised.

3.2.2. Minimum Standard

Article 17 of the Commission's proposal stipulates that the directive shall provide for merely a minimum standard for consular protection provided to unrepresented Union citizens stating that "Member States may introduce or retain more favourable provisions in so far as they are compatible with this Directive."

The Proposal reproduces the text of Article 5 of Decision 95/553/EC changing the order of the different precepts establishing that consular protection includes assistance in the situations of arrest or detention, being victim of crime, serious accident or serious illness, death, relief and repatriation in case of distress and as a novelty need of emergency travel documents. Furthermore, the Proposal mentions expressly the issue of

29 For instance the United Kingdom, see above, Chapter V.

ETDs as a consular protection under Article 23 TFEU although the draft-directive shall repeal only Decision 95/553/EC while Decision 96/409/CFSP will remain in force.[30] The only difference in the situations entitling to consular protection in comparison with Article 5 Decision 95/553/EC is that under draft-Article 6 para. 2 of the Proposal, consular protection is provided to victims of any crime and not only to victims of violent crimes as established by Article 5 para. 1 (d) of Decision 95/553/EC.

Conversely, the Proposal seems to suppose a setback in comparison with Decision 95/553/EC in so far as whereas Article 5 para. 2 Decision 95/553/EC expressly states that the situations listed in paragraph 1 are not exhaustive and that consular protection may be provided also in other circumstances,[31] this provision has disappeared in the Commission's Proposal for a directive. The express statement of the possibility to provide consular protection also in "other circumstances" is indeed not necessary since, as stated before, Article 19 of the Proposal clarifies that the directive shall establish a mere minimum standard so that Member States are not prevented from providing consular protection also in other circumstances beside those listed in Article 6 para. 2. Nonetheless, it would have been recommendable, for the sake of legal certainty, to add expressly this possibility as third paragraph into draft-Article 6 of the Proposal. Otherwise, the "minimum-standard clause" of Article 19 of the Proposal could be interpreted as applying merely to the measures to be undertaken by the national authorities in the situations listed exhaustively in Article 6 para. 2 of the Proposal.

3.2.3. Substantive Scope of the Right to Consular Protection

As stated above, the Commission's proposal integrates the former common practices issued by the Council of the European Union as legally non-binding guidelines as a minimum standard of consular protection. Whereas this approach is to be welcomed with view to the discrepancies among the national standards on consular protection, it fails to bridge the pitfalls of the right to consular protection as an equal-treatment right as regarding the question of whether there is an individual right to consular protection under the national law of the Member States. The Proposal focuses on establishing minimum common standards as to the question of how consular protection is provided but leaves the equal-treatment principle untouched as to the question of whether consular protection should be

30 Article 19 of the Proposal of a Directive on Consular Protection for Citizens of the Union abroad: "Decision 95/553/EC is repealed with effect from […]."

31 Article 5 para. 2 Decision 95/553/EC: "In addition, Member States' diplomatic representations or consular agents serving in a non-member State may, in so far as it is within their powers, also come to the assistance of any citizens of the Union who so request in other circumstances."

provided at all. This is all the most unfortunate taking into consideration the need for consular and diplomatic authorities to dispose of a wide scope of discretion regarding the concrete measures to be undertaken under due consideration of the circumstances of the case in question.

Rather, the directive should clarify that unrepresented Union citizens are entitled to consular protection by another Member State under Article 23 TFEU regardless of whether there is an individual right to consular protection under the national law of the Member State concerned, whereas the unrepresented Union citizen in distress should be treated as nationals of the Member State approached for help as regarding the measures to be undertaken in order to produce relief.

3.2.4. Judicial Remedies

The Proposal also fails to confirm that in case that consular protection under Article 23 TFEU has been refused to be provided to an unrepresented Union citizen or his/her family members or has been provided insufficiently, the persons concerned shall have access to judicial and, where appropriate, administrative redress procedures in the Member State approached for help. This provision could lean towards the text of Article 31 Directive 2004/38/EC.[32]

3.2.5. Other Cooperation and Collaboration Measures

The Commission's proposal dedicates the largest part of the text to local coordination among the consular and diplomatic representation, assistance in crisis situations and financial reimbursement. Positively to assess is first of all that Article 12 of the Proposal establishes a simplified procedure for granting financial advance to unrepresented Union citizens, abolishing the requirement to obtain first the permission of the Member State of nationality in order for an assisting Member State to be authorised to grant financial advance to an unrepresented Union citizen.

A novelty is the regulation of Article 12 (b) of the Proposal allowing for including in the sum to be paid back by the citizen concerned not only the financial advance and other costs incurred by the assisting Member State, but also the consular fees applicable to such cases in the home Member State.[33] This provision is based on the assumption that a financial advance

32 Article 31 para. 1 Directive 2004/38/EC: "The persons concerned shall have access to judicial and, where appropriate, administrative redress procedures in the host Member State to appeal against or seek review of any decision taken against them on the grounds of public policy, public security or public health."

33 Article 12 (b) of Proposal for a Directive on consular protection for citizens of the Union abroad: "if required by the assisting embassy or consulate, the citizen's Member State of nationality shall without delay provide the necessary information concerning the request, specifying whether any consular fee may be applicable;"

granted to an unrepresented Union citizen is provided on behalf of his/her Member State of nationality, so that the assisting Member State may not demand any consular fees for granting the financial advance but rather consular fees may incur on the part of the Member State of nationality. In this context, the Commission's proposal uses a complex legal fiction, involving the consular fees for a service that is actually provided by the national authorities of another Member States. Thus, it is at least questionable whether fictive consular fees are "fees" at all, since fees describe in terms of administrative law the effort made by the authorities to provide a real and not a fictive service. According to Article 13 para. 1 of the Proposal, in crisis situations the assisting Member State may seek reimbursement even if the unrepresented citizen has not signed an undertaking to repay.[34]

Worth mentioning is also that the Commission proposes the establishment of fix sums for consular protection provided in crisis situations where the costs of the services provided may not be calculated.[35] Besides, the reimbursement procedure shall be simplified by the use of a common format for reimbursement requests.[36]

Furthermore, the Proposal codifies some of the crisis coordination measures established so far by means of legally non-binding guidelines. Article 15 of the Proposal refers to the inclusion of unrepresented Union citizens in the contingency planning as well as the provision of information to those citizens on crisis preparedness arrangements. Moreover, Article 16 of the Proposal reproduces the most important provisions of the Union Guidelines on the Lead State concept, providing for a definition of a Lead State in a crisis situation as well as the procedure to be followed.

4. The European Parliament's Position

On 25 October 2012, the European Parliament adopted its amendments to the Commission's proposal.[37] The amendments introduced

---

[34] Article 13 para. 1, subparagraph 2 of the Proposal: "The assisting Member State shall submit any requests for reimbursement of the costs of such evacuation or support to the Ministry of Foreign Affairs of the citizen's Member State of nationality. The assisting Member State may seek reimbursement even if the unrepresented citizen has not signed an undertaking to repay pursuant to Article 12 (a)."

[35] Article 13 para. 3 of the Proposal: "Where costs cannot be calculated, the assisting Member State may request reimbursement on the basis of fixed sums corresponding to the type of support provided, as set out in Annex 2."

[36] Article 13 para. 5 of the Proposal: "For requests for reimbursement the common formats set out in Annex 2 shall be used."

[37] EUROPEAN PARLIAMENT, Legislative resolution of 25.10.2012 on the proposal for a Council directive on consular protection for citizens of the Union abroad (COM(2011)0881 – C7-0017/2012 – 2011/0432(CNS)). Available at: <http://www.eu

by Parliament (rapporteur Edit Bauer, Committee on Civil Liberties, Justice and Home Affairs (LIBE)) focus on improving the situation of unrepresented Union citizens in cases of distress, by for instance introducing a new Recital 14 a on any special situations that need to be taken into account in the case of detention and arrest, as e.g. being a victim of trafficking in human beings. Moreover, Parliament's amendments foresee a clarification that the Directive does not impose any obligations on the Member States to provide unrepresented citizens with those types of assistance which are not provided to their own nationals. In this way, Parliament correctly limits the equal-treatment character of the right to consular protection to the question of how consular protection is provided and not also to the question if consular protection is provided at all. To highlight is also the call upon the Commission to consider the creation of a "trust fund" for consular protection from which the representations of a Member State in a third country may advance its expenses for the protection offered to unrepresented Union citizens.

The main novelty proposed by Parliament is a newly created competence for the EEAS to provide consular protection itself.[38] As stated above, in the course of the negotiations on the rules on the staff and the budget of the EEAS as well as on the EEAS Regulation setting its competences, it was agreed upon the EEAS playing a mere coordination role instead of overtaking itself substantive consular tasks. The main argument at that time leading to this solution, beside some Member States reluctance to give up some of the very traditional competences of the nation states such as the protection of their citizens abroad, was also the consideration that the EEAS lacks sufficient staff and expertise to ensure effective protection of Union citizens in third countries. Some scholars argue that Parliament seeks with the newly raised question on the role of the EEAS in consular protection for unrepresented Union citizens to bring the EEAS closer to the citizens

---

roparl.europa.eu/RegData/seance_pleniere/textes_adoptes/provisoire/2012/10-25/0394/P7_TA-PROV(2012)0394_EN.pdf> (12.08.2013).

38 *Ibidem*. Amendment 25, Article 1: "This Directive lays down the cooperation and coordination measures necessary to facilitate the protection of citizens of the Union, in the territory of a third country in which the Member State of which they are nationals is not represented, by the diplomatic or consular authorities of another Member State on the same conditions as the nationals of that Member State. *Where relevant, Union delegations may also be entrusted with consular tasks for unrepresented citizens.*" (Parliament's amendment emphasised by author).

Amendment 29, Article 4: "Unrepresented citizens may choose the Member State embassy or consulate from which they seek consular protection. *They may also seek assistance from the Union delegation wherever necessary and relevant.*" (Parliament's amendment emphasised by author).

and at the same time to strengthen the citizens' sense of European identity while abroad.[39]

It remains to see whether the Member States are willing to make concessions on this aspect that they did not agree to during the negotiations on the set-up of the EEAS, or whether a compromise could be found by entrusting the EEAS with the consular protection only for unrepresented Union citizens from certain Member States.[40]

The second novelty introduced by Parliament's amendments is the replacement of the Lead State concept by coordination and consular protection provided by Union delegations (EEAS). The rapporteur was seeking in this way to remove the burden from a Lead State or other Member State present and entrusting instead with tasks as contingency planning and coordination the Union delegations.[41] The Report seems to overlook the voluntary character of the Lead State concept in the sense that a Member State suitable to overtake the lead in a third country cannot be obliged to do so. In this sense, it would have be more desirable from the point of view of effective consular protection to establish a co-existence between the Lead State concept and the assistance that could be provided by the Union delegations.

5. Transposition Requirements

The transposition of a directive on consular protection faces two main challenges: the first one is related to the lack of national legislation on consular protection in Member States where consular protection is provided as a matter of policy, and the second one is a more political one referring to the legal situation of the nationals of those Member States not recognising a legal right to consular protection.

As a general rule, a directive is not directly applicable in the legal orders of the Member States but must rather be transposed by national measures in order to deploy legal effects. As stated above, some of the Member States have no domestic legislation on consular protection but provide consular protection rather as a matter of policy based on internal instructions and guidelines issued by the Ministries of Foreign Affairs.

39 KRISTI, R., "Serving the citizens? Consular role of the EEAS grows in small steps", in *European Policy Center, Policy Brief*, 30.04.2013. Available at: <http://www.epc.eu/documents/uploads/pub_3488_consular_role_of_the_eeas.pdf> (12.08.2013).

40 *Ibidem*.

41 See EUROPEAN PARLIAMENT, Committee on Civil Libertice, Justice and Home Affairs, Report on the proposal for a Council Directive on consular protection for citizens of the Union abroad. 10.10.2012. Available at: <http://www.europarl.europa.eu/RegistreWeb/search/simple.htm?relName=DOSSIER&reference=LIBE/7/08241&language=EN> (12.08.2013).

Those internal guidelines and circulars have no external effect, i.e. deploy no effects towards citizens and prevent by this means the emergence of a subjective right to consular protection. Article 288 para. 3 TFEU, however, imposes the obligation upon the Member States to achieve by means of the transposition into national law the results prescribed by a directive.[42] The "choice of form and methods" left to the national authorities as to the achievement of the goals set by the directive means that the choice of the kind of measures to transpose the directive is at the discretion of the Member States.

This scope of discretion as regarding the means by which a directive is transposed into national law was inspired on the one hand by the desire to respect as far as possible the sovereignty and law-making power of the Member States and in particular the role of the national parliaments.[43] On the other hand, the freedom to choose the form of transposition allows the Member States to adapt to the "state of law" in the field object of the directive in question, taking into account the national social, economic and legal peculiarities.[44] This approach is the most respectful one for the different legal traditions of the Member States, encompassing also different legislative techniques, which on the other side is inherent to the directive as the mildest instrument of Union hard law.

The discretion of the Member States[45] as regarding the choice of the form of the national measures transposing a directive has faced during the last decades restrictions by the case-law of the Court of Justice. Already in 1980, the Court held in the "*motor vehicles*" case that the content of the directive in question may indeed establish requirements to the quality of the national transposing act.[46] According to the Court, it this regard, it is essential to transpose directives in a way which fully meets the requirements of clarity and certainty in legal situations.[47] The Court therefore went to conclude that mere administrative practices, "which by their nature can be changed as and when the authorities please" cannot be regarded as a proper transposition of a directive.[48] Rather, a proper transposition of a directive requires the adoption of legally binding

---

[42] Article 288 para. 3 TFEU: "A directive shall be binding, as to the result to be achieved, upon each Member State to which it is addressed, but shall leave to the national authorities the choice of form and methods."

[43] PRECHAL, S., *Directives in European Community Law*, Oxford/ New York, 2005, p. 73.

[44] *Ibidem*.

[45] Article 288, para. 3 TFEU speaks about "national authorities".

[46] Judgment of the Court of Justice of 6.05.1980 in the case C-102/79, *Commission of the European Communities v. Kingdom of Belgium*, ECR 1980, p. 1473.

[47] *Ibidem*, para. 11.

[48] *Ibidem*.

national measures. The discretion of the Member States as to the quality of the transposing measures is all the more restricted when the directive concerned is intended to create subjective rights. According to the case-law of the Court of Justice:

> [...] where the directive is intended to create rights for individuals, the legal position arising from those principles is sufficiently precise and clear and the persons concerned are made fully aware of their rights and, where appropriate, afforded the possibility of relying on them before the national courts.[49]

Accordingly, if a directive refers to individual rights, the Member States may not limit themselves in transposing the provisions by means of mere internal instructions, but the national transposing measures must rather enable the individuals to ascertain in a predictable manner the extent of the rights conferred on them and, if the case may be, take legal action against any refusal, etc.[50] In this sense, it is not sufficient that transposing measures are legally binding upon the national administration, as the case of internal guidelines might be, but they must rather be legally binding vis-à-vis the individuals concerned in the sense of having external effect.[51] Thus, Member States not having national legislation on consular protection may not meet the requirements for the transposition of a directive on consular protection by means of mere internal circulars. This applies also in the case where the existing administrative praxis on consular protection corresponds to or even goes beyond the minimum standards prescribed by the directive since, as pointed out by the Court of Justice, administrative practices are not capable of satisfying the requirement of legal certainty and transparency.[52]

In addition, the publicity and transparency of the provisions transposing a directive on consular protection are of particular importance taking into account that it refers to the rights of non-national Union citizens. The particular vulnerability of non-national citizens and its bearing on the requirements to the quality of transposing acts has been pointed out also by the Court of Justice stating that the condition of making individuals aware of their rights and the possibility to rely on them before national courts:

> [...] is of particular importance where the directive in question is intended to accord rights to nationals of other Member States because those nationals are not normally aware of such principles.

---

49 Judgment of the Court of Justice of 23.05.1985 in the case C-29/84, *Commission of the European Communities v. Federal Republic of Germany*, ECR 1985, p. 01661, para. 23.

50 PRECHAL, S., *Directives in EC Law*, p. 84, *op. cit.*, footnote 43.

51 *Ibidem*.

52 Judgment of the Court of Justice of 30.05.1991 in the case C-361/88, *Commission of the European Communities v. Federal republic of Germany (TA-Luft)*, ECR 1991, p. I-2567, para. 24.

Admittedly, the transposition of a directive on consular protection by those Member States not providing a legal right to consular protection under national law might place the ball in the Member States' court to adjust consular protection provided to nationals to the one established by the draft-directive. At the first sight, the provisions of the draft-directive on consular protection imply no better treatment of unrepresented Union citizens than nationals of the assisting Member States since the Commission's proposal establishes merely a common minimum standard, i.e. goes not beyond what is already provided under national law or practices to nationals. Nonetheless, the Proposal appears to presuppose the existence of a legal right to consular protection under Union law, otherwise the minimum standard as regarding the way consular protection is provided would be deprived of any sense. In any case, those Member States providing consular protection to their own citizens as a matter of policy and at the discretion of the competent authorities may be forced to change national rules on consular protection and establish a subjective right to consular protection also for their nationals. This would then be no legal but a political consequence of the implementation of the Union provisions on consular protection.

6. Conclusions

The Treaty of Lisbon paved the way for a further quantitative and qualitative development of the *acquis* on consular protection equipping the right to consular protection with the possibility to experience a legislative progress by means of a Council directive adopted upon the proposal of the European Commission and after consulting the European Parliament. The right to consular protection has lost by this means one of its particularities as the only citizenship' right not submitted to the legislative competences of the Union, confirming by this means the abandoning of the previous logic of intergovernmental decision-making in the field of consular protection provided to unrepresented Union citizens in third countries.[53]

The adoption of a directive on consular protection, although not necessary in order for Article 23 TFEU to produce effects directly on the relationship between Member States and citizens, is advisable in terms of legal certainty as well as with regard to the need to strengthen the practical effectiveness of the right to consular protection.

Bearing in mind these goals of the directive on consular protection, the specifications provided by Article 23 para. 2 TFEU as to the subject-matter of the directive need to be extensively interpreted subsuming

---

[53] See also EUROPEAN COMMISSION, Communication of 23.03.2011, p. 4, *op. cit.*, footnote 26.

under the coordination and cooperation measures authorised by the Treaty any provisions aimed at preventing and compensating the shortcoming deriving from the design of the right to consular protection as an equal-treatment right and the discrepancies among the Member States' legislations and practices on consular protection.

The Commission proposal for a directive on consular Protection for citizens of the Union Abroad of 14 December 2011, although supposing a qualitative legislative development by converting the numerous legally non-binding, intergovernmental, guidelines in the field of consular protection into legally binding Union law, falls short of the previously established goal to clarify the scope of consular protection under Union law.

Although the Proposal offers a positive development in the definition of the accessibility of the own diplomatic or consular representation of the Member State of nationality of the citizen concerned, it fails to effectively address the extension of the circle of right-holders to unrepresented family members of unrepresented Union citizens abroad. The Proposal chooses in this sense not to face the challenges stemming from the discrepancies among the Member States' legislations and practices regarding consular protection provided or not to family members of their nationals.

The abstract referral to the national legislations and practices in the Proposal is certainly the response to the Member States' reluctance to improve the legal situations of family members in light of the fear of a greater financial burden for the national budgets. The proposal thus misses the opportunity to improve the effectiveness of the right to consular protection by establishing that family members of Union citizens affected by the same situation of distress would be entitled to consular protection by the Member State assisting the unrepresented Union citizen if otherwise no consular protection might be provided effectively to the unrepresented Union citizen concerned.

Furthermore, it would have been recommendable to clarify in the Proposal that the establishment of a minimum standard of provision of consular protection to unrepresented Union citizens abroad presupposes the existence of a right to consular protection under Union law limiting the discretion of the Member States to the question of 'how' consular protection is provided in each case under consideration of the specific circumstances. The intended legal certainty for the citizens as right-holders of the right to consular protection will not be improved unless it is expressly established that unrepresented Union citizens are entitled to consular protection by another Member State under Article 23 TFEU and Article 46 of the Charter regardless of whether there is an individual right to consular protection under the national law of the Member State approached for help.

In this sense, the Commission proposal chooses rather an inappropriate field for further legislative development: the question of which type of consular protection may/should be provided in a situation of distress is as such capable of being left to the discretion of Member States' legislator respectively the competent diplomatic or consular authorities in order to enable them to take into account the circumstances of each concrete case. Besides, the common practices of the Member States as to how to provide consular protection identified in the Proposal for a directive show that the discrepancies among the Member States are not of particular relevance so that the identification of a common minimum protection-standard as to how consular protection is provided is indeed welcome with view to a better visibility for the citizens but is contradictory to the nature of the right to consular protection as a right to equal treatment regarding the type of assistance provided.

For the sake of legal certainty, which is one of the stated purposes of the Commission's proposal for a directive, it would have been much more important to clarify the existence of a legal right as to whether consular protection is provided not dependent on the recognition of such a right within the Member States' legal orders.

It is also unfortunate that the Commission's proposal fails to confirm the right of Union citizens to take redress against Member States' decisions not to provide consular protection or in case that the assistance provided has not been sufficient.

In contrast, the Proposal regulates satisfactorily the procedure for financial advance and its posterior reimbursement by the Member State of nationality simplifying the current procedure requiring the assisting Member State to obtain first the permission of the Member State of nationality of the Union citizen concerned. Moreover, folding the Lead State concept as well as other coordination arrangements in crisis situations into the body of the Council directive is appropriate and necessary for improving the legal certainty and the practical effectiveness of those specific guarantees aimed at ensuring the exercise of the right to consular protection.

Due to a negotiation stalemate in the Council, the adoption of the Commission proposal has been protracted. Member States are having a fairily hard time to agree on any provisions, even not very ambitious ones, that could potentially boost the claims to recognise the right-character of the provision of consular protection under EU law.

Chapter X

Final Remarks

In a globalised world, where State borders seem to have lost their inhibiting effect, and people, in particular, European Union citizens are travelling and/or living outside the territory of the EU Member States, the effective protection of those EU citizens have become a challenge for the national consular authorities, which has been illustrated by the experience gained from recent crises.

The financial burden involved by a wide net of diplomatic and consular missions providing consular protection abroad as well as the lack of traditional relationships among some Member States and some third States leading to the lack of such missions in many third States, has progressively attracted the attention to the instruments of protection provided under Union law. The right to consular protection established by Articles 23 TFEU and 46 of the Charter of Fundamental Rights of the European Union has turned out to be an appropriate instrument both to achieve a more effective protection of EU citizens abroad as well as by this means to strengthen the sense of European identity and promote an active European citizenship.[1]

In contrast to the particular relevance of the right to consular protection stands the legal uncertainty concerning the dogmatic classification of this institution of law leading to an uncertainty as regards its practical effectiveness. While the European Commission sees the right to consular protection as belonging to the "legal core of citizens' rights",[2] some Member States as well as many commentators regard consular protection as an unbinding programme that seeks to burden Member States with disagreeable tasks and as a silent attempt of the Union institutions to extend their field of action outside the European Union.

1 In this context it should be highlighted that initiatives such as the Community action programme to promote active European citizenship (Council Decision 2004/100/EC of 26.01.2004), which was implemented over 2004-2006 and the 'Europe for Citizens Programme' (Decision No. 1904/2006/EC of the European Parliament and the Council of 12.12.2006 establishing for the period 2007-2013 the programme 'Europe of citizens' to promote active European citizenship, Official Journal L 378/32 of 27.12.2006) for the period 2007-2013, provide the Union with important instruments to promote active European citizenship.

2 EUROPEAN COMMISSION, Fifth Report on Citizenship of the Union (1.05.2004-30.06.2007) of 15.02.2008, COM(2008)85 final. Available at: <http://eur-lex.europa.eu/LexUriServ/LexUriServ.do?uri=COM:2008:0085:FIN:en:PDF> (07.003.2009).

The legal complexity of the right to consular protection is based on its extraterritorial character on the one side and its design as an equal-treatment right on the other side. These two characteristics of the right to consular protection are challenging and promising at the same time. They both originate from and reflect the interaction of multiple legal orders within the shaping of a fundamental right.

The extraterritorial character of the right to consular protection conducts to the interaction within its legal framework of Union and international law rules whose hierarchical relationship or horizontal interaction is contentious and has been repeatedly subject of the case-law of the Court of Justice during the last years. In this regard, a comparison of the international law concept of diplomatic protection and the Union provisions on protection of unrepresented Union citizens abroad shows that while diplomatic protection under international law takes place in case of an internationally wrongful action of a State and is conceived of as a State power conferring no individual right to the person concerned, protection of Union citizens abroad shall be triggered rather by a human act, a natural disaster or another event not attributable to a State only and has been construed as a right deriving from Union citizenship. Besides, whereas the 'nationality rule' is strictly applied in the case of diplomatic protection, international law rules are not opposed to the provision of consular protection to non-national Union citizens. These conceptual divergences between diplomatic protection under international law on the one side and protection of Union citizens abroad on the other side require the establishment of hierarchical rules or rules of interaction between those two legal orders. Whereas international law shall have primacy over secondary Union law, both as regarding secondary Union law implementing the international law rules in question and secondary Union law provisions conflicting with relevant international law without a direct implementation link, international agreements may not have primacy over primary Union law where this would contradict the Union fundamental principles including fundamental rights. Thus, although the Court of Justice takes great care to respect the obligations that are incumbent on the Union and the Member States by virtue of international law, it seeks to preserve the constitutional framework created by the Treaties. Therefore, the reconciliation between the institutes of diplomatic and consular protection in their configuration established by Union and by international law should lead to their best possible unfolding and promote their coexistence as well as cooperation rather than the subordination of one concept to the other.

Regard being had of the conceptual differences between diplomatic protection and the protection of Union citizens abroad as a right stemming from Union citizenship, it seems that the protection intended by Article 23

TFEU could be rendered more effectively and would have a more positive bearing on the legal position of EU citizens if EU law covered consular protection only and not also diplomatic protection. Thus, the limitation of the material scope of Article 23 TFEU on consular protection would lead to a reinforcement of the regulatory depth of this legal provision by its personification and subjectivisation. This interpretation of the Union provisions on consular protection would bring the most practical effectiveness to European Union law.

In addition, the concept of consular protection provided to unrepresented Union citizens abroad needs to be distinguished from other consular functions under international and national law. Whereas consular officers are assigned a range of administrative functions, consular protection under Union law refers to action aimed at providing relief in a situation of distress.

The structural and functional traits of the provision of consular protection provide a comprehensive dogmatic framework for the definition of its legal character setting it in relation to the constitutional environment surrounding the provisions concerned and accounting for its function under due consideration of its capacity as a right deriving from the Union citizenship status. In this way, the particularities of the right to consular protection stemming from its extraterritorial character and its design as a positive claim against the Member States lead to an alleged legal uncertainty regarding its dogmatic classification. This legal uncertainty is however not implicit in the concept of the provision of consular protection to unrepresented Union citizens abroad but is based on the lack of a systematic structural and functional analysis of the provisions concerned.

Precisely the particularity of the right to consular protection as a legal concept construed under consideration of the distribution of competences between the European Union and the Member States regarding consular protection of Union citizens abroad in a multilevel-governance environment needs to be reflected in the analysis to be carried out. Therefore, the constitutional dimension of the right to consular protection as a right stemming from the "fundamental status of Union citizens" should be taken into account from a structural and from a functional perspective.

On the one side, the structural traits of the right to consular protection as included in the Treaties themselves, including the Charter of Fundamental Rights of the European Union, shed light on the dogmatic features of the right to consular protection as a subjective right under distinction with individual legal positions conferred by secondary Union law. The principles developed by the Court of Justice allowing for an exceptional procedural reliance on the provisions of a not transposed EU Directive in terms of an objective *invocabilité* find no justification within the framework of rights conferred upon individuals by the Treaties themselves. It should be therefore distinguished between the substantive right conferred by the Treaties, creating a subjective legal position conferred upon a determined or determinable circle of right-holders, and the judicial review of an alleged violation of the legal position granted as one of the guarantees effectively ensuring the enjoyment by the right-holders.

On the other side, the structural features of the right to consular protection give indication also about its functional environment as deriving from the Union citizenship status. Thus, the dogmatic concept of the right to consular protection may not disregard its function as a Union citizenship right taking into account the spirit and purpose not only of Union citizenship as such but also of its structural characteristics as a status embedded into the Union normative Constitution creating a real "multilevel citizenship". In this regard, and employing an institutional approach to consular protection as an institution of law integrated in a complex hierarchical and interpretative interaction with other legal norms at European and national level, the social function of the right to consular protection, pre-determined by its structural particularities as Union citizenship right, sets the context for the analysis of the different elements construing this right. Therefore, right-holders, exercise, scope, limits and guarantees of the right to consular protection should be construed under due consideration of the aim Union citizenship to facilitate a new stage of European integration based on a European identity created out of a qualitatively evolved Union of Rights.

The structure of the right to consular protection as a positive claim, against a liberalist approach conceiving it of as a negative right, poses a challenge to its multilevel-governance context involving action of Member States' national authorities according to national rules and practices. The balancing between the design of the right to consular protection as a positive claim on the one side and the legitimate State interest to remain Master of the political decision-making leads to the conceiving of the right to consular protection as a right to participate in existing consular and diplomatic facilities without establishing an obligation upon Member States to create new facilities which remains a policy option at State' disposal.

This being said, it should be noted that the exercise of the right to consular protection by its beneficiaries is narrowly linked to the capability of the legal provisions concerned to deploy direct effect on the relationship between Member States and citizens. The intention of those provisions as provisions of primary Union law to address not only Member States but also individuals, as held by the Court of Justice already in the *Van Gend & Loos* case, as well as the structure and function of the right to consular protection as deriving from the fundamental status of Union citizens, their Union citizenship, lead to the conclusion that the Union provisions on consular protection are directly effective.

Precisely taking into account the function of the right to consular protection to fill out with content the Union citizenship status providing an added value for the protection of Union citizens abroad by establishing a real solidarity relationship among Member States regarding consular protection in third countries, it must be concluded that the direct effect of the right to consular protection is inherent to its strive for effectiveness and to the pursuit of greater accomplishments to the benefit of Union citizens in distress beyond the borders of the European Union.

The alleged conditions imposed upon the exercise of the right to consular protection pose no objection to this conclusion. Rather, Article 23 TFEU establishes no constitutive conditions upon the right to consular protection which as a start shall "create" this right but rather mere implementing rules as well as guarantees in order to secure the effectiveness of the right to consular protection as a citizens' right established by the Treaties. In this regard it should be mentioned that neither the adoption of "necessary measures" by the Member States nor the international negotiations required to secure consular protection are dedicated to hinder the direct effect of the right to consular protection but rather shall guarantee its practical effectiveness and secure its unobstructed exercise. In addition, the inclusion of the right to consular protection into the rights' catalogue of the Charter of Fundamental Rights of the European Union would not be compatible with the lack of direct effect the provisions on consular protection. The aim of the now legally binding Charter to make the rights contained therein more visible by means of their effective enjoyment could not be achieved otherwise than by reaffirming the right to consular protection as a Union citizens' right that can be invoked by its right-holders before the national authorities of the Member States.

The Union provisions on consular protection identify as holders of the right to consular protection all Union citizens, being Union citizens all nationals of the EU Member States according to their national legislation and regardless of age and gender, whose Member State of origin is not represented in the third country concerned. The requirement of the "accessibility" of the representation of the Member State of nationality is thereby narrowly related to the extend of the circle of the right-holders, being those Union citizen having an accessible representation of their own Member State in the third country not entitled to ask for help the representation of another Member State. The extensive interpretation of the "accessibility" of the representation of the Member State of nationality of the person concerned facilitates a flexible and practical approach in each concrete case, accounting for the specific circumstances prevailing in the third country in question. An exception to the requirement of lack of an accessible representation of the Member State of nationality is the Lead State concept providing for the possibility to be assisted by a Member State different from the one of nationality in order to secure the effective and coordinated protection of all Union citizens in a third country. Besides, in order to guarantee the effective enjoyment of the right to consular protection by unrepresented Union citizens, the right to hold the right to consular protection should be extended to non-national family members of unrepresented Union citizens in third countries. The definition of the non-national family members, who should be awarded a right to consular protection under Union law, could be established in the likeness of the relevant provisions regarding freedom of movement and residence in the European Union, however, taking into account the different *rationale* behind the two citizens' rights. Thus, seeking to ensure the practical effectiveness of the right to consular protection conferred upon Union citizens, family members should be provided with consular protection under Union law merely in situations of "complicity" affecting both the Union citizen in distress as well as their family members, being the protection of the family members conditional for the effective enjoyment of the right to consular protection by the Union citizen concerned.

In contrast, third-country nationals entitled to consular protection by a Member State according to a bilateral or multilateral agreement as well as according to national legislation as long-term residents or recognised refugees may not invoke the right to consular protection under Union law.

The powers conferred upon the right-holders of the right to consular protection corresponding to an obligation imposed upon the Member States involve in their legal context besides international law and Union law provisions also national rules and practices due to the design of the right to consular protection as an equal-treatment right. This complexity as well as the demand for practical effectiveness of the right to consular protection as a citizens' right results in a distinction between the questions of if consular protection shall be provided and which type of protection is offered.

Whereas the first question is governed by Article 23 TFEU in conjunction with Decision 95/553/EC and Decision 96/409/CFSP and is not dependent on the recognition of a subjective right to consular protection in the legal orders of the Member States, the question of how consular protection shall be provided is regulated by the national rules and practices and shall be applied to unrepresented Union citizens in situations of distress in the same manner as to nationals of the assisting Member State. This approach prevents the right to consular protection under Union law from being deprived of any sense when unrepresented Union citizens ask for help Member States not conferring under their national rules a subjective right to consular protection so that a treatment equal to that of nationals would be of no avail for unrepresented Union citizens abroad.

The obligation upon the Member States corresponding to the subjective right to consular protection should be determined under due consideration of the function of the right to consular protection as a right aimed at guaranteeing the exercise of other fundamental rights such as the right to life, to physical integrity, property and human dignity. Thus, the violation of the obligation to protect these fundamental rights in a situation of distress as stipulated by Decision 95/553/EC and Decision 96/409/CFSP would constitute a violation of the right to consular protection.

The recognition of a substantive scope of the right to consular protection regarding the question of if consular protection is provided at all may, however, not result in conceiving of an absolute right to consular protection. Rather, the refusal to provide consular protection may be justified as complying with the principle of proportionality when the fundamental rights underlying the right to consular protection could be secured by means of the mechanisms of collaboration and coordination with regard to consular protection, such as Lead State concept, burden-sharing arrangements and pooling of resources. Thus, the obligation to provide consular protection to unrepresented Union citizens is not deemed to be violated by the refusal by the consular authorities of a Member State to provide protection with view to existent arrangements among the Member States' representations in the third country concerned aimed at guaranteeing effective consular protection under consideration of available capacities and infrastructures, provided the protection of the underlying fundamental rights is secured effectively.

As for the question of how consular protection is provided, the national rules of the Member States apply under equal treatment of unrepresented Union citizens. The discretion awarded by national rules to consular officers as to the choice among different means of protection needs to be exercised with regard to the principle of proportionality taking into account the suitability and necessity of the measures at disposal of the competent authorities to prevent or remedy the violation of the fundamental rights protected by the right to consular protection of the Union citizen concerned. Accordingly, an unrepresented Union citizen might be entitled to claim the provision of a specific measure, provided that that measure is the only one capable of providing efficiently relief. This would be the case if otherwise the fundamental rights of the citizen in distress underlying the right to consular protection may not be protected and the interest to prevent a threatening damage prevails over any conflicting public interests.

Furthermore, it should be pointed out that the enjoyment of the right to consular protection by its right-holders is effectively ensured by means of judicial and non-judicial guarantees. With the abolition of the pillar structure and the extension of the jurisdiction of the Court of Justice over the entire Union law, the controversy regarding the jurisdiction of the Court over the provisions on consular protection has been overcome so that the Court may rule in procedures of infringement of the provisions on consular protection brought by the European Commission as well as by a Member State. Moreover, a question for preliminary ruling may/must be referred to the Court of Justice by a national court in a case relating to the interpretation of Article 23 TFEU, Article 46 of the Charter as well as Decision 95/553/EC and Decision 96/409/CFSP. Member States are obliged under Union law to provide for the possibility for Union citizens to seek judicial review of the decisions of the national authorities regarding consular protection of unrepresented Union citizens. In case that unrepresented Union citizens or their family member entitled to consular protection have suffered a damage as a consequence of a denial to be provided with consular protection or of the insufficient protection, they would have the right to claim a compensation based on state liability.

The practices related to burden-sharing arrangements, Lead State concept and pooling of resources in the field of consular protection are also guarantees of consular protection insofar as they offer a major number of centres where consular protection may be requested or lead to a better efficiency of the protection measures. However, the utility of such arrangements in the practice as guarantees, although limiting the possibility of unrepresented Union citizens to choose among all Member States represented in the third country, need to be measured according to their capability to ensure the effective consular protection of the citizens concerned. Therefore, such arrangements would miss their own target, which is not the cooperation among Member States as an end in itself, but rather the effective protection of Union citizens, when representations of Member States abroad would invoke them in situations bearing an unreasonable risk for the physical integrity of the person concerned or the inviolability of his/her fundamental rights.

The legal framework of the right to consular protection could be modified and improved in the future by means of a Council Directive adopted upon the proposal of the European Commission and after consulting the European Parliament as a consequence of the entry into force of the Treaty of Lisbon. The adoption of a directive on consular protection, although not necessary in order for Article 23 TFEU to produce effects directly on the relationship between Member States and citizens, is advisable in terms of legal certainty as well as with regard to the need to strengthen the practical effectiveness of the right to consular protection.

The coordination and cooperation measures authorised by Article 23 para. 2 TFEU as a subject-matter of a directive on consular protection should comprise any provisions aimed at preventing and compensating the shortcoming deriving from the design of the right to consular protection as an equal-treatment right and the discrepancies among the Member States' legislations and practices on consular protection. The European Commission's Proposal for a Directive on Consular Protection for Citizens of the Union Abroad of 14 December 2011, although supposing a qualitative legislative development by converting the numerous legally non-binding intergovernmental guidelines in the field of consular protection into legally binding Union law, falls short of clarifying the scope of consular protection under Union law. The Proposal fails, for instance, to effectively address the extension of the circle of right-holders to unrepresented family members of unrepresented Union citizens abroad, disregarding the discrepancies among the Member States' legislations and practices regarding consular protection provided or not to family members of their nationals. In addition, the Commission Proposal for a Directive on consular protection unfortunately chooses to focus its efforts on establishing a common minimum standard of consular protection instead of clarifying the existence of a substantive scope of consular protection as regarding the question of if protection is provided regardless of conflicting national rules. In this regard, the character of the right to consular protection as a subjective right could have been underpinned by revisiting the right of Union citizens and family members to take redress against Member States' decisions not to provide consular protection or in case that the assistance provided has not been sufficient.

Moreover, the analysis of the provisions on consular protection showed that the obligation to provide protection to unrepresented Union citizens abroad should not be imposed on the Union delegations abroad within the EEAS as further passive subject of the right to consular protection besides the Member States. The lack of expertise of the EEAS diplomats as to consular protection and the better Member States' infrastructure in third countries resulted in authorising the EEAS to provide support to Member States in fulfilling their obligation to provide consular protection to unrepresented Union citizens. Therefore, the infrastructure of the new EEAS is likely to be used for coordination and information proposals, avoiding *inter alia* the pitfalls of consular coordination in major crisis situations but also in day-to-day consular business where complex burden-sharing arrangements among the Member States concluded in order to guarantee the effectiveness of consular protection under Union law in third countries raise concerns over their practicability in distress situations requiring rapid response in order to prevent or repair damages.

The construction of the right to consular protection as a fundamental right conferred upon Union citizens but also their family members is capable of turning into one of the most relevant projections of Union citizenship providing for a valuable advantage in terms of a subjective legal position to citizens in a difficult situation in a third country. But besides this importance of the right to consular protection for the achievement of the goals of Union citizenship, the complex legal framework of the right to consular protection is a prime example of multilevel constitutionalism based on complementarity of legal norms stemming from different legal orders and conceiving of in their interaction a fundamental right operating at different levels and capable of contributing to further juridification of the subject-matter concerned.

The conclusions of this legal analysis are, however, at odds with the reluctance of Member States to recognise the right-character of the provision of consular protection to unrepresented Union citizens abroad. Some Member States's governments give the impression of having underestimated the effect and the extent of legal provisions agreed upon within the Council. In this sense, several governments seem to still see Union citizenship mainly as a free-movement concept and deny the integrative power of other civic and political rights, perhaps due to the "legacy of the market citizen".[3] Many political actors refuse to recognise that Union citizenship is not a formalistic garment to show off when trying to capture citizens' votes and support. Rather, whether envisaged in this way or not, Union citizenship has turned into a constructive legal and socio-political concept. Consular protection is a case in point for this development and a test for Member States' commitment to the European project.

---

3 Shaw, J., "The Interpretation of European Union Citizenship", in *The Modern Law Review*, Vol. 61, No. 3 (1998), p. 304.

Bibliography

Monographs, Articles, Commentaries

ALEXY, Robert, *Teoría de los derechos fundamentales*, Centro de Estudios Constitucionales, Madrid, 1993.

ANDRÉS SÁENZ de SANTA MARÍA, Paz, "La protección diplomática y consular de los ciudadanos de la Unión en el exterior", in *Revista de Derecho de la Unión Europea*, No. 11-2° semestre 2006, p. 11.

BALAGUER CALLEJÓN, Francisco, "La construcción del lenguaje jurídico en la Unión Europea", in *Revista de Derecho Constitucional Europeo*, 2004, No. 1, pp. 307-320.

BARNIER, Michel, *For a European Civil Protection Force: Europe aid*, May 2006. Available at: <http://ec.europa.eu/archives/commission_2004-2009/president/pdf/rapport_barnier_en.pdf>.

BESSON, Samantha / UTZINGER, André, Introduction: Future Challenges of European Citizenship-Facing a Wide-Open Pandora's Box, in *European Law Journal*, Vol. 13 (2007), p. 573.

BETHLEHEM, Daniel, "International Law, European Community Law, National Law: Three Systems in Search of a Framework, Systematic Relativity in the Interaction of Law in the European Union", in *International Law Aspects of the European Union*, Martti Koskenniemi (ed.), p. 169, Springer, The Hague/London/Boston, 1998.

BLÁZQUEZ PEINADO, María Dolores, *La ciudadanía de la Unión (Los derechos reconocidos en los artículos 8.A a 8.D del T.C.E.)*, Tirant Lo Blanch, Valencia, 1998.

BÖCKENFÖRDE, Ernst Wolfgang, *Staat, Verfassung, Demokratie: Studien zur Verfassungstheorie und zum Verfassungsrecht*, 2. edition, Suhrkamp, Frankfurt a.M., 1992.

BÖCKENFÖRDE, Ernst-Wolfgang, "Grundrechtstheorie und Grundrechtsinterpretation", in *Neue Juristische Wochenschrift*, 1974, Heft 35, pp. 1529-1538, C.H. Beck, Frankfurt a.M., 1974.

BORISOV, Orlin, *Дипломатическо и консулско право*, Nova Svesda, Sofia, 2011.

BOSNIAK, L., "Universal Citizenship and the Problem of Alianage", in *Northwestern Law Review*, Vol. 94 (2000), pp. 963-984.

BOSNIAK, Linda, "Citizenship denationalized", in *Indiana Journal of Global Legal Studies*, Vol. 7 (2000), pp. 447-509.

BOSKIAK, Linda, "Persons and Citizens in Constitutional Thought", in *International Journal of Constitutional Law* (I-CON), Vol. 8 (2010), No. 1, pp. 9-29.

BUSSE, Christian, "Enthält Artikel 20 S.1 EGV – Amsterdam einen unmittelbaren Anspruch auf diplomatischen und konsularischen Schutz?", in *Europa-Blätter*, Vol. 1 (1998), p. 92.

CALLIES, Chriastian, *Schriftliche Stellungnahme zum öffentlichen Expertengespäch des Unterausschusses Europarecht des Rechtsausschusses des Deutschen Bundestages zum Thema "Prüfung des unionsrechtlichen Subsidiaritätsprinzips"* of 16.06.2010. Available at: <http://www.bundestag.de/bundestag/ausschuesse17/a06/ua_europarecht/anhoerungen/01_Subsidiaritaet/02_Stellungnahmen/Stellungnahme_Calliess.pdf> (13.03.2011).

DAVID, René, "Sources of Law", in *International Encyclopedia of Comparative Law*, K. Zweigert and K. Drobnig (ed.), Vol. II-3, Mohr Siebeck and Martinus Nijhoff Publishers, Tübingen/ The Hague, 1984.

DE BÚRCA, G., "Fundamental Rights and Citizenship", in *Ten Reflections on the Constitutional Treaty for Europe, Study by the European University Institute*, Bruno de Witte (ed.), presented by Vice-President Amato to the European Convention, CONV 703/03 of 28.04.2003, Robert Schuman Centre for Advanced Studies, European University Institute, San Domenico de Fiesole, 2003.

DENNINGER, Erhard, *Staatsrecht: Einführung in die Grundprobleme des Verfassungsrechts der Bundesrepublik Deutschland*, Vol. 1, 1. edition, Rowohlt, Reinbeck bei Hamburg, 1973.

DER DERIAN, James, *On Diplomacy: A Genealogy of Western Estrangement*, Basil Blackwell, Oxford, 1997.

DÍEZ-HOCHLEITNER, Javier, *La posición del Derecho Internacional en el Ordenamiento comunitario*, McGraw-Hill, Interamericana de España, Madrid, 1998.

DOLZER, Rudolf, "Diplomatic protection of Foreign Nationals" in *Encyclopedia of Public International Law (EPIL)*, Vol. 10 (1987), p. 121, Oxford University Press, New York/ Oxford, 1987.

DÖRR, Dieter / DREHER, Meinrad, *Europea als Rechtsgemeinschaft*, Nomos, Baden-Baden, 1997.

DOUGLAS-SCOTT, Sionaidh, "The Charter of Fundamental Rights as a Constitutional Document", in *European Human Rights Law Review*, Issue 1, 2004, pp. 37-50.

DOWNES, T. Antony / HILSON, Christopher, "Making Sense of Rights: Community Rights in E.C. Law", in *European Law Review*, 1999, pp. 121-136.

DUKE, Simon, "Providing for European-Level Diplomacy after Lisbon: The Case of the European External Action Service", in *The Hague Journal of Diplomacy*, No. 4 (2009), pp. 211-233.

DWORKIN, Ronald, *Taking Rights Seriously*, 8. edition, Harvard University Press, Harvard, 1996.

ELEFTERIADIS, Pavlos, "The Direct Effect of Community Law: Conceptual Issues", in *Yearbook of European Law*, Vol. 16 (1997), pp. 205-221.

FERNÁNDEZ, Ana Mar, "Consular Affairs in an Integrated Europe", in *Consular Affairs and Diplomacy*, Jan Melissen and Ana Mar Fernández (ed.), Leiden/ Boston, 2011, pp. 97-114.

FERNÁNDEZ, Ana Mar, "La dimensión externa del Espacio de Libertad, Seguridad y Justicia. El caso de la cooperación consular local", in *Revista CIDOB d'Afers Internacionals*, No. 91, 2010, pp. 87-104.

FERNÁNDEZ, Ana Mar, "Local Consular Cooperation: Administering EU Internal Security Abroad", in *European Foreign Affairs Review*, Vol. 14, No. 4 (2009), pp. 591-606.

FERNÁNDEZ, Ana Mar, "The Europeanisation of Consular Affairs: the Case of Visa Policy", in *Discussions Papers in Diplomacy*, Netherland Institute for International Relations Clingendael, The Hague, 2006, pp. 1-21.

FITZMAURICE, Gerald, *Recueil des Cours*, Collected Courses, Vol. 92 (1957-II), The Hague Academy of International Law, The Hague, 1957.

FREIXES SANJUÁN, Teresa, *Los derechos sociales de los trabajadores en la Constitución*, Ministerio de Trabajo y Seguridad Social, Madrid, 1986.

FREIXES SANJUÁN, Teresa, "La Constitución y el sistema de derechos fundamentales y libertades públicas", in *Administraciones Públicas y Constitución. Reflexiones sobre el XX Aniversario de la Constitución Española de 1978*, Enrique Álvarez Conde (Coord.), p. 141, Ministerio de Administraciones Públicas, Instituto Nacional de Administración Pública, Madrid, 1998.

FREIXES SANJUÁN, Teresa, "La europeización de los derechos fundamentales", in *La tutela miltilivello dei diritti. Punti di crisi, problemi aperti, momenti di stabilizzazione*, Paola Bilancia / Eugenio De Marco (a cura di), p. 21, Giuffré, Milano, 2004.

FREIXES SANJUÁN, Teresa, "Las principales construcciones jurisprudenciales del Tribunal Europeo de Derechos Humanos. El standard mínimo exigible a los sistemas internos de derechos en Europa", in *Cuadernos Constitucionales de la Cátedra Fadrique Furió Ceriol*, No. 11/12, p. 97, Universidad de Valencia, Valencia, 1995.

FREIXES SANJUÁN, Teresa, "Multilevel constitucionalism y principios fundacionales de los ordenamientos constitucionales: el caso de España", in

Federalismi e integrazioni sopranazionali nell'arena della globalizzazione; Unione Europea e Mercosur, Paola Bilancia (ed.), p. 43, Giuffrè, Milano, 2006.

FREIXES SANJUÁN, Teresa, "Multilevel constitutionalism as general framework for the ascertainment of the legal regulations in the European Union", in *Libertad, seguridad y transformaciones del estado*, Joan Lluís Pérez Francesc (coord.), p. 71, Institut de Ciències Polítiques i Socials, Barcelona, 2009.

FREIXES SANJUÁN, Teresa, *Constitución y derechos fundamentales. I – Estructura jurídica y función constitucional de los derechos. Introducción al sistema de derechos de la Constitución española de 1978*, Promociones y Publicaciones Universitarias, S.A. (PPU), Barcelona, 1992.

GALMOT, Yves / BONICHOT, Jean-Claude, "La Cour de Justice des Communautés européennes et la transposition des directives en droit national", in *Revue Française de Droit Administratif*, Vol. 4 (1) 1988, p. 1-19, Dalloz, Paris, 1988.

GAVARA DE CARA, Juan Carlos, *Derechos Fundamentales y desarrollo legislativo. La garantía del contenido esencial de los derechos fundamentales en la Ley Fundamental de Bonn*, Centro de Estudios Constitucionales, Madrid, 1994.

GEYER, Florian, "The External Dimension of EU Citizenship, Arguing for Effective Protection of Citizens Abroad" in *Centre for European Policy Studies (CEPS)*, No. 136, July 2007, p. 5, Centre for European Policy and Studies, Brussels, 2007.

GÓMEZ SÁNCHEZ, Yolanda, *Derecho Constitucional Europeo: derechos y libertades*, Sanz y Torres, Madrid, 2008.

HÄBERLE, Peter, *La garantía del contenido esencial de los derechos fundamentales*, traducción de Joaquin Brage Camazano, Dykinson, Madrid, 2003.

HÄBERLE, Peter, *Pluralismo y Constitución. Estudios de teoría constitucional en la sociedad abierta*, Icg Marge, Madrid, 2002.

HABERMAS, Jürgen, "The European Nation State. Its Achievements and its Limitations. On the Past and Future of Sovereignty and Citizenship", *Ratio Juris*, Vol. 9, Issue 2 (1996), pp. 125-137.

HALLSTEIN, Walter, *Der unvollendete Bundesstaat. Europäische Erfahrungen und Erkenntnisse*, Econ Verlag, Düsseldorf/ Wien, 1969.

HART, Herbert Lionel Adolphus, *Essays on Bentham: Studies in Jurisprudence and Political Theory*, Oxford University Press, Oxford/ New York, 1982.

HART, Herbert Lionel Adolphus, *The Concept of Law*, 6. edition, Oxford University Press, Oxford/ New York, 1975.

HATJE, Armin, "Kommentar zu Artikel 23 EUV", in *EU-Kommentar*, Jürgen Schwarze (ed.), 1. Auflage, Nomos Verlagsgesellschaft, Baden-Baden, 2012.

HAURIOU, Maurice, "La théorie de l'institution et de la fondation (Essai de vitalisme social)", in *Cahiers de la Nouvelle Journée*, Vol. IV, Librairie Bloud & Gay, Paris, 1925.

HESSE, Konrad, *Grundzüge des Verfassungsrechts der Bundesrepublik Deutschland*, 20. edition. C.F. Müller, Heidelberg, 1999.

HOHFELD, Wesley Newcomb, *Fundamental Legal Conceptions as Applied in Judicial Reasoning*, Yale University Press, New Haven CT, 1964.

IANNIELLO SALICETI, Alessandro, "The Protection of EU Citizens Abroad: Accountability, Rule of Law, Role of Consular and Diplomatic Services", in *European Public Law*, 17, No. 1 (2011), pp. 91-109, Kluver Law International BV, The Netherlands, 2011.

IPSEN, Jörn, *Allgemeines Verwaltungsrecht*, 6. Auflage, Carl Heymanns Verlag, Köln/München, 2009.

JELLINEK, Georg, *System der subjektiven öffentlichen Rechte*, Scientia Verlag, Aalen, 1979.

JIMÉNEZ PIERNAS, Carlos, "La asistencia consular al ciudadano de la Unión: de Maastricht a Amsterdam" in *Acción exterior de la Unión Europea y Comunidad Internacional*, Fernando M. Mariño Menéndez (ed.), p. 219, Universidad Carlos III, Madrid, 1998.

JIMÉNEZ PIERNAS, Carlos, "La protección diplomática y consular del ciudadano de la Unión Europea", in *Revista de Instituciones Europeas*, 1993, Vol. 20, No. 1, p. 9, Centro de Estudios Políticos y Constitucionales, Madrid, 1993.

JIMÉNEZ-UGARTE, Javier, *Práctica consular e inmigración*, Tirant Lo Blanch, Valencia, 2008.

KAUFMANN-BÜHLER, Werner, "Kommentar zu Article 20 TEC", in *EU-und EG-Vertrag Kommentar*, Karl Otto Lenz / Klaus Borhardt (Hrsg.), 4. Auflage, Bundesanzeiger Verlag/ Linde Verlag, Wien, 2006.

KELSEN, Hans, *Allgemeine Staatslehre*, Springer Verlag, Berlin, 1925.

KELSEN, Hans, *Reine Rechtslehre: Einleitung in die rechtswissenschaftliche Problematik*, Scientia Verlag, Aalen, 1985.

KINGREEN, Thorsten / STÖRMER, Rainer, "Die subjektiv-öffentlichen Rechte des primären Gemeinschaftsrechts", in *Europarecht*, 1998, pp. 263-290.

KLEINLEIN, Thomas / RABENSCHLAG, David, "Auslansschutz und Staatsangehörigkeit", in *Zeitschrift für ausländisches öffentliches Recht und Völkerrecht*, No. 67 (2007), pp. 1278-1337.

KLUTH, Winfried, "Kommentar zu Artikel 23 AEUV", in *EUV/AEUV Kommentar*, Christian Calliess/Matthias Ruffert (ed.), 4. Auflage, C.H. Beck, München, 2011.

KOCHENOV, Dimitry, "IUS Tractum of many faces. European Citizenship and the difficult relationship between status and rights", in *Columbia Journal of European Law*, Vol. 15, p. 213.

KOSTAKOPOULOU, Theodora, "European Union Citizenship: Writing the Future", in *European Law Journal*, Vol. 13 (2007), No. 5, pp. 623-646.

KRAHL, Matthias, *Tatbestand und Rechtsfolgen: Untersuchungen zu ihrem dogmatisch-methodologischen Verhältnis im Strafrecht*, Klostermann, Frankfurt am Main, 1999.

LEIRA, Halvard / NEUMANN, Iver B., "The many past lives of the Consul", in *Consular Affairs and Diplomacy*, Jan Melissen and Ana Mar Fernández (ed.), pp. 225-246, Martinus Nijhoff Publihsers, Leiden/Boston, 2011.

LENAERTS, Koen / DE SMIJTER, Eddy, "A 'Bill of Rights' for the European Union", in *Common Market Law Review*, 38 (2001), pp. 273-300.

LENAERTS, Koen / VAN NUFFEL, Piet, *Constitutional Law of the European Union*, Robert BRAY (ed.), 2. edition, Sweet & Maxwell, London, 2005.

LERCHE, Peter, *Übermass und Verfassungsrecht: zur Bindung des Gesetzgebers an die Grundsätze der Verhältnismässigkeit und der Erforderlichkeit*, Carl Heymann, Köln, 1961.

LOCKE, John, *The Second Treatise of Civil Government*, Thomas Hollis (ed.), A. Miller, London, 1690.

LUHMANN, Niklas, *Rechtssoziologie*, 3. edition, Westdeutscher Verlag, Opladen, 1987.

LUKE, T. Lee / QUIGLEY, John, *Consular Law and Practice*, 3. edition, Oxford University Press, Oxford/ New York, 2008.

MACCORMICK, Neil, *Institutions of Law: An Essay in Legal Theory (Law, State, and Practical Reason)*, Oxford University Press, Oxford/ New York, 2007.

MACCORMICK, Neil, *Legal Reasoning and Legal Theory*, Oxford University Press, Oxford/ New York, 1978.

MACCORMICK, Neil, *Legal Rights and Social Democracy*, Oxford University Press, Oxford/ New York, 1982.

MAGIERA, Siegfried, "Kommentar zu Artikel 46 der Charta der Grundrechte der Europäischen Union", in *Kommentar zur Charta der Grundrechte der Europäischen Union*, Jürgen Meyer (ed.), Nomos Verlag, Baden-Baden, 2003.

MAGNETTE, Paul, "European Citizenship from Maastricht to Amsterdam: The narrow Path of Legitimation", in *Journal of European Integration*, Vol. 21 (1998), pp. 37-69, Routledge, Oxford, 1998.

MAGNETTE, P., *La Citoyenneté européenne: Droits, politiques, institutions*, Éditions de l'Université de Bruxelles, Bruxelles, 1999.

MARSHALL, Thomas Humpfrey, *Citizenship and Social Class and other essays*, Cambridge University Press, Cambridge, 1950.

MARTENS, Wolfgang, Grundrechte im Leistungsstaaat. Die Dogmatik des Verwaltungsrechts vor den Gegenwartsaufgaben der Verwaltung by Martens/ Häberle/ Bachof/ Brohm (ed.), in *Veröffentlichungen der Vereinigungn der Deutschen Staatsrechtler*, No. 30 (1972), De Gruyter, Berlin-New York, 1972.

MASING, Johannes, *Die Mobilisierung des Bürgers für die Durchsetzung des Rechts- Europäische Impulse für eine Revision der Lehre vom subjektiv-öffentlichen Recht*, Duncker & Humblot, Berlin, 1997.

MAUERER, Hartmut, *Allgemeines Verwaltungsrecht*, 17. Auflage, C.H. Beck, München, 2008.

MAURER, Andreas / REICHEL, Sarah, The European External Action Service, Elements of a Three-Phase Plan, in *Stiftung Wissenschaft und Politik (SWP) Comments*, No. 36, December 2004, pp. 1-8. Stiftung Wissenschaft und Politik, Deutsches Institut für Internationale Politik und Sicherheit, Berlin, 2004.

MEEHAN, Michael, "(Un) Charted Waters: The Legal Background to Fundamental Rights Protection in the EU", in *An EU Charter of Fundamental Rights, Text and Commentaries*, Kim Feus (ed.), pp. 77-96, Federal Trust for Education and Research, London, 2000.

NETTESHEIM, Martin, "Subjektive Rechte im Unionsrecht", in *Archiv des Öffentlichen Rechts*, Band 132 (2007), pp. 333-392.

NETTESHEIM, Martin, "Der Grundsatz der einheitlichen Wirksamkeit des Gemeinschaftsrechts", in A. Randelzhofer/ R. Scholz/ D. Wilke (ed.), *Gedächtnisschrift für Eberhard Grabitz*, pp. 447-468, C.H. Beck, München, 1995.

NUÑEZ HERNÁNDEZ, Jesús / MARTÍ MARTÍ, Xavier, *La función consular en el derecho español*, 3. edition, Ministerio de Asuntos Exteriores y de Cooperación, Madrid, 2009.

OBWEXER, Walter, "Das Recht der Unionsbürger auf diplomatischen und konsularischen Schutz", in *ECOLEX Fachzeitschrift für Wirtschaftsrecht*, p. 323, Manz, Wien, 1996.

OKANO-HEIJMANS, Maaike, "Changes in Consular Assistance and the Emergence of Consular Diplomacy", in *Consular Affairs and Diplomacy*, Jan Melissen and Ana Mar Fernández (ed.), pp. 21-41, Martinus Nijhoff Publishers, Leiden/Boston, 2011.

OPERMANN, Thomas / CLAESSEN, Claus Dieter / NETTESHEIM, Martin, *Europarecht*, 4. Auflage, C.H. Beck, München, 2009.

PECES-BARBA, Gregorio, *Los valores superiores*, Tecnos, Madrid, 1986.

PERNICE, Ingolf E. A., The Treaty of Lisbon: Multilevel Constitutionalism in Action, in *Columbia Journal of European Law*, Vol. 15, No. 3/2009, p. 349-407, European Legal Studies Center, Columbia University School of Law, New York, 2009.

PERNICE, Ingolf E. A., "Multilevel Constitutionalism in the European Union", in *European Law Review*, No. 5, 2002, 511-529, Sweet & Maxwell, London, 2002.

PIEROTH, Bodo / SCHLINK, Bernhard, *Grundrechte, Staatsrecht II*, 16. edition, C.F. Müller Verlag, Heidelberg, 2000.

POLICASTRO, Pasquale, "Constitutionalism, Multi-Level Democracy and Fundamental Values", preface to J. Nergelius, P. Policastro and K. Urata (ed.), *Challenges of Multi-Level Constitutionalims, Proceedings of IVR 21st World Congress, Lund 2003*, Polpress Publisher, Kraków, 2004.

PORZIO, Giorgio, "Consular Assistance and Protection: An EU Perspective", in *The Hague Journal of Diplomacy*, 3 (2008), pp. 93-97.

PRECHAL, Sasha, *Directives in European Community Law*, 2. edition, Oxford University Press, Oxford/New York, 2005.

PREUSS, Ulrich, "Citizenship and Identity: Aspects of a Political Theory of Citizenship", in R. Bellamy/ V. Bufacchi/ D. Castaglione, *Democracy and Constitutional Culture in the Union of Europe*, pp. 107-120, Lothian Foundation Press, London, 1995.

KRISTI, Raik, "Serving the citizens? Consular role of the EEAS grows in small steps", in European Policy Center, Policy Brief, 30.04.2013. Available at: <http://www.epc.eu/documents/uploads/pub_3488_consular_role_of_the_eeas.pdf>.

RAWLS, John, *A Theory of Justice*, 2. edition, Oxford University Press, Oxford/London/New York, 1993.

REDDIG, Melanie, *Bürger jenseits des Staates? Unionsbürgerschaft als Mittel europäischer Integration*, Nomos Verlag, Baden-Baden, 2005.

RENGELING, Hans-Werner / SZCZEKALLA, Peter, *Grundrechte in der Europäischen Union. Charta der Grundrechte und Allgemeine Rechtsgrundsätze*, Carl Heymanns Verlag, Köln/Berlin/München, 2004.

RODRÍGUEZ BARRIGÓN, Juan Manuel, "La ciudadanía de la Unión Europea", in *Cuadernos y Debates*, No. 142, p. 559, Centro de Estudios Constitucionales, Madrid, 2002.

RODRÍGUEZ, Ángel, *Integración Europea y Derechos Fundamentales*, Civitas Ediciones, Madrid, 2001.

ROMANO, Santi, *El ordenamiento jurídico*, Instituto de Estudios Políticos, Madrid, 1963.

ROMANO, Santi, *Fragmentos de un diccionario jurídico*, Ediciones Jurídicas Europa-America, Buenos Aires, 1964.

ROVIRA VIÑAS, Antonio, *El abuso de los derechos fundamentales*, Ed. Península, Barcelona, 1983.

RUFFERT, Matthias, "Diplomatischer und konsularischer Schutz zwischen Völker- und Europarecht", in *Archiv des Völkerrechts*, 35 (1997), p. 459.

RUFFERT, Matthias, "Dogmatik und Praxis des subjektiv-öffentlichen rechts unter dem Einfluss des Gemeinschaftsrechts", in *Deutsches Verwaltungsblatt*, 1998, pp. 69-75.

SCHMITT, Carl, "Freiheitsrechte und institutionelle Garantien in der Reichsverfassung", in *Verfassungsrechtliche Aufsätze aus den Jahren 1924-1954. Materialien zu einer Verfassungslehre*, 3. edition, Duncker und Humblot, Berlin, 1985.

SCHMITT, Carl, *Verfassungslehre*, 6. edition, Duncker und Humblot, Berlin, 1983.

SCHÖNBERGER, Christoph, "European Citizenship as Federal Citizenship. Some Citizenship Lessons of Comparative Federalism", in *Revue Européenne de Droit Public*, 2007, Vol. 19 (1), p. 61-81.

SCHÖNBERGER, Christoph, *Unionsbürger. Europas Föderales Bürgerrecht in vergleichender Sicht*, Mohr Siebeck, Tübingen, 2005.

SCHWARZE, Jürgen (ed.), *The Birth of a European Constitutional Order*, Nomos Verlagsgesellschaft, Baden-Baden, 2001.

SCHWARZE, Jürgen, "Kommentar zu Artikel 19 EUV", in *EU-Kommentar*, Jürgen Schwarze (ed.), 1. edition, Nomos Verlagsgesellschaft, Baden-Baden, 2012.

SHAW, Jo, "The Interpretation of European Union Citizenship", in *The Modern Law Review*, Vol. 61, No. 3 (1998), pp. 293-317.

SILARD, John, "A Constitutional Forecast: Demise of the 'State Action' Limit on the Equal Protection Guarantee", in *Columbia Law Review*, Vol. 66 (1966), No. 5, pp. 855-872.

SILVEIRA, Alessandra / CANOTILHO, Mariana / MADEIRA FROUFE, Pedro, Citizenship and Solidarity in the European Union. From the Charter of Fundamental Rights to the Crisis: the State of the Art, P.I.E. Peter Lang, Brussels, 2013.

SIMON, Denys / MARIATTE, Flavien, "Le 'droit' à la protection diplomatique: droit fondamental en droit communautaire?", in *Europe*, 2006 (Novembre), Etude 11, pp. 4-7, Paris, 2006.

SMEND, Rudolf, *Constitución y Derecho Constitucional*, Centro de Estudios Constitucionales, Madrid, 1985.

STEIN, Thorsten, "Die Regelung des diplomatischen Schutzes im vertrag über die Europäische Union", in *Der diplomatische Schutz im Völker- und Europarecht. Aktuelle Probleme und Entwicklungstendenzen*, Georg Ress / Thorsten Stein (ed.), pp. 97-105, Nomos Verlagsgesellschaft, Baden-Baden, 1996.

STREINZ, Rudolf, *Europarecht*, 8. Auflage, C.F. Müller Heidelberg, 2008.

STRINGER, Kevin D., "Honorary Consuls in an Era of Globalization, Trade, and Investment", in *Consular Affairs and Diplomacy*, Jan Melissen and Ana Mar Fernández (ed.), pp. 63-96, Martinus Nijhoff Publishers, Leiden/ Boston, 2011.

SZCZEKALLA, Peter, "Die Pflicht der Gemeinschaft und der Mitgliedstaaten zum diplomatischen und konsularischen Schutz", in *Europarecht*, Heft 3, 1999, p. 325, Nomos Verlagsgesellschaft, Baden-Baden, 1999.

TERHECHTE, Jörg Philipp, "Kommentar zum Artikel 351 AEUV", in *EU-Kommentar*, Jürgen Schwarze (ed.), 3. edition, Nomos Verlagsgesellschaft, Baden-Baden, 2012.

THORPE, F. N. (ed.), *The Federal and State Constitutions*, Colonial Charters and Other Organic Laws of the United States, Washington DC, 1909.

VERMEER-KÜNZLI, Annemarieke, "Restricting Discretion: Judicial Review of Diplomatic Protection", in *Nordic Journal of International Law*, Vol. 75 (2006), p. 93, Martinus Nijhoff Publishers, Leiden/ Boston, 2006.

VERMEER-KÜNZLI, Annemarieke, "As If: The Legal Fiction in Diplomatic Protection", in *European Journal of International Law*, 2008, Vol. 18, No. 1, p. 37.

VERMEER-KÜNZLI, Annemarieke, "Exercising Diplomatic Protection, the Fine Line between Litigation, Demarches and Consular Assistance", in *ZaöRV*, 66 (2006), p. 321.

VILARIÑO PINTOS, Eduardo, "Representación exterior y cooperación diplomática y consular en el Tratado de la Unión Europea", in *Revista de Instituciones Europeas*, No. 2 (1995), Vol. 22, p. 418, Centro de Estudios Políticos y Constitucionales, Madrid, 1995.

VLADIMIROV, Ivan, *Дипломатическо и консулско право*, 3. edition, Romina, Sofia, 2007.

VON JHERING, Rudolf, *Abreviatura de "El espíritu del derecho romano"*, Revista de Occidente Argentina, Buenos Aires, 1947.

VON JHERING, Rudolf, *Geist des römischen Rechts auf den verschiedenen Stufen seiner Entwicklung*, 5. edition, Breitkopf und Härtel, Wiesbaden/ Leipzig, Paris, 1906.

WIENER, Antje, "Assessing the constructive potential of Union Citizenship – A Socio-Historical Perspective", in *European Integration Online Papers*, Vol. 1, No. 17 (1997), pp. 1-27.

WOLLENSCHLÄGER, Ferdinand, *Grunfreiheit ohne Markt: die Herausbildung der Unionsbürgerschaft im unionsrechtlichen Freizügigkeitsregime*, Mohr Siebeck, Tübingen, 2007.

ZOUREK, Jan, Report on Consular Intercourse and Immunities, in *Yearbook of International Law Commission*, 1957, Vol. II, Document A/CN.4/108, p. 71, United Nations, The Hague, 1957.

Institutional Documents (Chronological Order)

INTERNATIONAL LAW COMMISSION, Report Covering the Work of its Seventh Session 02.05 — 08.07.1955, Official Records of the General Assembly, Tenth Session, Supplement No. 9 (A/2934), Document A/CN.4/94, in Yearbook of the International Law Commission 1955, Vol. II, p. 19, 42. Available at: <http://untreaty.un.org/ilc/sessions/7/7docs.htm>.

ADONNINO COMMITTEE, Report submitted to the Milan European Council (Milan, 28/29.06.1985), in Bulletin of the European Communities 1985, No. Supplement 7/85. Available at: <http://www.ombudsman.europa.eu/en/resources/historicaldocument.faces;jsessionid=2FAF476D7F307335E43A6D9ED8D8862D>.

EUROPEAN COUNCIL, Conclusions of the Rome European Council (14/15.12.1990), Doc/90/6, available at: <http://europa.eu/rapid/pressReleasesAction.do?reference=DOC/90/6&format=HTML&aged=1&language=EN&guiLanguage=en>.

SPANISH DELEGATION, "Proposal of text with articles on European citizenship presented by the Spanish delegation to the Intergovernmental Conference on Political Union (20.02.1991)", in *Revista de Instituciones Europeas* (RIE), Vol. 18 (1991), p. 405.

COUNCIL OF THE EUROPEAN UNION, Guidelines for the protection of unrepresented EU citizens by missions of the Member States in third countries, 29/30.03.1993, Doc 7124/94 CFSP 161 COCON 2.

EUROPEAN COMMISSION, First Citizenship Report of the European Commission of 21.12.1993, COM(93)702 final. Available at: <http://eur-lex.europa.eu/LexUriServ/LexUriServ.do?uri=COM:1993:0702:FIN:EN:PDF>.

EUROPEAN COUNCIL, Presidency Conclusions, Cologne European Council, 3/4.06. 1999, available at: <http://www.consilium.europa.eu/ueDocs/cms_Data/docs/pressData/en/ec/kolnen.htm>.

CONVENTION on a Charter of Fundamental Rights, Proposal of the Presidium to the Convention, CHARTE 4360/00 of 14.06.2000, Convent 37.

EUROPEAN COMMISSION, Third Report on Union Citizenship of 07.09.2001, Document COM(2001)506 final. Available at: <http://eur-lex.europa.eu/LexUriServ/LexUriServ.do?uri=COM:2001:0506:FIN:EN:PDF>.

COUNCIL OF THE EUROPEAN UNION, Council Decision 2004/100/EC of 26.01.2004 on Community action programme to promote active European citizenship, Official Journal of 04.02.2004, L 30/6.

UNITED NATION'S INTERNATIONAL LAW COMMISSION, Seventh Report on Diplomatic Protection by John Dugard, Special Rapporteur of the ILC of 07.03.2004, A/CN.4/567. Available at: <http://untreaty.un.org/ilc/documentation/english/a_cn4_567.pdf>.

EUROPEAN PARLIAMENT, Resolution on the Institutional Aspects of the European External Action Service of 26.05.2005, published in the Official Journal of 18.5.2006, p. 232, C 117 E.

HIGH REPRESENTATIVE OF COMMON FOREIGN AND SECURITY POLICY AND EUROPEAN COMMISSION, Joint Progress Report by the High Representative and the Commission to the European Council on the European External Action Service, 9956/05, 9.06.2005. Available at: <http://www.epc.eu/pub_details.php?pub_id=424&cat_id=1>.

COUNCIL OF EUROPEAN UNION, Report of the Presidency of the Council of European Union to the European Council "Reinforcing the European Union's emergency and crisis response capacities", 15.06.2006, Document 10551/06. Available at: <http://www.consilium.europa.eu/uedocs/cmsUpload/st10551en06.pdf>.

COUNCIL OF THE EUROPEAN UNION, 2006 Guidelines on consular protection of EU citizens in third countries, Document of the Council 10109/2/06 REV 2 of 16.06.2006. Available at: <http://register.consilium.europa.eu/pdf/en/06/st10/st10109-re02.en06.pdf>.

UNITED NATION'S INTERNATIONAL LAW COMMISSION, Report on the work of the International Law Commission's fifty-eighth session (01.05. to 09.06. and 03.07. to 11.08.2006), UN General Assembly, Official Records, Sixty-first Session, Supplement No. 10 (A/61/10). Available at: <http://untreaty.un.org/ilc/reports/2006/2006report.htm>.

EUROPEAN COMMISSION, Flash Eurobarometer No. 188 on "Consular Protection" of July 2006. Available at: <http://ec.europa.eu/public_opinion/flash/fl188b_en.pdf>.

EUROPEAN COMMISSION, Green Paper "Diplomatic and consular protection of Union citizens in third countries", COM(2006)712 of 28.11.2006. Official Journal C 30 of 10.02.07.

EUROPEAN PARLIAMENT AND COUNCIL OF THE EUROPEAN UNION, Decision No. 1904/2006/EC of the European Parliament and the Council of 12.12.2006 establishing for the period 2007-2013 the programme 'Europe of citizens' to promote active European citizenship. Official Journal L 378/32 of 27.12.2006.

MINISTER FOR EUROPE OF THE UNITED KINGDOM, Letter in response to the Commission's Green Paper on Diplomatic and consular protection of Union citizens in third countries of 21.03.2007. Available at: <http://www.publications.parliament.uk/pa/cm200607/cmselect/cmeuleg/41-xvi/4104.htm>.

COUNCIL OF THE EUROPEAN UNION, General Affairs, Conclusions of the Luxembourg Council of 17/18.06.2007, Press Release 10654/07. Available at: <http://www.consilium.europa.eu/ueDocs/cms_Data/docs/pressData/en/gena/94803.pdf>.

EUROPEAN COUNCIL, Presidency Conclusions of the Brussels European Council 21/22.06.2007, 11177/1/07 of 20.07.2007. Available at: <http://register.consilium.europa.eu/pdf/en/07/st11/st11177-re01.en07.pdf>.

EUROPEAN COMMISSION, Action Plan 2007-2009 "Effective consular protection in third countries: the contribution of the European Union", Communication from the Commission to the European Parliament, the Council, the European Economic and Social Committee and the Committee of the Regions, COM(2007)767 final of 05.12.2007. Available at: <http://eur-lex.europa.eu/LexUriServ/LexUriServ.do?uri=COM:2007:0767:FIN:EN:HTML>.

EUROPEAN COMMISSION, "EU initiative to strengthen consular protection for citizens outside the European Union", MEMO/07/551 from 05.12.2007. Availableat:<http://europa.eu/rapid/pressReleasesAction.do?reference=MEMO/07/551>.

CONVENTION on a Charter of Fundamental Rights of the European Union, Explanations relating to the Charter of Fundamental Rights (2007/C 303/02), published in the Official Journal C303/17 of 14.12.2007.

EUROPEAN COMMISSION, Impact Assessment on "Effective consular protection in third countries: the contribution of the European Union. Action Plan 2007-2009", Document SEC(2007)16000 of 05.02.2008. Available at: <http://eur-lex.europa.eu/LexUriServ/LexUriServ.do?uri=CELEX:52007SC1601:EN:HTML>.

SLOVENIAN PRESIDENCY OF THE EU (2008), Press release: Evacuation of EU citizens from Chad and application of the consular Lead State concept, Press releases 11.02.2008. Available at: <http://www.eu2008.si/en/News_and_Documents/Press_Releases/February/0211MZZ_Chad.html>.

EUROPEAN COMMISSION, Fifth Report on Citizenship of the Union (01.05.2004-30.06.2007) of 15.02.2008, COM(2008)85 final. Available at: <http://eur-lex.europa.eu/LexUriServ/LexUriServ.do?uri=COM:2008:0085:FIN:en:PDF>.

COUNCIL OF THE EUROPEAN UNION, European Union Guidelines on the implementation of the consular Lead State concept, Document 2008/C 317/06, published in the Official Journal C 317/6 of 12.12.2008.

PRESIDENCY OF THE COUNCIL OF THE EUROPEAN UNION, General Affairs Council/European Council, The Stockholm Programme – An open and secure Europe serving and protecting the citizens, Document 17024/09 of 02.12.2009. Available at: <http://register.consilium.europa.eu/pdf/en/09/st17/st17024.en09.pdf>.

HIGH REPRESENTATIVE OF THE UNION FOR FOREIGN AFFAIRS AND SECURITY POLICY Proposal for a Council Decision establishing the organisation and functioning of the European External Action Service,

25.03.2010. Available at: <http://eeas.europa.eu/docs/eeas_draft_decision_250310_en.pdf>.

COUNCIL OF THE EUROPEAN UNION, Common practices in consular assistance outside the EU, adopted by COCON on 09.06.2010 and by the Council of the European Union on 14.06.2010, Document 10698/10, COCON 28, PESC 745. Available at: <http://register.consilium.europa.eu/pdf/en/10/st10/st10698.en10.pdf>.

EUROPEAN COMMISSION, Communication on Strategy for the effective implementation of the Charter of Fundamental Rights by the European Union of 19.10.2010, COM(2010)573 final, available at: <http://ec.europa.eu/justice/news/intro/doc/com_2010_573_en.pdf>.

EUROPEAN COMMISSION, Flash Eurobarometer No. 294 on "European Citizenship" of October 2010. Available at: <http://ec.europa.eu/public_opinion/flash/fl_294_en.pdf>.

EUROPEAN COMMISSION, EU Citizenship Report "Dismantling the obstacles to EU citizens' rights", COM(2010)603 final of 27.10.2010. Available at: <http://ec.europa.eu/justice/citizen/files/com_2010_603_en.pdf>.

COUNCIL OF THE EUROPEAN UNION, Guidelines on consular protection of EU citizens in third countries of 05.11.2010 (15613/10). Available at: <http://register.consilium.europa.eu/pdf/en/10/st15/st15613.en10.pdf>.

EUROPEAN COMMISSION, Communication to the European Parliament and the Council on Consular protection for EU citizens in third countries: State of play and way forward, 23.03.2011, COM(2011) 149/2. Available at: <http://ec.europa.eu/justice/policies/citizenship/diplomatic/docs/communication_consular_protection.pdf>.

EUROPEAN COMMISSION, Impact Assessment accompanying the document Proposal for a Directive of the Council on coordination and cooperation measures regarding consular protection for unrepresented EU citizens, 14.12.2011, Document SEC(2011)1556 final, not published.

HIGH REPRESENTATIVE OF THE UNION FOR FOREIGN AFFAIRS AND SECURITY POLICY, Report to the European Parliament and the Council of 22.12.2011. Available at: <http://www.eeas.europa.eu/images/top_stories/2011_eeas_report_cor.pdf>.

EUROPEAN PARLIAMENT, Committee on Civil Liberties, Justice and Home Affairs, Report on the proposal for a Council Directive on consular protection for citizens of the Union abroad. 10.10.2012. Available at: <http://www.europarl.europa.eu/RegistreWeb/search/simple.htm?relName=DOSSIER&reference=LIBE/7/08241&language=EN>.

EUROPEAN PARLIAMENT, Legislative resolution of 25.10.2012 on the proposal for a Council directive on consular protection for citizens of the Union abroad (COM(2011)0881 – C7-0017/2012 – 2011/0432(CNS)). Available at: <http://www.europarl.europa.eu/sides/getDoc.do?type=TA&language=EN&reference=P7-TA-2012-394>.

Court Rulings (Chronological List)

Judgements of the Court of Justice of the European Union

Judgement of 05.02.1963 in the case 26/62, *NV Algemene Transport – en Expeditie Onderneming van Gend & Loos v. Netherlands Inland Revenue Administration*, ECR 1963, p. 00001.

Judgement of 15.07.1964 in the case 6/64, *Flaminio Costa v. E.N.E.L.*, ECR 1964, p. 00585.

Judgement of 16.06.1966 in the case 57/65, *Alfons Lütticke GmbH v Hauptzollamt Sarrelouis*, ECR 1966, p. 205.

Judgement of 17.12.1970 in the case 11/70, *Internationale Handelsgesellschaft mbH v. Einfuhr- und Vorratsstelle für Getreide und Futtermittel*, ECR 1970, p. 1125.

Judgement of 04.12.1974 in the case 41/47, *Yvonne Van Duyn v. Home Office*, ECR 1974, p. 01337.

Judgement of 23.01.1975 in the case C-31/74, *Filippo Galli v. Pretore di Roma*, ECR 1975, p. 00047.

Judgement of 16.12.1976 in the case C-33/76, *Rewe-Zentralfinanz eG and Rewe-Zentral AG v Landwirtschaftskammer für das Saarland*, ECR 1976, p. 01989.

Judgement of 09.03.1978 in the case 106/77, *Amministrazione delle Finanze dello Stato v Simmenthal S.p.A.*, ECR 1978, p. 629.

Judgement of 07.02.1979 in the case 115/78, *J. Knoors v. Secretary of State for Economic Affairs*, ECR 1979, p. 00399.

Judgement of 05.04.1979 in the case 148/79, *Pubblico Ministero v. Tullio Ratti*, European Court reports 1979, p. 01629.

Judgement of 06.05.1980 in the case C-102/ 79, *Commission of the European Communities v. Kingdom of Belgium*, ECR 1980, p. 1473.

Judgement of 06.10.1981 in the case C-246/80, *C. Broekmeulen v. Huisarts Registratie Commissie*, ECR 1981, p. 2311.

Judgement of 19.01.1982 in the case C-8/81, *Ursula Becker v. Finanzamt Münster-Innenstadt*, ECR 1982, p. 53.

Judgement of 27.10.1982 in the joined cases C-35 and 36/82, *Elestina Esselina Christina Morson v. State of the Netherlands and Head of the Plaatselijke Politie within the meaning of the Vreemdelingenwet; Sweradjie Jhanjan v State of the Netherlands*, ECR 1982, p. 03723.

Judgement of 23.04.1986 in the case C-294/83, *Parti écologiste "Les Verts" v. European Parliament*, ECR 1986, p. 1339.

Judgement of 15.05.1986 in the case C-222/84, *Marguerite Johnston v. Chief Constable of the Royal Ulster Constabulary*, ECR 1986, p. 01226.

Judgement of 03.07.1986 in the case C-66/85, *Deborah Lawrie-Blum v. Land Baden-Württember*, ECR 1986, p. 2121.

Judgement of 02.02.1989 in the case C-186/87, *Ian William Covan v. Trésor Public*, ECR 1989, p. 000195.

Judgement of 11.07.1989 in the case C-265/87, *Hermann Schräder HS Kraftfutter GmbH & Co. KG v. Hauptzollamt Gronau*, ECR 1989, p. 2237.

Judgement of 13.07.1989 in the case C-5/88, *Hubert Wachauf v. Federal Republic of Germany, represented by the Bundesamt für Ernährung und Forstwirtschaft*, ECR 1989, p. 02609.

Judgement of 13.11.1990 in the case C-106/89, *Marleasing SA v. La Comercial Internacional de Alimentacion SA*, ECR 1990, p. I-04135.

Judgement of 26.02.1991 in the case C-292/89, *The Queen v Immigration Appeal Tribunal, ex parte Gustaff Desiderius Antonissen*, ECR 1991, p. I-00745.

Judgement of 30.05.1991 in the case C-361/88, *Commission of the European Communities v. Federal republic of Germany (TA-Luft)*, ECR 1991, p. I-2567.

Judgement of 19.11.1991 in the joined cases C-6/90 and C-9/90, *Andrea Francovich and Danila Bonifaci and others v. Italian Republic*, ECR 1991, p. 05357.

Judgement of 07.07.1992 in the case C-369/90, *Mario Vicente Micheletti and others v. Delegación del Gobierno de Cantabria*, ECR 1992, p. 04239.

Judgement of 24.11.1992 in the case C-286/90, *Poulsen and Diva Navigation*, ECR 1992, I-6048.

Judgement of 20.10.1993 in joined cases C-92/92 and C-326/92, *Phil Collins v. Imtrat Handelsgesellschaft mbH and Patricia Im- und Export Verwaltungsgesellschaft mbH and Leif Emanuel Kraul v. EMI Electrola GmbH*, ECR 1993, p. I-05145.

Judgement of 16.02.1995 in the joined cases C-29/94, C-30/94, C-31/94, C-32/94, C-33/94, C-34/94 and C-35/94, *Criminal proceedings against Jean-Louis Aubertin, Bernard Collignon, Guy Creusot, Isabelle Diblanc, Gilles Josse, Jacqueline Martin and Claudie Normand*, ECR 1995, p. 00301.

Judgement of 05.03.1996 in the joined cases C-46/93 and C-48/93, *Brasserie du Pêcheur and Factortame*, ECR 1996, p. 1029.

Judgement of 26.03.1996 in the case C-392/93, *The Queen v. H.M. Treasury, ex parte British Telecommunications*, ECR 1996, p. 1631.

Judgement of 30.07.1996 in the case C-84/95, *Bosphorus Hava Yollari Turizm v. Ticaret AS v. Minister for Transport, Energy and Communications and others*, ECR 1996, p. 03953.

Judgement of 08.10.1996 in the joined cases C-178/94, C-179/94, C-188/94, C-189/94 and C-190/94, *Dillenkofer and Others v. Federal Republic of Germany*, ECR 1996, p. 4845.

Judgement of 17.10.1996 in the joined cases C-283/94, C-291/94 and C-292/94, *Denkavit Internationaal and Others v. Bundesamt für Finanzen*, ECR 1996, p. 5063.

Judgement of 16.06.1998 in the case C-162/96, *A. Racke GmbH v. Hauptzollamt Mainz*, ECR 1998, p. I-03655.

Judgement of 24.11.1998 in the case C-274/96, *Criminal proceedings against Horst Otto Bickel and Ulrich Franz*, ECR 1998, p. I-07637.

Judgement of 13.04.2000 in the case C-292/97, *Kjell Karlsson and Others*, ECR 2000, p. I-02737.

Judgement of 26.09.2000 in the case C-443/98, *Unilever Italia S.p.A. v. Central Food SpA*, ECR 2000, p. I-07535.

Judgement of 20.02.2001 in the case C-192/99, *The Queen v. Secretary of State for the Home Department, ex parte: Manjit Kaur*, ECR 2001, p. I-01237.

Judgement of 20.09.2001 in the case C-184/99, *Rudy Grzelczyk v. Centre public d'aide sociale d'Ottignies-Louvain-la-Neuve*, ECR 2001, p. I-06193.

Judgement of the Court of First Instance of 11.09.2002 in the case T-13/99, *Pfizer Animal Health SA v. Council of the European Union*, ECR 2002, p. II-03305.

Judgement of the Court of Justice of 17.09.2002 in the case C-413/99, *Baumbast, R v. Secretary of State for the Home Department*, ECR 2002, p. I-07091.

Judgement of 22.10.2002 in the case C-94/00, *Roquette Fréres SA v. Directeur général de la concurrence, de la consommation et de la répression des fraudes*, ECR 2002, p. I-09011.

Judgement of 12.06.2003 in the case 112/00, *Eugen Schmidberger, Internationale Transporte und Planzüge v. Austria*, ECR 2003, p. I-05659.

Judgement of the Court of Justice of 02.10.2003 in the case C-148/02, *Carlos García Avello v. Belgian State*, ECR 2003, p. I-11613.

Judgement of 07.09.2004 in the case C-456/02, *Michel Trojani v. Centre public d'aide sociale de Bruxelles (CPAS)*, ECR 2004, p. I-07573.

Judgement of 19.10.2004 in the case C-200/02, *Kunqian Catherine Zhu, Man Lavette Chen v. Secretary of State for the Home Department*, ECR 2004, p. I-09925.

Judgement of 12.07.2005 in the case C-403/03, *Egon Schempp v. Finanzamnt München V*, ECR 2005, p. I-06421.

Judgement of the Court of First Instance of 21.09.2005 in the case T-306/01, *Ahmed Ali Yusuf and Al Barakaat International Foundation v. Council of the European Union and Commission of the European Communities*, ECR 2005, p. II-03533.

Judgement of the Court of First Instance of 21.09.2005 in the case T-315/01, *Yassin Abdullah Kadi v. Commission of the European Communities*, ECR 2005, p. II-03649.

Judgement of 08.11.2005 in the case C-443/03, *Götz Leffler v. Berlin Chemie AG*, ECR 2005, p. I-09611.

Judgement of 27.06.2006 in the case C-540/03, *European Parliament v. Council of the European Union*, ECR 2006, p. I-05769.

Judgement of the Court of First Instance of 12.07.2006 in the case T-253/02, *Chafiq Ayadi v. Council of the European Union*, ECR 2006, p. II-02139.

Judgement of 18.07.2006 in the case C-406/04, *Gérald De Cuyper v. Office national de l'emploi*, ECR 2006, p. I-06947.

Judgement of 12.09.2006 in the case C-145/04, *Kingdom of Spain v. United Kingdom of Great Britain and Northern Ireland*, ECR 2006, p. I-7917.

Judgement of 23.10.2007 in the joined cases C-11/06 and 12/06, *Rhiannon Morgan* (C-11/06) *v. Bezirksregierung Köln*, and *Iris Bucher* (C-12/06) *v. Landrat des Kreises Düren*, ECR 2007, p. I-09161.

Judgement of the Court of Justice (Grand Chamber) of 3.09.2008 in joined cases C-402/05 P and C-415/05 P, *Yassin Abdullah Kadi and Al Barakaat International Foundation v. Council of the European Union*, ECR 2008, p. I-06351.

Judgement of 03.12.2009 in the cases C-399/06 P and C-403/06 P, *Faraj Hassan v. Council of the European Union and European Commission, and Chafiq Ayadi v. Council of the European Union*, ECR 2009, p. I-11393.

Judgement of 23.02.2010 in the case C-310/08, *London Borough of Harrow v. Nimco Hassan Ibrahim and Secretary of State for the Home Department*, ECR 2020, p. I-01065.

Judgement of 23.02.2010 in the case C-480/08, *Maria Teixeira v. London Borough of Lambeth and Secretary of State for the Home Department*, ECR 2010, p. I-01107.

Judgement of 02.03.2010 in the case C-135/08, *Janco Rottman v. Freistaat Bayern*, ECR 2010, p. I-01449.

Judgement of 30.09.2010 in the case Kadi II, Judgement of the General Court (Seventh Chamber) in the Case T-85/09, *Yassin Abdullah Kadi v. European Commission*, ECR 2010, p. 00000.

Judgement of 08.03.2011 in the case C-34/09, *Ruiz Zambrano v. Office national de l'emploi (ONEm)*, ECR 2011, p. 00000.

Judgement of 05.05.2011 in the case C-434/09, *Shirley McCarthy v. Secretary of State for the Home Department*, ECR 2011, p. 00000.

Judgments of the International Court of Justice

Judgment of the Permanent Court of International Justice of 30.08.1924 in the case *Mavrommatis Palestine Concessions*, Publications of the Permanent Court of International Justice, Series A, A02.

International Court of Justice, case *Lichtenstein v. Guatemala* (*Nottebohm* case), ICJ Reports 1955.

International Court of Justice, case concerning the Barcelona Traction Light and Power Company Limited (*Belgium v. Spain*), Second Phase, Judgment, I.C.J. Reports 1970, p. 4.

International Court of Justice, LaGrand case (*Germany v. United States of America*) I.C.J. Reports 2001, p. 466.

International Court of Justice, case concerning Avena and Other Mexican Nationals (*Mexico v. United States of America*) I.C.J. Reports, 2004, p. 12.

Eu Member States' Legislation On Consular Protection

AUSTRIA

- *Bundesgesetz: Aufgaben und Organisation des auswärtigen Dienstes – Statut* [Federal Act on the Duties and Organization of the Foreign Office – Statute], Published in the State Official Gazette (Bundesgesetzblatt, BGBl) BGBl, I No. 129/1999. Available also at: <http://www.ris.bka.gv.at/GeltendeFassung.wxe?Abfrage=Bundesnormen&Gesetzesnummer=10001572>.

BELGIUM

- *Loi portant le tarif des taxes consulaires et des droits de chancellerie of 30 June 1999* [Act on Consular Fees]. Available at: <http://www.careproject.eu/database/scheda.php?caseother=137>.

BULGARIA

- Constitution of the Republic of Bulgaria, available at: <http://www.parliament.bg/en/const>.
- *Устройствен Правилник на Министерството на външните работи* [Statute of the Ministry of Foreign Affairs], Published in the State Official Gazette No. 64 of 18.07.2008. Available also at: <http://www.mfa.bg/bg/pages/view/528>.

CROATIA

- Constitution of the Republic of Croatia of 22.12.1990, consolidated version of 6.07.2010. Available at <http://www.sabor.hr/Default.aspx?art=2405>.
- *Zakon o vanima vanjskim poslovima*. Available at <http://www.zakon.hr/z/602/Zakon-o-vanjskim-poslovima>.

CZECH REPUBLIC

- *Směrnice o poskytování pomoci občanům CR, kteri se v zahranici ocitli v nouzi No. 301366/2000-KO/5* [Directive of the Ministry of Foreign Affairs on Consular Assistance to Czech Citizens in Case of Emergency] and *Směrnice o konzulární ochraně občanů členských států EU Č.j.: 300574/2004-KO/5* [Guidelines on consular protection of nationals of the EU Member States]. Available at: <http://www.careproject.eu/database/upload/CZguidelines/CZguidelinesTransEng.pdf>.

DENMARK

- *Lov om Udenrigstjenesten* [Foreign Service Act] No. 150 of 13.04.1983. Available at: <https://www.retsinformation.dk/Forms/R0710.aspx?id=72039>.
- *Bekendtgørelse om betaling for tjenestehandlinger i udenrigstjenesten No. 1228 of 10.12.2009*, [Ministry of Foreign Affairs, Executive Order]. Available at: <http://www.careproject.eu/database/upload/DAfees/DAfeesTransEng.pdf>.

ESTONIA

- Constitution of the Republic of Estonia, available at: <http://www.president.ee/en/republic-of-estonia/the-constitution/index.html>.
- *Konsulaarseadus* [Consular Act] published in *Riigi Teataja* (Official State Gazette, hereinafter RT) RT I 2009, 29, 175. Available at: <https://www.riigiteataja.ee/akt/13186034> (02.04.2011). In English: <http://www.careproject.eu/database/upload/ETlaw001/ETlaw001TransEng.pdf>.

FINLAND

- *Konsulipalvelulaki No. 498 of 22.04.1999* [Consular Services Act No. 498]. Available at: <http://www.finlex.fi/en/laki/kaannokset/1999/en19990498.pdf>.

  In English: <http://www.careproject.eu/database/upload/FIkonsulipalvelulaki/FIkonsulipalvelulakiTransEng.pdf>.

FRANCE

- *Le Décret No. 69-222 du 6 mars 1969 relatif au statut particulier des agents diplomatiques et consulaires (version consolidée le 23 février 2008)* [Decree on statute of diplomatic and consular officers]
- *Le Décret No. 76-548 du 16 juin 1976 relatif aux consuls généraux, aux consuls et vice-consuls honoraires et aux agents consulaires* [Decree on general consuls, honorary consuls and vice-consuls and consular officers]

  Both available at: <http://admi.net/jo/20020503/MAEF0210016D.html>.

GERMANY

- *Gesetz über die Konsularbeamten, ihre Aufgaben und Befugnisse of 11.09.1974* [Act on Consular Officers, their Functions and Powers], published in the State

Official Gazette (*Bundesgesetzblatt*) I 1974, 2317. Available also at: <https://www.juris.de/purl/gesetze/_ges/KonsG>.

- *Auslandskostengesetz* of 28.02.1978 [Act on Fees for Public Services Abroad] of 1978, published in the State Official Gazette 1978 Part I No. 11, Page 301 ff. Available also at: <http://www.gesetze-im-internet.de/bundesrecht/akostg/gesamt.pdf>.

GREECE

- *Οργανισμός του Υπουργείου Εξωτερικών της Ελληνικής Δημοκρατίας No. 3566/2007* [Act on the Organisation of the Ministry of Foreign Affairs], published in the Official Gazette of the Government of the Hellenic Republic, Vol. I, No. 117, 5.06.2007. Available also at: <http://www1.mfa.gr/organismos-ypex/>.

HUNGARY

- Constitution of the Republic of Hungary, available at: <http://www.mkogy.hu/parl_en.htm>.
- *2001. évi XLVI. törvény a konzuli védelemről* [Act on Consular Protection], available at: <http://www.mfa.gov.hu/kum/hu/bal/Konzuli_informaciok/Kulfoldiek_beutazasa/Jogszabalyok/2001_evi.htm>.

IRELAND

- Diplomatic Relations and Immunities Act of 1967 available at: <http://www.irishstatutebook.ie/1967/en/act/pub/0008/index.html>.

ITALY

- *Ordinamento dell'amministrazione degli affari esteri d.p.r. 5 gennaio 1967, No. 18 e successive modificazioni e integrazioni* [Decree of the President of the Republic "Organization of Administration of Foreign Affairs"]. Available at: <http://www.esteri.it/mae/normative/Normativa_Consolare/ParteGenerale/DPR_18_1967.pdf>.
- *Decreto Legislativo of 03.12.2011, No. 7, Ordinamento e funzioni degli uffici consolari, ai sensi dell'articolo 14, comma 18, della legge 28 novembre 2005, No. 246 (GU No. 110 del 13-5-2011)* [Legislative Decree on Organisation and Functions of Consular Services]. Available at: <http://www.careproject.eu/database/upload/ITdpr200/ITdpr200Text.pdf>.

LATVIA

- Constitution of the Republic of Latvia, available at: <http://www.saeima.lv/en/legislation/constitution>.
- *Konsulārais reglaments of 03.07.1994 [Act on Consular Regulations], published in Latvijas Vēstnesis* (Official Gazette) on 06.11.1996. Available also at: <http://www.likumi.lv/doc.php?id=57318&menu_body=KDOC>.

LITHUANIA

- Constitution of the Republic of Lithuania, available at: <http://www3.lrs.lt/home/Konstitucija/Constitution.htm>.
- Lithuanian Citizenship Act of 17.09.2002, No. IX-1078. Last amendment: 15 July 2008, No. X-1709. Available at: <http://www.coe.int/t/dghl/standardsetting/nationality/National%20legislation/Lithuania-Law%20on%20Citizenship%202003.pdf>.
- *Konsulinis Statutas of 09.05.1995 No. I-886* [Act on Consular Statute], published in *Valstybės Žinios*, 1995, No. 43-1047. Last amendment: Act of the Republic of Lithuania modifying the Consular Statute, 25 May 2006, No. X-169, published in Valstybės Žinios, 17 June 2006, No. 68-2492. Available also at: <http://www3.lrs.lt/pls/inter3/dokpaieska.showdoc_l?p_id=17774>.

LUXEMBOURG

- *Convention entre le Grand-Duché de Luxembourg et le Royaume de Belgique relative à la coopération dans le domaine consulaire of 30.09.1965* [Agreement between the Grand Duchy of Luxembourg and the Kingdom of Belgium on consular cooperation]. Available at: <http://www.legilux.public.lu/rgl/1966/A/0954/1.pdf>.

MALTA

- Consular Conventions Act, Chapter 144 of the Laws of Malta (enacted by Act XXXI of 1955, as amended by Emergency Ordinance XV of 1958; Ordinance XXV of 1962; Legal Notice 46 of 1965 and Act I of 1966). Available at: <http://www.imldb.iom.int/viewDocument.do?id=%7BD6DC23DD-EFBD-4D91-A42A-E34D1D88286A%7D>.

THE NETHERLANDS

- *Wet van 25 juli 1871, houdende regeling van de bevoegdheid der consulaire ambtenaren tot het opmaken van burgerlijke akten, en van de consulaire regtsmagt* (Consular Act of 25 July 1871 governing the powers of consular officers to establish civil status records and the consular jurisdiction), available at: <http://www.wetboek-online.nl/wet/Consulaire%20Wet.html>.
- *Besluit van 23 november 1981, tot vaststelling van een nieuw Consulair besluit* (Royal Decree of 23 November 1981 on the adoption of a new consular decree. Available at: <http://lexius.nl/consulair-besluit>.

POLAND

- Constitution of the Republic of Poland, available at: <http://www.sejm.gov.pl/prawo/konst/angielski/kon1.htm>.
- *Ustawa o funkcjach konsulów Rzeczypospolitej Polskiej z dnia 13 lutego 1984, Dz. U. No. 9 poz. 34* [Act on the Functions of Consular Officers]. Available at: <http://isap.sejm.gov.pl/DetailsServlet?id=WDU20022151823>

(01.12.2010). In English: <http://www.careproject.eu/database/upload/PLfunctionsofconsuls/PLfunctionsofconsulsTransEng.pdf>.

PORTUGAL

- Constitution of the Republic of Portugal, available at: <http://app.parlamento.pt/site_antigo/ingles/cons_leg/Constitution_VII_revisao_definitive.pdf>.
- *Ministério dos Negócios Estrangeiros Decreto-Lei No. 162/2006 de 8 de Agosto* [Decree-Act 162/2006], published in *Diário da República* (State Official Gazette), 1.a série – No. 152-8 August 2006, p. 5658. Available also at: <http://www.dre.pt/pdf1s/2006/08/15200/56585670.pdf>.
- *Ministério dos Negócios Estrangeiros Decreto-Lei No. 71/2009 de 31 de Março* [Decree-Act 71/2009], published in *Diário da República*, 1.ª série – No. 63 – 31 March 2009, p. 1961. Available also at: <http://dre.pt/pdf1s/2009/03/06300/0196101973.pdf>.

ROMANIA

- Constitution of the Republic of Romania, available at: <http://www.cdep.ro/pls/dic/site.page?id=371>.

SLOVAKIA

- *Zákon o organizácií činnosti vlády a organizácií ústrednej štátnej správy No. 575/2001 of 12 December 2001* [Act on Powers of the Ministries], available at: <http://www.vyvlastnenie.sk/predpisy/zakon-o-organizacii-cinnosti-vlady-a-organizacii ustrednej-statnej-spravy>.

SLOVENIA

- *Zakon o zunanjih zadevah – 7.6.2001 (spremembe in dopolnitve: 8.8.2003, 25.7.2008, 28.12.2009); neuradno prečiščeno besedilo objavljeno: 12.1.2010 – ZZZ-1-NPB3* [Foreign Affairs Act], published in the Official Journal of the Republic of Slovenia No. 113/03 (20.11.2003). Available in English at: <http://www.careproject.eu/database/upload/SLforeignaffairsact/SLforeignaffairsactTransEng.pdf>.
- *Navodilo za častne konzularne funkcionarje Republike Slovenije – of 21.03.2007 – ZKD-1154/07* [Instructions for Honorary Consular Officers of the Republic of Slovenia]. Available at: <http://www.mzz.gov.si/fileadmin/pageuploads/Zakonodaja_in_dokumenti/INSTRUCTION_Honorary_Consular_Officers_2007.pdf>.
- *Zakono potnih listinah uradno prečiščeno besedilo* (ZPLD-1-UPB3) [Act on Travel Documents]. Consolidated text, published in the Official Journal No. 3/06 (10.01.2006). Available also at: <http://www.uradni-list.si/1/objava.jsp?urlid=200962&stevilka=2959>.

SPAIN

- *Ley 40/2006 de 14 de diciembre, del Estatuto de la ciudadanía española en el exterior* [Act on the Statute of Spanish Citizens Abroad], published in *Boletín*

Oficial del Estado (BOE) (Spanish State Official Gazette) of 15.12.2006, No. 299. Available at: <http://www.boe.es/boe/dias/2006/12/15/pdfs/A44156-44166.pdf>.

- *Orden AEX/1059/2002 de bases reguladoras de las ayudas de protección y asistencia consulares en el extranjero* [Order AEX/1059/2002 of 25 April of the Ministry of Foreign Affairs on basic regulation of financial aid for consular protection and assistance abroad], published in BOE of 14.05.2002, No. 115. Available at: <http://www.boe.es/boe/dias/2002/05/14/pdfs/A17475-17477.pdf> (30.10.2010). Order AEX/1059/2002 was amended by Order AEC/3119/2005, of 26 September, published in BOE of 10.10.2005, No. 242. Available at: <http://www.boe.es/boe/dias/2005/10/10/pdfs/A33180-33180.pdf> (30.10.2010).
- *Real Decreto 1748/2010, de 23 de diciembre, por el que se desarrolla la estructura orgánica básica del Ministerio de Asuntos Exteriores y de Cooperación* [Royal Decree on basic organizational structure of the Ministry of Foreign Affairs and Cooperation], published in BOE of 14.01.2011, No. 12. Available at: <http://www.boe.es/boe/dias/2011/01/14/pdfs/BOE-A-2011-696.pdf>.

SWEDEN

- *Lag om konsulärt ekonomiskt bistånd of 26.06.2003* [Act on Consular Financial Assistance], available at: <http://62.95.69.3/SFSdoc/03/030491.PDF> (14.10.2011). In English: <http://www.careproject.eu/database/upload/SV2003_491/SV2003_491TransEng.pdf>.
- *Förordning med instruktion för utrikesrepresentationen 1992:247* [Regulation containing Instructions for the Foreign Representations], available at: <http://se.vlex.com/vid/ouml-1992-utrikesrepresentationen-50448809>.
- *Proposition 2002/03:69 En ny lag om konsulärt ekonomiskt bistånd* [Draft bill 2002/03:69 on the Swedish Consular Financial Assistance Act]. Available at: <http://www.riksdagen.se/webbnav/index.aspx?nid=37&dok_id=GQ0369>.